"How do we worship God? It seems common sense that we listen as God tells us what pleases him. *How Majestic Is Your Name* helps us listen as McConnell presents a topical survey of biblical teaching on worship. This book is well structured, comprehensive in its contents, and contemporary in its applications. Anyone teaching on worship or leading services will gain from this book. Likewise for believers who are serious about treating God as God."
—DAVID BURKE, Christ College, Sydney

"'The Bible sees worship as the beginning and the end of mission,' asserts McConnell. But what is worship? Driven by a deep commitment to learn what the living God desires of his worshipers, McConnell looks carefully at both Testaments and provides rich theological reflections. McConnell presents the contemporary church with a reliable and inspiring guide as to what Scripture teaches about the width and depth of biblical worship."
—MICHAEL WIDMER, Hokkaido Bible Institute

"This is a much-awaited, highly-recommended book for pastors, seminary students, worship leaders, and all who seek biblical and theological studies on the worship of God, as well as its practical implications and contemporary applications in individual and corporate worship life."
—MYRLEENE GRACE YAP, Singapore Bible College

"*How Majestic Is Your Name* is a rich, expansive, and profoundly biblical book on true worship as service, reverential fear, and bowing down to our God. It reminds us that worship is not a forty-five-minute event each week but a twenty-four-hour-a-day awareness of the presence of God in everything we do. The church has been waiting for this book for a very long time."
—MICHAEL CARD, singer-songwriter and author

"Carefully written and biblically thorough, *How Majestic Is Your Name* will prove to be a valuable resource for anyone seeking a comprehensive biblical theology of this vital but easily misunderstood theme."
—ALAN WILSON, Irish Bible Institute

"Walter McConnell has written a wonderful and much-needed theology of worship.... Readers will learn new things about worship and be challenged to bring their own patterns of worship into greater conformity with biblical models. *How Majestic Is Your Name* would make an excellent textbook. Passionate, competent, and clearly written, here is a book that will have lasting impact."
—TIMOTHY WIARDA, Gateway Seminary

"Walter's book is a timely reminder of the richness and depth of God's understanding of worship. There is nothing shallow or 'me-centered' in this book. We swim in the depths of biblical teaching and experiences.... I honestly believe that as we read, new doors of understanding will be opened. We will worship the Lord more wholeheartedly. We will serve him more obediently. We will love him more passionately. Thank you, Walter, for this great book!"
—KEN (FANTA) CLARKE, Bishop, Church of Ireland

"*How Majestic Is Your Name* invites readers to know the triune God whom we worship and proclaim. Such a theological disposition is evidence of the God-centered commitment of the author that has been crystallized after years of ministry as a church planter, theological educator, and director of international mission research.... I highly recommend this book because McConnell ushers us into worship that is Trinitarian, scriptural, and pastoral."
—BUDIANTO LIM, Reformed Theological Seminary, Indonesia

How Majestic Is Your Name

How Majestic Is Your Name

An Introduction to Biblical Worship

WALTER LESLIE McCONNELL

WIPF & STOCK · Eugene, Oregon

HOW MAJESTIC IS YOUR NAME
An Introduction to Biblical Worship

Copyright © 2021 Walter Leslie McConnell. All rights reserved. Except for brief quotations in critical publications or reviews, no part of this book may be reproduced in any manner without prior written permission from the publisher. Write: Permissions, Wipf and Stock Publishers, 199 W. 8th Ave., Suite 3, Eugene, OR 97401.

Wipf & Stock
An Imprint of Wipf and Stock Publishers
199 W. 8th Ave., Suite 3
Eugene, OR 97401

www.wipfandstock.com

PAPERBACK ISBN: 978-1-60899-907-1
HARDCOVER ISBN: 978-1-4982-8720-3
EBOOK ISBN: 978-1-7252-4601-0

12/02/21

All scripture quotations, unless otherwise indicated, are taken from the Holy Bible, New International Version®, NIV®. Copyright ©1973, 1978, 1984, 2011 by Biblica, Inc.™ Used by permission of Zondervan. All rights reserved worldwide. www.zondervan.com. The "NIV" and "New International Version" are trademarks registered in the United States Patent and Trademark Office by Biblica, Inc.™

For Claire, with whom I worship our Triune God daily. Thanks for stimulating me through the process of thinking and writing so that this book has become an act of worship.
In memory of Karen, whose worship was transformed by meeting her Lord face to face.

Contents

Preface		ix
Acknowledgments		xiii
Abbreviations		xv
1	What is Worship?	1
2	The God Who is Worshipped	15
3	The Worship of Jesus	30
4	The Holy Spirit in Worship	44
5	The People Who Worship	59
6	The Place of Worship	72
7	Times and Seasons of Worship: The Holy Days of Israel	105
8	Worship and Praise	132
9	Worship and Lament	155
10	Worship and Sacrifice	166
11	Worship and Baptism	191
12	Worship and the Lord's Supper	207
13	Worship and the Word	222
14	Worship and Prayer	233
15	Worship and Spiritual Gifts	249
16	Conclusion: A Life of Worship	256
Appendix: Times and Seasons of Worship: The Church Year		265
Bibliography		285
Subject Index		295
Name Index		303
Scripture Index		309

Preface

The worship of God has always played a central role of my life. Growing up in a Christian family, my earliest recollections include attending Sunday School classes and worship services where we gathered with friends and neighbors to sing praise to God, hear his word read and expounded, and reach out to him in prayer. But even though we came together every week to worship, I don't remember anyone explaining what worship was or how we should do it. As children, we were taught to put our hands together and close our eyes during prayer and we were instructed to stand or sit or do something else during different parts of a service, but that was about it. Worship was just one of those things Christians did even if they didn't really understand it.

Only later did I begin to question what worship is all about. These thoughts were greatly stimulated by a course that helped me see that worship entailed much more than what we do on a Sunday morning and that worship has a history. Its practice developed from the time of Adam and Eve to the call of Abraham and the giving of the Law. More changes arose during the time of David and Solomon. Then, with the Advent of Christ and the coming of the Holy Spirit, the contours of worship were redrawn. When the church fathers and later theologians reflected upon the biblical documents, they also developed a number of practices to help Christians worship God.

While I had learned some of these practices from my childhood, others felt foreign as they were not part of the tradition in which I was raised. This often made me feel that other churches—as a friend once put it—practiced a different religion. How can Christians worship God in such dissimilar ways? How can we discover which worship style is right? Am I the only one who wonders about these things?

The answers to my questions didn't come immediately. However, as time went on I became more and more involved in both leading worship and teaching it. For several years, I served in a church where I led worship three or four times a week in both formal and informal settings. And while I frequently prepared the order of worship, it largely reflected our denominational norms. The history of worship was set aside for what was known and comfortable. The theological foundations for worship remained unexplored. We continued to practice our form of worship without really understanding it.

When I began to teach others about worship, I discovered that I wasn't the only one with unanswered questions. Fellow worshippers at church and students preparing for ministry admitted their ignorance about the subject and their desire to learn more. Despite the renewed interest in worship that has grown during the past couple of decades, despite the new worship songs, books, and seminars, despite the development and implementation of new liturgies and non-liturgical forms, despite the establishment of worship committees and worship teams in local congregations, we remain unclear about how to worship God.

Should our worship style be liturgical or charismatic? High or free church? Regulated or Spirit-led? Should we strike a happy medium that blends a little bit of this and a little bit of that? Does adopting any particular style, or even attempting to achieve a more "balanced approach," throw more light on our personal preferences than on God's design for worship?

Where should we go to learn the right way to worship? Many recent books on the subject turn to the development of liturgical formulas in the early centuries or the transformation of worship during the time of the Reformation. Others present us with the thoughts and practices of modern worship leaders. While many of these books are helpful, they reveal only part of the picture. If we want to understand what worship is and how we should do it, we need more than historical reflection and technical direction; we need the theological grounding that only comes from the Bible. The Bible is our guide to worship because it is our guide to God. It should impact our understanding and practice far more than any other work, ancient or modern. The Bible's narrative passages introduce us to God's worshippers in action, its laws show us how the holy God desires to be approached by a holy people, the psalms provide words for individuals and groups who draw near to God believing he will hear and receive their prayers, and the New Testament documents realign the earlier revelation by showing how it points to Jesus Christ. In this book, we will explore the Bible's teaching on worship so that it won't be one of those things we do without understanding. Here, we will learn what God wants us to know so that we can worship him the way he wants us to worship.

This book was written for students, pastors, worship leaders, and everyone else who wants to grow as a worshipper of God. While it goes beyond the historical, technical, and experiential study of worship, it does not simply recount biblical evidence, but asks modern Christians to allow the information to influence their thinking and practice. Where relevant, examples show how the Bible's teaching on worship has been applied historically and how it can be used now.

Our study begins by looking at the biblical words for worship, as they lay a foundation for all that follows. Three chapters will take us deeper as we focus on the God who is worshipped as Father, Son, and Holy Spirit. He is the only proper object of worship, and he both teaches us how to worship and equips us for worship. Following our consideration of the God we worship, three chapters will consider the people who worship, the physical setting for worship, and the times and seasons Scripture sets aside for worship. Worship, we will see, is a spiritual and physical act that requires a holy people to interact with a holy God in holy space and time. A final eight chapters will examine a number of biblical themes and practices that are central to worship. We will thus discuss the age-old practices of praise, lament, and sacrifice, and the distinctly Christian rituals of baptism and the Lord's Supper. Our study will conclude as we reflect on the role that God's word, prayer, and spiritual gifts play in worship.

My fervent desire and prayer is that this book will help you become not just a more knowledgeable worshipper of God, but a worshipper who knows God better and desires to love and worship him with all of your heart, soul, mind, and strength. May God accept this book as my labor of worship and use it so that your reading becomes an act of worship that grows as you apply the teachings of his word to your life.

Acknowledgments

I would like to express my deepest thanks to a number of people who have helped in the preparation of this book. I am particularly grateful to the leaders and members of the churches in the United States, Taiwan, Singapore, and Northern Ireland, where I have worshipped as a member of God's family. I have learned much from this international and interdenominational community and have counted it an honor to join with them in worshipping our wonderful Lord. Many thanks to the students from Singapore Bible College and Belfast Bible College who attended the classes where I developed many of my ideas and who raised questions I had not considered. Special recognition is due to my friends and colleagues Drs. Rick Griffiths and Timothy Wiarda, who commented on parts of this work, and particularly to my friend and former pastor Rev. David Burke who has given me feedback on the whole. Thanks also to Alan Robinson and Wai Ying Lee for their keen eyes to detail and to Marven Harkness for her sage editorial advice. While I have been helped much, all errors in fact and interpretation remain my own responsibility.

Abbreviations

1 Apol.	Justin Martyr, *First Apology*
AB	Anchor Bible
BNTC	Black's New Testament Commentaries
BST	The Bible Speaks Today
BTCL	Biblical and Theological Classics Library
BTDB	*Baker Theological Dictionary of the Bible.* Edited by Walter A. Elwell. Grand Rapids: Baker, 2000
CSB	Holman Christian Standard Bible
Did	*Didache*
DOTP	*Dictionary of the Old Testament: Pentateuch.* Edited by T. Desmond Alexander and David W. Baker. Downers Grove and Leicester: IVP, 2003
DOTWPW	*Dictionary of the Old Testament: Wisdom, Poetry and Writings.* Edited by Tremper Longman III and Peter Enns. Downers Grove: IVP Academic and Nottingham: IVP, 2008
DPL	*Dictionary of Paul and His Letters.* Edited by G. F. Hawthorne, R. P. Martin, and D. G. Reid. Downers Grove and Leicester: IVP, 1993
DTIB	*Dictionary for Theological Interpretation of the Bible.* Edited by Kevin J. Vanhoozer. Grand Rapids: Baker Academic and London: SPCK, 2005
EBC	Expositor's Bible Commentary
EQ	*Evangelical Quarterly*
ESV	English Standard Version

ERT		*Evangelical Review of Theology*
HBT		*Horizons in Biblical Theology*
IBD		*Illustrated Bible Dictionary*. 3 vols. Edited by J. D. Douglas. Leicester: IVP; Wheaton: Tyndale House; Lane Cove, New South Wales: Hodder & Stoughton, 1980
ICC		International Critical Commentary
Ign. *Magn.*		Ignatius, *To the Magnesians*
ISBE		*International Standard Bible Encyclopedia*. 4 vols. Edited by G. W. Bromiley, Grand Rapids: Eerdmans, 1979–1988
IVP		InterVarsity Press or Inter-Varsity Press
JAET		*Journal of Asian Evangelical Theology*
JSOT		*Journal for the Study of the Old Testament*
JSOTSup		Journal for the Study of the Old Testament: Supplement Series
NASB		New American Standard Bible
NDBT		*New Dictionary of Biblical Theology*. Edited by T. D. Alexander and Brian S. Rosner. Leicester and Downers Grove: IVP, 2000
NDT		*New Dictionary of Theology*. Edited by S. B. Ferguson and D. F. Right. Leicester and Downers Grove: IVP, 1988
NIBC		New International Biblical Commentary
NICNT		New International Commentary on the New Testament
NICOT		New International Commentary on the Old Testament
NIDNTT		*New International Dictionary of New Testament Theology*. 4 vols. Edited by Colin Brown. Grand Rapids: Zondervan, 1975–1986
NIDOTTE		*New International Dictionary of Old Testament Theology and Exegesis*. 5 vols. Edited by W. A. VanGemeren. Grand Rapids: Zondervan, 1997
NIGTC		New International Greek Testament Commentary
NIV		New International Version
NLT		New Living Translation
NRSV		New Revised Standard Version
OTL		Old Testament Library
PTSB		*Princeton Theological Seminary Bulletin*

RSV	Revised Standard Version
RTRSupSer	*Reformed Theological Review* Supplement Series
TDNT	*Theological Dictionary of the New Testament.* 10 vols. Edited by Gerhard Kittel and Gerhard Friedrich. Translated by Geoffrey W. Bromiley. Grand Rapids: Eerdmans, 1964–76
TDOT	*Theological Dictionary of the Old Testament.* 14 vols. Edited by G. Johannes Botterweck and Helmer Ringgren. Translated by Geoffrey W. Bromiley et al. Grand Rapids: Eerdmans, 1974–2004
TLOT	*Theological Lexicon of the Old Testament.* 3 vols. Edited by Ernst Jenni and Claus Westermann. Translated by Mark Biddle. Peabody, MA: Hendrickson, 1997
TNTC	Tyndale New Testament Commentary
TOTC	Tyndale Old Testament Commentary
Trad. ap.	*Apostolic Tradition*
TWOT	*Theological Wordbook of the Old Testament.* 2 vols. Edited by R. Laird Harris, Gleason L. Archer Jr., and Bruce K. Waltke. Chicago: Moody, 1980
TynBul	*Tyndale Bulletin*
UBS	United Bible Societies
WBC	Word Biblical Commentary
WTJ	*Westminster Theological Journal*
κτλ	καὶ τά λοιπά, "and the rest"

1

What is Worship?

What is worship? Ask this question of a group of Christians from the average congregation and you will receive a wide spectrum of responses. For some, it is the action of ascribing worth to God. Others understand it to be the activities one does during a worship service, or the part of the service that is made up of singing and prayers as distinct from Bible reading, preaching, and announcements. Still more equate worship with the singing of choruses or "worship songs." And while some believers only connect worship with certain celebratory acts performed during a weekly service, others insist that it should reflect our response to the Creator for who he is and what he has done in every activity of life.

That Christians have such a splintered understanding of something as important as worship is far from satisfactory. Many of us have worshipped God for a long time, some of us regularly lead worship, others are church pastors or students taking an academic course on worship. Yet, in spite of all we have learned and experienced, it is probably accurate to say that we are all only novice worshippers. The fact that there is still so much to learn has motivated me to write this book. My goal is to increase our understanding of worship and provide some practical suggestions that will help us become better worshippers of the Lord in public and in private.

Most of us have accepted certain ideas about worship or adopted a particular style of worship simply because it is practiced by our family, congregation, or denomination. Some are unacquainted with other worship styles and have never considered alternatives; others are familiar with other practices but retain the cherished forms they feel comfortable with or believe are most pleasing to the Lord. Other worshippers have decided to adopt a new style after experiencing it in another setting. And though they may not be sure what they should replace it with, some have determined that the style of worship they had originally experienced has become stale, past its use-by date.

Our feelings toward and understanding of worship are guided by both theological and social influences. In many cases, they are determined more by personal experience than biblical revelation. Is it possible to develop an understanding of worship that will be acceptable or even considered valuable to all Christian communities? Can we find a way to think about and practice worship in its public and private forms that will be accepted in charismatic fellowships and liturgical high churches? What about churches that identify themselves as being somewhere in between, those that see themselves situated in a totally different orbit from either, or those that maintain they are both charismatic and liturgical at the same time? Assuming that such an understanding of worship might possibly exist, where can we look to find it?

As is usually true when one considers complex questions, much can be gained by examining a variety of sources. We could, for instance, turn to current and historical sources to add to our understanding and give us a more solid basis for our worship practices. Or we could consider the way scholars have understood the definition or etymology of the English word. But while they may stretch our thinking about worship, investigations into such things may also prove misleading since the biblical authors used Hebrew and Greek when they addressed the worship of God and some of our historical and liturgical questions may distract us from the concerns of Scripture.

This book is written to present the modern church with a biblical theology of the worship of God and to demonstrate how that teaching can be applied today. And though the biblical texts provide scant liturgical direction for Christian worship, I am convinced that what they say should influence contemporary practice far more that either the standardization of liturgy in the fourth century or the various worship renewals that have sprung up at other times in history. It is for this reason that we will begin by examining the words used in the Bible for worship. Unless we appreciate the rich vocabulary used by biblical authors as they expressed themselves in worship and bore witness to the way Israel and the church worshipped God, our understanding of the subject will always remain flawed.

THE WORDS OF WORSHIP

The problem is, one can scour the Bible from Genesis to Revelation without exposing even one definition of worship. Nevertheless, readers are left in no doubt that God requires certain kinds of worship and rejects others. We see this in the various literary genres of the Bible. The narrative sections tell of people engaged in worship activities that included sacrifice, prayer, praise, fasting, and feasting. The laws often record that God, whether directly or indirectly, commanded his covenant people to follow certain worship forms and practices faithfully. Compiled over several centuries, the psalms provided resources for corporate and private worship to guide God's people through the seasons of life whether they experienced joy or sorrow, hope or fear. The Gospels and Epistles make it clear that the one God revealed in the Old Testament should be worshipped through Jesus Christ and by the power of the Holy Spirit. They further show that even though Christian worship retained much of what had been required of Israel, God's new revelation through his Son demanded the adoption of some new forms and the abandonment of others. The book of Revelation, building upon imagery found throughout Scripture, envisions the worship of God and of the Lamb being perfected in the new heavens and new earth where all rivals will be decisively eliminated when the kingdom is fully ushered in.

In addition to the instruction and examples it gives about the worship of God, the Bible shows that ancient Israel and the early church maintained a vibrant vocabulary of worship terms. These words indicate that biblical worship is essentially a proper response to the person of God and his actions that results in a person falling or bowing down before him in humble submission, expressing fear or reverence due to his majesty and power, and serving him through various religious activities and in one's day-to-day life. Understanding the Greek and Hebrew words for worship is crucial if we are to grasp the Bible's teaching on the subject and allow it to impact the way we worship today.

To bow down

The most common Hebrew word for worship in the Old Testament is *ḥāwâ*, which carries the basic meaning "to bow down," or "to prostrate oneself."[1] Found some 170 times in the Old Testament, it is almost universally

---

1. Although many older works relate this word to the hithpael form of the Hebrew verb *šāḥah*, "to bow down," modern scholarship identifies it as a rare eshtaphal stem of *ḥāwâ*. Preuss, "חוה *ḥwh*," 249.

translated in the Septuagint[2] (148 times) by *proskuneō*, the Greek word that is used for worship sixty times in the New Testament. The much rarer Hebrew word *sāgad*, and its Aramaic cognate *sĕgid*, are similar in meaning to *ḥāwâ*, but usually used of those who bow down in submission to idols (Isa 44:15, 17, 19; 46:6; Dan 3:5–7, 10–12, 14–18, 28). In the Old Testament, *ḥāwâ* is regularly paired with one of the other words for worship, indicating that they are treated as synonyms.

The basic action required by these Hebrew and Greek verbs is for a person to fall to the knees and then lower his forehead to the ground. Living in an age when etiquette required bowing before honored guests and protocol made it incumbent upon commoners to lower the head before a king to lessen the risk of having it removed, it was natural for biblical authors to use these words in their standard sense as part of a secular greeting in which one person bows before another out of respect or to acknowledge authority (Gen 23:7, 12; 42:6; 43:26, 28; 1 Sam 24:9). By extension, they employed the terms for bowing before the awesome greatness of Yahweh and before the images of false gods. Since people knew what it meant to bow down before a human king who possessed great power, they knew how to respond to a God who exercised even greater power. By bowing before God, they were surrendering themselves before his greatness and submitting themselves to do his will. And whereas the terms are frequently used for literal prostration in the presence of God, they can simply denote inward religious attitudes and actions that in many contexts can rightly be translated "to worship" or even "to pray." Indeed, in Old Testament times, prostration usually preceded prayer, which was normally offered as one knelt or stood.

The Bible frequently describes people bowing to Yahweh in response to his manifest presence or as a response of thanksgiving for something he had done. Thus, Abraham's servant bowed down to worship God for answering his prayer to provide a bride for Isaac (Gen 24:26–27). Similarly, after Moses returned to Egypt with God's promise to set his people free, the Israelites bowed down and worshipped the Lord (Exod 4:31). After the building of Solomon's temple, when the glory of God descended and filled the house so that not even the priests could enter, all the Israelites who gathered there "worshiped and gave thanks to the LORD, saying, 'He is good; his love endures forever'" (2 Chr 7:3). In most cases, God's people are not said to fall down to worship him in a formal worship service, but in what should be considered spontaneous responses of prayer and praise.

---

2. The Septuagint—abbreviated LXX—is the name given to the ancient Greek translation of the Hebrew Bible.

The Bible makes it clear that Yahweh is the only proper object of worship and prohibits Israel from bowing down before any other gods. This was first explicitly stated in the second commandment and then regularly repeated throughout Israel's history (Exod 20:4–6). However, in spite of frequent warnings, God's chosen nation regularly adopted the worship practices of the people around them and bowed down to other gods. In the end, their refusal to worship Yahweh alone was cited as a major reason why both the Northern and Southern Kingdoms were driven into exile (2 Kgs 17; Jer 22:8–9). Worship of Yahweh was not, however, thought to be required of Israel alone. The Psalms and prophets regularly looked forward to a day when foreign nations, indeed all the earth, would worship Yahweh (Pss 22:27, 29; 86:9; 96:9; Isa 45:14; 49:7; Zeph 2:11). Even the heavenly beings (Neh 9:6) and the beings that others worshipped as gods are either said or commanded to bow down to Yahweh (Ps 97:9).[3] Every part of creation should bow before the Lord to acknowledge that they are subject to him.

Fear

The next biblical word related to worship is the Hebrew *yārē'*, and its Greek counterpart *phobeō*: "to fear, to be afraid." Like *ḥāwâ* and *proskuneō*, the semantic range of these words is quite broad. They can be used in response to everyday threats such as animals, enemies, punishment, sickness, and death. They can reveal one's feeling in the presence of a king or on a battlefield. Fear can strike through nightmares or when facing the unknown. Finally, they can be used of the fear of God.[4] The fear of God or fear of Yahweh is a concept that ranges in meaning from being afraid of God's power as judge or as the master of creation to expressing reverential awe because of his power to deliver. For the most part, those who are outside the covenant are terror-stricken when they realize that Yahweh personally leads his people

---

3. Falling into a similar category are the "sons of the mighty" (*běnê 'ēlîm*) in Psalm 29:1–2. While the term may refer to angels, Canaanite usage suggests that it points to other deities of the divine council. Whatever the exact meaning of the term, worshippers who use this psalm call upon heavenly beings to join them in their worship of God. See Craigie, *Psalms 1–50*, 242, 246.

4. Notice how the last two concepts come together in Jonah 1:5–16. The sailors were afraid because of the storm. News that Jonah feared (i.e., worshipped, so NIV) Yahweh, the Creator God, and was fleeing from him made the sailors even more afraid. The sailor's realization that they must throw Jonah in the water so that they could be saved, caused them to cry out to the Lord that he would not hold them accountable for Jonah's blood. After the sea was calmed, they feared Yahweh and sacrificed animals to him. Though the versions do not indicate it, the parallelism with sacrifice and vows provides good reason to understand this final act in the sense of worship.

and fights for them (Exod 15:13–16), while those in covenant relationship with Yahweh experience the fear of God as a proper reverence based upon their trust in his ability to deliver them from their enemies whom he will judge. The fear of the Lord leads God's people to surrender to his sovereign will and humbly do his bidding. In conjunction with the other biblical words for worship, fear of the Lord leads a person to bow before him in humility and serve him.

In many contexts, the word approximates worship as is seen by its frequent use in conjunction with *ḥāwâ* and *'ābad* (see below). Thus, throughout their history, Israel was regularly told they could choose to fear and bow down to, or to fear and serve, either Yahweh or other gods—they could worship one or the other, but not both. That fear is an important part of worship is especially seen in the Psalms where "you who fear the LORD" or "you who fear him" is virtually synonymous with being a worshipper (Pss 22:23; 115:11; 135:20). While the Old Testament almost exclusively limited people who feared Yahweh to believing Israel, the phrase took on a wider connotation in the New Testament, so that "God-fearing" is used in the book of Acts for Gentiles who attended synagogue worship but had not submitted themselves to be circumcised (Acts 10:2, 22, 35; 13:16, 26).[5] In other contexts, the New Testament uses the term for anyone who worships God (Rev 11:8; 19:5).

In Wisdom literature, fearing God requires that one lives in a proper relationship with him because he is known experientially. This is reflected in the most basic thought found in biblical Wisdom:

> The fear of the LORD is the beginning of wisdom,
> and knowledge of the Holy One is understanding.
> (Prov 9:10; cf. Job 28:28; Ps 111:10; Prov 1:7; 2:5)

Living in God's fear extends to the whole of life and becomes "a virtual synonym for righteous living or piety."[6] This is seen most clearly in the book of Job, which identifies its title character as a man who "was blameless and upright; he feared God and shunned evil" (Job 1:1). Using almost equivalent wording, Proverbs 3:7 exhorts the student of wisdom: "Do not be wise in your own eyes; fear the LORD and shun evil" (cf. Prov 8:13). And to illustrate what this looks like, the book frequently makes statements that are comparable to the injunctions found in the Ten Commandments. The basic Wisdom teaching that one should come into relationship with Yahweh

---

5. Although "Gentiles" is not found in the original, the NIV often translates "you who fear God" with "Gentiles who worship God" or "God-fearing Gentiles" to provide a more idiomatic interpretation of the phrase (Acts 13:16, 26).

6. Boling, "יָרֵא *yārē'*," 400.

and reject all other gods reflects the first and second commandments. As in the fifth commandment, the wise person will listen to his parents' teaching (Prov 1:8; 2:1; 3:1; 4:1–4; 5:1, 20:30). Following the sixth, seventh, and eighth commandments, he will not murder (Prov 1:11–12, 16–18; 6:17), commit adultery (Prov 2:16–19; 5:3–23; 6:24–35; 7:5–27), or steal (Prov 1:13–14, 19). From the standpoint of Wisdom, the one who fears God lives morally because he knows God, maintains a right relationship with him, and is fully intent on obeying his commandments and doing whatever he requires.

The connection between the fear of the Lord and biblical Wisdom literature reminds us that this aspect of worship can be learned. Indeed, God had instructed Israel in the wilderness that they were to learn to fear him (Deut 4:10; 14:23; 17:9). In both Wisdom and Law, this was not just an accumulation of knowledge about God, but was closely linked to obeying his commands, particularly about how he should be worshipped. And though the laws of worship include the tabernacle sacrifices, they were not limited to them. Thus, the fear of God was to encompass all of life, as Qohelet, the Preacher in Ecclesiastes, concludes after his survey of all manner of wisdom concepts.

> Now all has been heard;
> here is the conclusion of the matter:
> Fear God and keep his commandments,
> for this is the whole duty of man. (Eccl 12:13)

The connection between morality and the fear of God is maintained by New Testament writers. Thus, Paul warns the Corinthian church to remain distinct from the unbelievers around them since God had promised to live among them and be their Father. He further exhorts them by saying, "let us purify ourselves from everything that contaminates body and spirit, perfecting holiness out of reverence [lit. 'fear'] for God" (2 Cor 7:1). As in the Old Testament, one's entire life should express a positive fear of God. Those who do not, like the judge in Jesus' parable who claimed neither to fear God nor respect people, are understood to have no real religion (Luke 18:2, 4; cf. Luke 23:40; Rom 3:9–18). Fear of God results in proper religious practice and moral uprightness.

Service

The final group of biblical words for worship center around the idea of service. The main Hebrew verb for working or serving is *'ābad*, which is found some 290 times in the Old Testament. Noun forms include *'ebed*, in reference to a servant, slave, or worker (800 times), *ʿăbôdâ*, for work, service, or bondage (145 times), and several other forms. In the Septuagint, the word is variously translated by words related to *douleuō* when referring to slavery, *ergazomai* when referring to work, and words of the *latreuō* group when referring to the cultic service of the priests. All these Greek terms find further service in the New Testament when worship is in view.

Another Hebrew word used for service is *šārat*, which is used ninety-seven times in the Hebrew Bible. Twenty of these times, the word is a participle acting as the noun "minister." In ritual settings, the Septuagint almost exclusively translates it with *leitourgeō*.[7] The word differs from *ʿābad* in that *ʿābad* can be used for menial labor, while *šārat* only refers to a higher level of service. Though it can be used of personal service to an important person (e.g., Joseph serving Potiphar, Gen 39:4; Elisha serving Elijah, 1 Kgs 19:21), it is usually reserved for cultic worship performed by a priest or Levite at the tabernacle or someone else who has a special relationship with God (including angels; Ps 103:21). And while it was understandably used for sacrificial service, *šārat* could also be used for those who ministered to Yahweh with song and praise (1 Chr 6:32; 16:4, 37).

Like the other biblical words for worship, those related to service have a broad semantic range. In Genesis 2:5 and 15 *ʿābad* was used when God told the man to "till" or "work" the garden. More frequently, the words are used for someone who serves another human, such as a slave serving his master, a man his employer (Gen 29:15), a courtier or subject his king (1 Sam 11:1), or one nation serving another (1 Chr 18:2, 6, 13). By extension, they could be used for the spiritual realm to indicate service of gods, idols, or even heavenly bodies (Acts 7:42). Even created things can be served as though they were gods (Rom 1:25). Rather than worshipping those things, Israel was specifically called out of Egypt to "serve" Yahweh (Exod 3:12; 4:23; 7:16, 26; 10:26). Throughout their history, the Israelites were regularly instructed to choose to serve Yahweh or other gods (Josh 24:14–24), that is, to acknowledge one or the other as lord.

Even though the word can be used in so many ways, its most important use, from our perspective, pertains to service rendered to Yahweh. The Bible proclaims that all God's people are his servants. In the thought world of the ancient Near East, the status of a servant is always viewed in his relationship to his lord. God's servants are therefore related to him, acknowledge him as master, and aim to obey him in all things. And while a human master may treat his servant harshly, this will never happen to God's servant as Yahweh

---

7. The noun form of this Greek word provides the root for the English word "liturgy."

is always a good lord.[8] Although a servant of God can simply be related to him as vassal, he might also serve the Lord through cultic rituals (e.g., by offering sacrifices or celebrating the appointed festivals) and performing other types of service. Frequently, the type of service rendered differed depending on the status of the individual involved. Thus, the Aaronic priests served Yahweh by offering sacrifices in the tabernacle and later temple. Other Levitical clans served at the tent of meeting by bearing burdens and taking care of the items of furniture placed there (Num 4:4, 23–24, 30–33). One passage informs us that the Levites took part in the Lord's worship by literally "serving in the service of the tabernacle" (Num 3:7–8). They thus worshipped God through their performance of what many might consider mundane labor. Much later in Israel's history, the Levites served by writing and performing music for the temple cult. The people—as one—performed their service when they came together to celebrate the Passover and other feasts (Exod 12:25–26). Serving God was thus not restricted to performing "religious rites" such as offering sacrifices but included a wide range of activities that pleased God.

The second commandment and other passages make it clear that no one should bow down before or serve any other god or image (Exod 20:4–6). Despite continual reminders, Israel regularly failed to obey. A key passage presenting those who entered the land with the paradigmatic challenge of serving the gods of the nations or Yahweh is found in the book of Joshua.

> But if serving the LORD seems undesirable to you, then choose for yourselves this day whom you will serve, whether the gods your forefathers served beyond the River, or the gods of the Amorites, in whose land you are living. But as for me and my household, we will serve the LORD. (Josh 24:15)

While the bulk of the Bible's teaching about service comes from the Old Testament, the New Testament also considers different ways in which God's people should serve him. One can thus serve God through preaching the gospel (Rom 1:9) or by fasting and praying (Luke 2:37; 2 Tim 1:3). Many activities that are not performed in overtly religious settings should also be recognized as Christian service. Paul specifically identifies caring for the material needs of others as serving them and thus a means to worship the Lord (Rom 15:27; Phil 2:25).

The New Testament writers were clear that all service to God was spiritual (Rom 1:9; 12:1; Phil 3:3). This is because only those whose consciences have been cleansed through the blood of Christ can engage in them (Heb

---

8. Westermann, "עָבַד ʿebed servant," 826.

9:14). Service was never limited to something done in a particular meeting or performed only on special occasions. Rather, people should serve God continually—both "night and day" (Luke 2:37; 2 Tim 1:3; Rev 7:15). Service can therefore include the things God's people do when gathered as a community of the faith, what is performed as part of one's private relationship with God, and what is done in the public realm as long as it is done unto the Lord. All of this is worship.

THE WORDS OF WORSHIP AND THE CHURCH TODAY

Discovering that the major biblical words for worship are concerned with bowing down to God, fearing him, and serving him can come as a surprise to many. Though the English term "worship" may come from an ancient Anglo-Saxon word meaning "worth-ship," biblical worship is concerned with a lot more than ascribing worth to God.[9] If we are to worship God according to biblical patterns, we must discover how to bow down before him in submission; express our fear through recognition of his power as creator, judge, and defender, and by living out his moral demands; and serve him through acts of devotion and in our earthly vocation.

Bowing Down before God

Although people throughout the world formerly bowed to others in greeting, reserving the lowest bows for those of the highest rank, for the past couple of centuries, these actions have been replaced as many societies have adopted the modern democratic idea that "all men are created equal." Those influenced by this concept have, to a large degree, lost the sense that certain people should be honored simply because they have been born into a noble family or elected to a high position. The handshake, with its concrete symbolism of solidarity and equality, and the hug, exuding nearness and intimacy, have replaced bowing and kneeling before one's superiors in much of the world. While these modern symbols have their positive aspects, the loss of esteem for leaders in society can easily cause us to lose perspective when it comes to God's majesty. Since we have not learned to bow down before men, we do not know how to fall on our faces before God in humble

---

9. Only four verses in the entire Bible explicitly proclaim the worth of God the Father or Son (Heb 3:3; Rev 4:11; 5:9, 12). Some English translations have added the concept to a few more verses even though it does not appear in the original (2 Sam 22:4; 1 Chr 16:25; Pss 18:3; 48:1; 96:4; 145:3).

submission to his person and his will. This problem is compounded as the lack of a modern physical symbol of submission makes proposing a culturally relevant replacement for bowing difficult.

Christians who live in democratic societies are not the only ones who struggle with the concept of bowing before God. Believers who come from nations where the majority of the population adhere to other religions and commonly bow to or prostrate themselves before idols, ancestors, and/or other gods, often recoil at the thought of kneeling down to God as they perceive it to be an activity that non-Christians do. They therefore often reject it in order to be seen as a distinct people who separate themselves from such actions.

It should be clear, however, that the lack of a particular action in one culture or the ascription of a different meaning to that action in another culture does not necessarily negate its use. Just as Old Testament believers did not stop sacrificing animals to Yahweh because their Canaanite neighbors sacrificed to Baal and other deities and New Testament believers added the Lord's Supper to their worship practices, modern Christians can attach new significance to old practices and take on new practices to make worship more meaningful. Even so, when old practices are redefined or new forms adopted, it is essential to instruct believers about the meaning of the act. Bowing and kneeling are significant acts because they remind us of God's greatness and our insignificance before him. Any physical discomfort we might feel should make us recall our position before him as his creatures and servants.

While Christians were formerly taught to kneel during prayer, that training is often lacking today. Even believers from traditions that follow a liturgy calling for kneeling at certain times during a service can find themselves standing or returning to their seats at the point the liturgy instructs them to kneel. Other congregations have never experienced any more than bowing the head during a worship service, and many Christians probably never physically bow to God, even in private. Could it be that bowing in church is deemed irrelevant since people today are not used to bowing to anyone? Or is it simply a sign of laziness or ignorance or that church seating is not designed to provide room to kneel?[10]

Service leaders often erase a natural opportunity for bowing, kneeling, or lying prostrate simply by what they say. The case of changing the words of the prayer book so that one stands or sits instead of kneels stands out.

---

10. This leads to a whole series of questions on how the construction of our places of worship impacts the worship that takes place there. Although modern architectural design lies outside the scope of this work, it appears that worship space is often designed for practical, aesthetic, or economic rather than theological reasons.

Further incongruity results when a worship leader instructs the congregation to stand and sing a song that exhorts us to worship and bow down. If we use psalms or choruses that speak of bowing down, we should not instruct the congregation to do the opposite. Rather, we should explain why we should bow and then make it possible to do so while we sing.

While some may object that kneeling or bowing is not practical, this was not always the case. Throughout history, many churches were supplied with kneelers or pads, though it is possible to kneel almost anywhere, just as it is possible to bow one's head anywhere. Postures of submission can be taught and space provided in our building plans so that people can worship God through these simple gestures and motions.

No matter what reasons we may have for not bowing, kneeling, or falling prostrate before God, the fact that this is a major biblical word for worship should give us pause for reflection. To incorporate this physical symbol of submission in our public and private worship of God, our starting point should be to educate our congregations about the meaning of this symbol and provide them with opportunities to bow before their sovereign Lord in deep heartfelt worship.

Expressing Fear of God

Many Christians will be surprised to find that the Bible considers the fear of the Lord to be a major aspect of worship. Perhaps this is because it focuses more on one's relationship with God and obedience to his instructions in everyday life than with one's actions or feelings during a service. Even so, the Bible regularly associates the fear of God with both serving and bowing down (Deut 6:13; 10:12, 20; Pss 2:11; 5:7; Rev 14:7; 15:4). To fear God is always to hold him in proper respect. This includes our attitude toward him during worship services and throughout the week. To fear God is to know and obey his commands. It therefore requires us to pay attention to and obey his word through reading, meditation, and practice. To fear God is to live a moral life, following the Ten Commandments and other biblical ethical teaching. We therefore need to be sure that everything we do is in accordance with God's will. The life of worship is a life of obedience and personal holiness.

The fear of God begins with recognizing that he is the Judge who will prosecute those who have sinned against him. This is why it requires submission and obedience. Those who fear God draw near to worship the Father out of respect because he is the Creator and Lord who removes the fear of punishment from those who come to him through Jesus Christ. The fear of God makes it possible for believers in Jesus, like their spiritual father Abraham, to be unafraid of their circumstances since God is their shield, their protector (Gen 15:1). To fear God is to put oneself in his care. In response to God's gracious provision of protection and direction for living, those who fear him should do that which pleases him out of love and gratitude. This includes assembling with others to remember what God has done for his people and serving him in the world regardless of the consequences. The fear of Christ will also prompt us to submit to one another (Eph 5:21).

Though the fear of God has no tangible symbol like bowing down in humility and submission, it can be seen through one's actions, attitudes, obedience, and righteous living. As the fear of God produces active conformity to God's will, it naturally leads to the third major aspect of biblical worship—service—because those who fear God will serve him, his church, and the world.

Serving God

Many Christians today do not recognize service to be one of the main expressions of biblical worship. And yet it makes a lot of sense. People serve God when they lead or otherwise take part in the rituals of the church. Preaching, praying, reading Scripture, singing in the choir, leading the service, and dispensing the elements of the Lord's Supper are obvious avenues of service that are performed during a worship service. Not so obvious ones include sharing the gospel, writing sacred songs, playing musical instruments, running the sound, lights, or computer system, assembling slides for projection, handing out bulletins, greeting visitors, and helping to park cars. As with the Levites who worshipped God through their mundane service, whatever we do to serve his cause is worship. When used for the advancement of his kingdom, even the secular is sacred.

What is important is that we serve the Creator God and not the gods of the nations. As we acknowledge him to be Lord and master, we recognize ourselves to be his servants, his bond slaves, who should do everything we can to please him. This includes everything we do when we meet and what we do when we go out into the world. Spiritual gifts, as we will see in a later chapter, should thus be recognized as a means to worship God. Gifts used for God's service include teaching and prophecy as well as the more commonplace ones such as encouragement, giving, leadership, and showing mercy. Our vocations should similarly be recognized as vehicles of worship as we live for Christ in the workplace. We therefore worship God as we come together to serve him and one another in the assembly and when we depart to serve him and the world.

CONCLUSION

Everyone begins the journey of worship at a different starting point and with different preunderstandings. Whereas the churches we attend, the people we talk to, and the books we read can greatly influence our consideration and practice of worship, it is essential that we give ear to what the Lord has revealed about worship in his word. As most Christians are ignorant of the concepts and actions associated with worship that were known and practiced in biblical times, we have much to learn. Worship is not merely something we do during a weekly service. It is certainly not limited to singing. Worship is an activity of the heart and mind, the emotion and will, that brings us to God in his majesty, causes us to bow before him as our God and master, to express an attitude of reverence and fear because of his power and love, and to obey his commands in daily and seasonal acts of service that embrace both the sacred and the secular.

Our communal gatherings should flow from our understanding that worship encompasses everything we do for God. Both Old Testament and New Testament communal worship services provided believers with opportunities to unite with others to listen to God's words to them through Scripture, song, exposition, and perhaps prophecy, and respond by humbly realigning their ideas and actions to match God's desire for them. Communal worship thus allowed them to be reconciled to God and to one another. It also gave them a venue where they could be more fully equipped so that they could go forth to serve God in the world. Christian congregations today could have no higher aim.

This study of the words of worship has only given us a brief introduction to the Bible's teaching on this subject. In the chapters that follow, we will consider the God whom we worship, the people who worship him, the times and places set aside for worship, and a number of biblical themes that inform our practice. We now turn to the biblical narratives, laws, and psalms used by Israel as they worshipped God and the New Testament documents that realigned earlier revelation by showing how it points to Jesus Christ. We will see how the believing response of God's people throughout the ages provides us with a model of worship for us to reflect on and emulate.

2

The God Who is Worshipped

Some years ago, when I lived in Taiwan, I learned that when new acquaintances discovered I was a missionary, the conversation was likely to head in one of two directions. Some had no interest in Christianity and intended to shut down any discussion of the topic. "All religions are the same," they would tell me. "They teach us how to be good. We Chinese have our religions and you Westerners have yours." The statements came across as a polite way to say that they might accept me as being a good guy, but they had no interest in my religion as it was foreign. Apparently, in their desire to change the topic, they never took the time to consider that there are great differences between religions and that the main purpose of religion is not simply to teach people to be good. Similarly, they probably never considered that Christianity was not Western but that its roots are in Asia and that one of the most popular religions among the Chinese—Buddhism—was a foreign import from India.

The other potential conversation began with my new friend availing himself of the opportunity to hear the answer to a question he had long found to be quite puzzling. "What is the difference between a Christian and a Catholic?" I soon discovered that they were not curious about the causes of the Reformation or the resultant division of the church into various branches, but simply desired to understand why different Chinese terms were used by Protestants and Roman Catholics for the religion of those who follow Jesus. Why do some call it *Tian Zhu Jiao*—the Heavenly Lord Religion—and others refer to it as *Jidu Jiao*—the Christ Religion? Are these distinct faiths that worship different Gods? Or is the difference simply a matter of nomenclature?

This brief recollection highlights two essential aspects of biblical worship. First, it points out that the object of worship matters. Even as it is wrong to say that every religion is the same, so it is wrong to think that every deity is the same. The God of the Bible is distinct from the other gods worshipped in the ancient Near Eastern and the ones worshipped in the world today. Second, it reminds us that since the Bible uses several different names for God, it is permissible, indeed essential, that different names are used for him today as long as we make it clear that only one God is in view. By using various names or titles for God, we follow biblical precedent and recognize that no one name can adequately express God's attributes and greatness.[1] This chapter will build upon these two concepts as it examines what the Bible says about the one God who alone is to be worshipped.

THE GOD OF CREATION

"In the beginning God created the heavens and the earth" (Gen 1:1). With these words, the Bible begins its narrative about God and the people he chose to be his own. As the first subject of Scripture, God's existence is never questioned and no attempt is made to explain where he came from. This is undoubtedly because the first readers of Genesis were well acquainted with God as they had experienced his power and presence in Egypt, at Mt. Sinai, and in the wilderness. They knew that the God of their ancestors had revealed himself anew to Moses at the burning bush and to the whole nation through the exodus. So when they read about the God of creation, they knew exactly who he was—the God of Abraham, Isaac, and Jacob who revealed himself as Yahweh to his chosen people.[2] That the God who entered into covenant relationship with Abraham and his descendants was the God of creation is seen in the main Hebrew words for the divine—Elohim and Yahweh—usually translated in our Bibles as "God" and "the LORD." As Elohim,

---

1. For an examination of how a number of names for God found in the Bible compare to names of certain Canaanite gods, see McConnell, "You Shall Have No Other Gods," 25–31.

2. Israel's faith began, not with the understanding that Yahweh is Creator, but with the confession, based on their exodus experience, that he is Redeemer. See Anderson, *From Creation to New Creation*, 26. This does not, however, lessen the importance of their belief in him as Creator. "Yahweh is not the God of creation because he is the God of the humans or of human history. He is the God of the humans and of human history because He is the God of creation." Knierim, "The Task of Old Testament Theology," 40, quoted in Fretheim, *God and World*, xiii.

he is the God of creation, the God who is over all (including the nations that do not acknowledge him). As Yahweh, he is the God of the covenant, the God who is relational. At times, the two are combined as Yahweh Elohim, which in most English Bibles is translated "the Lord God." The implication is that the God of creation is the God of the covenant. Though he is referred to in different ways, only one God is in view.

Who is the God of creation? During the nineteenth and twentieth centuries, creation accounts from other ancient Near Eastern cultures were discovered that lead some scholars to conclude the primeval history in Genesis contained little that was original.[3] Later studies demonstrated that there was more to distinguish the Genesis creation accounts from the other stories than unite them. The differences have been rightly accentuated by a number of scholars who point out that the biblical creation stories were not written to imitate the other versions, but to serve as a polemic against them.[4] As a diatribe against the other religious worldviews of its day, Genesis provides information about God that his worshippers needed to know. First, it distinguished him from the gods in other accounts as he was the sole Creator who needed no help. Genesis further sets the God of Israel apart by showing that he is powerful rather than impotent, just instead of capricious, concerned for the lot of humankind rather than intent on using them for his own benefit.[5] As described in the early chapters of Genesis, Yahweh was neither a tribal deity nor one god among many. Rather, he was the one true God, the Creator of all things, the only proper object of worship.

A second thing that Genesis 1 teaches about the God who is worshipped is that he is transcendent—above and distinct from everything else. That a deity could be distinct from creation was unknown to Israel's neighbors who worshipped gods that were connected to heavenly bodies, geographic features, and living organisms. A totally different vision is revealed in the Bible, which describes God creating the things that other people worshipped as divine. By simply speaking the word, God made the light and separated it from darkness, divided the heavens from the earth, separated the water in the seas from dry land, caused seed yielding plants to grow, made the luminaries to light the day and night, and created the sea creatures, birds, land animals, and humankind. That God speaks into existence the things

---

3. For other creation accounts, see Heidel, *Gilgamesh Epic*; Gunkel, *Legends of Genesis*; Smith, *Chaldean Account*; Clifford, *Creation Accounts*; Simkins, *Creator and Creation*, 41–81. See also the many articles in Hess and Tsumura, *Inscriptions*.

4. See Hasel, "Polemic," 81–102; Wenham, *Genesis 1–15*, xlvii. For an argument that the Old Testament may not be a polemic but "simply giving its own account of creation and the Creator," see Walton, *Old Testament Theology*, 77.

5. Wenham, *Genesis 1–15*, 1.

worshipped as deities says something about him and about them. As the Creator, the whole world and everything in it belongs to him (Ps 24:1). He is the Lord of all. In addition, by declaring that the parts of creation commonly identified as divine were made by God, Genesis insists that they have no independent existence and should not be worshipped or fashioned into idols (Exod 20:4–5; Deut 4:15–19). Since the gods are not gods but created things, polytheism—in both its ancient and modern forms—is negated and people are freed from servitude to a multiplicity of gods. Whether the gods that are worshipped are part of the natural world, are made of wood, metal, or stone, or have more in common with the modern pursuits of sex, success, and security, God's creative transcendence liberates his people from them. It further reminds them that since the things worshipped as gods were made by God, they are should not be feared but recognized as "good" when allowed to fulfill the purposes for which God made them.

Genesis makes a third point about God that should impact our worship: he is not what deists described as a distant watchmaker who put everything together and then left it to run on its own. Far from being a wholly transcendent being that is unknowable and uncaring, God is intimately involved in the world. His immanence is seen in the presence of the Spirit hovering over the waters and through his personal acts of speaking, naming, evaluating, and blessing the various things he makes. By speaking creation into existence, "God shows his 'heart', demonstrates his intelligence, and inaugurates the communication of himself which he will make by speaking to mankind."[6] He begins communicating to Israel and the rest of humankind through his act of creation so that he can be known by what he has made. By evaluating his work and proclaiming it "good," he shows that he enjoys his achievements. "God the great artist is pictured admiring his handiwork."[7] And though the word translated "good" can be used for moral or aesthetic categories, in this context, it seems best to say it indicates that the different parts of creation accomplish what God intended them to do.[8] His pleasure with creation demonstrates his care for it. By blessing the various parts, God shows that he loves the things he has made and endows them with life. God explicitly blesses the animals and humans so that they can reproduce and fill the earth (Gen 1:22, 28).[9] Humans receive the further blessing of subduing

---

6. Blocher, *In the Beginning*, 68.

7. Wenham, *Genesis 1–15*, 18.

8. Westermann, *Creation*, 61. Thus, the light worked like light should. The land and water separated like God wanted them to. The sun, moon, and stars shone and moved about the heavens just like God designed them to. The plants grew and produced seed, and animals, fish, and birds grew and had offspring, just like God desired.

9. A close reading of the passage reveals that God blesses the sea creatures, birds,

the earth and ruling over all the other living creatures, a task that the wider context indicates is to be fulfilled by relating to the nonhuman world with compassion and care.[10]

God's immanence is portrayed in a slightly different way in Genesis 2, where anthropomorphic terms are used to show his relation to the earth and particularly to the man he creates. After creating the earth, God stoops down, collects a handful of dust, and, like a potter, forms the man. He then breathes life into the nostrils of the man so that he could live. The narrative next portrays Yahweh God as a gardener, planting a beautiful, bountiful garden that would be an ideal place for the man to live. God then places the man in the garden, speaks to him, instructs him to tend and keep the garden, brings all the animals before him so that he can name them, and performs a surgical operation through which he makes a companion suitable for him.

God's involvement with creation and with humankind indicates that he is a relational God who can be known and therefore worshipped by those he creates.[11] This could not be true of a god who was exclusively transcendent or immanent: the first would be unknowable to the worshipper and the second would be indistinguishable from creation and perhaps even from the worshipper.

A fourth way in which Genesis 1–2 hints that God should be worshipped is grounded in its brief reference to seasons and to the seventh day. On the fourth day of creation, God said, "Let there be lights in the expanse of the sky to separate the day from the night, and let them serve as signs to mark seasons and days and years, and let them be lights in the expanse of the sky to give light on the earth" (Gen 1:14–15). What is important for worship is that one of the God-ordained functions of the sun and moon was to mark seasons. The Hebrew word translated seasons is commonly used to designate the religious feasts that Israel celebrated according to the lunar calendar.

That God created the lights that enabled Israel to mark their seasons of worship would not have been missed by the original readers. Neither would

---

and humans. Blocher suggests that "if the various animals that walk on the earth receive no particular blessing, it is without doubt because the blessing of humanity spills over on to them, so close is their association." Blocher, *In the Beginning*, 76.

10. For an in-depth examination of the way the Genesis creation passages view the relationship between humans and the rest of creation, see McConnell, "Ecological Ethics," 189–222.

11. For some aspects of what it means for God to be relational in creation, see Fretheim, *God and World*, 13–22. There is a sense in which even nonhuman creation, though it is not personal, is able to express praise through humans. "Creation's non-personality means that it is unable to realise its destiny, the praise of its Creator, apart from persons. It is not personal, but requires persons in order to be itself." Gunton, *Trinitarian Theology*, 114.

the reference to the seventh day. Though some have cautioned against locating the "institution of the Sabbath" here,[12] the fact that the account was written at a time when Israel celebrated the seventh day as the Sabbath makes it unlikely that early readers would have understood it in any other way. Since God blessed the day and proclaimed it holy, it was set apart from the other days so that the six days for work found their goal in the one day for rest.[13] There is a sense in which the blessing of the day flows over into the lives of people who accept the rest so that their lives and work become more fruitful.[14] The seventh day exists for all humankind to enjoy, and in the context of the later Sabbath command (Exod 20:8–11; Deut 5:12–15), may also serve as a blessing for the animals. The importance of time to the worship of God will be examined more closely in a later chapter.

A fifth way in which the creation stories inform readers that God should be worshipped is found in the parallels between the Garden of Eden and later sanctuaries.[15] Though a number of other similarities could be identified, the following should suffice to indicate the link between Eden and the Mosaic tabernacle—the place that served as God's dwelling place in the midst of his people. (1) God walks about in Eden and amongst his people Israel in their camp and particularly in the tabernacle (Gen 3:8; Lev 26:12; Deut 23:15; 2 Sam 7:6–7). (2) Both the garden and the tabernacle are entered from the east. (3) After Adam and Eve are expelled from the garden, cherubim, which frequently guarded ancient Near Eastern holy places, are stationed there to prevent them from reentering. Cherubim are also present in the tabernacle and Solomon's temple where they are closely associated with God. (4) Connections can be made between the garden and the tabernacle as places where life is bestowed upon God's people. In Eden, the fruit of the tree of life gives life, as do the rivers that flow through the Garden. In the tabernacle, life comes through sacrificial offerings. There are reasons to believe that the menorah found in the tabernacle was a stylized tree of life. It is also clear that later biblical passages connected the temple with life-giving water (Ps 46:5; Ezek 47). This symbolism comes to its climax in Revelation 22:1–2, which speaks of the river of life flowing from the throne of God and of the Lamb, and of the tree of life planted on both sides of the river. Though there is no temple in the New Jerusalem (Rev 21:22), the presence of the Lord God Almighty and of the Lamb replaces the temple and is associated with the things formerly found in Eden.

12. Rad, *Genesis*, 60.
13. Westermann, *Genesis 1–11*, 171.
14. Wenham, *Genesis 1–15*, 36; Westermann, *Genesis 1–11*, 172.
15. See Wenham, "Sanctuary Symbolism," 19–25.

A final lesson the creation passages teach about God comes from the story of the first sin. In contrast to the greatness of Yahweh Elohim, Genesis 3 portrays the serpent as nothing more than a creature, even if it "was more crafty than any of the wild animals the LORD God had made" (Gen 3:1). And though it is not a rival divinity, when the man and woman chose to accept the snake's word over the LORD God's, the creational hierarchy—which placed God at the top, people underneath him as the image of God ruling on earth, and the rest of creation under them—was subverted. The snake assumes the position that only God can rightfully hold (cf. Exod 20:3). By accepting its word over God's, Adam and Eve chose to rise above their created position, a decision that would have tragic consequences as it would bring their life in the garden to an end, result in an existence of painful toil, and eventually see them return to the dust in death.

Several implications arise from this story that should inform our understanding of the God who is worshipped. (1) People have always had the capacity to displace the God of creation with another god or gods. (2) Everyone who raises the status of other beings over God becomes alienated from God and unable to know him and appreciate him in his fullness. (3) The worship of other beings as gods neither negates God's real existence nor lessens his sovereignty. He will still judge those who reject him, and can graciously intervene in the lives of sinners so that they can return to fellowship with him.

Even though the creation passages in Genesis do not explicitly command people to worship God, they portray the Creator as distinct from all other deities and as the only proper object of worship.

THE GOD OF THE COVENANT

The transcendent God of creation relates intimately to the world he made by forming and naming it. He evaluates it and speaks to it. God is no distant deity who is disconnected from his handiwork. Rather, he cares for it deeply and personally. One of the ways God cares for his handiwork is through his covenant relationship. Although mainly developed through the covenants he makes with people, God's covenants embrace the rest of creation as well.

In the ancient Near East, covenants were drawn up between individuals or nations in order to bring them into relationship and testify that each party was committed to uphold certain obligations toward the other party.[16] Frequently, a written document—which was duly signed, witnessed,

---

16. Covenant obligations could be unilateral or bilateral—binding on either one or both parties.

and sealed—was drawn up to stipulate what each side was required to do. While the Bible mentions covenants drawn up between humans,[17] it is more concerned with the covenants God makes with his chosen people.[18] Five such covenants are explicitly mentioned: (1) between God and Noah (Gen 6:18; 9:9–17); (2) between God and Abraham (Gen 15:8–18; 17:1–14); (3) between God and Israel at Sinai (Exod 20:1–17);[19] (4) between God and David (2 Sam 7:12–17); and (5) the new covenant (Jer 31:31–37).[20]

In addition to supporting the claim that God is personal, the Bible's teaching about the covenants reflects three things about him that should impact worship. First, it describes them in the context of a sovereign-servant relationship. Biblical covenants, echoing ancient Near Eastern practice, were often made between rulers and their vassals (Josh 9:6, 11, 15; 2 Sam 5:1–3). This is similar to the covenant established between Israel and Yahweh at Mt. Sinai in that God is the king and ruler of his people.[21] Israel was responsible to keep the stipulations laid out in the covenant, particularly those found in the Ten Commandments (Exod 20:1–17) and the Book of the Covenant (Exod 21:1—23:33). If they kept the covenant, God would bless them, but if they disobeyed, they would be cursed (Lev 26; Deut 27:9—28:28). Their failure to keep the covenant by worshipping other gods is often cited as the major reason Israel suffered at the hands of other nations (Judg 2; 2 Kgs 17).

Second, when Israel comes into covenant relation with God, they are set apart as God's treasured possession who will serve him as a kingdom of priests and a holy nation (Exod 19:5–6). God's choice suggests that Israel was reckoned the "crown jewel" or masterpiece of his works simply because they assented to be his covenant people.[22] As he holds them to be precious, they should respond in kind. As a kingdom of priests, they are responsible

---

17. For a list of types of biblical covenants established between people, see Thompson, "Covenant (OT)," 791.

18. Covenant is such an important concept in the Bible that Walter Eichrodt identified it as the center of Old Testament theology. Though few today accept Eichrodt's conclusion, the importance of the theme cannot be overestimated. Eichrodt, *Theology of the Old Testament*.

19. At various times during Israel's history, this covenant was renewed (Deut 29; Josh 24; 2 Kgs 11; 23:3; 2 Chr 29:10).

20. Reformed theologians often point to a "covenant with creation" or a "covenant of works" said to have existed before the fall. For some of the arguments for this position, see Dumbrell, *Covenant and Creation*, 11–46. Exegetical and other reasons can be given for concluding that these claims often go beyond the evidence. See Williamson, "Covenant," 141–43.

21. Other relationships that can be used to describe God's covenant relation with his people include husband-wife (Jer 31:32) and father-son (Hos 11).

22. Durham, *Exodus*, 262.

to extend Yahweh's kingdom throughout the world (Exod 19:6). This they will do by representing God to the nations, and representing the nations to God. Their priestly role indicates that theirs is a kingdom of service rather than of power. As a holy nation, they will be set apart from the other peoples to demonstrate how obedience to Yahweh's covenant changes people. It also sets them apart to be like their holy God.

Third, the covenantal language about God indicates that he is faithful and will keep his covenant with those who obey his commands (Deut 7:9).[23] God's faithful, covenantal love is regularly expressed by use of *ḥesed*, a word that conveys a breadth of ideas from kindness to mercy. Abraham's servant finds Rebekah due to Yahweh's *ḥesed* and responds by bowing in worship (Gen 24:12, 26–27). In the Song of the Sea, Israel rejoices that God led them through the waters because of his *ḥesed* (Exod 15:13). The connection between God's covenant and *ḥesed* is made clear in Deuteronomy 7:9. "Know therefore that the LORD your God, He is God, the faithful God, who keeps His covenant and His lovingkindness [*ḥesed*] to a thousandth generation with those who love Him and keep His commandments" (NASB). Yahweh is distinct from the gods of the Near East who are exceedingly capricious. That God can be trusted to keep his word and to act for the benefit of his people is good news. This is so even for those who sin against him. Though his people will inevitably fail to fulfill their covenant obligations, Yahweh never will. And since the failure of his people is certain, God provides a sacrificial system designed to repair the breach.

THE GOD WHO IS HOLY

Throughout the Bible, God is consistently portrayed as holy. He proclaims himself to be holy (Lev 19:2; 20:26). He is known as the Holy One (Job 6:10; Ps 22:3) or the Holy One of Israel (2 Kgs 19:22; Ps 71:22; Isa 1:4).[24] He is proclaimed holy by the seraphim and other heavenly beings (Isa 6:3; Rev 4:8). Even his name is said to be holy (Lev 20:3; 22:2, 32). Since names in the ancient Near East were considered an aspect of a person's identity, linking God's name and holiness indicates that it is one of the basic aspects of his nature. And just like his person, God's name is to be praised (Pss 30:4; 103:1;

---

23. As Childs says, "the covenant is a means of revelation whose major function is to demonstrate God's faithfulness to his word." Childs, *Old Testament Theology in a Canonical Context*, 43.

24. The translation "Holy One" comes from the Hebrew adjective *qādôš*, which, used as a substantive, can refer to God as the Holy One or to heavenly beings or saints as holy ones.

105:3). Holiness, which is the most basic characteristic of God, conveys both separateness and ethical righteousness. Neither concept is adequate, as the first does not identify what God is separate from, and righteousness is not as broad as holiness. Even so, these ideas help us understand what God's holiness is and what it requires of his worshippers.[25]

On the one hand, God's holiness "becomes an expression for His perfection of being which transcends everything creaturely."[26] As he is wholly other, he should not be confused with the gods of the natural world or the idols made by human hands. God's holiness is experienced as he exhibits his majestic power, whether through salvific acts, establishing his covenant, or providing instructions for the building of the tabernacle and its holy furnishings. On the other hand, God's holiness has a moral aspect that points to the purity of his being which cannot abide the presence of sin in any form. Sinners can only come into his presence when they acknowledge their unholiness and are cleansed from their sin.

Both the otherness and purity of God come across in Isaiah's vision in which the seraphim called out to each other: "Holy, holy, holy is the Lord Almighty; the whole earth is full of his glory" (Isa 6:3). Though they are sinless beings, the seraphim recognize their creatureliness in the presence of the Almighty. Isaiah's response shows that he was not only aware that God was set apart on high, but that he was morally destitute in the Lord's presence. "Woe to me! . . . I am ruined! For I am a man of unclean lips, and I live among a people of unclean lips, and my eyes have seen the King, the Lord Almighty" (Isa 6:5). By dating his vision to the year of the death of the most prosperous Judean king since Solomon, Isaiah likely intended to contrast dependence upon a successful earthly king and reliance upon Yahweh of Hosts who rules over all. Though the sin that the prophet and his fellow citizens needed to be cleansed of was more extensive, it undoubtedly included their recognition of who was the true king.[27] While the seraphim continually reminded themselves of God's holiness, the citizens of Judea had been satisfied to follow a man who long occupied a throne. The prophet's encounter with Yahweh pointed out his need to reassess his allegiance and reflect the moral purity displayed by God. His need for cleansing was met when one of the seraphim touched his lips with a live coal and proclaimed that his guilt was taken away and his sin atoned for (Isa 6:7). Significantly, Isaiah was not cleansed by offering up a sacrifice for himself, but by God's intervention through a seraph.

---

25. Hartley, "Holy and Holiness," 420. For an in-depth study of the concept, see North, "חָדָשׁ *chādhāsh*; חֹדֶשׁ *chōdhesh*."

26. Procksch, "ἅγιος," 91.

27. Dumbrell, "Worship and Isaiah 6," 59.

This cleansing has a counterpart in the New Testament that insists one can be purified only by coming into relationship with the Holy One, Jesus Christ, who makes people holy (Heb 2:11; 10:10, 14).

The Bible repeatedly declares that God makes people and things holy (Exod 31:13; Lev 20:8; 21:8). Holiness is part of his divine nature that can only be transferred to people or things at his direction and will. A place, thing, or person becomes holy due to the presence of God. The high priest, priests, Levites, and even the entire nation of Israel are made holy. The tabernacle and camp around it are holy. Those whom God makes holy are to keep themselves separate from the nations around them, refusing to worship any other gods and being careful to obey God's righteous statutes. Since they come from God, Israel's laws are intrinsically holy. Repeatedly, individual laws are given with the reminder to "Be holy because I, the LORD your God, am holy" (Lev 19:2; 1 Pet 1:16). When Israel obeys God's holy laws, they express his righteousness by doing what pleases him. Obedience is thus a means of worshiping through daily service. To help them maintain their holy standing before him, God instituted the Old Testament sacrificial system that required his people to discern between what is holy and what is not, and mandated that they approach God only in the way he prescribed—with clean hands and clean heart.

In the New Testament, God's holiness is taken for granted to the extent that it is rarely mentioned except in reference to the Holy Spirit. When found, it usually reflects Old Testament usage. Thus, when Mary prays what is known as the Magnificat, she praises God for the great things he has accomplished for her and acknowledges that "holy is his name" (Luke 1:49). Jesus makes a similar recognition in his great high priestly prayer by petitioning his "Holy Father" to protect the disciples by his name, which he gave to the Son (John 17:11).[28] While Jesus and Mary recognize the Father's intrinsic holiness through his works of provision and protection, a different light is thrown upon the holiness of God's name in the Lord's Prayer where we find, not so much an acknowledgement that God's name *is* holy, but a request that his name be considered holy by his children and by the world (Matt 6:9). This is surely because those who pray to the Father need to know what his holiness is like before they can reflect it in their own lives. The desire that God's people demonstrate his holiness is expressed by Peter who echoes the common refrain from Leviticus that they should be holy since the God who called them is holy (1 Pet 1:15–16).

---

28. This name is undoubtedly the divine name which Jesus shares with the Father and the Spirit.

The book of Revelation speaks of God's holiness more than any other New Testament book. The creatures in heaven echo the seraphim of Isaiah when they cry out "Holy, holy, holy is the Lord God Almighty" (Rev 4:8). In response, the twenty-four elders bow down before God in worship and cast their crowns before the throne in recognition that he is the true king. Later in the book, those martyred for their testimony about Jesus cry out to the Lord, asking how long it would take until he "judge the inhabitants of the earth and avenge our blood?" (Rev 6:10).[29] That they recognize him as "holy and true" indicates their conviction that he would bring vengeance. Those who overcame the beast exalted God with a song in which they declare, "Who will not fear you, O Lord, and bring glory to your name? For you alone are holy. All nations will come and worship before you, for your righteous acts have been revealed" (Rev 15:4). God's holiness, observed through his righteous acts, results in fear, glory, and the worship of the nations.

The New Testament writers recognize both the Father and Son to be holy. During the annunciation of Jesus' birth, the angel told Mary that the "holy one" she would bear would be called the Son of God (Luke 1:35). When Jesus asked the Twelve whether they wanted to stop following him as did many other disciples, Peter responded with what can only be called a confession of faith: "We believe and know that you are the Holy One of God" (John 6:69). Jesus' standing was evident to a band of unclean spirits residing in a man who encountered Jesus in the synagogue in Capernaum. They could sense that he was "the Holy One of God," probably because he uniquely possessed the Holy Spirit who is diametrically opposed to their work and existence (Mark 1:24; Luke 4:34).[30] After Pentecost, the apostles continued to use the title "Holy One" for Jesus. They signified that Old Testament passages applied to him (Acts 2:27; 13:35), used the term in evangelistic sermons (Acts 3:14), and even recounted the work of "your holy servant Jesus" to the Father in prayer (Acts 4:27, 30). Holiness is as much a part of Jesus' essential nature as it is the Father's and similarly makes him the object of worship.

The biblical concept of holiness sets the people of God apart from those who do not know him. Other ancient people could not conceive of a personal God or a holy God, as they mainly experienced holiness as a feeling of awe (which at times produced aversion) when one came in contact with the divine realm. A priest was a holy person simply because he had contact with

---

29. Note that "How long?" is frequently used in Old Testament laments by those who want to know when God will judge oppressors and vindicate the righteous. We will later examine the place of lament in worship.

30. Procksch, "ἅγιος," 101–102.

the divine realm, not because of his moral character.[31] In contrast, Israel and the church saw God's holiness linked to his person, his transcendence, and his activity as Creator. His worshippers are required to know him and reflect his holiness just like they reflect his image. They similarly need to keep themselves apart from the worship of other gods and from all that would make them impure. Whereas they may feel awe in his presence, they are also to pursue the moral purity that characterizes their Lord.

THE GOD WHO IS ONE

Sometimes, living in a pluralistic world where different religions and belief-systems vie for our attention makes us feel uneasy. If Jesus is the only way to God, why do so many people refuse to follow him, choosing instead to worship other gods or no god at all? Could there be saving truth in other religions? Is it possible for people to come to God using different names, like some of my Chinese friends implied? Can Christians access God through Jesus Christ while followers of other religions come to God using other names or forms? Such questions are nothing new. The Bible was written for people who continually interacted with those who served other gods and wondered about their place in such a world. The early Israelites pondered the identity of Yahweh and how he fit into the pantheon of gods worshipped by the Egyptians, Canaanites, and their other neighbors. The biblical testimony stated that their God was unique—the Creator, covenant maker, and rescuer. By way of contrast, everything the nations worshipped as divine was part of the created order and therefore of no consequence in the light of Yahweh's power.

Since Yahweh was the only God, laws were established to prohibit the worship of other gods and the worship of Yahweh through images (Exod 20:3–5).[32] Though Israel's early practice is at times said to reflect henotheism or monolatry—the exclusive worship of one deity without denying the existence of others—it is clear that the Bible treats Yahweh as the only true God and insists that all the nations should worship him (Isa 45:18–23; Zech 14:9). This conviction was such an integral part of Israel's creed that it was codified in a statement that was central to their faith—the *Shema*. "Hear,

31. The Bible at times uses *qādēš* and *qĕdēšâ* for male and female cult prostitutes to indicate that they were set apart for a god, while making it clear that this practice should be rejected by worshippers of Yahweh (Deut 23:17).

32. Biblical and archaeological evidence makes it clear that even though the biblical writers demanded worship of Yahweh alone, many (and at times a majority) in Israel failed to comply. Both idols (e.g., the golden calf) and other gods (e.g., Baal and the Asherah) were worshipped throughout their history. See Smith, *History of God*.

O Israel: The Lord our God, the Lord is one" (Deut 6:4).[33] Yahweh was to be the sole object of Israel's worship. All other gods were rejected. Furthermore, the Bible views Yahweh as the one, unique, or indivisible God. He is like no other deity and is always consistent within himself. In later Judaism, the *Shema* was looked on as the most important prayer in the liturgy and was required to be repeated twice daily. Jesus highlighted its importance when he used the *Shema* in his response to the teachers of the law who asked him which was the greatest commandment (Mark 12:28–29).

New Testament writers make direct statements about God being one or over all (Eph 4:4–6; 1 Tim 1:17; 2:5). At times, they contrast him to the so-called gods that other people worship in the form of idols (Rom 1:18–25; 1 Cor 8:4–6). And even though the gods of Rome differed from the ones of Canaan, the apostles and their associates stringently defended God's preeminence. While they followed the Old Testament teaching about one God, they embraced a radically new idea when they proclaimed that the one God revealed himself and his redemptive power in the person of Jesus Christ who is to be worshipped along with the Father and the Holy Spirit (1 Tim 2:5–6; Rev 5:13; 7:10–12; 21:22–23).

Trinitarian Worship

That the one God is worshipped in three persons has been a distinguishing mark of Christianity from the time Jesus instructed his disciples to baptize new believers "in the name of the Father and of the Son and of the Holy Spirit" (Matt 28:19). Immediately after Pentecost, the disciples began to proclaim a gospel that spoke of the work of the Father, Son, and Spirit, which cut their hearers to the heart so that they repented and joined the apostles in worship (Acts 2:22–42). A Trinitarian formula was used at the end of Paul's second letter to the church in Corinth (2 Cor 13:14).[34] "May the grace of the Lord Jesus Christ, and the love of God, and the fellowship of the Holy Spirit be with you all." The "Grace," as this expression has become known, is a regular part of the liturgy of many churches.

Although the Christian doctrine of the Trinity took several centuries to develop and has been attacked on several fronts, its essential principles have been consistently defended as the only adequate explanation of the

---

33. The Hebrew is somewhat difficult to translate as it contains no verbs and the relationship between the words is not always clear. As the NIV marginal note makes clear, four translations are possible.

34. Note the similar "grace" in Revelation 1:4–6 which places the Spirit between the Father and Son.

New Testament witness that Jesus Christ and the Holy Spirit work together with the Father in creation and salvation, share his glory, and deserve universal worship. Our inability to articulate how the members of the Godhead can be three persons yet one essence is due to the mystery that is God. It is therefore important to realize that "the triune God is far more capable of worship than rational explanation."[35] For this reason, we should spend more time developing our practice of worshiping God the Father through Jesus Christ the Son by the power and leading of the Holy Spirit than attempting to explain the mystery.

CONCLUSION

In this chapter, we have seen the necessity to identify the object of our worship. In contrast to those who claim that all religious are alike, the Bible insists that there is but one God and Creator who alone is to be worshipped. Not only does religion differ from religion, the God of the Bible is distinct from all other deities, as they have no independent existence and are, at best, creatures, while he is transcendent over all. And though some have understood transcendence in deistic terms, the Bible makes it plain that Yahweh is equally an imminent God who desires to relate to what he has made and has chosen to establish a series of covenants with his own people, culminating in the New Covenant enacted by Jesus. In the light of scriptural usage, it is right to refer to God by multiple names, particularly Father, Son, and Holy Spirit, since no one name can capture his essence or character.

As we experience God's creative power and acknowledge his transcendent majesty, we need to acknowledge our creatureliness, bow before his greatness, and put away everything that attempts to usurp his authority. Since he is the relational Lord of all, everyone made in his image should acknowledge and walk with him as Adam did in Eden before the fall. Since he is the giver of life, we should respond to him with thanks and lifelong obedience. As he appointed the days and seasons, we should worship him throughout the weeks and years. As he extends grace to disobedient sinners, we should revere him with humble gratefulness. As he is the holy God who enters into covenant relationship with us, we should strive to uphold our part in the covenant as his holy, faithful servants. The best model we have of this life of worship is none other than Jesus Christ. In the next chapter, we will consider how our worship should be impacted by Jesus' worship of the Father and the way he was worshipped by others.

---

35. Seitz, *Word without End*, 16.

3

The Worship of Jesus

Although the Christian faith clearly springs from the religion of Israel and retains a fair level of continuity with it, it also exhibits areas of great discontinuity, particularly when it comes to the worship of Jesus. The biblical testimony about the worship of Jesus can be viewed from two different vantage points because Jesus appears as both the subject and the object of worship. As the subject of worship, Jesus worshipped the Father through his adherence to the religion of the old covenant, through his daily service of God and others, and by sacrificially offering himself for the sins of others. As the object of worship, Jesus displays his unity with the Father and the Holy Spirit—the one God of creation and redemption who allows, indeed welcomes, people to worship him. If we are to understand biblical worship, it is imperative that we examine the way in which Jesus worshipped his Father and the way in which people in Bible times, and since, worshipped him.

JESUS THE WORSHIPPER

The Gospels portray Abraham's first-century descendants faithfully adhering to the forms of worship introduced in the Old Testament. Mary followed directions given in Leviticus when she brought a purification sacrifice to the temple after giving birth to Jesus (Luke 2:21–24; Lev 12:3, 8). Joseph and Mary joined the annual Passover pilgrimage to Jerusalem so they could sacrifice and eat a Passover lamb. Jesus joined them at the Passover celebration when he was twelve years old,[1] but remained in the temple courts, listening

---

1. Care is needed when interpreting Luke 2:41–42. While the text does not necessarily

to and questioning the religious teachers, when Mary and Joseph began their return journey to Nazareth. When Mary reproved Jesus for mistreating her and Joseph, he made it clear that his Father's house—the temple—was the place where he should be. Thus, from an early age, he associated himself with the place where God was worshipped and identified God as his Father. In the light of his future ministry, we can conclude that what Jesus did at the age the Jews considered to be threshold of manhood, he continued to do as he grew up. Throughout the Gospels, Jesus frequently visited Jerusalem to celebrate the feasts and undoubtedly joined the sacrificial meals that accompanied those celebrations. While he had no need to present sin offerings, he would have rightly participated in the peace offerings and could well have sponsored them.

In addition to attending the annual Jewish feasts at the temple, Jesus regularly took part in services held in various synagogues.[2] As Luke reports, it "was his custom" to attend synagogue worship on the Sabbath (Luke 4:16). Like other Jews of the time, Jesus went to the synagogue to hear the word of God read and expounded. In addition, his synagogue visits served as opportunities to heal people of various diseases, free them from demonic control, and teach them about the kingdom of God (Matt 4:23; 12:9; 13:54). Jesus' worship in the synagogue went beyond impacting mind and heart to bringing God's shalom to people by healing their bodies and spirits. As his ministry progressed, synagogue services marked some of Jesus' greatest disputations with the Scribes and other Jewish religious leaders, mainly over what could or could not be done on the Sabbath. At issue was not whether God should be worshipped, but how.

Jesus understood worship to be an integral part of his relationship with God as expressed by obedience to the Father's will and demonstrated by concrete acts of service. This comes out vividly in the story about Jesus being tempted in the wilderness immediately after being baptized by John. In many ways, the temptation narrative parallels the Old Testament story of Israel's wandering in the wilderness.[3] The account in Matthew's Gospel echoes Deuteronomy 6 and 8 that detail how Moses informed the

---

imply that this was the first time Jesus celebrated the Passover in Jerusalem (see Marshall, *Gospel of Luke*, 126), it does not warrant the conclusion that Jesus went to Jerusalem with his parents every year for the feast (as in Peterson, *Engaging with God*, 110).

2. See the chapter "The Place of Worship" for a description of the development of synagogue worship and its practice in the first century AD.

3. It is also possible to see parallels between Jesus' temptations and the temptation faced by Adam and Eve and the three types of temptation mentioned in 1 John 2:16, "the lust of the flesh and the lust of the eyes and the boastful pride of life" (NASB). Blomberg, *Jesus and the Gospels*, 223.

generation about to enter the promised land to "Remember how the LORD your God led you all the way in the desert these forty years, to humble you and to test you in order to know what was in your heart, whether or not you would keep his commands" (Deut 8:2). The God who led Israel out of Egypt led Jesus into the wilderness by his Spirit. The God who tested the descendants of Jacob to see if they would obey his commands allowed Jesus to be tempted by the devil. While forty years of wilderness wanderings demonstrated that Israel failed God's test, forty days and forty nights fasting in the wilderness was sufficient to demonstrate that Jesus was God's humble servant who would faithfully keep his commands.

Jesus' interaction with the devil after his long fast shows his devotion to obeying the Father's will. Three times Jesus is tempted and three times he responds, "It is written," and quotes words to God's ancient children recorded in Deuteronomy (Matt 4:4, 7, 10; cf. Deut 8:3; 6:13, 16). His use of Scripture after each temptation shows that he knew God's commands and was determined to obey them. The third temptation is of special importance, as the devil promised to give Jesus all the kingdoms of the world if he would only bow down and worship him. Unlike the Israelites who fell before the golden calf in the shadow of the mountain where the Lord had instructed them to have no other gods before him and to make no idols, Jesus refused to worship any but the one who gave the law that said to "Worship the Lord your God, and serve him only" (Matt 4:10).[4] When Jesus thus dismissed his adversary, angels came and ministered to him.[5] In marked contrast to the devil's claim that angels would come to him if he jumped off the temple, they came because he worshipped his Father alone.

When the third temptation is interpreted in the context of Matthew's Gospel as a whole, Satan promised to give Jesus something he had no right to give. The authority belonged to the Father who gave it to his Son in response to his humble service, obedient death, and triumphant resurrection (cf. Matt 28:19-20). Once he received his rightfully earned power over all

---

4. Note the difference between the quote of Jesus in Matthew 4:10 and the original found in Deuteronomy 6:13, which says, "Fear the LORD your God, serve him only and take your oaths in his name." We have seen that to fear God is to worship him. That these terms were often used as synonyms is seen in the way the text of Matthew (and Luke 4:8) differs from the Septuagint by replacing *kurion ton theon sou phobēthēsē*, "Fear the LORD your God," with *kurion ton theon sou proskunēseis*, "Worship the LORD your God."

5. It is tempting to take *diakoneō* as "to serve," link it with the Old Testament word for worship, and conclude that the angels in Matthew 4:11 came to worship Jesus. This inviting interpretation fails because the Septuagint never uses the word and even though later Jewish writers and New Testament authors used it in the extended sense of "to serve," its basic meaning is "to wait at table" (cf. Luke 17:8; John 12:2). See Beyer, "διακονέω," 84–85, who understands that the angels ministered to Jesus by serving him food.

creation, Jesus returned to heaven to reign with his father and continue his priestly ministry of interceding for the saints (Rom 8:34; Heb 8:2).

Jesus' worship was based upon the close relationship he shared with the Father from all eternity. This is especially evident in John. According to Begbie, "The Fourth Gospel . . . opens up a vision in which the worship Jesus offers God is grounded in the eternal Son's loving communion with the Father."[6] John thus portrays Jesus as the Word, the *Logos*, who was with God and was God from the beginning (John 1:1). By coming into the world as God incarnate, Jesus reveals his Father's glory so that the invisible God could be made known (John 1:14, 18).[7] Jesus is able to show the world what God is like because he is willing to be sent by the Father. This idea pervades the Gospel and is frequently found on the lips of Jesus.[8] Accordingly, the fact that Jesus did not come on his own initiative but was sent by the Father supports his claim to know the Father (John 7:28–29). Similarly, he did not speak his own words but the words of the one who sent him (John 7:16–17). The sender and sent one are so intimate that Jesus can say that the one who sent him is with him (John 8:29; cf. 8:16), that one who believes in him believes in the one who sent him (John 12:44), that to see him is to see the sender (John 12:45), and to receive him is to receive the sender (John 13:20).

John demonstrates this close relationship in several ways. Jesus works in unity with the one who sent him in a spirit of humble obedience. Jesus never ceased to perform works that testified of his devotion to and reliance on the Father and service to both God and humankind. He was sent by the Father who ensures that he judges rightly (John 8:16, 18). He performs miracles in his Father's name (John 10:25). As the good shepherd, he lays down his life for the sheep and is able to take it up again because of his Father (John 10:14–18). He testifies, "I do nothing on my own but speak just what the Father has taught me" (John 8:28; cf. John 12:49; 14:23). When a group of Jews were planning to stone him for blasphemy, Jesus granted that they should "not believe me unless I do what my Father does" (John 10:37). But since he does obey the Father, they should accept him. This idea sums up his life work as is seen in his declaration prior to Gethsemane: "I do exactly what my Father has commanded me" (John 14:31). Everything Jesus does is an expression of his worship actualized through concrete acts of service in obedience to his Father's will.

6. Begbie, "Worship," 857.

7. Jesus also reveals his glory by performing miraculous signs. In response to these signs, such as when he turned the water to wine at the wedding feast in Cana, "his disciples put their faith in him" (John 2:11).

8. Leon Morris says that John's Gospel includes "forty-one references to the sending of the Son." Morris, *New Testament Theology*, 251.

The service Jesus performs distinguishes him from everyone else and prompts his followers to identify him with the Servant of Yahweh spoken of by the prophet Isaiah. The self-giving, suffering service performed by Jesus was so unexpected that not even his closest followers understood it. Reflecting the world's aspirations, the apostles James and John requested that Jesus allow them to sit on his left and right when he established his kingdom.[9] Jesus' response that "the Son of Man did not come to be served, but to serve, and to give his life as a ransom for many" (Matt 20:28; cf. Mark 10:45) demonstrates that the apostles' ambition for power runs counter to a proper kingdom ethic. The disciples' place under God is to serve others, not themselves. The one who wants to be great must become a servant (Matt 20:26; cf. Matt 23:11). And as Jesus reminded them and would soon demonstrate, service for the sake of others could very well lead to one's death (Matt 20:28). He would present himself as an offering so that others could be freed from their service to sin and restored to a proper place as members of God's family.

Though serving others in a sacrificial manner is an essential part of a life of worship, not even Jesus found it easy. Frequent rejection by religious leaders and citizens alike made service difficult, and the prospect of death was tougher still. On numerous occasions, he informed the disciples that he would return to Jerusalem where he would be rejected and killed. On the night before he was crucified, Jesus instructed his disciples to wait while he prayed. He then asked the Father that if it was possible to take his cup away (Matt 26:39, 42). But even as he expressed his desire to evade death, he steeled himself to obey the Father's will. Secure in his Father's desire for him, he stepped forward and engaged the gang that came to arrest him. Though he could have called twelve legions of angels to come to his defense (Matt 26:53), he did what was necessary for Scripture to be fulfilled. He performed his major act of worship by going to the cross to die as the perfect sacrifice for sin.

Jesus and Prayer

Jesus' life was characterized by obedient service from beginning to end. To ensure that his service would always be pleasing to the Father, Jesus frequently engaged in another aspect of worship—prayer. Jesus consistently modeled what it means to worship God through prayer. Since prayer was a

---

9. Though the other disciples rightly expressed indignation that the brothers would make such an audacious request, they were probably motivated by their own desire to attain the exalted positions for themselves.

means of accessing God's power for service, he regularly prayed for himself and for others (Luke 22:32, 40–46; 23:34, 46), all the while asking that his Father's will be done. Even though he came to seek and save those who were lost, at times he felt the need to get away from people and pray in solitude (Matt 14:23; Mark 1:35; 6:46–48; Luke 5:16; 6:12).[10] As Grenz puts it, "Jesus' ministry oscillated between engagement and disengagement. He was alternately with the people, teaching and healing, and alone for times of prayer."[11] At the beginning of his ministry, Jesus withdrew to fast and pray for a period of forty days and nights (Matt 4:2). On other occasions, his prayer extended late into the night, and often came at significant moments in his ministry (e.g., before he chose his twelve apostles; Luke 6:12–13).[12]

Jesus prayed before his baptism (Luke 3:21) and before many of his miracles (Matt 15:36; John 11:41–42). During his transfiguration, the appearance of his face changed "as he was praying" (Luke 9:28–29). The phraseology indicates that the apostles made a connection between his prayer and transformation. In Luke's Gospel, Jesus' private prayer formed the backdrop against which he asked his disciples who the crowds thought he was. While some thought he was John the Baptist and others that he was Elijah, Peter declared that Jesus was "the Christ of God" (Luke 9:20). Jesus responded by warning his disciples not to tell anyone else and then reminding them that he, the Son of Man, would be rejected and killed (Luke 9:18–22). Jesus prayed before his arrest, trial, and crucifixion (Matt 26:36–44; Luke 22:40–46). Even on the cross, he called out to his Father (Matt 27:46; Mark 15:34; Luke 23:34, 46). The initial echoes of the psalmist's lament, "My God, my God, why have you forsaken me?" (Matt 27:46; cf. Ps 22:1) are transformed into the triumphant exclamations, "It is finished" (John 19:30) and "Father, into your hands I commit my spirit" (Luke 23:46).

Though Jesus prayed for the major events of his life, he also prayed for simple everyday things like the provision of food and drink (Matt 14:19; 15:36; 26:26–27). Because he considered the needs of others, he prayed for little children (Matt 19:13–15) and especially for his disciples. In his great

---

10. His teaching that his followers should pray to God in the privacy of their homes rather than in public places (Matt 6:5–6) is a further sign that Jesus believed that prayer was a private engagement with God.

11. Grenz, *Prayer*, 12.

12. A comparison of the stories of Jesus appointing the twelve apostles in Mark 3:13–19 and Luke 6:12–16 links the night-long prayer (Luke only), the call of the apostles out of a larger group of disciples (both Evangelists), and the service the apostles would render—"that they might be with him and that he might send them out to preach and to have authority to drive out demons" (Mark 3:14–15). Along with the other things he prayed for, Jesus devoted time to praying for the men he chose and the mission they would perform.

high priestly prayer, Jesus asked the Father to protect his disciples as they remained in a world that hated them as it hated him, to keep them safe from the evil one, and to sanctify them in God's truth (John 17:11–17). Jesus continued by praying for those who would believe the message the disciples would preach and requesting unity so that the world might know that the Father sent the Son and loves those who follow the Son (John 17:20–23). Jesus' intercession for his disciples immediately before the crucifixion is perhaps the first installment of his role of heavenly intercessor that he would take up after his ascension (Rom 8:34; Heb 7:25; 1 John 2:1).[13]

Jesus, moreover, taught others to pray. The most noteworthy example being what we call the Lord's Prayer (Matt 6:9–13; Luke 11:1–2). Luke records the Lord's Prayer in the context of Jesus' personal prayer. After he had finished praying, he taught the prayer that everyone who wants to learn to pray should copy because it focuses on the Father and his kingdom. Jesus also taught his disciples to pray for other workers to be sent out so that the harvest could be brought in (Luke 10:2). And when the disciples struggled with the reality that some evil spirits are extremely difficult to cast out, Jesus reminded them that some demons come out only by prayer and fasting (Mark 9:28–29).[14] In order to encourage his disciples "that they should always pray and not give up," Jesus told them a parable about a widow who entreated an unjust judge to hear her case (Luke 18:1–8). If one who feared neither God nor man would listen to the cries of an importune woman, surely the loving Father would hear his children's requests and meet their needs. The disciples should thus continually call upon God, trusting that he would help them.

JESUS THE ONE WHO IS WORSHIPPED

The New Testament writers were all Jewish monotheists who accepted the teaching of the Old Testament prophets, priests, and sages that there was only one God who alone should be worshipped.[15] For this reason, it would

---

13. In addition to interceding for his disciples, Jesus also interceded for those who persecuted and killed him (Luke 23:34; cf. Matt 5:44).

14. Though most ancient manuscripts and versions have "prayer and fasting," many scholars reject this reading as containing an addition that was influenced by the early church's growing emphasis on fasting. The shorter reading is given an "A" ("virtually certain") reading by Metzger, *Textual Commentary*, 101. For a good argument for retaining the longer reading and an explanation of the difference it makes in the interpretation of the passage, see France, *Mark*, 361, 369–70.

15. For an account of the nature of Jewish monotheism and its role in shaping Christian devotion to Jesus, see Hurtado, *Lord Jesus Christ*, 29–53.

have been unthinkable for them to produce clear statements about Jesus being worshipped unless they reckoned him to be divine.[16] There is no way they could have considered Jesus to be another god or even a lesser god. Yet, their conviction that there was only one God did not make them reticent to worship Jesus, describe others who worshipped him, and encourage their readers to do the same. Jesus was none other than the God of creation, the God who entered into a covenant with his people Israel, and who had now come to earth as a man for the sake of his people. While the apostles could not have fully understood this concept until after the resurrection, the Gospels provide many examples of people worshipping Jesus all through his earthly life.[17]

The earliest indications that Jesus was considered divine are found in the announcements of his birth to Mary and Joseph. According to the heavenly messenger, Mary's son "will be called the Son of the Most High," will receive David's throne, and "will reign over the house of Jacob forever" (Luke 1:32–33). The messianic language used here, along with the supernatural nature of the conception, and the indication that her child will be the Son of God, point to his divine nature. An angel later encouraged Joseph that he should not be afraid to take Mary as his wife: "She will give birth to a son, and you are to give him the name Jesus, because he will save his people from their sins" (Matt 1:21). The subject of, "he will save," is almost certainly the child. However, as the Hebrew for Jesus' name means "Yahweh saves," Joseph may well have understood this to mean that Yahweh intended to save his people through the child. Could he have deduced that the child was in some special way Yahweh himself—the one who saves?

While his name and birth connect Jesus with Yahweh, several passages indicate that he is the true temple, the place where God dwells with his people. This is surely the implication of the name Immanuel—"God with us" (Matt 1:23). The idea is also to be found in the introduction to John's Gospel that speaks of the Word being with God and being God and records that he dwelt among us so that his glory could be seen (John 1:1–14). The

---

16. As France says, "Monotheism was the hallmark of Judaism. To be a Jew was to be committed, often fanatically committed, to the maintenance of faith in only one God, in the face of a surrounding hellenistic culture which worshipped many gods, not to mention many semidivine heroes, and a deified emperor. . . . For a Jew then, as now, to speak of a man of his own times as divine was as impossible as it is for a Muslim to welcome the Christian doctrine of the Trinity or of Jesus as the Son of God." France, "The Worship of Jesus," 24.

17. Though France says that "the gospels do not provide clear evidence that Jesus was worshipped in the formal sense during His lifetime," he admits that this changed rapidly after his death and resurrection when his followers worshipped him in response to what they had seen and heard in his ministry. France, "The Worship of Jesus," 25–26.

phrase translated "and made his dwelling" in verse 14 includes the word *eskēnōsen*, which is the verbal form of the word for tent or tabernacle. Thus, Jesus "set up his tabernacle" among us so that we could experience God's presence on earth. The Son of God who dwells among us in glory, reigns forever, and brings Yahweh's salvation to the earth is regularly recognized in the New Testament as deserving and receiving worship.

Jesus first received worship as a baby. When Magi came from the east searching for the newborn king of the Jews, they explained to King Herod that, "We saw his star in the east and have come to worship him" (Matt 2:2).[18] After ascertaining that the Messiah would be born in Bethlehem, Herod requested that after the Magi saw him they should return and let him know where the child could be found since he too wanted to go and worship him (Matt 2:8).[19] Following the star to Bethlehem, the Magi entered the house where they saw Jesus and Mary. When they set their eyes on the child "they bowed down and worshiped him," and presented him with treasure fit for a king (Matt 2:11). While the Greek word here translated worship has a secular meaning that can denote paying homage, its use undoubtedly goes beyond mere respect. Matthew regularly uses the word for people who bow down to worship Jesus and it can plausibly be argued that it is only used in the New Testament for the worship of a deity.[20]

Matthew's Gospel has by far the most references to people bowing down to Jesus and is thus an important source for information about his being worshipped. After delivering the Sermon on the Mount, Jesus was approached by a leper who bowed down before him and said, "Lord, if you are willing, you can make me clean" (Matt 8:2). His realization that Jesus had the power to cure him, in concert with his actions and address, makes it likely that actual worship is in view.[21] In answer to the man's prayer, Jesus

---

18. How many Magi came, their original homeland, how long they travelled, and the nature of the star that guided them have been variously interpreted. The tradition of three Magi is based upon the three gifts they brought—gold, frankincense, and myrrh. Later Christian tradition give names to the "wise men" (and different names were used in the East and the West).

19. Only later would the Magi be warned not to return to Herod and Herod would show his true intent by killing all the young boys around Bethlehem to eliminate a potential threat to his rule.

20. Greeven says that the object of *proskuneō*, in the New Testament "is always something—truly or supposedly—divine." Greeven, "προσκυνέω," 763. He overcomes the apparent exception in Matthew 18:26 by saying that God can be glimpsed behind the king in the parable. Nolland presents a more nuanced position, arguing that Matthew's use blurs "the distinction between deferential respect and religious worship" when applied to Jesus. Whereas Matthew's ultimate goal is that his reader worships Jesus, the characters in his story may not have all come to that position. Nolland, *Matthew*, 111.

21. While *kurios* can mean "mister" or "sir," the context indicates divine status.

affirms his willingness, cleanses him of leprosy, and sends him to the priest so that he can worship God by offering the gifts specified in the Mosaic law.

The story of Jairus's daughter recounts a similar recognition that Jesus possessed power not only to heal, but, even more impressively, to raise someone from the dead (Matt 9:18–26). A synagogue ruler came to Jesus, bowed down, and pleaded that his daughter might be restored to life.[22] In the compound narrative, Jesus brought the young girl back to life after healing the woman who was ceremonially unclean due to her flow of blood. His power over disease and death are parallel signs of his divinity. As people recognized this, news about him spread all over the region.[23]

Though at times the disciples seemed confused about Jesus' identity, at other times they recognized his divinity and worshipped him. After feeding five thousand men plus women and children with just five loaves and two fish, Jesus sent the disciples away in their boat, and set off to pray privately. The disciples' progress across the lake was hindered by a great storm that threatened their existence. When Jesus approached, walking on the water, their fear of the waves was quickly overshadowed by the appearance of what they took for a ghost. Immediately, Jesus called out to them, "Take courage! It is I. Don't be afraid" (Matt 14:27). Impulsive as always, Peter responded that if it was the Lord, he should bid him to walk on the water too. Though initially able to traverse the wave tops, when Peter realized what he was doing, fear filled his heart and he began to sink. Responding to his desperate cry, "Lord, save me!" Jesus caught him up and chastised him for his doubt (Matt 14:30–31). After they climbed back into the boat, everyone onboard worshipped Jesus, saying, "Truly you are the Son of God" (Matt 14:33).

While Jesus was visiting the vicinity of Tyre and Sidon, a Canaanite woman came and pleaded for him to heal her demon-possessed daughter. Like the Jewish leper, this Gentile woman bowed down before him, addressed him as Lord, and begged for his help (Matt 15:25). More significantly, her first encounter with Jesus is marked by messianic language—"Lord, Son of David" (Matt 15:22). And though Jesus initially ignored her and then put her off by declaring that he had only been sent to the lost sheep of Israel, the woman's demonstration of faith moved him to grant her request. She,

22. While Matthew simplifies the account found in Mark, he is the only Evangelist who records that Jairus worshipped Jesus; the other synoptic Gospels have him fall at Jesus' feet. Mark and Luke singularly inform us that the man's name was Jairus and that he was the ruler of a synagogue (Mark 5:22; Luke 8:41). They also record that Jairus first came to Jesus to ask him to heal his daughter as she was sick. Only after the girl died did he ask Jesus to raise her from the dead.

23. John records a similar miracle that led to the spread of Jesus' reputation as a healer. After the man born blind was healed and put out of the synagogue, he came to believe that Jesus was the Son of Man and worshipped him (John 9:1–38).

like the Magi, was a foreigner who was allowed to worship him. Another story provides a potential contrast to this woman. The mother of James and John at one point bowed down to Jesus and asked him to help her sons by granting that they might sit at his right and left hand in the kingdom (Matt 20:20). While she probably made her request in the light of Jesus' promise that his disciples will sit on twelve thrones and judge the twelve tribes of Israel (Matt 19:29), it was likely a sign of ambition rather than faith. Even so, by prostrating herself in front of Jesus, she may well have been indicating her belief that he would set up his kingdom and that he was the proper object of worship.

The last two examples of Jesus being worshipped in Matthew are found in the post-resurrection narratives. After Mary Magdalene and the other Mary discovered Jesus' empty tomb early on the Sabbath morning, an angel instructed them to return to tell the disciples that Jesus would meet with them in Galilee. Hurrying back to Jerusalem, they were surprised when the Lord himself greeted them. Immediately, "They came to him, clasped his feet and worshiped him" (Matt 28:9). Obviously, they recognized that the crucified Lord had risen from the dead and that he deserved worship.

The second post-resurrection account describes the eleven remaining disciples on the mountain in Galilee where they were to meet Jesus (Matt 28:16–20). Once there, they worshipped him.[24] Like the women who met him on the morning of his resurrection, the disciples' encounter with the risen Christ convinced them that he should be the object of their worship. Jesus then declared that all authority in heaven and on earth had been given to him. As the one who wielded this authority, he sent them out to make disciples of all the nations of the world so that others would also recognize and worship him.

A further post-resurrection appearance of Jesus identifies him as the object of worship, although no words of worship are used. According to John, when the disciples had locked themselves away for fear of the Jews, Jesus appeared to them, gave them a greeting of peace, and showed them the scars on his hands and sides (John 20:19–20). When the missing Thomas was later informed that Jesus had appeared, he expressed the doubt that has ever since been attached to his name. Sadly, the faith he expressed after seeing Jesus is seldom noticed, even though it surpassed what the other disciples had shown up to that point. When the one who said he would not believe unless he saw and touched the nail marks in Jesus' hands and put

---

24. Luke similarly records that at the time of his ascension, Jesus' disciples worshipped him before returning to Jerusalem with great joy (Luke 24:52). Though some versions (e.g., NASB [but not the 1995 revision], RSV) omit "they worshipped him," the manuscript evidence for this omission is very weak.

his hand into Jesus' side was confronted by presence of the one who told him to stop doubting and believe, he gasped, "My Lord and my God" (John 20:28). No one in the Gospels provides a stronger witness that Jesus should be worshipped as God.

It is striking that Jesus willingly received the worship of his disciples and others. This is something that neither the apostles nor angels would permit anyone to do. Peter rebukes Cornelius's attempts by saying, "I am only a man myself" (Acts 10:25-26; cf. Acts 14:14-15). The angel before whom John bowed similarly responded, "Do not do it! I am a fellow servant with you . . . Worship God!" (Rev 22:8-9). If those who identify themselves merely as men and fellow servants are not to be worshipped, the only possible explanation for Jesus welcoming the worship of others is that he understood himself to be God. That Jesus was widely recognized as God is seen clearly in the opening chapter of John's Gospel and in the scenes of heavenly worship recorded in Revelation that portray the elders, mysterious living creatures, angels, and "every creature in heaven and on earth and under the earth and on the sea, and all that is in them" bowing down before the living God who is recognized as holy and worthy to receive praise and glory and honor and power forever and ever (Rev 4:11; 5:13). This picture of the universal worship of God is expanded in Revelation 5:6-14, where Jesus is portrayed as a Lamb standing on God's throne and worshipped by the four living creatures and the twenty-four elders because he was worthy to take the scroll that no one else could open, since he was slain and had purchased "men for God from every tribe and language and people and nation" (Rev 5:9). In response, myriads of angels sang that the slain Lamb was worthy and were joined by every creature who voiced their praise "to him who sits on the throne and to the Lamb" (Rev 5:11-14). Seated with the Father on the throne of authority and worshipped by all, the Lamb is regularly equated with God in Revelation (Rev 5:13; 6:16; 7:10, 17; 14:1, 4; 17:14; 21:22-23; 22:1, 3).

Recognition that Jesus is God is also found in Paul's epistles (Rom 9:5; Phil 2:5-6; Col 1:15-17, 19-20; 2:9), the book of Hebrews (Heb 1:1-12), and Peter's letter (1 Pet 3:15).[25] This understanding of Jesus, which was in place from the earliest days of the Christian religion, was the feature that distinguished Christian worship from Judaism and every Roman cult of the time. And since Jesus was acknowledged to be God, he became not only the object of worship but also the one to whom prayer was offered (Acts 7:59-60; 2 Cor 12:8-9; 1 Thess 3:11-12; 2 Thess 3:5, 16, 18). Prayer to Jesus was so characteristic that, from an early time, Christians could be identified

---

25. While the juxtaposition of Jesus and Lord do not always refer directly to the divinity of Christ, the reference from 1 Peter does, because, in this context, Lord is an explicit reference to Yahweh.

as those "who call on the name of our Lord Jesus Christ" (1 Cor 1:2). That Jesus receives our prayers and passes them on to his Father as our intercessor reinforces the idea that he is the only way we can approach God. Only as we pray in his name, aware of our natural unworthiness to come before God and of our need for his redemptive cleansing, can we gain confidence that the Father will hear our prayers.

THE WORSHIP OF JESUS AND THE CHURCH TODAY

The New Testament gives the church reason to understand Jesus as the model worshipper who should be emulated and the one who should be worshipped as God. It also makes it clear that one can worship God only as he reveals himself in Jesus Christ. Thus, Jesus' frequent use of "I am" in the Gospel of John indicates that he is the right way, the only way, to experience God. When Israel was in the wilderness, God gave them manna. Aligning himself with this experience, Jesus declared, "I am the bread of life" (John 6:35), the one sent from heaven who provides eternal life for all who come to him. By claiming further that, "I am the light of the world" (John 8:12), Jesus promises to take away darkness and give people the light of life. "I am the gate for the sheep" (John 10:7, 9) and "I am the good shepherd" (John 10:11, 14) affirm his watchful care for those the Father has given him. "I am the resurrection and the life" (John 11:25) asserts his power over death and gives assurance that those who believe in him will attain to the resurrection. While all these statements indicate that Jesus is the means by which God can be known, his response to Thomas's question about where he was going makes it clear that no other means exists. "I am the way and the truth and the life. No one comes to the Father except through me" (John 14:6). The exclusiveness of this statement indicates that access to God is limited to those who believe in Jesus. Indeed, Jesus goes on to say that to know him is to know the Father and to see him is to see the Father (John 14:7, 9). Without Jesus, it is impossible to know or worship God.

The author of Hebrews provides more detail to the picture of Jesus being the only way to God when he explains that Jesus is greater than any angel, human leader, or cultic artifact from any age. Since he is greater than the angels, the revelation that he brings is more trustworthy than theirs. As he surpasses Moses, he builds a greater house than the ancient prophet. Since he is both the greatest priest and the most perfect sacrifice, he provides never-ending access into the very throne room of the living God (Heb 8:1–13; 10:1–10). The unmistakable aim of the book is to demonstrate that people can be reconciled to God only because of Jesus' death and resurrection. Genuine worship is only possible through him.

Christians need to examine how they worship in the light of what the New Testament teaches about the worship of Jesus. As we have seen, Jesus followed the directions for worship that were recorded in the Old Testament. Though he did not need to offer up sacrifices for sin, he did take part in the festivals, partake of peace offerings, and actively lived out his worship through practical and humble service to God and others. Like their Lord, Jesus' modern-day disciples need to work out their faith in the light of Scripture. This includes meeting regularly with other believers to hear God's word read and expounded and to praise him. We should also emulate our Lord's ministry of restoring people to physical and spiritual wholeness. Like him, we should develop a life of prayer that brings us into close relationship with God and enables us to align our wills and actions with his. If these practices are lacking from our worship, we cannot call it biblical worship. And any worship that is not biblically based can hardly be considered Christian worship.

Alongside our questions about our practice of worship, we need to raise the question of our entry point to worship. Everyone who desires to worship in a biblical manner must recognize that Jesus is the only way to the Father. They must further acknowledge the Triune God—Father, Son, and Holy Spirit—to be the sole object of worship. This worship should include praise to Jesus for his works in creation and redemption. It should also be guided by the power of the Holy Spirit who was sent by the Son and the Father to be with the church after Jesus returned to heaven (John 14:15–26). As the Son was sent to serve the Father and the world, the Spirit was sent to be with the church to teach them all they needed to know and to be in the world to bear witness to Jesus and to convict people of sin, righteousness, and judgment (John 14:26; 15:26; 16:8). The return of Jesus to heaven makes the presence of the Spirit essential so that worship can continue in his name.

4

The Holy Spirit in Worship

Christian worship, as we have seen in the previous two chapters, centers on God the Father and Jesus Christ his Son. Even so, worship would be impossible without the presence of the third person of the Trinity—the Holy Spirit. There are many reasons for this. He is the giver of life and the source of the new—spiritual—life which is essential for worship. He is the one who inspired the authors of the Bible, making it possible for us to know who God is and how he is to be worshipped. He is the one who convicts us of sin, judgment, and righteousness so that we become aware of our need to know God and worship him (John 16:8). He empowers us to serve God by endowing us with spiritual gifts. The Holy Spirit is thus our essential guide and instructor who leads us to worship, teaches us how to worship, and equips us to worship.

Who is this Holy Spirit, this *rûaḥ* or *pneuma* of God? The basic meaning of the Hebrew *rûaḥ* and Greek *pneuma* is breath or wind.[1] By extension, the words encompass human vitality (since people breathe), personal disposition or character (such as having a "spirit of wisdom" or a "spirit of jealousy"), and the center of one's emotions, intellect, and will. These biblical words are used for God's Spirit as they express his energy, invisibility, and creative power. Though "Holy Spirit" is used only three times in the Old Testament (Ps 51:11; Isa 63:10–11), there are frequent references to the "Spirit of God," "Spirit of Yahweh," or "my Spirit." New Testament writers use "Holy Spirit" more than ninety times and "Spirit," referring to the third person of the Trinity, many more times.

---

1. For an in-depth study of the term, see Schweizer, "πνεῦμα."

Though the Spirit is mentioned throughout the Bible, it took a deep and sustained reflection on God's saving activity for Christian theologians from the time of Tertullian (*ca.* 160–*ca.* 225 AD) and Irenaeus (second century–*ca.* 202 AD) to solidify our understanding that the Holy Spirit is the third person of the Trinity. Indeed, Tertullian invented the term *Trinitas* to express more succinctly what the New Testament writers said about the involvement of the Father, Son, and Holy Spirit in the process of salvation from beginning to end.[2] While early creeds (e.g., the Apostles' Creed) acknowledged belief in the Father, Jesus the Son, and the Holy Spirit, they said nothing explicit about the divinity of the Son or Spirit. However, when Arias (*ca.* 250–336) asserted that, since Jesus was begotten by the Father, there must have been a time when he did not exist, it became clear that the relationship between the Father and Son needed to be stated more explicitly. The Councils of Nicea (325) and Constantinople (381) were convened so that the church could come to a consensus on this and other important issues. The creed developed at the first ecumenical council and revised at the second council is commonly known as the Nicene Creed. It recognizes all three members of the Godhead as distinct persons who are nonetheless unified in their being, equally active in creation and regeneration, and the object and source of worship.

Though it took several centuries for the church to formulate a doctrinal statement recognizing the Spirit as divine and the object of worship, this affirmation was based upon biblical teaching about his person and work. The goal of this chapter is to examine the biblical testimony about the Holy Spirit as the object of worship and the one who makes worship possible.

THE HOLY SPIRIT IN THE OLD TESTAMENT

The Spirit of God first appears in the creation accounts as God's powerful presence hovering over the waters to protect and sustain the cosmos and its contents (Gen 1:2). His power is further revealed as God speaks things into existence. The co-mingling of God's word and Spirit testify that the eternal Son and Spirit engaged harmoniously from the very act of creation. This was understood by the psalmist who wrote, "By the word of the LORD were the heavens made, their starry host by the breath (*rûaḥ*) of his mouth" (Ps 33:6). When God speaks, his Spirit works and makes himself known. And

---

2. Though other proof texts are often given for the existence of the Trinity, Matthew 28:19 and 2 Corinthians 13:14 stand out. Even so, the use of these texts "can hardly be thought of as constituting a doctrine of the Trinity" which must be built upon the whole New Testament's witness to the divine activity in salvation. McGrath, *Christian Theology*, 248.

even though Jesus is rightly called Immanuel—"God with us"—the Spirit, as the breath of God, is equally imminent and knowable.

The Spirit is not merely God's power to speak things into existence or God's expression of care for creation; he is the giver of life. While he gives life to all living creatures, he especially gives life to humankind. Genesis 2:7 records that God instilled life into the man he formed from the dust of the earth by breathing into his nostrils. Although the word *rûaḥ* is not found in this passage, the parallelism between spirit and breath identifies the Spirit of God as the life-giving breath of God. This parallelism is made plain when Job acknowledges that "The Spirit (*rûaḥ*) of God has made me; the breath (*nĕšāmâ*) of the Almighty gives me life" (Job 33:4). He similarly maintains that "as long as my breath (*nĕšāmâ*) is in me, and the spirit (*rûaḥ*) of God is in my nostrils, my lips will not speak falsehood, and my tongue will not utter deceit" (Job 27:3-4, ESV). The Spirit gives us life and the ability to keep on living. We find a similar idea reflected in Jesus' words recorded in John 6:63 and Paul's reflections in 2 Corinthians 3:6—the "Spirit gives life." Both physical and spiritual life are gifts of God's Spirit.

The Spirit who gives life is the Spirit who empowers people for service and worship. Although Old Testament saints never received the Spirit in a way comparable to Pentecost, God's Spirit enabled leaders—prophets, priests, judges, kings, and others—to serve the nation of Israel. The Spirit provided these leaders with wisdom to act or build, power to deliver Israel from their enemies, and the ability to speak for God or foresee future events. At times, the Spirit's presence moved them to states of ecstasy or endowed them with unusual strength (1 Sam 10:6, 10; Judg 14:6, 19; 15:14). By empowering these God-chosen leaders, the Spirit brought them and those to whom they ministered into an active relationship with himself.

Beginning with Moses, Israel's leaders are regularly identified as being empowered by the Spirit. At one point, God told Moses that he would put the Spirit upon seventy of Israel's elders so that they could help him carry the burdens of the people (Num 11:16-17, 25). Later, the Lord told Moses to lay his hands upon Joshua, "in whom is the spirit," and commission him so that he would have the ability to lead the whole assembly (Num 27:18-23; Deut 34:9). The Spirit similarly endowed a series of judges with power so that they could defeat Israel's foes and lead the nation in the period between the settlement and the rise of the monarchy (Judg 3:9-10; 6:34; 11:29; 13:25). When the first of Israel's kings were crowned, the Spirit came upon them with power so they could rule over the people of God (1 Sam 10:6, 10; 16:13). But the Spirit's power didn't only come upon the political or community leaders of Israel. He also provided men like Bezalel and Oholiab with the wisdom and skill needed to design the furnishings, clothing, and other things used in tabernacle worship, and direct the craftsmen who would make them (Exod 31:2–11).

Another characteristic work of the Spirit was his enabling the prophets to speak for God to Israel and to the nations (Num 11:25; 2 Chr 15:1; Isa 48:16; Ezek 11:5). True prophets were clearly distinguished from the false, as when Micah denounced those who proclaimed whatever their listeners wanted to hear, even though they had seen no visions and received no answers from God, and further declared that he was filled with power, with the Spirit of Yahweh, and with justice and might so that he could reveal the people's sin (Mic 3:5–8). The Spirit played such an important role in prophetic proclamation that Hosea used "prophet" and "man of the spirit" synonymously (Hos 9:7).[3] Prophets were so attuned to God's word and Spirit that they recognized when God spoke to them and could highlight the failure of God's people to obey what earlier prophets had said (Zech 7:12).

Whether a prophet's career as God's spokesman was long or brief, he was set apart from the average person by the Spirit's work in his life. Even so, the Spirit did not limit his work to recognized seers. He could empower any member of society to speak for God. In the early monarchy, King Saul and some of his messengers temporarily joined the ranks of the prophets (1 Sam 10:1–13; 19:18–24).[4] King David was expressly counted among the prophets for transmitting the word of the Lord through songs (Acts 2:29–30). Though a limited number of people are mentioned as exhibiting prophetic power, Israel maintained the hope that all of God's people would prophesy (Num 11:24–27, 29; Joel 2:28–29). The great desire was to see everyone empowered by the Spirit to receive God's word—whether through direct speech, dreams, visions, or in some other way—and communicate it to others who needed to hear it. As prophecy served Yahweh and his people, it was demonstrably an act of worship.

The Spirit, whose ways were as unfathomable as the workings of the wind, gifted people for service and at times took the gifts away. Samson and Saul are examples of men who not only experienced the Spirit's presence and power in their lives, but lost it due to disobedience (Judg 16:20; 1 Sam 16:14). Having witnessed Saul's demise, David expressed his fear that

---

3. Though the NIV and some other translations translate *'îš hārûaḥ*, "inspired man" or something similar, there is good reason to maintain the literal "man of the spirit" or even "man of the Spirit," as "Prophets were frequently associated with the Spirit of God in the Old Testament." McComiskey, "Hosea," 145. McComiskey lists Numbers 11:25, 29; 24:2; 1 Samuel 10:6–8; 19:23; 1 Kings 22:24; and 2 Kings 2:9 among Old Testament passages that link the term *rûaḥ* with the prophets.

4. It is quite possible that the prophecy of these individuals consisted of songs of praise, as the Spirit moved them in the context of prayer, music, and perhaps ritual dance. Smith, "Prophet," 996.

the Spirit might be taken away after his sin with Bathsheba (Ps 51:11). The inspired prayer in Psalm 51 expresses his desire that God would have mercy on him, cleanse him of his sin, create a clean heart within him, and neither cast him out of his presence nor take his Spirit away.[5] As a penitential psalm of lament, it expresses grief for the sin that separates a person from God and expresses hope that God will bring the sinner back to the center of worship and praise. Without the Spirit's presence, this would be impossible.

Many of the kings who followed David failed to echo his expressed desire to live in the presence of God and his Spirit. Eventually, their rejection of God's word and ways moved Yahweh to send his people into exile. But despite their expulsion from the land, the Lord did not utterly forsake them. Throughout the exile, the Spirit continued to speak through prophets, encouraging his people to remain faithful to their God and prepare to return to the promised land. An angelic vision received by the prophet Zechariah declared that the Spirit of God would bring his people back to their land and they would worship at the restored temple where the lampstand would again burn as a sign of God's presence (Zech 4:1–6; cf. Isa 32:15). The restoration of worship is taken up by Ezekiel who foresaw a time when God would give his people a new heart and spirit, and enable them to put away their sins and keep his laws (Ezek 11:19–20; 18:31; 36:26–27). As Israel anticipated being restored to their land, God, through the prophet Joel, let them know he was about to reveal his presence in a startling new way.

> And afterward, I will pour out my Spirit on all people. Your sons and daughters will prophesy, your old men will dream dreams, your young men will see visions. Even on my servants, both men and women, I will pour out my Spirit in those days (Joel 2:28–29).

Quoted by Peter in his Pentecost sermon, this passage announces God's intention to empower all his people with his Spirit. Neither age, gender, nor social status would separate people from God's protective presence. When the Spirit is poured out, prophecy—the mark of a "man of the Spirit"—and visions will become commonplace. Though Joel discerns that the coming age of the Spirit would usher in the day of the Lord, he also realizes that the signs of the Spirit's presence are given to pave the way for deliverance, as "everyone who calls on the name of the LORD will be saved" (Joel 2:32).

As the prophets looked forward to the coming age of the Spirit, they anticipated the arrival of a kingly, prophetic figure who would be specially endowed with the Spirit's power and wisdom—the Messiah (Deut 18:15, 18–19; Isa 11:1–5; 42:1). This "son of man" would receive divine glory and

---

5. For a survey of the way Psalm 51 has been used in the worship of the church throughout the ages, see Waltke and Houston, *The Psalms*, 446–62.

sovereign power, be worshipped by all people, and have an everlasting kingdom (Dan 7:13–14). And since the Righteous One would be filled with the Spirit, he would speak God's words, liberate his people, bring justice to the nations, and unite both Jew and Gentile in worship.

The Old Testament thus portrays the Spirit as the power of God who endows humanity and the rest of creation with life and as the loving presence of God who sustains the world that he made. Anticipating the spiritual gifts that would emerge in the church age, he is described as empowering people to rule, prophesy, and speak and work wisely. As the Old Testament age ended, the prophets turned their eyes to a future age of the Spirit in which salvation would be realized, justice would prevail, and all of God's people would be empowered for ministry and worship. When we turn to the New Testament, we find that the age foreseen by Israel's prophets was fulfilled through the life and ministry of Jesus the Messiah and the outpouring of the Holy Spirit.

THE HOLY SPIRIT IN THE NEW TESTAMENT

Like the Hebrew Scriptures, the New Testament reveals some important truths that link the third person of the Trinity with God's service and worship. And like the earlier revelation, it makes no attempt to link them systematically. As N. T. Wright has pointed out, "when worship is either discussed or evidenced in the New Testament, the Spirit is not mentioned, and mostly when the Spirit is mentioned, worship is not."[6] This does not, however, mean that there is no connection. In fact, a wider view of the material makes it clear that the Spirit is present during New Testament worship even when he is not mentioned.[7] And though the New Testament authors may not mention explicit liturgical rites, they frequently refer to the Spirit in conjunction with acts of worship.

This is readily seen in the Gospels. The writers of the Synoptic Gospels almost exclusively connect the Holy Spirit's work with the birth and ministry of Jesus. Though rarely noticed, their description of the Spirit and his work often comes in the context of worship or results in a renewed worship of God. This is clearly seen in the prophecies that immediately preceded or followed the Savior's birth.[8] Luke's birth account begins with an angel visit-

---

6. According to Wright, this may explain why so few books on the Holy Spirit pay attention to worship and so few books on worship make any reference to the Holy Spirit. Wright, "Worship and the Spirit," 3.

7. Wright, "Worship and the Spirit," 4.

8. Prophetic utterance is, of course, a sign of the Spirit moving someone to worship.

ing Zechariah as he was "serving as priest before God" while other worshippers were gathered in the temple courts at the time of prayer (Luke 1:8–10). The angel informed the startled priest that his long-awaited son would "be filled with the Holy Spirit" from his mother's womb, that he would bring many people back to the Lord, and that he would go before the Lord in the spirit and power of Elijah "to turn the hearts of the fathers to their children and . . . make ready a people prepared for the Lord" (Luke 1:15–17). Zechariah's son would be like the Old Testament "man of the Spirit" who steered his countrymen back to the right worship of God. And though Zechariah was for many months struck mute for unbelief, after his son's birth, the Holy Spirit opened his mouth and enabled him to utter a prophecy filled with praise to God for the salvation that would be announced through John (Luke 1:67–79).

Not long after Zechariah heard that he would have a son, the angel Gabriel informed the virgin Mary that "The Holy Spirit will come upon you, and the power of the Most High will overshadow you. So the holy one to be born will be called the Son of God" (Luke 1:35; cf. Matt 1:18). Mary responded to the annunciation with humility and willingness to perform what God desired, a patent act of worship as is evident in the hymn of praise—the Magnificat—which she uttered while visiting Elizabeth (Luke 1:46–55).[9] Shortly thereafter, an angel came to minister to the distraught Joseph, who was thinking of divorcing Mary. The heavenly messenger first comforted the carpenter by saying that his fiancée's child was "from the Holy Spirit" and then encouraged him to take her as his wife and name the baby Jesus—"Yahweh saves"—because he would save his people from their sins (Matt 1:20–21). Joseph's obedience to the heavenly command should be understood as his service or worship of God.

After Jesus was born, Mary and Joseph waited the time stipulated for purification after childbirth and took their son to Jerusalem to present him to the Lord. While there, they met a man named Simeon who had been told by the Holy Spirit that he would not die before he saw the Christ. When Mary and Joseph were bringing Jesus to offer the sacrifice prescribed by the law, the Holy Spirit again came upon Simeon and moved him to enter the temple courts (Luke 2:25–27). Not only did the Spirit prepare Simeon to see Jesus as the one who fulfills the messianic promises, he also inspired Simeon's prophecy concerning the child and his mother.[10] This prophecy—often

---

9. The ascription of praise, use of poetic parallelism, and even phraseology found in the Magnificat echo forms found in the Hebrew Psalter.

10. Marshall, *Gospel of Luke*, 118. Simeon's prophecy is filled with allusions from the Old Testament. "For my eyes have seen your salvation" alludes to Isaiah 52:10 (cf. Luke 3:6). The phrase, "which you have prepared in the sight of all people" recalls Psalm 98:2.

called the *Nunc Dimittis* from the first two words in Latin that mean, "now dismiss"—has entered the liturgy of many Christian traditions, usually as part of evening prayer or a funeral or memorial service. Simeon's act of worship, performed when he saw the Christ child, is thus regularly repeated by many modern congregations.

The Spirit who hovered over the water at creation and came upon Mary when she conceived remained with Jesus from the time of his baptism, which marked the beginning of his earthly ministry, until his ascension. "The Holy Spirit descended on him in bodily form like a dove" (Luke 3:22) and led him into the wilderness where he was tempted by the devil (Matt 4:1; Mark 1:12; Luke 4:1). Although Jesus was promised authority over the whole world in exchange for worship, he insisted that the Lord God was the only true object of worship (Luke 4:8). After defeating the devil, "Jesus returned to Galilee in the power of the Spirit" to teach in all the synagogues (Luke 4:14–15). The Spirit who led him out into the wilderness to face the devil brought him back so that he could inform others where his power came from. Jesus thus instructed the worshippers at the synagogue in Nazareth that the words of Isaiah 61:1 were fulfilled in their hearing. "The Spirit of the Lord is on me, because he has anointed me to preach good news to the poor. He has sent me to proclaim freedom for the prisoners and recovery of sight for the blind, to release the oppressed, to proclaim the year of the Lord's favor" (Luke 4:18–19). All aspects of Jesus' earthly ministry were performed as an expression of the Spirit's presence in his life. Even his sacrifice on the cross was a demonstration of the power of the Spirit acting through him (Heb 9:14).

The Holy Spirit empowers followers of Jesus for service

As the Holy Spirit empowered Jesus for service, he also enabled Jesus' followers to serve God and the church. The New Testament repeatedly promises that the Holy Spirit would live within those who believe in Christ. John the Baptist was to be filled with the Spirit from his mother's womb (Luke 1:15). As he grew, John prepared the way for Jesus' coming and testified that the one who would follow him would take away the sin of the world and "baptize you with the Holy Spirit and with fire" (Matt 3:11; Mark 1:8; Luke 3:16; John 1:6–9; 19–34). When Jesus taught his disciples how to pray, he informed them that the Father would always give them good things, including the Holy Spirit if they asked him (Luke 11:13). Toward the end of his

---

The statement that Jesus would be "a light for revelation to the Gentiles and for glory to your people Israel," echoes words found in Isaiah 42:6; 49:6.

ministry, he told his disciples that he and his Father would send the Spirit to them to be another *Paraclete* to live in them and to teach them what they needed to know about who Jesus was and what he taught (John 14:15–18, 26; 16:7–15).[11] Among the final instructions Jesus gave before ascending to his Father was the command for his disciples to wait in Jerusalem until they received the gift of the Holy Spirit who would give them "power from on high" so that they could be witnesses for him throughout the world (Luke 24:49; Acts 1:4–5, 8).

Though John and the disciples had preached the good news about God's kingdom while Jesus was with them, the mission of the Spirit began in earnest on the day of Pentecost when Jesus' followers were baptized with the Holy Spirit and began to preach the gospel with such conviction and power that many found new life in Christ (Acts 2:14–41; 4:31; 9:17–22; 11:24). Without the Spirit, the disciples would not have been able to lead one person to Christ.[12] But after the Spirit filled them on the day of Pentecost and other occasions, they witnessed great crowds and individuals come to faith. People believed their preaching, not because of human persuasion, wisdom, or manipulation, but because of the Spirit's power (1 Cor 4–5). The Spirit was sent by the Father and the Son in order to testify about Jesus in concord with the testimony of the disciples so that people could believe (John 15:26–27). Indeed, as the disciples tell others about Jesus, the Spirit convicts "the world of guilt in regard to sin and righteousness and judgment" so that their listeners can come to faith (John 16:8). The testimony of the Spirit does not merely support the witness of the disciples, but directs their witness both with respect to "chance" conversations and in directing the mission of the early church as it spread from Jerusalem to "the ends of the earth" (Acts 1:8).

While it is easy to recognize that the Spirit's role in the proclamation of the gospel is essential, it is equally important to see that no one can truly worship God without the Spirit's work in their hearts. The giver of life is the giver of new spiritual life. The one who convicts of sin is the one who bears

---

11. Variously rendered "another Counselor" (CSB, NIV, RSV), "another Helper" (ESV, NASB), "another Comforter" (KJV), and "another Advocate" (NLT, NRSV), *paraklētos* is difficult to translate accurately due to its legal overtones and rare use. (It is only found in the Bible in John 14:16, 26; 15:26; 16:7; and 1 John 2:1.) While at times it can refer to an advocate, counselor (at law), or witness who defends another in a court setting or serves as prosecuting attorney (cf. John 16:7–11; 1 John 2:1), in John 14 the usage appears to be much broader, as the Spirit will abide with the disciples, teach them all things, and help them remember what Jesus had said. That he is "another" Counselor implies that the disciples already have a Counselor in Jesus. The Spirit comes to replace the Counselor who was taken from them.

12. Oswald Sanders thus writes, "apart from the Spirit's co-witness, there can be no effective witness to Christ." Sanders, *The Holy Spirit and His Gifts*, 85.

witness with our spirits that we are God's children and enables us to cry out "Abba, Father"—the simplest of all prayers (Rom 8:15–16; Gal 4:6–7). We begin to worship God when we are adopted into his family and his Spirit gives us the vocabulary we need for worship. Along with learning from the main biblical words of worship, the stories, psalms, prayers, and prophesies recorded in Scripture impact our thought and practice.

Our worship vocabulary enables us to respond to God's revelation of himself through the Spirit and his word. It makes it possible for us to build up and encourage one another as we obey the command to be filled with the Spirit and "Speak to one another with psalms, hymns and spiritual songs. Sing and make music in your heart to the Lord, always giving thanks to God the Father for everything, in the name of our Lord Jesus Christ" (Eph 5:18–20). Singing, like sharing the gospel, is a sign of a Spirit-filled life. And it is essential to recognize that Christian psalmody is not limited to the praise of God. Paul places songs that edify Christians ahead of songs sung to praise and thank the Lord. The Spirit enables us to sing so that we can serve one another through "edification, instruction, and exhortation."[13] He also ordained that the hymns and songs found in Paul's writings brimmed over with doctrine so that those who sang or heard them might be built up in truth.[14] Biblical worship thus envisions Spirit-filled individuals building others up through Spirit-inspired music. And while Spirit-led worship will abound with joyful songs that edify others, it will also result in heart-felt praise and warm thanksgiving expressed to God.

The Holy Spirit gives God's people new life, a new message, a new vocabulary, and new songs. He also distinguishes them from those who do not worship in spirit and in truth. Paul makes a radical distinction between true believers and "those dogs, those men who do evil, those mutilators of the flesh," to whom worship is a matter of performing external rites, such as circumcision and obeying the Mosaic law (Phil 3:2). As Paul considers these acts, he concludes that, far from being a sign of family membership or of adherence to God's covenant, "Circumcision of the flesh has become pagan lacerations" that actually exclude those who trust in it from being counted among God's people.[15] Contrary to contemporary Jewish beliefs, Paul insisted that "it is we who are the circumcision, we who worship by the Spirit of God, who glory in Christ Jesus, and who put no confidence in the flesh" (Phil 3:3). Being a member of God's covenant people is not a matter of

---

13. Lincoln, *Ephesians*, 345.

14. See particularly Philippians 2:6–11; Colossians 1:15–20; Ephesians 5:14; and 1 Timothy 3:16.

15. O'Brien, *Philippians*, 357.

physical circumcision, but of being filled with the Spirit, engaging in Spirit-inspired worship, boasting in Jesus, and refusing to take pride in personal advantage or attainment. Many Jews ultimately failed in worship because they trusted in the flesh—"their God-given privileges and achievements"—instead of their position in Jesus Christ and the power of the Spirit.[16]

The Holy Spirit fills God's people and moves them to worship, to perform their religious service of God.[17] True worship is performed when God's Spirit empowers his people to perform religious acts, such as prayer and praise, *and* to work so that their whole lives are exemplified by service. While the motivation for this worship comes from the Spirit's work within, it is directed by God's revelation in Scripture, the words set in writing by men who were moved by the Spirit.

The Spirit reveals God's word to men

> "In the past God spoke to our forefathers through the prophets at many times and in various ways" (Heb 1:1).

The Old Testament is filled with examples of how God, through his Spirit, spoke to prophets and other people directly or through dreams, visions, and other ways. Both the writing prophets and other prophets frequently set off the revelations they received by saying, "Thus said the Lord," or "The Lord says," or "The word of the Lord came to me, saying . . ." At times, the biblical authors declared that they had recorded a message sent from God (Exod 24:4; Isa 30:8). By revealing God's word, the Spirit continues the work he performed at creation. This is what gives Scripture its authority. The Bible is "penetrated and filled with the Holy Spirit. It is God-breathed, and the creative breath of God remains in and with Scripture."[18] As the Spirit speaks, the word of the Lord is revealed to the human mind and passed on orally or in writing. Thus, the author of Revelation records: "On the Lord's Day I was in the Spirit, and I heard behind me a loud voice like a trumpet, which said: 'Write on a scroll what you see and send it to the seven churches: to Ephesus, Smyrna, Pergamum, Thyatira, Sardis, Philadelphia and Laodicea'" (Rev 1:10–11). The phrase, "in the Spirit," as used here, refers to John being

---

16. O'Brien, *Philippians*, 364.

17. The word translated "worship" in Philippians 3:3 (from *latreuō*) is only used in the Bible to refer to religious cultic service, whether it is offered to God or pagan gods. Strathmann, "λατρεύω." For an instructive deliberation on what it means to worship by the Spirit, see Motyer, *Philippians*, 150–51.

18. Bloesch, *Holy Scripture*, 129.

in a trance-like state.[19] "It is certainly a state in which the Seer is specially open to the Holy Spirit and ready to see visions."[20] As a result of his visions, he wrote down what he saw and passed it on to the church.

By penning the words of Scripture, the original authors performed an act of worship in response to the Spirit's out-breathing. The texts they produced lead more people into worship as the Spirit uses them to reveal the God they are to worship and to enable them to worship him. Paul's teaching on Scripture in 2 Timothy 3:14–17 asserts the twin truths that the text has its origin in the Spirit's communication and that its purpose is to profit its readers.[21] The Bible benefits its readers by giving them wisdom for salvation through faith in Jesus, without which no one can worship God. It is also "useful for teaching, rebuking, correcting and training in righteousness, so that the man of God may be thoroughly equipped for every good work" (2 Tim 3:16–17). As Scripture instructs us, we discover how to rightly relate to God and serve him.

The Spirit acts to build the Church

The Holy Spirit breathes out the Scriptures so that the church can hear the words of God. He also breathes life into men and women so that they can respond to the gospel by acknowledging their sinful condition before God, their need of a Savior, and the fact that Jesus is the Savior who is sufficient for them and for the world. The Spirit's aim in bringing people into relationship with God is not merely the salvation of individuals. He also gathers them into active fellowship with God and other believers in the church. The book of Acts describes how Jews and Gentiles respond to the gospel, are filled with the Spirit, and are added to the number of other believers with whom they share, eat, learn, worship, and spread the gospel. Their source of unity is the Holy Spirit who indwells both individuals and the church.

While the Spirit is the gift of the Father to the church (Luke 11:13; John 14:16; Acts 1:4; 2:33), he in turn gives gifts to the church so that it can grow in numbers and in knowledge of and relationship with God. A couple of important lessons follow. First, since all believers are given the Spirit and his gifts, there is a sense in which everyone has a part in the *missio Dei*, even if they are not considered missionaries in the way that term is usually understood. I. Howard Marshall says:

19. Aune, *Revelation 1–5*, 82–83.
20. Morris, *Revelation*, 51.
21. Stott, "2 Timothy," 100–104.

this gift of the Spirit to every believer has the same effect as in the case of the apostles. Its purpose is to constitute a church composed of missionaries... It therefore seems likely that Luke especially understood the gift of the Holy Spirit as equipping the church for mission, and consequently that he regarded the essence of being a Christian as the activity of mission.[22]

From the day of Pentecost, the Spirit no longer empowered only a few individuals for special ministry as in Old Testament times, but confirmed his presence through all of God's people as they delivered prophetic words about God's salvation through Jesus Christ that would free more people to worship God and cause the church to grow.[23] The theological basis for gospel ministry being an aspect of worship is found in Paul's reflection in Romans 15:15–16 that recognizes the essential role of the Holy Spirit in this.

> I have written you quite boldly on some points, as if to remind you of them again, because of the grace God gave me to be a minister of Christ Jesus to the Gentiles with the priestly duty of proclaiming the gospel of God, so that the Gentiles might become an offering acceptable to God, sanctified by the Holy Spirit. (Rom 15:15–16)

At least five words used in this passage carry priestly and sacrificial overtones.[24] Paul viewed himself as God's chosen *minister* who would perform the *priestly service* of proclaiming the gospel to the Gentiles so that they might become an *offering* that was *acceptable to God* because it was *sanctified* by the Holy Spirit. Stott's reflections on how worship and witness are united in Paul's thought are of tremendous value.

> Although Paul's priestly ministry as apostle to the Gentiles was unique, the principle he enunciates has a vital contemporary application. All evangelists are priests, because they offer their converts to God. Indeed, it is this truth more than any other which effectively unites the church's two major roles of worship and witness. It is when we worship God, glorying in his holy name, that we are driven out to proclaim his name to the world. And when through our witness people are brought to Christ, we then offer them to God. Further, they themselves join in his worship, until they too go out to witness. Thus worship leads to witness, and witness to worship.[25]

22. Marshall, *Luke: Historian and Theologian*, 200.
23. Schweizer, "πνεῦμα," 412–13.
24. Stott, *Romans*, 379.
25. Stott, *Romans*, 379–80.

Although it is essential to understand that worship and witness go hand in hand, we also need to appreciate that this is only possible because of the work of the Spirit. It is only because he sanctifies the people who respond to the gospel that they become an offering that is acceptable to God. It is only because the Holy Spirit speaks that God's grace is passed on through the minister who preaches the gospel to the people who respond to it. God's gift of the Spirit empowers people to worship God through gospel ministry and ensures that others will be saved to worship him too.

Second, in addition to being God's gift to his people, the Holy Spirit has given various spiritual gifts or charisms so that Christians are enabled to worship God through their service. These gifts are given by the Spirit at his discretion (1 Cor 12:11; Eph 4:11) and are intended "for the common good" (1 Cor 12:7) so that the whole church might be built up (1 Cor 14:12; Eph 4:12). By giving us these gifts, the Spirit makes it possible for us to serve God and each other for the benefit of the whole body.

Third, as the Spirit works within the hearts of Christians, he sanctifies them, changing their lifestyles and causing them to become more like Jesus. In an earlier chapter, we saw that worship is intimately related to morality since God is holy and requires that we live as his holy people. That the third person of the Trinity, who leads us into worship, is recognized as the *Holy* Spirit supports the deep ethical nature of worship.[26] Those who live by the Spirit "will not gratify the desires of the sinful nature" (Gal 5:16–17) but will crucify it along with its desires. In its place, they will display the fruit of the Spirit: "love, joy, peace, patience, kindness, goodness, faithfulness, gentleness and self-control" (Gal 5:22–23).

In 1 Corinthians 6:9–11, Paul reminds his readers that before they were washed, sanctified, and justified "in the name of the Lord Jesus Christ and by the Spirit of our God," they performed many evil acts. Marking the change that took place through redemption, their post-baptismal life should be free from the sins of sexual immorality, idolatry, theft, greed, drunkenness, slander, swindling, and no doubt many more. Belief in Christ does not pave the way for libertinism, but frees people from slavery to sin. Paul then develops his thought about Christians being cleansed by the Spirit by focusing on the problem of sexual immorality, a sin that a man commits "against his own body" (1 Cor 6:18). Adopting unambiguous worship terminology, he asks, "Do you not know that your body is a temple of the Holy Spirit, who is in you, whom you have received from God? You are not your own; you were bought at a price. Therefore honor God with your body" (1 Cor 6:19–20). Instead of living as slaves to sin, Christians are to serve the Lord

---

26. Morris, *Jesus is the Christ*, 160.

with their bodies because their bodies have become the holy place where the Spirit of God dwells. Everything we do is therefore a spiritual act of worship, performed to please the God who has called us to be his own, who has given us the Holy Spirit so that we could become holy, and who has endowed us with gifts so that we can serve him and the world.

CONCLUSION

Through their interaction with the Scriptures, the Fathers who gathered for the Council of Constantinople in 381 broadened the Nicene Creed's teaching about the Holy Spirit when they wrote that Christians believe "in the Holy Ghost, the Lord, and Giver of life, who proceedeth from the Father, who with the Father and the Son together is worshiped and glorified, who spake by the prophets."[27] They thus codified biblical teaching on the Spirit that had been understood in Trinitarian terms from the time of Tertullian. The Holy Spirit is the third person of the Trinity who is to be believed in, worshipped, and glorified along with the Father and Son. But the Spirit is not merely to be worshipped as God. As the one who "spake by the prophets" and apostles, he is the one who reveals God's word to people so that they can know who God is, what he has done, and how to rightly respond to him in worship. This is particularly true when it comes to the revelation of God through his Son Jesus Christ. The Spirit leads us to Jesus by convicting us of sin, judgment, and righteousness, and convincing us that Jesus' death and resurrection makes it certain that we will receive forgiveness and be restored to a right relationship with God. Our response to his promptings initiates our first acts of true worship.

Once the Spirit brings people into God's family, he makes all things new for them. In addition to giving them a new life, he gives them a new message—the gospel—that involves all believers in God's mission and effectively draws others into God's kingdom. He also gives them a new vocabulary and new songs so that they can join others in worship and express their relationship with God for mutual benefit. The Spirit further gives spiritual gifts to his people that empower them to perform works of service so that others can be built up in Christ. The Spirit is the Lord, the Giver of life, who, along with the Father and Son, is to be worshipped and glorified. He is also the one who leads people to, provides the means for, and empowers them for worship. But if God—Father, Son, and Holy Spirit—is to be worshipped and glorified, and he makes it possible for people to worship him, we may need to ask what his worshippers should look like. We will examine this question in the next chapter.

27. Schaff, *The Creeds of Christendom*, 50.

5

The People Who Worship

"*Who may ascend the* hill of the Lord?" the Psalmist asks. "Who may stand in his holy place?" (Ps 24:3). The person who raises such questions knows deep within that not just anyone can rightly worship God. As the poet observes, worship is limited to, "He who has clean hands and a pure heart, who does not lift up his soul to an idol or swear by what is false" (Ps 24:4). While the passage does not provide a comprehensive list of actions required of those who want to worship Yahweh,[1] the questions and answer make it clear that worship is not to be profaned by illegitimate worship or worshippers. Without personal holiness and wholehearted devotion to God, it is impossible to worship him. How then are the people of worship to be recognized? What does one need to do or be in order to join them? Should those who do not conform to the standard be removed from the assembly that worships God in truth? These are questions that this chapter is written to answer.

In the Bible, people worship God because he makes himself known to them by his presence, his word, and his acts of power. From the very beginning, Adam and Eve experienced God's presence in Eden where he walked and talked with them. Even after they rebelled by eating the fruit he told them not to eat, God sought them and called out to them because he desired to restore their relationship with him. As throughout Scripture, God extended his hand of grace to undeserving sinners and thereby drew them to himself so that they might know him and worship him.

---

1. See Psalm 15 for a more extensive list of actions worshippers are either required to do or prohibited from doing.

Even though we can locate the beginnings of worship in the feeble human response to God's call, it properly starts when they invoke his name, an act that has been called "the foundation of every act of divine service."[2] Just as worship would be impossible without God first acting on behalf of his creation, all other acts of worship are inconceivable without a person responding to him by calling on his name. From a very early time, Genesis records, "men began to call on the name of the Lord" (Gen 4:26). The Bible thus recognizes "Yahweh worship as the primeval religion of mankind in general,"[3] even though it did not remain so for long. Though "calling on the name of the Lord" explicitly refers to invocation, it also points to worship acts that follow the invocation, such as prayer and sacrifice.[4]

People called upon the Lord as individuals and in groups. Cain and Abel brought offerings to God from the proceeds of their work (Gen 4:3–4). After being safely delivered from the flood, Noah built an altar to Yahweh and sacrificed burnt offerings (Gen 8:20). Once he reached the promised land, Abraham built a series of altars and called on the name of the Lord (Gen 12:7–8; 13:4, 18; 22:9). Abraham's obedient response to God's call by leaving his family and homeland was an act of worship. Abraham's servant, "bowed down and worshiped the Lord" when he learned that God had led him back to his master's family who would provide a wife for Isaac (Gen 24:26). In the time of the judges, Gideon bowed down and worshipped when he heard the interpretation of a dream indicating that Israel would defeat the Midianites (Judg 7:15). During the exile, Daniel prayed in solitude three times a day (Dan 6:10). These examples illustrate the wide range of individuals who worshipped God throughout biblical history.

More frequently, the Old Testament speaks of groups worshipping together. The laws given to Israel include a sacrificial system that united people in their worship. While sacrifices were sometimes shared within a family, they were offered publically under the direction of a priest at the central sanctuary. The great festivals brought people together so they could worship the Lord with feasting and communal celebrations. By the second temple period, people ascended the temple mount when they celebrated the feasts, singing songs like those recorded in the book of Psalms.[5] Other psalms prompted communal praise or lament to unite the people in their

---

2. Westermann, *Genesis 1–11*, 340. Westermann comments that calling on God's name has influenced Christian liturgy which frequently begins with the invocation "In the name of the Father, and of the Son, and of the Holy Spirit," a call which replaces the name Yahweh with the Trinitarian name. *Genesis 1–11*, 340–41.

3. Rad, *Genesis*, 109.

4. See Genesis 13:4; 21:33; 26:25; Zephaniah 3:9.

5. See particularly the Songs of Ascents in Psalms 120–134.

worship of God. Old Testament worship was designed so that the nation of Israel could relate to the holy God who called them into covenant relationship with himself.

BE HOLY AS GOD IS HOLY

Holiness was a *sine qua non* of biblical worship. The Scriptures regularly command everyone in relationship with God to "Be holy because I, the LORD your God, am holy" (Lev 19:2; 1 Pet 1:16). Since Yahweh is the Holy One of Israel, his people are to be distinct from the nations as God's chosen people and special possession (Deut 7:6; 14:2) and serve him as "a kingdom of priests and a holy nation" (Exod 19:5-6). Though the descendants of Aaron would perform the priestly duties within Israel, the rest of the nation was consecrated so that they might be priests to the world.[6] As Israel demonstrated what it meant to be God's holy people, the nations would recognize that Yahweh is holy and righteous and desire the blessings that God promised would come to the world through Abraham's offspring (Gen 12:1-3).

For Israel, being a holy people meant living in a holy land, obeying God's holy laws, worshipping at a holy sanctuary where holy priests ministered, celebrating holy festivals, and resting on a holy day. It also required, as made clear in Leviticus, that they adopt the categories holy, clean, and unclean as a grid for viewing life. While being clean was considered normal, and therefore good, being holy was better and should be pursued, not only by priests and Nazirites, but by the whole nation. There was no hiding the fact, however, that a person could become unclean through sin and more everyday causes, such as having bodily discharges, giving birth, contacting someone or something dead, eating certain foods, or contracting a skin disease. To maintain holiness, God's people were required to obey the laws that warned against contact with that which is unclean and to offer up sacrifices that would atone for their sins and engage in other rituals that would take away all uncleanness.

In spite of the command to be holy and the provision of rituals to take away uncleanness, God's people were often guilty of going through

---

6. Note the similarities between the consecration of the whole nation (Exod 24:6-8) and the consecration of the priests (Exod 29:19-21). In both cases, blood was applied to an altar and then to the people involved—the people being sprinkled, and the priests being anointed on the lobes of their right ears, right thumbs, and right big toes. Further connecting the people to the priests is the ritual by which those who had become unclean were permitted to reenter the camp after presenting an offering and then being anointed with blood on the same extremities as the priests when they were consecrated (Lev 14:1-20).

the motions of worship because their hearts were not in it. At times, they brought offerings to Yahweh and also sacrificed to other gods. They performed ceremonies designed to deal with sin, but did not lead lives of justice and righteousness. Placed in the land of Canaan where they were to be distinct, they were often guilty of emulating the nations. The prophets thus frequently pointed out that their worship activities were an offence to the Lord and therefore unacceptable. While Isaiah recognized a remnant of the people as holy (Isa 4:3), the nation was driven from their holy land and their holy sanctuary destroyed because they failed to live up to their holy calling. Even so, God extended grace and made it possible for the sinners to be sanctified and promised to bring his renewed people back from captivity.

WORSHIP OF GOD BY NON-ISRAELITES

Even though Old Testament worship centers on Israel, others could encounter God along with them. In part, this reflects God's plan for all humankind from the time he created them in his image, blessed them, and gave them stewardship over the rest of creation. These promises, which were reiterated to Noah after the flood, were passed on to Abraham when God pledged to make him into a great nation, bless him, and bless the other nations through him (Gen 12:2–3). God's covenant was to be ratified by the sign of circumcision. Every circumcised male—including Abraham's descendants and his servants, whether born into his household or purchased—was considered a member of God's covenant people (Gen 17:9–14). The idea that those not physically related to Abraham can become part of the people of God is often repeated in the Old Testament. At the time of the exodus, "many other people" accompanied Israel out of Egypt (Exod 12:38). Those who were integrated into the nation through circumcision were allowed to celebrate the Passover and other festivals with native-born Israelites (Exod 12:43–49). Thus, we frequently read that "The same law applies to the native-born and to the alien living among you" (Exod 12:49; cf. Exod 12:19; 20:10; 23:12; Lev 24:22; Num 15:14–16, 29; Deut 5:14; 16:10–11).

Foreigners were added to Israel through circumcision and obedience to the law or through marriage. For example, during the conquest, the men sent to spy on Jericho were protected by Rahab who expressed her belief in Yahweh (Josh 2:11). Rahab and her family were spared and from that time on counted among the Israelites (Josh 6:25). A similar example is the young Moabitess Ruth, who declared to Naomi: "Your people will be my people and your God my God" (Ruth 1:16). When she later married Boaz, the elders proclaimed that Ruth should be likened to Rachel and Leah, two of the matriarchs of the nation (Ruth 4:11). Other foreigners who rose to prominent positions in Israel include Doeg the Edomite (1 Sam 21:7), Uriah the Hittite (2 Sam 11:3–24), Ittai the Gittite (2 Sam 15:19–21), and Araunah the Jebusite (2 Sam 24:16–24). These may all have been proselytes as they are mentioned in the context of worship or personally confess that Yahweh is God.

An instance of a person who recognizes Yahweh as the true God and yet does not become a part of Israel is Naaman the Syrian (2 Kgs 5:2–3). Sent to Israel with a great treasure to pay for the cure for his skin disease, Naaman's rage when Elisha refused to greet him was transformed to praise when his ablutions in the Jordan River cleansed him entirely. The miracle performed in Elisha's absence convinced him that his healing came from God, not the man (2 Kgs 5:15).[7] From now on, he would sacrifice to no god but Yahweh.

In addition to those who came to know God through their interaction with Israel, the Old Testament mentions Yahweh worshippers who received their knowledge of him independently of the chosen people. It is neither possible nor necessary to discern whether these people knew of Yahweh because his worship had been preserved from ancient times or whether God revealed himself to them directly as he did to Abraham. Two of these independent believers are Melchizedek and Job. Like Naaman, these men remained distinct from Israel even though they worshipped the same God.

After defeating the kings of Shinar, Ellasar, Elam, and Goiim, Abraham met Melchizedek, the priest of God Most High,[8] and presented him with a tithe of the booty taken in battle. Abraham thus recognized Melchizedek to be greater than he and "the legitimate priest and king of his God."[9] Melchizedek is further mentioned in Psalm 110:4, which connects him to the Davidic line of kings and ascribes to him an eternal priesthood. The psalm becomes for Jesus and several New Testament authors a prophecy about the coming Messiah (Matt 22:44–45; Acts 2:34–35; Heb 5:6–10; 6:20; 7:1–17). The author of Hebrews treats the ancient priest-king typologically as greater than Abraham and the Levitical priests, and thus pointing to the need for a greater priest to come—Jesus Christ.

The other major Old Testament character who developed a close relationship with God outside of Israel is Job. The book of Job, which is set in the Patriarchal age, introduces the title character as being from Uz, an area

7. "Ambiguity would have remained, had Elisha been involved." Provan, *1 and 2 Kings*, 192–93.

8. That is, El Elyon.

9. Waltke, *Genesis*, 235. Not all scholars agree with this conclusion. For more on the identity of El Elyon and Yahweh in Genesis 14, see McConnell, "You Shall Have No Other Gods," 26–30.

to the east of Canaan (Job 1:3). Several times the book identifies Job as a man who was "blameless and upright . . . feared God and shunned evil" (Job 1:1, 8; 2:3). His worship life apparently centered around sacrifice, praise, and doing what he knew pleased God. Job routinely acted as a priest for his family, sacrificing burnt offerings for their sins (Job 1:5). He further mediated between God and his friends because they sinned by failing to speak rightly for God (Job 42:7–9). Although he complained bitterly after his testing, he refused to charge God with wrongdoing and, despite his personal tragedy, brought himself to praise Yahweh's name (Job 1:21–22). Though a foreigner, the faith he expressed, despite the loss of his loved ones, wealth, and health, surpassed what could be found in Israel during most of its history.

In addition to recounting Israel's worship of Yahweh and relating a few of his worshippers who were not descendants of Abraham, many psalms and the prophets envisioned a time when people from all over the earth would bow before the Lord. As the prophets looked forward to the regathering of national Israel, which divided in the wake of Solomon's reign and was later exiled to the nations, they foresaw that many Gentiles would worship Yahweh with them. Israel would no longer serve foreigners in exile, but return home accompanied by Gentiles bearing costly gifts to worship the Lord in Jerusalem (Isa 60:3–6). At that time, the nations would learn God's ways and do his commands (Isa 2:2–3; Mic 4:1–3). As all the earth comes to recognize him as God, Yahweh's worship would become universal (Pss 22:27; 66:4; 72:11; Isa 11:10; 45:22–23; 56:3–8; 66:23; Zeph 2:11; Zech 2:11). In what has been called "the clearest Old Testament statement of the theme of missionary outreach,"[10] Isaiah proclaims that the survivors of the Diaspora, "will proclaim my glory among the nations" (Isa 66:19), resulting in Gentiles being brought as an offering to God (v 20). Amazingly, some of the Gentiles would serve as priests and Levites (v 21), not only uniting with Israel in worship, but even leading the worship.

WORSHIPPERS IN THE NEW TESTAMENT

The Old Testament expectation that worship of God would spread to the whole earth began to be fulfilled with the dawning of the church age. Before ascending to heaven, Jesus informed his apostles that they would "be my witnesses in Jerusalem, and in all Judea and Samaria, and to the ends of the earth" (Acts 1:8). These words highlight the structure Luke used to write his second book as they point to the worship of God spreading beyond the Jews to Samaritans and Gentiles. From the day of Pentecost, the gospel

---

10. Motyer, *Isaiah*, 541. See also Westermann, *Isaiah 40–66*, 425.

was preached to Jews and Gentile proselytes, many of whom responded by repenting of their sins and being baptized in the name of Jesus Christ. Immediately they devoted themselves to worship acts such as listening "to the apostles' teaching and to the fellowship, to the breaking of bread and to prayer" (Acts 2:42). From its very start, the church was a community centered on worship.

As Paul understood relations within the church, Jews and Greeks, slaves and freedmen, men and women, were united in Christ as the spiritual descendants of Abraham (Gal 3:28–29). Believing Gentiles were ingrafted into the people of God. Paul believed his priestly duty was fulfilled as these former outsiders were presented as an offering to God that was sanctified by the Holy Spirit (Rom 15:16). He further understood that it fulfilled Isaiah's eschatological vision of people coming from all over the world to worship in Jerusalem (Isa 66:20). Along with representative believers from different lands, monetary gifts were brought to Jerusalem in fulfillment of the ancient prophecies (Rom 15:25–31; 1 Cor 16:1–4; 2 Cor 8–9; Gal 2:10).[11]

The New Testament describes how God's expectations for his chosen people were transferred to the New Covenant community who have taken over from Israel as "a chosen people, a royal priesthood, a holy nation, a people belonging to God" (1 Pet 2:9). Like Israel, they were called by God to be a holy people (Rom 1:7; 1 Cor 1:2). Accordingly, the characteristic New Testament term for believers in Jesus was *hagioi*, "holy ones" or "saints." The first Christians understood holiness in the standard Old Testament categories of separation and ethical righteousness. Christians are separate from the world positionally since they are united with God through Jesus Christ, and instructed to live as holy, obedient children because God their Father is holy (1 Pet 1:14–16). Holy living is thus a response to God that springs from one's recognition that he is a merciful Lord, and results in worship that combines holy living and nonconformity to the world's pattern (Rom 12:1–2).

Like Israel, the church is to live as a holy people before the world. But there is a difference between the Old Testament and New Testament people of God. The former did not intentionally go out to convince others to enter covenant relationship with Yahweh, while the church was founded on Christ's commission to compel both Jews and Gentiles to worship God together. Though they at times struggled with the implications of being a people united under God—demonstrated by Peter's need of the vision of a sheet containing unclean food (Acts 10), the deliberations of the council in Jerusalem (Acts 15), and Peter's refusal to eat with Gentile believers (Gal 2:11–14)—within twenty years of Christ's resurrection, the gospel had made

---

11. Bruce, "Paul and Jerusalem," 22–25.

such inroads into the Roman world that opponents in Thessalonica could bewail, "These men who have caused trouble all over the world have now come here" (Acts 17:6). The spread of Christianity in such a short time was remarkable. God's creational intent that everyone made in his image could worship him was fulfilled in Jesus Christ. Worship is thus tied to the gospel, as its ends and means. When people come to salvation through Jesus Christ, they become worshippers. When the church carries out its mission of making disciples, it is engaged in worship.[12]

Since the New Testament was completed before the end of the first century, it does not record the extent of the church's growth. It does, however, anticipate that people from every tribe, language, people, and nation will worship God. Revelation foresees a broad section of humanity redeemed by the Lamb of God and gathered to worship him on this earth and in the new heavens and new earth. Along with its report of the universal worship of God, the book proclaims that the worship of all other deities will cease. In addition, it joins other biblical books in declaring that the worship of God is not limited to humans.

WORSHIP NOT LIMITED TO HUMANS

Biblical worship is characterized by responding to God's majesty by bowing before him and calling on his name, expressing an attitude of reverence and fear because of his power and love, and obeying his commands through holy living. These responses are not limited to humans, but can be engaged in by angels, other spiritual beings, and by creation itself. That angels worship is almost axiomatic as they are "ministering spirits" (Heb 1:14) sent by God to carry messages to humans and, in particular, his covenant people. That service is their basic function can be located in the Hebrew and Greek words used to refer to them: *mal'āk* and *angelos* both mean "messenger," and can refer to human or spiritual beings who engage in temporal or spiritual affairs on behalf of another.[13] In addition to serving the Lord by taking

---

12. Shedd correctly writes that, "all that the church does to fulfil its mission can be rightly considered worship." Shedd, "Worship in the New Testament Church," 146.

13. Other biblical terms used for angels include *běnê hā 'ělōhîm*, "sons of God" (Job 1:6; 2:1; 38:7; Ps 29:1); *qědōšîm*, "holy ones" (Job 5:1; 15:15); and *ṣěbā 'ōt*, "hosts" or "armies." Different opinions exist as to whether *'ělōhîm* in Psalm 97:7 refers to angels or the gods of the nations doing obeisance to Yahweh. Most English versions interpret it as "gods." If taken this way, the idea is that since the foreign gods fall before Yahweh's majesty, those who worship idols should cast them aside as worthless. So, Weiser, *Psalms*, 634. That it could be interpreted as a reference to angels is supported by its translation *angeloi* in the Septuagint, which is followed by the author of Hebrews who quotes the

messages to his people or looking after them, the angels are at times entreated to worship Yahweh (Pss 29:1–2; 103:20–21; 148:2). Revelation describes angels joining the living creatures and the twenty-four elders to bring glory, honor, and power to God, falling down before him, and singing the praises and worth of God and the Lamb (Rev 4:6–11; 5:6–14; 7:11–12; 11:15–18). In addition, their worship is expressed by obeying the Lord's command to inform people about his will or otherwise serve him.

The Bible's vision of worship does not end with humans and angels, but extends to all creation. The heavens, the earth, the sea, and everything in them are enjoined to praise God (Pss 96:11–13; 98:4–9; 148). Even though the hills cannot literally break into song or trees clap their hands (Isa 55:12), their splendor confirms the existence of a mighty Creator. Their singing or clapping can be taken symbolically that they approve of God and his great acts.

While creation mainly praises God in poetic passages, different parts of creation clearly worship by simply doing what they were created to do. The sun and moon perform their worship by dividing day from night and marking seasons, days, and years. Birds, fish, and animals worship God by being fruitful and multiplying and taking their rightful place in the created order. Though they don't raise an audible voice, created things worship God through service and obedience, and by declaring God's existence and might (Ps 19:1–6).

Eastern Orthodoxy often describes creation's part in the worship of God by speaking of humans who act as the "microcosm" of creation. From this perspective, humankind stands "on the boundary (*methorion*) between the material and the spiritual worlds as a connecting link, directly related to the earthly aspect of created existence as well as to the uncreated existence of the Creator."[14] Humans and the rest of creation exist in a dynamic relationship in which human actions affect the whole of creation positively and negatively in both material and spiritual ways. Human sin negatively impacts the created order; human praise benefits the other creatures. Humans serve as priests of creation "to sanctify the creation and to draw it into the fullness of the life of the Kingdom of God, to bring it into communion with its maker."[15] Through human mediation, creation can worship and glorify God. As Orthodox Bishop Kallisto Ware says, humans "give to physical objects a voice which in themselves they lack."[16] Human praise is therefore

---

verse to argue that angels worship Jesus (Heb 1:6).
    14. Prokurat, "Orthodox Perspectives on Creation," 335.
    15. Harakas, "Creation and Ethics," 33.
    16. Quoted in Harakas, "Creation and Ethics," 35.

essential so that the created world can attain the relationship that God, from creation, intended it to have with him.

PEOPLE AT WORSHIP IN THE CHURCH TODAY

From the beginning, God intended that humankind should worship him along with the rest of creation. Though sin damaged our relationship with God, he intervened so that worship is possible for those who are restored through Jesus Christ. The initiative God took to make worship possible requires that we consider how this impacts our gathered services to meet with God and our dispersion to serve him in the world.

The Bible is clear that God instigates worship by creating people in his image and calling them into relationship with himself. He reaches out to sinners who do not know their need for him, gives them knowledge of himself, and empowers them for worship as the Holy Spirit regenerates them. Since worship begins with God's desire to engage us, it is not something we can produce or stimulate through our actions or words. There is no formula for inducing praise. It is not a matter of the right kind of atmosphere or music or lighting or techniques, but of recognizing the presence of the God who calls us to himself and responding to him rightly. Many liturgies thus commence with a simple invocation or call to worship because worship begins as we enter God's presence in response to who he is and what he has done and call upon his name.

As the presence of God is necessary for worship, so also is the presence of those who are in a right relationship with him. Only those who have been called by God can worship. Unbelievers are, by definition, excluded. This does not mean that churches should dissuade non-Christians from attending services,[17] but insists that designing "worship" services for the sake of unbelievers makes little sense. While non-Christians may join believers who pray, sing praises, and hear the Bible read and expounded, their words and actions are no more acceptable to God than were the attempts of the ancient Canaanites who sacrificed their children under sacred trees or the Israelites who performed the rituals with uncircumcised hearts. Communal services should be designed so that believers can engage the Lord on his terms and be prepared for works of service to be performed when they reenter the world. Worship that is focused on God cannot be reduced to entertainment. Worship that is designed for believers to respond to God can only be evangelistic insofar as unbelievers are given an opportunity to see

---

17. It should be noted, however, that the early church often dismissed those who were not communicants after the service of the word and before the Lord's Supper.

God's people expressing their love for him, hear about his greatness through song, word, and testimony, and witness the change that a relationship with God can make in one's life. When this happens, non-Christians can experience Christian worship as a means by which God draws them to himself. Only when they enter his family can they respond in worship.

Worship cannot take place without a relationship with God because sin distances us from God. It is impossible to defraud a business partner, cheat on a spouse, or lie to one's parents and worship God with clean hands and heart. Though one might put on a good face, God knows what is going on inside. For this reason, personal holiness must never be separated from worship. Following biblical injunctions to confess sin and pray for one another (Jas 5:16; 1 John 1:9), many worship services include appointed times for confession and absolution. In some cases, the sinner may confess to the person sinned against or to a minister in private. At other times, a public confession may be required. Many liturgies include a general confession that acknowledges sins of commission and omission and leaves time for introspection and personal confession to the Lord. This is immediately followed by the reminder that God forgives our sins through the work of Christ. Through confession, one's relationship with God and others is restored so that these impediments to worship melt away.

The reminder that only holy people can properly worship leads to a consideration of church discipline. How should a church respond to a member who continues to live a sinful life? Though not popular today, many traditions have held that the committal of certain sins requires excommunication.[18] Indeed, for many early Protestants, the exercise of church discipline was—along with the preaching of the gospel and the proper administration of the sacraments—considered one of the marks of a true church.[19] Discipline is an essential part of growing a family and of growing the church. The goal of church discipline is not condemnation, but restoration and training in righteousness. The sinning brother or sister is informed of the error(s) committed so that they can repent and return to fellowship with God and others. As a result, when everyone concerned sees sin exposed for what it is and the individual restored, they will praise God. When the penitent is restored to fellowship, the worship of the whole body is enhanced.

As the church spread throughout the Mediterranean world in the first century, the apostles discerned that the "dividing wall of hostility" that had

---

18. This could be practiced in several ways. The most severe form of excommunication would require that the sinning individual no longer be considered a Christian. A less harsh form would be to put the person out of the fellowship or refuse to serve them communion until confession and restoration are made.

19. See the Belgic Confession, article 29.

separated Jews and Gentiles was broken down by Jesus' atoning sacrifice (Eph 2:14). Though misunderstanding and prejudice could raise their heads at times, people from all nations who believed in Jesus were united as the one people of God. This was best seen in churches like Antioch and Philippi that were composed of believers from diverse backgrounds (Acts 13:1; 16:12–34). In the following centuries, the church spread throughout the world. And even though many churches today are well integrated, others struggle with some of the issues faced by the first generation of Christians. Though our faith in Christ unites us with believers of other races, cultures, and language groups as members of the family of God, we often find it difficult to worship with those who are different. Where linguistic differences make communal worship impractical or impossible, monocultural worship may be unavoidable. However, where races and cultures mix within a single language group, refusing to worship with others goes against biblical teaching and re-erects barriers that Christ tore down. In Christ, there is no Jew or Greek, slave or free, black, white, or brown. There is no male or female, young or old. Perhaps we should add that there is also no Baptist or Brethren, Presbyterian or Pentecostal, Methodist or Mennonite, Evangelical or Ecumenical. While some of these distinctions are age-old, others have been erected in more recent history and may create bigger stumbling blocks than the others.

For the church to be the church, we need to do away with the things that separate us and unite in our worship of Christ the Savior who set us an example of humbly serving others. As Paul instructed the saints in Corinth, all factions must be put aside so that the church can be recognized as the unified work of God (1 Cor 1:11–13; 3:3–9). This requires those from majority and minority cultures to be willing to learn from others whom Christ has accepted. Those who are older need to be aware of the gifts and training the younger have received; the younger should similarly respect the wisdom and traditions of their elders. Those from different theological backgrounds should attempt to understand why others have come to divergent conclusions on certain—and often key—issues and spend more time rejoicing in what they share in common than in what divides them. This does not mean that we should stoop to a lowest common denominator set of practices that are so watered down they cannot be recognized as Christian. Rather, our unity should come from our common salvation and our possession of the Spirit who calls us into one family and has given us his word that lays the foundation for our faith. Our unity should likewise be based on our common confession of the historical creeds that are grounded in Scripture.

Such unity, though biblical and desirable, does not come easily. Not only does it call for sensitivity to the needs of people from different backgrounds, it may also require that we put aside our personal preferences and pet doctrines, and put on the humility of Jesus Christ who gave up all to be a servant. No one is exempt. Like the twenty-four elders whom John witnessed bowing down and laying their crowns before the throne of God, we are required to give up our authority as we together worship the only one who is worthy (Rev 4:10). Only then will we be recognizable as the people of God at worship.

6

The Place of Worship

The Bible informs us about God's person and works and instructs how we should respond to him. It teaches us about worship by giving examples of people who rightly worshipped God and of others who didn't. Similarly, Scripture's teaching about the physical setting of worship should influence our worship environment. As physical beings, our worship will of necessity be tied to a physical location. What clues does the Bible provide about where God prefers to be worshipped and how one's physical environment influences worship? Are some places more holy than others? Does Christian worship require a holy city or holy building? Should our worship places resemble a holy temple, a teaching hall, theater, or something else? Should we take Jesus' words to the Samaritan woman, "a time is coming when you will worship the Father neither on this mountain nor in Jerusalem" (John 4:21), to mean that identifying a particular place for worship is irrelevant?

The New Testament provides no explicit information about where Christians should meet or what a Christian place of worship should look like, how it should be constructed, or what furnishings or fixtures should be included. This differs greatly from the instructions God gave in the Old Testament about the building of the tabernacle and temple. But even though details are given about the size and construction materials used for the tabernacle and temple, they were so rough that a heavy dose of imagination would be required for either of them to be built. And though these structures were designed for worship, lay people were not permitted to enter. Individuals, families, and larger groups could only bring their offerings to the courtyard where sacrifices took place. For this reason, neither the tabernacle nor temple provides Christians with a viable model for designing community worship space.

This does not mean that the Bible has nothing to say about worship space. In Scripture, people met with and worshipped God in many different places. Adam and Eve met God in the Garden of Eden. Cain and Abel presented their offerings in the open air. Abraham erected altars all over Canaan and was preparing to offer up Isaac as a sacrifice on a mountain before God stopped him. Moses and others also worshipped on mountain tops. After leaving Egypt, the children of Israel worshipped God in the wilderness where they erected the tabernacle that signified God's presence. And though the Israelites did not actually gather to worship *in* the tabernacle, it became the focal point of their worship both in the wilderness and after the conquest of the land of Canaan.

Once the tribes were settled in their own inheritance, the central site where priests helped people present their offerings to God changed from time to time (Josh 8:30; 18:1; 1 Sam 7:17; 2 Chr 1:3). In addition to the bronze altar of the tabernacle, altars were constructed in many places so that families and individuals could sacrifice burnt, peace, grain, and drink offerings. And even though Israel at times conducted syncretistic practices at some altars, others were constructed and maintained at God's instruction (Josh 8:30–35; Judg 6:25–29).

When the monarchy was firmly in David's hands, Jerusalem became the hub of Israel's cultic worship. The central place of Jerusalem did not mean that people did not worship elsewhere. Scripture describes in great detail the throng that went with David to Baalah in Judah in order to bring the ark to Jerusalem (2 Sam 6; 1 Chr 13; 15–16). The procession was marked by an exuberant celebration of the Lord until Uzzah was killed for touching the ark. At that point, David and his retinue returned to Jerusalem, leaving the ark at Obed-Edom's house to see what might transpire. Three months later, when David heard how God had blessed this household, he returned to bring the ark up to his capital, leading the crowds who were dancing, shouting, singing, and playing musical instruments in worship.

Once the ark was situated in a new tent in Jerusalem, David ensured that Asaph the priest and a number of Levites were available to perform the required rituals (1 Chr 16:37). Even so, the centralization of worship in Jerusalem did not signal the end of worship in other parts of the kingdom. David ensured that the morning and evening burnt offerings prescribed by the law were performed under the supervision of Zadok and other priests at the high place in Gibeon, where the tabernacle—minus the ark—remained (1 Chr 16:39–42).

The construction of Solomon's temple strengthened the importance of David's city as the center for worship. Even so, worship was not restricted to the building. Following the instructions for tabernacle worship, only priests could enter the temple. The rest of the people worshipped God in the temple courts where they offered their sacrifices and sang praises. As they approached the temple site, worshippers filled the streets of the city with praise to God.

The Old Testament never limited the worship of God to the land of Israel or the Israelites as a people. Individuals like Job and Naaman worshipped the Lord outside of the land. Similarly, the exiled Daniel engaged in private worship (in the form of prayer) three times a day (Dan 6:10). Also, in Babylon, Ezekiel fell on his face to worship when the Lord appeared to him beside the Kebar River and gave him a vision that he was to communicate to his people (Ezek 3:15–23). The prophets were not the only ones who worshipped Yahweh outside of the land of Israel. It is probable that synagogues were first organized during the exilic period as the exiled people gathered to worship, pray, and read the holy Scriptures. Synagogue worship was a main part of the lives of God's people during the exile, the postexilic period, in Jesus' day, and beyond.

In the New Testament, Jesus and his disciples worshipped at the temple and in synagogues. Jesus spent time in prayer on mountains and in gardens. The book of Acts tells of believers gathering in private homes to pray and learn about the faith (Acts 1:13; 10:22; 12:12). At other times, people gathered beside a river to pray and, we suspect, to engage in other acts of worship (Acts 16:13). Paul and Barnabas discovered that it was possible to worship God while chained up in a prison (Acts 16:24–25).

The Bible makes it clear that God's worship cannot be restricted to one type of building—whether tabernacle, temple, synagogue, or church. One can worship God indoors, out of doors, in a home, on a mountain, in exile, in prison, in Jerusalem, in Samaria, or anywhere else. The rest of this chapter focuses on some of the places where people worshipped God. As we consider them, we will attempt to bridge the gap between the ancient and modern world to see how the earlier practices and concepts can influence our worship today.

WORSHIP AT ALTARS

Some of the earliest glimpses the Bible gives us of worship are associated with the offering of sacrifices on altars. After the flood waters dispersed, Noah built an altar to sacrifice burnt offerings "of every clean animal and of every clean bird" to Yahweh who accepted it as a pleasing aroma (Gen 8:20–21). At times, altars are connected with God's promises to his people, as when Abraham built a series of altars after entering Canaan (Gen 12:7–8; 13:18) and erected another on Mt. Moriah where he prepared to sacrifice Isaac in response to the Lord's command (Gen 22:9). Demonstrating that he had taken up his part in the promise, Isaac built an altar at Beersheba (Gen 26:25), as did Jacob at Shechem and Bethel (Gen 33:20; 35:1–3, 7). While it is not expressly stated that offerings were burned on all these altars, the Hebrew word for altar—*mizbēaḥ*—is derived from the word for sacrifice and is mainly used for a place where animals are sacrificed, whether to Yahweh or to other gods.[1] Though originally a place for animal sacrifice, the word also denotes a place for burning incense. In some instances, an altar was built as a memorial or witness of some event, as when Moses constructed an altar to mark Israel's victory over the Amalekites (Exod 17:15) and the two-and-a-half tribes that settled east of the Jordan built "an imposing altar" after returning to their territory following the conquest (Josh 22:10–11, 27–28).

The Bible mentions several types of altars. The simplest was an "altar of earth," evidently constructed by piling up earth and stone or perhaps of bricks made from mud (Exod 20:24).[2] In other cases, one stone (Judg 13:19) or a pile of stones might serve as an altar (Deut 27:5–6; Josh 8:30–31). According to the Mosaic law, altars were not to be built of cut stones (Exod 20:25–26). Neither were they to be approached by steps. While no reason for these strictures is given, it was likely made in response to some rejected aspect of Canaanite worship.

While no particular size or shape was required for earthen or stone altars, the altar constructed for use in the tabernacle had fixed measurements and design.[3] According to the instructions found in Exodus 27:1–2, the bronze altar was to be constructed of acacia wood covered with bronze, measuring five cubits wide, five cubits long, and three cubits tall (approximately seven-and-a-half feet by seven-and-a-half feet by four-and-a-half feet). Integrated into the construction of the bronze altar were four horns located on the corners. While their precise purpose is unclear, blood was to be smeared on the horns during consecration ceremonies and some sacrifices.[4] Furthermore, fugitives seeking asylum were permitted to cling to the horns for protection before they stood trial. A bronze grating attached to

---

1. The Greek for altar—*thusiastērion*—similarly refers to a place of sacrifice, whether actual or metaphorical (cf. Heb 13:10).

2. For a discussion of their construction and use, see Zevit, "Earthen Altar Laws," 53–62.

3. See Durham, *Exodus*, 375–76.

4. For suggestions on the purpose of the horns, see Ball, "Horns of the Altar," 758.

the interior of the altar held the burning coals and the offerings presented, while allowing ash and drippings to pass through to the ground beneath and air to circulate to keep the fire going. Rings were affixed to the outside of the altar through which poles were inserted so that it could be carried. This altar apparently served as the model for the one built on a much larger scale for Solomon's temple. According to 2 Chronicles 4:1, Solomon's altar was twenty cubits by twenty cubits by ten cubits high (thirty feet by thirty feet by fifteen feet).[5]

During Israel's history, the bronze altar served as a thermometer for measuring the nation's spiritual temperature. Reformers such as Asa and Hezekiah repaired or purified the altar that had been neglected during the reigns of earlier kings (2 Chr 15:8; 29:17). This contrasted sharply with Ahaz, who exchanged the altar built by Solomon with one based on a design he had seen in Damascus and reserved the earlier one for personal divination or prayer (2 Kgs 16:10–15).[6]

In addition to the bronze altar for burnt offerings, the Old Testament speaks of a smaller altar of acacia wood covered with gold for burning incense in the tabernacle (Exod 30:1–10) and for Solomon's temple (1 Chr 28:18). The altar of incense or "gold altar" was one cubit square and two cubits high (eighteen inches by eighteen inches by three feet). Like the bronze altar, it was made with four horns that were consecrated by sacrificial blood and was built to be easily moved by inserting poles into rings attached to its sides. Placed inside the tabernacle, the incense burned on the altar obscured the curtain before the most holy place.

As the bronze and incense altars are frequently associated with the work of the priests in the tabernacle and temple, it is often assumed that only the descendants of Aaron were permitted to offer sacrifices on altars. However, individuals from outside the priestly family were permitted, and at times instructed, by Yahweh to present sacrifices on earthen or stone altars not connected with the central shrine. The patriarchs used such altars, as did individuals such as Joshua, Gideon, David, and Elijah (Josh 8:30–31;

---

5. It is possible that the altar was twenty by twenty cubits at the base and then rose in tiers like the altar described in Ezekiel 43:13–17 so that it was smaller at the top. See Dillard, *2 Chronicles*, 34. That the account of the building of Solomon's temple in 1 Kings 6–7, which is the source for the similar account in 2 Chronicles 3–4, omits the construction of the bronze altar and its size may be explained by the phrase being lost in the transmission of the earlier account. So, Hurowitz, "Yhwh's Exalted House," 67.

6. Commenting on Ahaz's use of the bronze altar, T. R. Hobbs says that in the context of 2 Kings 16:15, "The word לבקר 'to pray at' is puzzling." It has been variously interpreted as indicating divination by examining animal entrails and seeking God through prayer. Hobbs, *2 Kings*, 217.

Judg 6:24–26; 2 Sam 24:18–25; 1 Kgs 18:30–32).[7] It is quite possible that these altars were governed by the instructions for building an earthen or stone altar found in Exodus 20:24–26. If so, the instructions applied to individual Israelites in the same way the Ten Commandments given at the beginning of Exodus 20 and the instructions about Hebrew servants and personal injuries in Exodus 21 did. Altars thus used by lay people would have been constructed of earth or stone and used only for burnt offerings and peace offerings that did not require a priest to officiate.

The New Testament occasionally mentions the altars at Herod's temple used for sacrificing animals and burning incense. Jesus declares that since the altar makes the gift holy, anyone who swears by the altar or something offered on it should keep their word (Matt 23:18–20). When Zechariah entered Herod's temple to offer incense, he learned of the upcoming birth of his son who would be the forerunner of the Messiah (Luke 1:11). In addition to mentioning the altars in the temple of their day, New Testament writers also refer to Old Testament altars to express theological concepts. The author of Hebrews includes the altar of incense in his description of the tabernacle's furnishings to show that Jesus is greater (Heb 9:4). James refers to Abraham offering Isaac on the altar to show that since he was considered righteous because of his works, we should also do works of righteousness (Jas 2:21). Hebrews implies that the cross is an altar to which Christians approach "outside the gate" to be sanctified by the blood of Jesus (Heb 13:10–12).

The biblical witness about altars indicates that they are formal (though at times crude) places for offering animal sacrifices or burning incense to a deity, whether that is Yahweh or some other. They are physical (and at times metaphorical) locations where a person engages the deity, be it to ask for blessing and/or forgiveness, offer up thanksgiving, or merely to call upon his name in prayer. And though Christians do not burn animal sacrifices as they worship the Lord, the altar concept has remained a part of our religious vocabulary. Even in churches where the Lord's Supper is not understood to be sacrificial in nature, the table upon which the elements are placed and where the words of consecration are spoken is often called the altar or altar-table.[8] In many churches, the place where congregants kneel to receive communion or where a couple kneels during a wedding ceremony is called an altar rail. The terminology is likewise retained when family devotions are referred to as the family altar and when a preacher gives an altar call to

---

7. It has been suggested that Naaman may have transported soil back to Aram to build this type of altar. Zevit, "Earthen Altar Laws," 56.

8. For a brief discussion on the use of altar-tables by many traditions, see White, "Spatial Setting," 806–10.

encourage people to consecrate their lives to Christ, whether for the first time or as a recommitment to his cause.

In each of these cases, "altar" is used to indicate a place where God is encountered. Modern Christian use is therefore more metaphorical than literal. Since the Old Testament indicates that altars were places to meet God or memorials of what he did for his people, it is proper to use the term in this way. However, as the Christian church came into being because of Jesus' work on the cross, the most important metaphorical use of altar is the one alluded to Hebrews 13:10–12. The sacrifice of Christ allows Christians to encounter God in a way that was more effective than any offered under the old covenant. We have a memorial of God's work among us that speaks more clearly than any pile of stones or earth in Palestine. We have a testimony that God has fulfilled his promise of forming us into his people by adoption through his Son. Our altar is the cross. It is the place that we should return as we accept the once-for-all sacrifice he provided and as we offer up to him our sacrifice of praise (Heb 13:15).

TABERNACLE WORSHIP

Tabernacle worship is introduced in the book of Exodus—a book that centers on Yahweh's self-revelation to Israel (and others) and their response to him. Early in the book, Yahweh reveals himself to Moses at the burning bush where he declares his name and charges Moses to free his people from Egypt. Yahweh reveals his power to Israel and their enemies when he strikes the Egyptians with the plagues and parts the sea. Yahweh reveals himself to Israel at Mt. Sinai where he gives the law and provides directions for building the tabernacle that would signify his abiding presence. Yahweh reveals his anger against Israel when they shape and worship the golden calf. And when Moses prays for the people, Yahweh shows himself to be the God who will punish them for sin and yet deigns to travel with them, reminding them of their need to continually obey the obligations of his covenant.

Though Israel's response to God's self-revelation throughout Exodus can teach us much about worship, our focus here is the tabernacle. This tent, which along with its courtyard and furnishings is described in two lengthy passages in Exodus (Exod 25–31; 35–40), was essentially a portable sanctuary for the worship of God. The Hebrew word for tabernacle (*miškān*) simply means a dwelling place.[9] Although other terms used for the tabernacle

---

9. This word is not used of the whole complex, but only of the tent—the "dwelling place"—in the middle of the court.

include "tent of meeting" (*'ōhel mô 'ēd*, Exod 27:21),[10] the compound designation, "tabernacle, the tent of meeting" (*miškān 'ōhel mô 'ēd*, Exod 39:32), "sanctuary" (*miqdāš*, Exod 25:8), and "holy place" (*qōdeš*, Exod 38:24),[11] the main idea was that the tent was God's dwelling place on earth. As the Hebrew for tabernacle is derived from the word for "to dwell" (*šākan*), a term that evokes ideas of closeness, the Bible's common description of God dwelling among his people in the tabernacle highlights his immanence. His presence at the tabernacle is understood to be so close that it is at times specifically referred to as the "tabernacle of Yahweh" (*miškān YHWH*, Lev 17:4; Num 17:13; 31:47) or the "house of Yahweh your God" (*bêt YHWH 'ĕlōheykā*, Exod 23:19; 34:26).

Since the tabernacle is God's dwelling or house, it should be likened to a king's royal pavilion pitched amidst the tents of his people (Exod 25:8). While exhibiting similar features to the tents of others, it differed in its royal features. The presence of precious metals such as gold and silver and costly fabric made of blue, purple, and scarlet linen with skillfully embroidered cherubim exudes kingly wealth. Like the tents of a common man, the tabernacle housed a number of different pieces of furniture. The most important of them was the box usually called the ark of the covenant.[12] This movable chest, which would later hold the tablets of the covenant, served as God's throne.[13] God spoke to his covenant people from between the two cherubim. Two other pieces of furniture in the tabernacle, the table and the lampstand, were also similar to those found in the homes of everyday

---

10. Scholars divide on whether there are two tents of meeting—one in the center of the camp and the other pitched by Moses "outside the camp" (Exod 33:7)—or whether there was one tent described by two different traditions. Most critical scholars consider the tent in the center of the camp where the priests performed their duties to be part of the Priestly tradition, while the one where Moses alone met with God is usually identified as part of the Elohistic tradition, though Krauss considers it Yahwistic. Kraus, *Worship in Israel*, 128. Even so, there are good reasons to conclude that two tents are in view. See Averbeck, "Tabernacle," 810–12, 818; Durham, *Exodus*, 440–41.

11. It should be noted that while *miqdāš* and *qōdeš* are sometimes used synonymously for the whole tabernacle (or temple), *qōdeš* alone is used to refer to the "holy place" as distinct from the "most holy place" or "holy of holies."

12. In the Hebrew Bible, several different terms are used for the ark. It is called "the ark of the testimony" (*'ărōn hā 'ēdut*; 18x, especially in Exodus), "the ark of the covenant" (*'ărōn habbĕrît*; 184x), "the ark of Yahweh" (*'ărōn YHWH*), "the ark of God" (*'ărōn hā 'ĕlōhîm*), and simply "the ark" (*hā 'ārōn*).

13. While some passages liken the ark to God's footstool (1 Chr 28:2; Ps 132:7), others clearly say that the ark is God's throne (Num 7:89; 1 Sam 4:4; 2 Sam 6:2; 2 Kgs 19:15; Pss 80:1; 99:1). That many ancient Near Eastern cultures considered cherubim—composite creatures similar to the sphinx of Egypt—to serve as guardians of a king's or deity's throne supports the conclusion that the ark served as God's throne.

people. The difference being that the ones placed in the tabernacle were made of very costly materials as befit a king. The final piece of furniture designed for the tabernacle was the altar of incense upon which incense was burned twice a day.

Another difference between the tabernacle and the tents in which the Israelites lived was that the tabernacle was surrounded by a courtyard. This appears to have served as a sort of "buffer zone" that would protect the Israelites from coming too close to God.[14] Since Yahweh was holy, it was dangerous to draw too near. Only when bringing an offering to Yahweh could the average Israelite go into the tabernacle courtyard. Usually only priests wearing special sacred clothes and who had been purified according to a strict ritual could enter its confines to carry out their work. It was even more dangerous to enter the holy place and the most holy place. The latter could only be entered by the high priest once a year to make atonement.

Even though the Israelites considered the tabernacle to be God's home, they never thought of it as his only dwelling place. Rather, they understood the tabernacle to be a type or copy of God's home in heaven, an earthly representation built according to the plan shown to Moses. It is possible that the perpetually burning lamp and incense along with the bread laid out on the table signified that God was at home.[15] An even greater demonstration of God's presence in the tabernacle was the cloud that had covered Mt. Sinai with his glory and had moved from the mountain to the tabernacle, indicating that "What happened at Sinai is continued in the tabernacle."[16] The God who saved Israel from Egypt and established his covenant with them on Sinai would remain with them as long as they obeyed his covenant regulations. He would dwell in his holy tent as he had dwelt on the holy mountain. He would meet with his people in his earthly home as he had met with Moses and the elders on the mountain. And significantly, as Israel had been delivered from Egypt so that they could worship God at the mountain (Exod 3:12), they would continue to worship him at the tabernacle. After the tabernacle was completed, the pillar of cloud descended upon it and filled it with God's glory to signify the transference of his presence from the mountain to the tent. As a result, no one, not even Moses, could enter. From that time on, whenever and wherever the Israelites traveled, the presence of

---

14. The layout of the camp also protected the average Israelite from approaching too near, as the priests and Levites set up their tents immediately outside the tabernacle courtyard with the other tribes camping at a greater distance (Num 2–3; see particularly Num 2:2 which says, "the Israelites are to camp around the Tent of Meeting some distance from [*mineged*] it.").

15. So, Averbeck, "Tabernacle," 815.

16. Childs, *Exodus*, 540.

the cloud by day or pillar of fire by night visibly reminded them that Yahweh lived in their midst and that his presence went before them.

Strangely, from the time Israel emerged from the wilderness until the building of Solomon's temple, Scripture rarely mentions the tabernacle.[17] It is never mentioned in Deuteronomy,[18] and only twice in Joshua after the three tribes built an altar east of the Jordan as a memorial (Josh 22:19, 29; cf. Josh 22:27 where it is referred to as the sanctuary). Even so, its presence is at times indicated by reference to the ark of the covenant (Judg 20:26–27). At other times, the tabernacle and the ark are clearly in different locations as when the ark was taken into battle and when David pitched a tent for the ark in Jerusalem even though the tabernacle was at Gibeon (1 Chr 16).

There is evidence that the tabernacle continued to move according to God's instructions. Though not expressly stated, it seems clear that the tabernacle was erected at Gilgal, where the Israelites camped after crossing the Jordan (Josh 4:15–19). At various times, the tabernacle was set up at Shiloh (Josh 18:1; Ps 78:60), (presumably) Nob (1 Sam 21), and Gibeon (1 Chr 16:39; 2 Chr 1:3). Evidently, the tabernacle was moved for its last time when Solomon had it brought to Jerusalem with all its sacred furnishings (1 Kgs 8:4; 2 Chr 1:3–6).

The tabernacle's position in the camp, materials used for construction, and the personnel allowed to enter set it apart as a holy place. While the camp of Israel was considered clean, the tabernacle area was reckoned holy, and the innermost part of the tent was "most holy." The progression from clean to holy to most holy is reflected in the materials used. Bronze and silver are found in the courtyard. Though valued metals, they are nowhere near as precious as the gold found inside the holy place or the "pure gold" found in the holy of holies. A similar progression can be seen regarding God's people. All Israelites who were clean could remain in the camp,[19] but

---

17. Though the reality is not quite as negative as von Rad's statement that "After the settlement of Israel in Canaan the Tent disappears from the history," his assessment is generally accurate. Rad, *Old Testament Theology*, 236.

18. But see Deuteronomy 31:14, where Yahweh tells Moses and Joshua to go to the tent of meeting for Joshua to be commissioned to replace Moses. This lone reference to the tent in Deuteronomy does not explicitly state whether the tabernacle or the other tent of meeting is in view. The LXX apparently interprets it as the first and emends the text to read *"para tas thuras tēs skēnēs tou marturiou,"* "at the door of the tent of meeting," presumably because of the theological problem of having Joshua and Moses enter the holy place since they were not priests (cf. Exod 29:42, where God says he would speak to Israel "at the doorway of the tent of meeting" in reference to the tabernacle). However, since Exodus 33:11 states that Joshua regularly remained at the tent of meeting which was outside of the camp, it is likely that it is also in view here.

19. Israelites who became "unclean" for any reason were required to live outside the camp so that they would profane neither it nor others who lived there.

only the priests and individuals who were offering sacrifices could enter the outer courtyard of the tabernacle. Only the priests were allowed to enter the sacred tent, and even they could not enter any time they wanted, but only when serving the Lord as he required. What is true of the holy place is particularly true of the holy of holies that could only be entered by the high priest—the most holy person in Israel—once a year when making atonement for the tabernacle and people.

The presence of the tabernacle in their camp did several things for Israel. First, it provided a physical reminder that God lived in their midst. Although they were aware that God was not restricted to the tabernacle, the fact that it was a tent like the ones they lived in, only much grander and located right in the middle of their camp, showed that he was with them as their king and would lead them wherever they went. Second, God directly gave Moses the design of the tabernacle (Exod 25:9, 40; 26:30; 27:8). As God was the king of his people, only he had the right to determine how the tabernacle should be built and how worship should be performed. God's revelation at Sinai must be carried out in history. To worship God in any other way was beneath his dignity. Any such "worship" was false worship— a form of rebellion against God.[20] Third, the tabernacle was set apart as a holy place in the center of the camp to remind Israel that they were to be holy as God is holy. The holy nature of the tabernacle was reflected in its common designation "the sanctuary,"[21] a term usually applied to the whole complex but that could also be used for the tent in the middle of the courtyard. Fourth, the construction of the tabernacle was carried out as the people gave gifts of gold, silver, bronze, cloth, wood, etc. Though God commanded that the tabernacle be built, it required the gifts of his people to be completed. What is true of the materials is also true of the workmen. God specially gifted craftsmen to work with the material provided and build the tabernacle according to his design. They needed to enlist the help of others to ensure that the design was carried out.

---

20. The account of the golden calf, coming as it does in the middle of the tabernacle passages (Exod 32), highlights the fact that God could reject worship that his people considered desirable and that paralleled many aspects of true worship. Such worship is for this reason all the more dangerous.

21. The Hebrew word *miqdāš* is derived from the word for holy, *qōdeš*, signifying that a sanctuary is a holy place. This is true even when it is used for sanctuaries where Yahweh was worshipped improperly or where foreign gods were worshipped. It can also be used for the items in the tabernacle used for worship (Num 10:21), and the holy part of sacrifices (Num 18:29).

Tabernacle Worship's Lessons for Today

One of my earliest memories of the church my family attended when I was young is of finding a scale model of the tabernacle in a back room of the church basement. Arrayed on a plywood sheet, a series of wooden dowels were joined by strings and strips of cloth. It is likely that at one time miniature replicas of the various pieces of furniture were placed in their appropriate positions and the cloths were several layers deep in multiple colors. Models like this can make it easier for Christians to visualize what the ancient tabernacle looked like and how it would have been used. A similar attempt to come to grips with the tabernacle's symbolism in Israel was attempted by a woman who reconstructed the tent in her six-hundred-square-foot apartment to remind her that God is always present in her home.[22]

While attempts to help modern Christians visualize the tabernacle or provide a tangible reminder of God's abiding presence may be commendable, they are of limited value. I have no doubt but that the model of the tabernacle I found in the church basement had once helped the congregation as they studied Exodus or Israel's worship. However, it did not take long before it was relegated to a backroom where it spent years collecting dust and occasionally stimulating the interest of a few young boys until it was eventually dispensed with altogether. The lady who erected a tabernacle in her living room discovered that after a while she stopped seeing it. As she put it, "Like a bad piece of art or a roommate's ugly lamp, this crazy tabernacle that I had constructed to be a daily reminder of God dwelling *with* me—something I couldn't ignore if I tried—had become just like another piece of furniture, part of the backdrop of my life."[23] While intended to help people understand Israel's worship or experience God's presence, these tools had an early sell-by date after which their benefits diminished greatly.

The biblical accounts about the building of the tabernacle and its furnishings and their place in Israel's society were not written to instruct us how to build similar structures. Neither were they written because people in later times might be curious about how things were done in the past. Rather, these accounts were shaped by theological considerations. As stated above, the important issue was to inform future generations that God dwelt in the midst of his people, that one must worship God according to the patterns he prescribes, that God's people should be holy as he is, and that they should be personally involved in providing gifts and performing the rites he required of his worshippers. The amount of instruction given concerning the design

---

22. Harrell, "Leviticus Challenge," 32.
23. Harrell, "Leviticus Challenge," 33. Italics are in the original.

and building of the tabernacle as compared to other biblical themes demonstrates its relative importance in the text. Two chapters of the Pentateuch are devoted to God's creation of the world, while thirteen are required for the building of the tabernacle and many more to describe the sacrifices that would be offered there and the priestly personnel who would do it.

The near word-for-word repetition of the instructions about building the various pieces of the tabernacle (Exod 25–31) found in the confirmation that the various parts were indeed constructed "just as the Lord had commanded Moses" (Exod 35–40) is not the result of sloppy editorial work, nor of the author's enthusiasm for recording minute details. Rather, the passages show that what God commands, his people should do. His instructions about worship should guide their practice. When taken together, the two long sections about building the tabernacle indicate that when Israel obeyed God's instructions about worship, the cloud of his glory came down upon the newly constructed tabernacle so that the glory of the Lord filled the whole place. And as long as Israel obeyed God and moved camp any time the cloud lifted up from the tabernacle, his glory remained with them throughout their travels.

This approach to reading the Exodus narratives about the tabernacle makes sense, particularly when one considers their placement on either side of the account of the golden calf. When Moses was delayed on the mountain where God instructed him about building the tent, many Israelites expressed their desire to find another way to worship God under a different leader. Their yearning to worship without waiting for God's instructions led to the manufacture and worship of an idol, directly contradicting the first and second commandments that Yahweh had recently given them. This action also serves as an illustration of what can happen when God's people try to approach God in their own way—they lapse into idolatry and apostasy. Aaron's attempt to connect the worship of the golden calf with the worship of Yahweh, by announcing the fabrication of the calf in conjunction with a festival to the Lord, failed miserably.[24] God was so displeased by their lusty worship that he threatened to destroy the nation and make a new and greater nation from Moses. And even though he relented in response to

---

24. Notice the parallels between the worship of the calf and the worship required by God. (1) The people presented an offering of gold to build the object of worship (Exod 32:2–4). (2) The worship of the calf was equated with Yahweh worship as he had brought them up from Egypt and a festival was held in his honor (Exod 32:4–5). The idol was thus to represent God's presence in their midst. (3) As was common in the worship of Yahweh, burnt offerings and fellowship offerings were presented, though not according to the pattern he gave (Exod 32:6). But note that as a result of idol worship, the Israelites indulged in revelry and "running wild" (Exod 32:6, 25) instead of living as God's holy people.

Moses' intercession, 3000 people fell by the swords of the Levites who defended the Lord's honor. Additionally, the nation that had been liberated to worship Yahweh—while the Egyptians faced plague after plague for refusing to recognize that Yahweh was God or allow Israel to worship him (Exod 5:2)—was struck by a plague because they confused their Savior with an idol shaped like a calf.

Like the original readers, modern Christians who read this account should pause and consider where they stand as worshippers of God. Do we succumb to the temptation to worship other things in a style similar to that which God desires or do we worship him in the way he has revealed? Like Israel, we need to recognize that the tabernacle teaches us some important truths about worship. First, it shows us that God is in our midst, not in the form of a tent and furnishings, but in the person of Jesus Christ who was the Word who "became flesh and made his dwelling among us" and displayed the Father's glory (John 1:14). John intentionally compared Jesus to the tabernacle by using the Greek word *skēnoō*, "to live in a tent." He "made his dwelling among us" is thus more literally translated, "he tabernacled among us." The one whom the first evangelist called Immanuel—"God with us" (Matt 1:23)—was likened by John to the tabernacle where God's glory was revealed "to show that this is the presence of the Eternal in time."[25] The center of Christian worship becomes the person of Jesus Christ rather than a tent or edifice. The glory of God is seen in his person, not in a cloud.

Second, biblical teaching on the tabernacle should remind us that God is the designer of worship in the same way that he is the designer of the created world. As the one who knows what we need to come into relationship with him, he reveals his will so that we can relate rightly to him. Ancient Israel approached him through the sacrificial system associated with the tabernacle and later the temple. Christians approach him through the gospel of Jesus Christ as recorded in his word. Our thoughts concerning worship should be primarily based upon God's revelation, so that we are not led into idolatrous or misshaped worship.

Third, the requirement for holiness in tabernacle worship reminds us that Christians should emphasize personal holiness before their holy God. The holy tent has been replaced by the Holy One (Luke 1:35; John 6:69; Acts 2:27) who should be emulated by those who follow him (1 Pet 1:15). Jesus models holiness, demands holiness, and sanctifies his people so that they can live holy lives for his Father. Actions that do not reflect his holiness fall outside of true worship.

---

25. Michaelis, "σκηνή," 386.

Fourth, the tabernacle stories remind us that God's people contributed their gifts and talents so that the tent and its furnishings could be constructed and used in the worship of God. Even after the completion of the tabernacle, people continued to give gifts so that the ministry of sacrifice could continue. As all good gifts come from God, we simply return to him from what we have been given—money, time, talents, etc. As we use them in his service, they become expressions of our worship of God.

Many of the theological concepts associated with the tabernacle accounts should be applied to the worship of the Christian church. Anyone who wishes to worship God in a way that pleases him should consider how to do this. Although some of these can be readily applied, others may need to be implemented in a much more nuanced manner. In later chapters, we will develop some of these concepts and suggest how they can be applied in the church.

TEMPLE WORSHIP

The tabernacle served as the focal point of much of Israel's worship from its construction in the wilderness until Solomon's temple was built around 960 BC. Though built on a much larger scale and more richly ornamented than the tabernacle, the proportions and the furnishings of the temple closely resembled the structure it replaced. More importantly, the theology attached to the tabernacle was transferred to the temple. It thus remained the sign that God dwelt among his people, a reality most clearly seen by the descent of the cloud upon the temple after it was dedicated by Solomon (1 Kgs 8:1–11).[26] As the temple was the place for offering sacrifices, it became the center of religious activity during the kingdom period and was considered the most holy site in Israel. Only those with clean hands and a pure heart could draw near to it (Ps 24:3–4). The link between the temple and Jerusalem led to David's royal city being recognized as the city of God (Pss 46:4; 87:3), the city of the great King (Ps 42:8), and the holy city (Neh 11:1, 18; Isa 48:2: 52:1). Indeed, it was the center from which God reigned over all people on earth (2 Kgs 19:15; Pss 9:11; 99:1–2; Isa 37:16). God's presence and holiness were to have a central place in the minds of the Israelites who came to the temple to offer sacrifices and to celebrate the annual feasts.

As the hub of Israel's worship, individuals came to the temple to present their sacrifices, pay their vows, and offer personal prayers to God. As

---

26. Note that Solomon was just as clear as Moses that God did not dwell in the temple, as even the heavens could not contain him. The temple was simply the place God chose put his name and where his people would pray to him (1 Kgs 8:27–30).

the place Yahweh chose for his name to dwell, the temple gave his people an opportunity to witness his beauty and experience his goodness and blessings. It also gave them security when they considered the possibility that their neighbors might attack them.[27] While the temple was always open, Israelites chiefly drew near on Sabbath days and to celebrate the great feasts. Often, their worship was marked by great rejoicing and dancing before the Lord (Pss 149:3; 150:4). At other times, they drew near to the Lord individually or in groups to lament the difficulties they faced in life. After the temple was built, women came to be purified after childbirth and brought their baby boys to be circumcised (Luke 2:21–24). The temple was also a place where God's prophets confronted his people with the words of the Lord (Jer 7:2; 19:14; 26:2).

The time came when God's chosen people chose not to approach him in holiness or worship him in the way he prescribed. Disregarding his laws, they built altars and temples to other gods that they worshipped along with or instead of Yahweh. At times, they worshipped the foreign gods inside the Jerusalem temple. Reacting against their continual breaking of his covenant, God eventually withdrew his presence from the temple and sent them into exile (Ezek 10:18–19). While in exile, with no temple at the center of the worshipping community, the Israelites learned to assemble for worship in small communities and discovered that Yahweh was not limited to one city or sanctuary, but ruled even where they had been taken as hostages. These assemblies gave rise to the synagogues.

Although synagogues would eventually become the main centers for religious education and worship, temple worship was not forgotten. When the people returned to their homeland after the exile, they immediately set out to rebuild the temple. This cause was supported by various priests and governors like Zerubbabel and Nehemiah, in addition to the Persian king Cyrus who is credited for promoting the idea in the first place (Ezra 1:1–2). The second temple would be the center of Jewish worship for nearly five hundred years. Though the temple was desecrated by Antiochus IV Epiphanes who erected an altar to Zeus there (167 BC), it was repaired and rededicated by Judas Maccabeus (164 BC). The relighting of the menorah in the temple at this time is yearly celebrated during the Jewish Feast of Hanukkah. Desecrated on several other occasions, the second temple was partially destroyed by Herod the Great when he attacked and entered Jerusalem in

---

27. At times, this sense of security was denounced as deceptive; God would not always protect those who had broken his covenant (Jer 7:3–8; 26:2–13; Mic 3:11–12). While God's presence could bring protection, it could also bring judgment upon sinners. The temple in Jerusalem could fall in the same way the worship center in Shiloh had (Jer 7:12–15; 26:6).

37 BC. Then, starting around 19 BC, Herod rebuilt the temple in an attempt to gain support of Jews who did not readily accept him as king due to his Idumaean bloodline. Though the main part of the temple building was complete within about ten years, different parts of the project continued until about AD 64, not many years before the whole building was destroyed when Titus invaded Jerusalem.[28] Though the three temple buildings shared a number of architectural features and furnishings, differences in size and style indicate that the function was more important than the structure.

NEW TESTAMENT WORSHIP AND THE TEMPLE

Although its importance would decline after the resurrection of Jesus, the New Testament, particularly the Gospels and Acts, features the temple as a prominent place for worship. Luke begins his birth narratives with the announcement of the birth of John the Baptist to Zechariah who was serving in the temple as a priest of the Aaronic order.[29] Chosen by lot to enter the temple to burn incense in accordance with the rules laid down in the Mosaic legislation and the division of priests into orders by King David (Exod 30:7–8; 1 Chr 24:1–19), Zechariah was amazed to see an angel standing alongside the altar. The angel announced that his prayers had been answered so that his barren wife would give birth to a son who would "be great in the sight of the Lord" (Luke 1:15).[30] He would also live the life of a Nazirite—abstaining from wine and other fermented drink—and be filled by the Holy Spirit from his mother's womb. The child, who would be named John—"God is gracious"—would fulfill the prophecy of Micah 4:5 by going forth in the spirit of Elijah to restore relationships between people and with God.

Though Zechariah received a special vision, he wasn't the only faithful person to visit the temple on that day. Other priests, who had not been selected to enter the temple, remained in the courtyard, awaiting his return. In addition, a number of laypeople had come to worship and to hear the priest pronounce a benediction upon them. Undoubtedly, they were all shocked

---

28. The on-going nature of the building project is reflected in the Jews' response to Jesus' remark, "Destroy this temple, and I will raise it again in three days." "It has taken forty-six years to build this temple, and you are going to raise it in three days?" (John 2:19–20).

29. Significantly, Luke begins and ends his Gospel with people worshipping God at the temple.

30. Later in the Gospel of Luke, Jesus upheld this prophecy by saying that John was a prophet "and more than a prophet," as he had been sent before the Messiah to prepare the way for his coming (Luke 7:26–27). Jesus thus considered him the greatest of those who were alive at the time.

when Zechariah emerged from the temple unable to speak. The astonishment at having a priest who couldn't pray quickly gave way to the realization that something spectacular had happened—God had given Zechariah a vision.

The appearance of the angel while Zechariah was performing his worship ministrations alerts us to two things about the place the temple held in the thinking of New Testament authors regarding worship. First, it was a place for the worship of the true God of Israel. Second, it was a place where God revealed himself, a revelation that particularly highlighted Jesus' role as Savior.

More than a year after Zechariah's vision in the temple, Mary and Joseph took Jesus to Jerusalem to worship. Eight days after his birth, they had Jesus circumcised and offered a sacrifice at the temple to acknowledge that their firstborn son belonged to the Lord. Their faithfulness in obeying Old Testament revelation is reflected in the fact that they did not return home until they had done everything the law required (Luke 2:30).

While in Jerusalem, Mary and Joseph met two individuals among the great crowds of worshippers: the "righteous and devout" Simeon to whom it had been revealed that he would not die before he saw the Messiah and the prophetess Anna who "never left the temple but worshiped night and day, fasting and praying" (Luke 2:25-26, 37). These two elderly worshippers realized that God's promises had been fulfilled in the baby Jesus. Simeon praised God that he had the opportunity to see the one through whom salvation for Israel and the Gentiles would come, and asked that he could now depart in peace. Anna thanked the Lord for what she had seen and informed the gathering crowds that God was about to do wonderful things through this child.

The New Testament frequently describes Jesus and his disciples going to the temple during the feasts and at other times (Luke 2:41-42; John 2:13; 5:1; 7:10-14; 10:22-23; Acts 20:16). Jesus often identified the temple as a place of prayer and piety. His parable of the Pharisee and tax collector never questions that the temple was the right place to pray, but simply asks whether the worshipper's heart is properly prepared (Luke 18:9-14). Similarly, his exhortation to leave a gift at the altar until one is reconciled with a brother identifies the altar as the proper place to present gifts as long as one's heart and relationships are right (Matt 5:23-24). Like Solomon and the prophets, Jesus understood the temple to be God's dwelling place (Matt 23:21), the place where one could meet God. It was for this reason that he cleansed the temple to remove all abuses in worship (Matt 21:12-13; Mark 11:15-17; Luke 19:45-46; John 2:14-17).

As Jewish men, the disciples were brought up to share Jesus' view of the temple. Their reverence for the place was only strengthened as they accompanied their rabbi to the temple and heard what he said about it. Temple worship was such a natural part of their lives that even after the resurrection and ascension, they returned to Jerusalem with joy and "stayed continually at the temple, praising God" (Luke 24:52-53). In the book of Acts, Luke frequently records that the early believers in Jesus as Messiah met together at the temple (Acts 2:46) where they prayed (Acts 3:1) and preached the gospel about Jesus (Acts 3:12-26; 4:1-2; 5:42). Late in his career, the Apostle Paul, encouraged by other Christian leaders, went to the temple to bring alms and purify himself according to the Mosaic laws (Acts 21:23-26; 24:17-18). Through much of the first century, the church shared much in common with traditional Jewish temple and synagogue worship. The major difference between the first Christians and their fellow Jews was their belief that the Messiah had come in the person of Jesus, while the others believed that the Messiah was yet to come.

The Temple as a Place of Revelation

A second thing Luke reveals about the temple is that it was a place of revelation. This was true for Zechariah and for Simeon and Anna who bore witness about the child who would bring salvation for Israel and the nations (Luke 2:21-38). Twelve years later, after Mary and Joseph traveled to Jerusalem to celebrate the Passover, the temple became the place where the missing boy Jesus was revealed to his parents. After spending three days desperately searching for their son, they found him at the temple "sitting among the teachers, listening to them and asking them questions" (Luke 2:46). His questions and answers amazed those who heard him and revealed Jesus' supreme promise as a student of Scripture, a promise that would yield much fruit in the years to come when he again entered into dialogue with the rabbis at the temple and in other places. When asked why he had abandoned his parents, Jesus' answer that he needed to be in his Father's house shows that from an early age he was aware of his special relationship with God and his need to be associated with the temple.

The temple was frequently the location where Jesus revealed himself—to his disciples, the Jewish leaders, and others—as one who came to teach and heal in the spirit of the prophets (Matt 21:14, 23; 26:55; Mark 12:35; Luke 19:47; 20:1; 21:37-38). Following Old Testament teaching, Jesus viewed the temple as the place where God dwelt, and, following the lead of the prophets, he was determined to rectify its misuse. He thus overturned the tables and benches of those who carried out business there and blocked its use as a thoroughfare for carrying merchandise. Quoting Isaiah and Jeremiah, he told them, "It is written . . . 'My house will be called a house of prayer,' but you are making it a 'den of robbers'" (Matt 21:13; cf. Isa 56:7; Jer 7:11).

The Temple eclipsed as a Place of Worship

Even though the temple retained a central place in the worship of the first Christians, its importance was eclipsed for several reasons. First, it lost its position for theological reasons—Jesus took its place. The New Testament commonly regards Jesus as the temple, the "place," where God is present in the midst of his people. The old order would pass away because Jesus was greater than the temple (Matt 12:6). After cleansing the temple of profit makers, he was asked to perform a miracle to prove that he had authority to do so. He answered, "Destroy this temple, and I will raise it again in three days." Though the Jews (along with Jesus' disciples) misunderstood his meaning, he was clearly speaking of his own body as the temple they would destroy and which would be raised again in three days (John 2:14–22).

In addition to equating the temple with Jesus, the New Testament also indicates that the temple in Jerusalem would not always be the center of God's worship. When the Samaritan woman questioned Jesus about the proper place for worship, he informed her that in the "time [that] is coming and has now come," the setting would no longer be of primary importance. In the kingdom he was establishing, neither the mountain revered by Samaritans nor the temple venerated by Jews would be essential in the worship of God.[31] Though the temple in Jerusalem had been the place God set apart for worship, it (and Mt. Gerizim) would become irrelevant.[32] Of greater importance than worshipping in a particular physical setting would be one's spiritual relationship to God (John 4:20–24). Since God is spirit, only those who come to him in spirit and in truth can worship him. God can only be known and truly worshipped as the Holy Spirit—the Spirit of Truth—empowers his people for worship. God can only be known and worshipped as one encounters the One who is the Truth and whom Scripture proclaims to be Redeemer. Worshipping in a particular place is thus replaced by worshipping a particular person. Those whom the Father

---

31. While Jesus nullifies the geographic argument about the place of worship, he insists that "salvation is from the Jews." God's revelation has come through the agency of Jewish and not Samaritan (or other) religion.

32. Jesus here follows the path of the prophets who had said that a central sanctuary would not always be required.

desires to worship him will come to him through the person of the Son, not the location of the temple.

In the book of Acts, the story of Stephen shows that Jesus replaced the temple. In Acts 7:49–50, Stephen quotes Isaiah 66:1–2 to show that neither the temple nor the land was the most important part of God's promise to David to build him a house. God's work among his people could not be restricted to one locality or building. To restrict him in this way is to deny Isaiah's pronouncement that God does not live in houses constructed by humans. Instead, Stephen sees a vision of Jesus standing at the right hand of the Father in heaven. He, not the building, is the way to God.

The writer of Hebrews—though he uses the term tabernacle instead of temple—makes it clear that the Old Testament worship system was superseded by Jesus, who is greater than Moses, the priests, the sacrifices, and the entire tabernacle/temple cult of the Old Covenant. By worshipping Jesus, we have access into the very throne room of God and join the worship of heaven (Heb 12:22–29). As Paul understands it, Christians—individually and corporately—make up the temple of God (1 Cor 3:16–17; 6:19; 2 Cor 6:16; Eph 2:19–22; cf. 1 Pet 2:5). God is thus experienced, not in a sacred building, but in the fellowship of believers—the church.

Seen from the perspective of Revelation, the future new heaven and new earth will be home to a new Holy City where God dwells with his people. In this New Jerusalem, which is said to be the bride of Christ, there will be no temple, because "the Lord God Almighty and the Lamb are its temple" (Rev 21:1–2, 22). Ultimately, no building will be needed to remind God's people that he dwells in their midst because he will be immediately present and they will see his face (Rev 22:4). The New Testament thus understands that the physical temple has been replaced by Jesus Christ and by the Spirit-filled people who make up his body on earth. Theologically, the temple has been replaced by Christ and his church as the only way to experience God's presence today.

A second reason the Jerusalem temple lost its importance in the life of the church was that it was destroyed by the Romans in AD 70 as Jesus foretold (Matt 24:1–2; Mark 13:1–2; Luke 21:5–6). One of his prophecies to this effect came in response to the comments of one of his disciples about the size and beauty of the temple building (Mark 13:1). Like the messages of the Old Testament prophets, Jesus' response would have shocked the men who considered the building to be the dwelling place of God. Even so, Jesus denounced the very temple he had cleansed and where he had taught and performed many miracles. Mark's inclusion of Jesus' pronouncement against the temple at the end of a section (Mark 11:27—13:2) that tells of his last visit to the temple may be significant. The section begins with the Jewish leaders questioning Jesus about the source of his authority. Jesus turns their question around with the result that they refuse to comment on the source of John the Baptist's authority (Mark 11:27–33). He then presents the parable of the vineyard in which the tenants refused to pay the owner and either beat or killed those sent to collect the proceeds, including the owner's son (Mark 12:1–12). Realizing the parable was spoken against them, the Jewish leaders looked for a way to arrest him. Later, Jesus responded to a series of questions by different parties of Jews who tried to trap him in his answers (Mark 12:13–34). When they were all silenced and unwilling or unable to ask any more questions, Jesus probed them about the nature of the Messiah, commented on the coming punishment of the teachers of the law who were not sincere in their profession, and observed that a poor woman gave more to the temple treasury than the rich who gave of their surplus (Mark 12:35–44). That Jesus pronounced judgment against the temple at this time may indicate his conviction that the whole Jewish way of worship—including that which was associated with the temple—had come to an end and would be reoriented in God's new Kingdom where his worshippers would not focus on a man-made structure but on the one who is greater than the temple.[33]

It is possible that the destruction of the temple partially fulfilled Jesus' statement to the Samaritan woman about the future of worship. Without a centralized temple, there could be no centralized worship. And after the Holy Spirit was sent, there was no need for all of the people of God to gather together in one place for worship.

Third, even before its destruction, the temple's role in the life of the church began to wane. This was in part because mainstream Judaism more and more considered Christianity to be a heretical sect. Shortly after Pentecost, Jewish leaders began to exert enormous pressure on the followers of Jesus, forbade them from preaching in Jesus' name (Acts 4:18; 5:40), and gave their audience reason to distance themselves from them (Acts 5:13). Even so, until the martyrdom of Stephen, the apostles and other believers continued to meet and teach in the temple and synagogues throughout Jerusalem. But after Stephen's death, the church faced open persecution and believers were forced to flee from the city. Under such conditions, it became more and more difficult to meet openly in the temple.

A fourth reason the temple lost its importance for the church is tied to the expansion of Christianity among the Gentiles. As more Gentiles turned to Christ, it became clear that their lack of a Jewish cultural and theological background exempted them from performing many of the Jewish rites and laws. Since regular pilgrimages to Jerusalem were unnecessary for Gentile

---

33. France, *Mark*, 494–96.

believers, the Jerusalem temple became less important for the early church, and meetings followed the style of synagogue gatherings instead of temple assemblies.

Lessons from Temple Worship for Today

Like the tabernacle before it, the temple was the place God chose to dwell among his people. This concept must guide our considerations regarding how to adopt biblical teaching about the temple for the church today. As we have seen, the early church portrayed the temple less as a physical building and more in terms of the spiritual dwelling place of God. Christian worship should therefore embrace the theology developed by New Testament writers who identified the temple with the person of Christ and his body, the church. New Testament teaching about living as the temple of God should be given more weight than Davidic or Solomonic practices developed for the sanctuary in Jerusalem.

The authors of the New Testament often turned to temple imagery to deliver ethical instruction that was integrated with worship practice. Paul thus urged Christians to live holy lives since the holy God dwells in them (1 Cor 6:19–20; 2 Cor 7:1). He specifically reminded the Corinthian church that since their bodies are the temple of God, they should separate themselves from prostitutes and all sexual immorality. Though modern believers may miss the implications of this for worship, first-century Christians would not, as ritual prostitution was common at pagan temples. Paul's warning against this form of impurity was not the extent of his concern. Since Christians are "the temple of the living God," they should also resist all forms of idolatry (2 Cor 6:16). The apostle thus recalls that Old Testament promises of God's presence with his people are tied to injunctions to be separate from that which is unclean (2 Cor 6:17–18). But even separation from idolatry is not enough. Paul implores his readers to purify themselves "from everything that contaminates body and spirit, perfecting holiness out of reverence [lit. "fear"] for God" (2 Cor 7:1). Holiness and fear are inextricably linked. As the holy God takes up his dwelling in a living temple, holy living, seen through proper worship and the fear of God, should be the result.

Paul also makes use of temple imagery when he cries out for unity in Christian worship (1 Cor 3:3–17). Though it is unthinkable that believers today might divide over their association with Paul or Apollos, followers of Christ frequently divide along denominational lines and for other reasons. According to Paul, schism is tantamount to desecration of the temple, and since Christians are God's temple, those who separate believers will receive

God's punishment (1 Cor 3:16–17).[34] Christians must do everything in their power to ensure that the temple is properly built upon the foundation that was laid by the first workers. It is similarly essential to remove every obstacle that separates believers in the same way that Christ destroyed "the dividing wall of hostility" that kept Jews and Gentiles apart (Eph 2:14). Barriers of race, culture, class, age, etc., are out of place in the church. In an age when new churches are planted in order to reach distinct social groups and others divide over issues of style that appeal to some but not others, a sound biblical theology of the church, linked with creative thinking about how all can be included, is sorely needed. Our spiritual unity in Christ should move us to work for the restoration of individuals and groups who believe in him yet remain divided. As those who share a common faith, we should be willing to meet with and worship with those who differ with us on minor issues, removing as many obstacles as we can.

SYNAGOGUE WORSHIP

A synagogue was an assembly or "gathering" of Jewish believers. Only later did the word come to be used for the buildings where the congregation met.[35] The English word is never used in the Old Testament,[36] primarily because synagogues, as we understand them, most likely came into existence during the exilic or postexilic period when the Jews lived away from their homeland and were not able to participate in temple worship.[37]

---

34. Thus R. J. McKelvey says of this context, "To cause disunity in the church is to desecrate the temple of God, and desecration of a holy place leads to its destruction." McKelvey, "Temple," 809. Is it possible that God might withdraw from the church (or sections thereof) in the same way he departed from the earthly temple?

35. Usage sometimes makes it difficult to distinguish between the worshipping assembly and the synagogue building, particularly since a congregation and the building where it met used the same term. Schrage, "συναγωγή," 807.

36. Although the word "synagogues" can be found in Psalm 74:8 in the KJV, the Hebrew word behind this, *mo'ed*, expresses a different concept. The Hebrew word was used for the "tent of meeting," and for an "appointed time" for a festival or meeting. Most modern versions rightly translate the word "meeting place" or something similar, though the LXX renders it *heortas*, "festivals" (though how these could be burned up is unclear). The Greek term *synagōgē*, which is the source of our English word, is usually found in the Septuagint as a translation of *'edah*, a "gathering" or "congregation," or (less frequently) *qahal*, an "assembly" or "convocation" (which is more commonly translated *ekklēsia*). In later times, the rabbis used the word *keneset* for the "gathering" of the people. This term is used today for the Hebrew parliament—The Knesset—in addition to modern synagogues.

37. While Jewish traditions assign the beginnings of synagogue worship to the time of Moses or even the Patriarchs, most modern scholars find no trace of the concept

Two of the most important aspects of synagogue worship were prayer and the reading and study of Hebrew Scripture.[38] For this reason, synagogues were often referred to as the house of prayer or house of instruction. From the beginning, the primary aim of instruction was to acquaint the community with the Torah—the books of Moses. Synagogues were also centers where young people learned to read so that they could study the Prophets and other Scriptures. In time, other aspects of Jewish culture and traditions were passed on in synagogues. The focus on prayer influenced the construction of synagogue buildings which were usually oriented toward Jerusalem or were erected so that the ark which held the Torah was affixed to a wall facing Jerusalem.[39] Synagogues were established wherever Jews could be found. As a gathering for prayer and instruction, a minimum of ten men who wanted to meet was required to start one. During the first century AD, dozens, even hundreds of synagogues, were found in large cities like Jerusalem.

Although the literary and archaeological evidence is sparse, even before the destruction of the temple in AD 70, many synagogues apparently patterned their worship after temple worship and their buildings after the temple. Synagogues timed their prayer services with the morning and evening sacrifices offered at the temple. Synagogue services did not require a priest to take the lead as they were more lay oriented, and allowed women and children to read Scripture.[40] In the first century, they were mainly administered by the Pharisees; the Sadducees taking charge of the temple cult. At that time, it is probable that synagogue services contained the following elements.[41]

(1) A recitation of the *Shema*. This prayer, which most Jewish men would recite at least twice a day, comes from Deuteronomy 6:4 and takes its name from the first word in Hebrew which means "hear." "Hear, O Israel:

---

until after the destruction of Jerusalem. See Schrage, "συναγωγή," 810–11; Rowley, *Worship in Ancient Israel*, 211–18, 224–27.

38. Beckwith reminds us that "all the elements of synagogue worship—prayer, Scripture reading and teaching—had a Temple background." Beckwith, *Calendar, Chronology and Worship*, 178. Since these elements were more developed in the synagogue than the temple and synagogues were more widely distributed, more Jews could take part in gathered worship than was possible with the temple as the sole venue.

39. This follows the known habits of Jews who prayed facing the temple or Jerusalem (1 Kgs 8:38, 44, 48; 2 Chr 6:34, 38; Dan 6:10).

40. Schrage, "συναγωγή," 823.

41. Both archaeological and literary evidence have led many scholars to conclude that there was no regular Sabbath liturgy in synagogues until the third century. See Bradshaw, *Origins of Christian Worship*, 36–38.

The LORD our God, the LORD is one." It was used at the beginning of a service after the men put on their prayer shawls.

(2) After saying the *Shema*, the men would recite several other psalms and prayers, including a series of Eighteen Benedictions. Some of the prayers followed fixed forms; others did not. The prayers were said with the congregation standing and responding with a unified "Amen."

(3) Scripture passages from the Torah (a scroll containing the Pentateuch) and Haftarah (a scroll of the Prophets) were read. After being taken out of the holy ark in the front of the synagogue, the "king of books" was removed from its special royal robe and crown and read for the congregation to hear. Where it was necessary, the reading was interpreted for those who did not understand Hebrew.[42] The passage read was long enough so that the whole Torah could be read in either one or three years, depending on the congregation. After the Torah was replaced in its ark, a reading from the prophets followed. When Jesus read the portion of Isaiah's prophecy in the synagogue in Nazareth, he was probably participating in this part of the synagogue service (Luke 4:16–21; cf. Isa 61:1–2). Psalms were probably regularly read during synagogue services. Other passages would be read in conjunction with specific festivals.

(4) As the service focused on prayer and instruction from the Scriptures, synagogue worship regularly included a sermon or homily, usually explaining some portion of the day's reading. Any member of the synagogue could give the sermon, but it was usually given by someone who had taken time to the study the passage or a visiting rabbi. Its purpose was to help listeners understand and apply the text to their daily life.

(5) Although the Jews made use of several different benedictions, synagogue services concluded with the priestly blessing from Numbers 6:24–26.

> The LORD bless you and keep you;
> the LORD make his face shine upon you and be gracious to you;
> the LORD turn his face toward you and give you peace.

In addition to their importance for worship and learning, synagogues served as centers for justice and punishment. While this stretched beyond punishment for believing that Jesus was the Messiah, the New Testament indicates that Christian Jews were tried in synagogues. Jesus informed his disciples that they would be put on trial and beaten for their faith (Matt 10:17; Luke 12:11). And though Stephen was eventually tried by the Sanhedrin, the original accusations against him came from the members of the

---

42. The translation of the Hebrew text of Scripture to Aramaic led to the development of the Targumim in both Palestine and Babylon. These translations could differ widely from the original due to added explanations and allegorical interpretations.

Synagogue of the Freedmen (Acts 6:9). Acknowledging his role in persecuting believers in Jesus, Paul testified before Agrippa that "Many a time I went from one synagogue to another to have them punished, and I tried to force them to blaspheme" (Acts 26:11).

As an institution, the synagogue was extremely important to the early church. Jesus often visited synagogues during his ministry in order to worship, teach the people assembled there, and, on some occasions, heal people and cast out demons. The apostles similarly visited synagogues when they wanted to join with God's people and teach others about God's revelation of himself in Jesus Christ. Paul characteristically visited the local synagogue in every city before taking the gospel to the Gentiles. In many of these cities, while some Jews, proselytes, and "God-fearers" responded positively to the gospel, others reacted so negatively that Paul was forced to turn from these assemblies to proclaim Christ to those who were outside. Even so, synagogues were usually the first point of contact for first-century missionaries.

It is not surprising that the synagogues became the models for Christian meetings which, in addition to the breaking of bread, also centered on prayer, Bible reading, and instruction.[43] But even though the church took its main worship forms from the synagogue, it rarely used the term for gatherings of Christians, preferring to call itself an *ekklēsia*.[44] Though this word was used somewhat synonymously with synagogue in the LXX, Christians apparently preferred it, as it distinguished them from their Jewish kin and gave them a term broad enough to designate both the universal and local church.[45] In addition, the early church adopted the Greek Septuagint which was used in many synagogues. New Testament writers often drew upon this version when quoting the Old Testament and it was extensively used in Greek-speaking churches.

HOUSE CHURCHES

From creation, people have worshipped God in many different settings. The same is true for Christians in the first century. In addition to outdoor gatherings and taking part in services at the temple or in synagogues, early

---

43. For more information on the influence synagogues had on Christian worship, see Beckwith, "Jewish Background," 39–51 and Beckwith, *Daily and Weekly Worship*.

44. See James 2:2 for the only time that the term synagogue may have been used in the New Testament to refer to the church. It may, however, have referred to a Christian meeting. For other instances of early Christian writers referring to the church as a synagogue, see Davids, *James*, 108.

45. Schrage, "συναγωγή," 829.

believers gathered in homes to pray, break bread, and praise God (Acts 1:13–14; 2:46–47). Christians frequently met in the houses of prominent believers who in many cases also served as leaders. We know of churches meeting in the houses of Aquila and Priscilla in Ephesus (1 Cor 16:19), Philemon in Colossae (Phlm 2), Nympha[46] in Laodicea (Col 4:15), and Gaius in Rome (Rom 16:3–5). The houses of Lydia in Philippi (Acts 16:15, 40) and Titius Justus in Corinth (Acts 18:7–8) were apparently used in the same way.[47] Commonly referred to as house churches, these assemblies served as centers for worship, instruction, and the proclamation of the gospel (Acts 5:42; 20:20). Since "house," in biblical times, could be used to refer to the building and the family that dwelt there, a house church could point to the residence where believers gathered or to the gathered believers, which would consist of the head of a household along with his or her family, relatives who lived with them, servants, and friends who joined them for worship.

The importance of households in the early church is evident both regarding their place in the salvation of new believers and as a training ground for church leadership. New Testament writers record the response of those who heard the gospel message.[48] People opened their homes in order to explain the gospel to specific individuals or groups (Acts 18:26; 28:17–31). When Paul was turned away from synagogues, he visited private homes to demonstrate that the Scriptures pointed to Jesus (Acts 18:7; possibly Acts 17:5). On several occasions, whole households came to faith in Jesus, usually following the conversion of the head of the house (Luke 19:9; John 4:53; Acts 11:14; 16:15; 16:30–33; 18:8; 1 Cor 1:16; 16:51). Homes were truly the ground in which the seed of the gospel was sown and nurtured. Travelers who heard the good news about Jesus often took it home with them. Others, who heard of Jesus from the apostles and evangelists who roamed far and wide, responded by opening their hearts and homes to Jesus and his church (Acts 16:14–15).

In addition to seeing a household as a place for proclamation and teaching, the early church also understood that the way one maintained

---

46. Or perhaps Nymphas. Whether this person was male or female is somewhat unclear as the accusative form of the name used in Colossians 4:15—*Numphan*—was the same for either sex. The presence of an accent mark would have clarified the person's gender, but they were not included in first-century texts. The problem is made somewhat more difficult because the following pronoun is subject to variant readings. Thus, some manuscripts have "her," others have "his," and a few more have "their." Many scholars today believe that Nympha was a wealthy woman who had possibly been widowed and who opened her home for church gatherings.

47. No evidence exists for buildings specifically constructed for Christian worship until the third century.

48. See Green, *Evangelism in the Early Church*, 318–38.

his household should play an important part in determining whether the person should serve as a church leader. Instructions were given that only those who managed their own houses well should be permitted to serve as deacons and overseers (1 Tim 3:4–5).[49] This requirement distinguishes those who can legitimately lead a church from others who are considered rebellious and deceitful people who should be silenced for "ruining whole households by teaching things they ought not to teach" (Titus 1:11). The ruination spoken of may well have engulfed both families and churches.[50] For the church to remain pure, both individual households and the house churches that met together required leaders who held fast to apostolic truth and taught others to do the same.

The fact that people could travel without difficulty in the Roman world made it easy for the Christian faith, along with house churches, to spread. It is not clear how long it would have taken for house churches in one city to multiply. However, since it would have been scarcely possible for large numbers to meet in one place, many cities undoubtedly contained several house churches from very early times. Thus, the apostles went "from house to house" as they taught about Jesus being the Messiah (Acts 5:42; 20:20). These small groups of believers were considered part of the church in a particular locale and would have been under the leadership of the deacons and elders of that place. As the church grew, the house churches might have needed to relocate. For example, the church that met in the house of Aquila and Priscilla in Ephesus (1 Cor 16:19) would probably have found a new meeting place after its hosts returned to Rome (Rom 16:3).

As noted above, the house churches met to share the Lord's Supper, hear the apostles' teaching about Jesus,[51] and pray. While the New Testament says nothing about the order in which these acts were performed, it mentions several acts of worship that were used. To the church in Corinth, Paul wrote, "When you come together, everyone has a hymn, or a word of instruction, a revelation, a tongue or an interpretation" (1 Cor 14:26). Singing biblical psalms or more recent compositions was apparently common (Eph 5:18–20; Col 3:16). Instruction probably included teaching about Jesus or how to live as a Christian. Paul sometimes uses the word for revelation to refer to the eschatological day when God's judgment will be complete, his children made known, and Jesus will return (Rom 2:5; 8:19; 1 Cor 1:7; 2 Thess 1:7). He also uses the word to refer to supernatural revelations of the

---

49. This is somewhat obscured in the NIV which has "his own family" for *tou idiou oikou*, in 1 Timothy 3:4–5, but uses "his household" for the plural form in 1 Timothy 3:12.

50. Towner, *Timothy and Titus*, 697.

51. If an apostle was present, they would receive the teaching directly. Otherwise, they might hear the apostles' teaching read to them as instructed in their letters (Col 4:16).

gospel message (Rom 16:25), of ecstatic visions of heaven (2 Cor 12:1), or of information about what he should do (Gal 2:2). It isn't clear what he had in mind in 1 Corinthians 14, though the second appears to be more likely. Speaking in tongues and interpretation point to the practice of a number of spiritual gifts that were deemed an essential part of church life. We will say more about them in a later chapter. What is clear in Paul's presentation is that these actions should be performed in such a way that there is order in the meeting, God is praised, and the body is built up. This Paul saw as the essence of community worship.

PRACTICAL IMPLICATIONS OF WHAT THE BIBLE SAYS ABOUT THE PLACE OF WORSHIP

In this chapter, we have seen that although God can be worshipped anywhere, humans, who exist in time and space, need a particular place to worship God. This place may change from day to day, week to week, or year to year. But whether we worship in private or as congregations, a physical setting is essential. We will conclude the chapter by considering some practical issues regarding how our theology of the place of worship can influence our practice.

Although the places Christians worship today differ from those used in the first century, biblical instruction about worship places highlights several important truths. First, it shows that places of worship remind us that God is accessible to his people right where they are. The Old Testament teaching about the tabernacle and temple as God's house is spiritualized in the New Testament where the church becomes the temple where God dwells. We find God where we find Christ in one another. A building or specific locale is therefore unnecessary, though useful, as it gives us a place to gather. Second, the fact God gave instructions about the design of altars, the tabernacle and temple, and various worship rites instructs us that the basis for worship comes from God himself. This is reflected in the Westminster Confession of Faith.

> The acceptable way of worshipping the true God is instituted by himself, and so limited by his own revealed will, that he may not be worshipped according to the imaginations and devices of men, or the suggestions of Satan, under any visible representation, or any other way not prescribed in the holy Scripture.[52]

---

52. The Confession of Faith, 21.1, 90.

While the Bible is not explicit about every aspect of worship that God requires or desires of us and the Puritans who wrote this document clearly adopted some worship practices that go beyond scriptural warrant, their reflection on the source of worship should guide ours.[53] Where the Bible is silent, there should be a degree of freedom in worship styles, but where God speaks, we should ask whether or not our practice follows. To worship in a way that is contrary to his demands is idolatry no matter what we may feel about it.

Third, ethics and worship should not be separated. Holiness is just as important in the church as it was in ancient Israel. As the tabernacle and temple were considered holy places that needed to be sanctified on a regular basis, individual Christians and the church have been made holy through Jesus Christ and must remain so if he is to be rightly worshipped. This will be seen through personal righteousness and corporate unity. Fourth, as the building and maintenance of the tabernacle and temple required that people present various gifts to the Lord so that worship could take place, believers today need to bring gifts of money, kind, and/or service in their worship of God.

A Building for Christian Worship

If the church of Jesus Christ is God's temple on earth, there is no need for a particular type of building to be used for worship. Neither is there a need for specific furnishings or fixtures to be used in a place of worship. Even so, it is probably best for a local congregation to have a regular meeting place in a fixed location, if for no other reason than to allow people to know where the meeting will be held and when.[54]

Believers in Jesus who desire a place to worship are free to rent, buy, or design and build any suitable structure that will provide them with a venue to worship God. It may be small or large. It may be constructed of mud, grass, cloth, wood, stone, concrete, steel, glass, or whatever other materials are available. It may be in a house, a lecture hall, a natural amphitheater, the ballroom of a grand hotel, or somewhere else. Its floor plan may outline

---

53. For a basic introduction to Puritan approaches to worship, see McConnell, "Facing New Paradigms," 331–46. The Puritans identified the basic biblical essentials for worship as prayer; the reading, preaching, and hearing of the Scriptures; catechizing; singing psalms; administering and receiving the sacraments of baptism and the Lord's Supper; and keeping the Sabbath.

54. It may be possible that Christians in some parts of the world will find it beneficial not to have a regular meeting place for political, religious, or other reasons. Biblically, this is perfectly acceptable.

a cross, a rectangle, a circle, or an octagon. It may resemble a boat, a yurt, or a warehouse. It may have a square, pointed, or onion-shaped spire, or none at all. It may have fixed, flexible, or no seating. And whereas, from an aesthetic or even a practical point of view, questions about the choice of construction materials, size, or shape are important, there are no biblical directions to follow.

We are, therefore, left to our own choices regarding what our worship place will look like. Any decision on this matter will probably combine practical, theological, aesthetic, and economic issues. While it is not always a primary motivation in design, a church building's physical layout may reflect the theology of worship of a congregation. Do congregants sit in uniform rows to focus upon what is happening in front of them or in some other pattern that allows them to more freely interact with each other? Are lofty spaces designed to inspire worshippers to lift their eyes and hearts to God or a broader expanse intended to unite believers with one another? Is architectural design and ornamentation considered important or an impediment? Similar questions can be asked about the way those who worship in a particular building think about it as they relate to society around them. Is the building a metaphorical ark into which believers gather for safety, a lighthouse from which the gospel can shine upon a community, or something else? While somewhat irrelevant from a biblical perspective, questions like these are useful as we consider the way our places of worship influence our worship of God.

The same is true for worship held in an outdoor setting. For instance, many churches hold sunrise services on Easter morning with the hope that the natural setting will help worshippers feel closer to the women who went early to the tomb and were greeted by angels who proclaimed that Jesus had risen from the dead. Similarly, an evening service in a quiet place with the stars for a ceiling can help us visualize the greatness of God and the expanse of his creative power. But outdoor services are not only designed to replicate biblical scenes or to help us contemplate God as Creator. Large-scale meetings can be held in sports stadia, marquees, or in the open air. These may function to unite believers from different traditions so they can worship together, or as a means of reaching out to the larger society evangelistically.

The time has come when the worshippers of God do not have to go to Jerusalem or Mt. Gerizim or any other particular place to worship him. This is because we can find God wherever we meet. Since he is the Creator, there is nowhere we can go to escape his presence. Since he is the Savior, he lives in the hearts of the people whom he has made to be his temple, his dwelling place. But even though he lives within us, we still need to gather in a physical place to worship him as a body. Apparently, some believers in the first century were guilty of thinking they could get on in their lives all on their own. The writer of Hebrews therefore encourages his readers, "Let us not give up meeting together, as some are in the habit of doing, but let us encourage one another—and all the more as you see the Day approaching" (Heb 10:25). Gathering together in a physical location demonstrates our desire to worship God in relationship with others. It also shows that we desire to encourage others and be encouraged as we meet in God's presence. Let us be sure to do just that as we wait for the day of Christ's return when we will all be gathered together to worship God face to face.

7

Times and Seasons of Worship: The Holy Days of Israel

In the previous chapter, we saw that since life is lived in the physical world, we need a place for worship. Life in the world is also lived within time. Whether we measure it accurately with an expensive chronograph or an atomic clock, or simply note the position of the sun in the sky, the phases of the moon, and the turn of the seasons, humans are inextricably tied to time. Even though we do not follow the same patterns throughout the year or throughout our lives, there is a time to rise for a new day, a time to eat, a time to work, a time to rest. There are seasons for planting and harvesting. There are times for births and birthdays, weddings and anniversaries, funerals and holidays. There are times for being educated and times to complete one's education and enter the workplace. And there is a time to worship God.

While, from one perspective, time marches forward in a linear fashion and commands that we keep up with it, there is a degree in which it is also experienced with a certain amount of circularity. The change to a new day, new month, or new year, does not bring totally unique experiences. Thus Qohelet, the Preacher in Ecclesiastes, notes that:

> What has been will be again,
> what has been done will be done again;
> there is nothing new under the sun. (Eccl 1:9)

The passage of time will naturally bring new technologies, new ideas, and new ways of doing things. Even so, we recognize that each day has much in common with the one that preceded it and the one that will follow it. Each year reflects the one before. Each generation faces the same kind of life events as their predecessors. The sun rises and sets. We prepare food and eat only to prepare more food to eat. The patterns in life are pervasive and inescapable. As Qohelet describes it,

> There is a time for everything,
> and a season for every activity under heaven:
> a time to be born and a time to die,
> a time to plant and a time to uproot,
> a time to kill and a time to heal,
> a time to tear down and a time to build,
> a time to weep and a time to laugh,
> a time to mourn and a time to dance,
> a time to scatter stones and a time to gather them,
> a time to embrace and a time to refrain,
> a time to search and a time to give up,
> a time to keep and a time to throw away,
> a time to tear and a time to mend,
> a time to be silent and a time to speak,
> a time to love and a time to hate,
> a time for war and a time for peace. (Eccl 3:1–8)

Life, the Preacher tells us, is arranged according to the patterns of what one does at different times in life. Although many readers of Ecclesiastes find his musings about time to be very beautiful, Qohelet may not be quite so optimistic. Life, despite its patterns, is unpredictable (Eccl 5:13–14; 6:1–2; 7:14; 8:14; 9:11–12). And even though we know that God has planned everything and that everything he does will endure, we are no closer to understanding how it all works or what it all means. God's ways are cloaked in mystery.

The Preacher's conclusion was that the circularity and unpredictability of time should lead people to fear or revere God (Eccl 3:14). When we examined the biblical words of worship, we saw that fearing the Lord is synonymous with worshipping him. What the sage unearthed from his wisdom perspective was spelled out earlier in the Old Testament laws that set apart a number of days throughout the year as occasions to cease from all regular activities so that God could be worshipped. The laws about the feasts are set in the Pentateuch so that the Israelites could worship Yahweh in the land he promised to give their forefathers. The holy days set aside in the law—from the weekly Sabbath, to the monthly New Moon celebration, to the yearly feasts and festivals—were all tied to the calendar. Even though other ancient Near Eastern people celebrated religious festivals through the seasons of the year, Israel's festivals were unique in that their focus was not on the actions of the gods in nature—actions that needed to be maintained by fertility rites—but on the actions of Yahweh in history as the Creator who called them to be his people. As they traversed the seasons and years, they were reminded of his choice of them in the past and their need to live each day, season, and year for him.

In ancient Israel, the Sabbath, the New Moon, Passover and Feast of Unleavened Bread, Firstfruits, Feast of Weeks, Feast of Trumpets, Day of Atonement, and Feast of Tabernacles were set apart as feast days. These "appointed feasts" were to be proclaimed as "sacred assemblies" or "holy convocations" (Lev 23:2)—days on which God's people were to put aside their normal occupations and come together as a nation to worship the Lord. Toward the end of the Old Testament age, the Feast of Purim was added in memory of Israel's deliverance from the machinations of Haman. A final feast mentioned in the Bible (John 10:22)—the Feast of Dedication or Hanukkah—developed in the intertestamental period. This chapter examines the special times and seasons established in the Old Testament so that Israel could worship God. Where possible, we will show how Jesus and the early church understood these holy days and consider how the church today can think about these days and celebrate them.

THE SABBATH

Although the beginnings of Israel as the people of God can be traced to Abraham's call in Genesis 12, there is a sense in which they only attained nationhood after they were delivered from slavery in Egypt. As they met with Yahweh at Mt. Sinai, Israel was given a series of stipulations—the Ten Commandments—that enabled them to demonstrate and maintain covenant loyalty to the God who revealed his name to them, fought for them, and set them free to worship him. These stipulations included the injunction to "Remember the Sabbath day by keeping it holy" (Exod 20:8).[1] In Hebrew, "remember" is a strong command. The Israelites were duty bound to keep this day since they agreed to do "everything the LORD has said" when the covenant was established (Exod 19:8). How they were to keep the Sabbath as a holy day is stated in both positive and negative terms. Positively, all work was to be performed on the other six days. Negatively, they were not to do their regular work activities on the Sabbath.

---

1. Although the Sabbath command was given in Exodus 20, Israel was familiar with the concept before they arrived at Sinai as is clear from the instruction to observe the Sabbath found in Exodus 16:23–30. For an in-depth study of the word, see Lohse, "σάββατον" or Stott, "Sabbath, Lord's Day."

As the only holy day singled out in the Decalogue, the Sabbath has a unique place in Israel's relationship with God. Its importance is enhanced as the fourth commandment is supplemented by extensive instruction about its purpose and use in both its Exodus and Deuteronomy versions. As the longest of all the Decalogue commands, some scholars consider it the central commandment both in position and in its relationship to the other commands. Its connection to the first three links it to Yahweh's rule in the world. Its tie to the following commands anticipates what life in the community of Israel should be like. As the holy day that God gives so that all his people can rest, it helps build the ethical community in which shalom characterizes relationships between humans.[2]

The Exodus version of the Decalogue connects the Sabbath to creation. Israel was to rest on the Sabbath to reflect God's rest on the seventh day after creating the universe in six (Exod 20:8–11; cf. Gen 2:2–3). Through Sabbath keeping, God's people align themselves with the Creator and his purpose for the world. Just as God worked to bring everything into existence and instructed the first man to work in the Garden so that it would remain a beautiful and bountiful place, Israel was to carry on this work in the same way they were to fulfill the creation blessings. Their existence was thus not to be defined solely by their physical or cultural accomplishments. All work was to be completed in six days and the seventh given to rest. The setting aside of one day as holy made it clear that God is sovereign over time and that all days were to be lived in God's presence and all tasks were to reflect his image.

The provision of rest on the Sabbath is both liberating and limiting, as it combines freedom with responsibility. The liberation that rest brings is best seen in the Deuteronomic wording of the fourth commandment that connects it with redemption from Egypt. "Remember that you were slaves in Egypt and that the LORD your God brought you out of there with a mighty hand and an outstretched arm. Therefore the LORD your God has commanded you to observe the Sabbath day" (Deut 5:15). In Egypt, Israel was subject to Pharaoh's whims about when and how they should work, and were denied the privilege of worshipping Yahweh. Their request to sacrifice to Yahweh resulted in a cynical remark that offering sacrifices would take them away from their work. If they had time enough to think of worship, they must be lazy and in need of increased labor (Exod 5:1–9). But once Yahweh set them free, their existence was no longer defined by the work they performed for someone else; they could now serve him.[3] As described

---

2. See Miller, "The Human Sabbath," 81–97.
3. For a stimulating discussion on the difference between Pharaoh's rule and Yahweh's,

earlier, service and worship go hand in hand. When Israel was freed to serve Yahweh, the Sabbath command became an integral part of their worship.

While the Sabbath regulation freed God's people from the tyranny of perpetual labor, it also placed them under a set of limitations that made them responsible to ensure that no one was captivated by ceaseless work. As freed slaves, they were not to exploit others. Neither were they to allow themselves to become enslaved to any other nation, person, or deity. Furthermore, they were to ensure that even the weakest in society were to receive their rest—their sons and daughters, servants, animals, and even the aliens who lived among them (Exod 10:10).[4] God freed his people so that they could free others in turn. Instead of focusing only on their own needs and wants, they were to consider the needs of others to ensure that everyone is released from any form of work that might prevent them from worshipping and serving him and from receiving their needed rest. The Sabbath command thus had extensive social ramifications; it required that everyone be treated on the same level before God.

As stated above, God gave the fourth commandment in the context of the Sinaitic covenant. The covenantal aspect of the Sabbath is of tremendous importance. Along with circumcision, keeping the Sabbath became a sign of keeping God's covenant (Exod 31:12–17; Ezek 20:12–20).[5] Every Sabbath was a reminder that Yahweh's chosen people were required to obey his laws. It also reminded them that the God who set the seventh day apart as holy was the one who set them apart as holy. The importance of remembering the Sabbath as an aspect of keeping the covenant is highlighted by the passages that insist that those who break the Sabbath should suffer the penalty of death (Exod 31:14–15; 35:2; Num 15:32–36). To reject the sign of the covenant is to reject the Lord of the covenant. Those who are so guilty deserve to be cut off from the covenant community.

The Old Testament says little about particular cultic acts to be performed on the Sabbath day. For the most part, instructions about the Sabbath detail work that is *not* to be done: no one is to plow or harvest crops (Exod 34:21), light fires (Exod 35:3), gather firewood (Num 15:32–36), or carry burdens of any kind (Jer 17:22).[6] During the postexilic period, all

---

see Brueggemann, *Theology of the Old Testament*, 181–86.

4. Note that Deuteronomy 5:14 is more specific in adding "your ox" and "your donkey" to the animals and that it refers to manservants and maidservants twice, evidently to reinforce God's desire that servants and working beasts be allowed to rest.

5. In postexilic Judaism, these two covenantal signs became the distinguishing marks separated Jews from Gentiles.

6. The Old Testament identifies some work that was performed on the Sabbath. Priests offered sacrifices (Num 28:9–10, cf. Matt 12:5), the army of Israel marched into

types of commerce were prohibited on the Sabbath (Neh 10:31; 13:15–22). From the standpoint of the Mosaic law, the major difference in the cultic activities of the Sabbath and other days was the requirement for priests to offer extra sacrifices (Num 28:9–10) and for showbread to be laid out in the tabernacle "Sabbath after Sabbath" (Lev 24:8; cf. 1 Chr 9:32). Nowhere are the common people given instructions regarding how they should spend the day, except to keep it holy as a day of rest. The only indication as to how some preexilic Israelites might spend the day is found in the passing statement that one might on occasion visit a prophet on the Sabbath or New Moon (2 Kgs 4:23).

There is evidence that Sabbath remembrance during the postexilic period extended beyond rest to include sacrificial rites and the gathering of the people for worship (Ezek 46:1–9). Beyond sacrifice, we can only speculate as to the nature of these gatherings. As synagogues probably came into existence during the exilic period, formal meetings in which the exiles gathered to pray and read the Scriptures grew in importance. Even so, the Bible nowhere legislates how these congregations should be organized or what acts of worship should be included. The rise of the importance of synagogues and Sabbath assemblies in the worship of Israel is frequently linked to the loss of the temple during the exile. As the people were separated from the temple and other "holy places," "holy time" became more important.[7] The change in focus from location to day ensured that Jews could worship even in exile.

Though the Old Testament says little about how people spent the Sabbath, by New Testament times, it was a day on which to assemble, pray, read Scripture, and explain its meaning (Mark 1:21; Luke 4:16–21; Acts 13:14–48; 15:21; 16:13; 17:2–3; 18:4). This aspect of Sabbath keeping was such an integral part of first-century Jewish devotion that Jesus customarily went to the synagogue on that day, where he at times read and explained Scripture to those in attendance (Luke 4:16). However, Jesus' opinions about how one should keep the day clearly differed from the Pharisees' detailed list of what could or could not be done. By what he did and taught, Jesus rejected an absolute cessation of work. He frequently healed on the Sabbath (Mark 3:1–5; Luke 6:6–10; 13:10–13; 14:1–4; John 5:1–9; 9:1–14). He

---

battle (Josh 6:3–4), and the gates were guarded and military action was threatened due to people who tried to buy and sell on the Sabbath (Neh 13:19–21). The New Testament adds that baby boys are circumcised on the eighth day to fulfil God's command (John 7:22; Lev 12:3). When the synagogue ruler complained that since there are six days to work people should not come to be healed on the Sabbath, Jesus countered by saying that just as people untied and led their oxen and donkeys to water on the Sabbath, so the woman who had been bound by Satan with illness should be freed from her even greater bondage (Luke 13:14–16).

7. Kraus, *Worship in Israel*, 87.

allowed his disciples to pick and eat grain, though the Pharisees interpreted it as reaping—one of the thirty-nine "main tasks" the Mishnah tractate *Sabbath* 7.2 forbade on the Sabbath (Matt 12:1–8; Mark 2:23–28; Luke 6:1–5).

It is not clear whether Jesus purposely broke the Sabbath to demonstrate his messianic authority or whether the works he performed on the day were simply to show that the Pharisees' interpretation of Sabbath laws were in error. Jesus' statement that "the Son of Man is Lord of the Sabbath" (Matt 12:8) highlights his belief that he had power to determine how to keep the day. John's Gospel links Jesus' authority over the Sabbath to his relationship with the Father. After healing the man at Bethesda, Jesus told the Jewish leaders, "My Father is always at work to this very day, and I, too, am working" (John 5:17). The implication of his use of "My Father" was not lost on his hearers who determined that he should be killed, not only for breaking the Sabbath, but also for claiming equality with God. But if he *is* God, the Sabbath belongs to him as it was God's holy day. Jesus is therefore able to return it to its original purpose of being a benefit to humankind rather than a burden for the Jews to bear. As he stated, "The Sabbath was made for man, not man for the Sabbath" (Mark 2:27). It existed to meet people's needs for rest, for food, for healing, or for other things. On the Sabbath, it was therefore lawful "to do good" and "to save life" (Mark 3:4). To Jesus, love and mercy are important motivations for obeying the Fourth Commandment, as it was originally given as a demonstration of God's love and mercy to Israel (Matt 12:7).

It seems likely that early Jewish Christians continued to observe the Sabbath for quite some time after Jesus' resurrection and ascension. Apart from two references to Christians breaking bread or setting aside money for the poor "on the first day of the week" (Acts 20:7; 1 Cor 16:2), the New Testament gives no indication that they gave up a seventh day Sabbath. Gentile believers, however, were freed from strict obedience. While the Council of Jerusalem agreed that they should "abstain from foods polluted by idols, from sexual immorality, from the meat of strangled animals and from blood" (Acts 15:21), they made no comment about the Sabbath. Later, Paul was to argue that religious festivals, the New Moon observance, and the Sabbath were simply shadows that pointed to the spiritual reality found in Christ (Col 2:16–17). True Sabbath rest was experienced by coming to Jesus in faith (cf. Matt 11:28–30).

Since the Sabbath points to this completed rest in Jesus, the day set aside does not come across as of primary importance in the light of the spiritual realities. The person we celebrate and who gives us rest is the reality, the ultimate meaning of the Sabbath. For this reason, Paul insists that those who consider one day as special and those who consider every day the same should do so to the Lord (Rom 14:5–6). His ideas reflect the Old Testament teaching that links creation and the sanctity of the seventh day in order to help Israel understand that every day is to be lived for God. Of more importance than consecrating one particular day of the week is remembering that each day is the Lord's and that when God's servants celebrate what he has done for us as Savior and Redeemer, they have no right to judge each other.

By the time the book of Hebrews was written, the Sabbath rest had become an eschatological hope for people of faith (Heb 4:1–11). In many ways, Hebrews 3 and 4 show that the Christian life parallels the exodus from Egypt. While the Israelites were led by Moses, the new people of God are led by Jesus. While the Israelites hardened their hearts in the desert and forfeited their promised rest, Christians are encouraged to press on to the heavenly rest God desires to give to his people. In Hebrews, heaven becomes a new and better Canaan. The future, heavenly Sabbath is an eternal rest that ensures that God's people can cease from their labors. God's people cannot and should not strive to earn recognition from God by observing a particular day. Rather, they should believe and obey the gospel they received. Only by accepting God's living Word that comes through hearing God's written word can anyone enter his rest.

In the first century, the church's practice, vis-à-vis contemporary Judaism, underwent significant changes. This is clear from Jesus' challenge to the rabbis and the determination that the two major signs of the covenant—Sabbath and circumcision—were not required of Gentile believers. It seems that some early Christians began to worship Jesus on the first day of the week in commemoration of his resurrection from the dead (Acts 20:7; 1 Cor 16:2; cf. Rom 14:5–6). It is certain that by the middle of the second century, Christians regularly gathered on Sunday for worship.[8] Even so, third-century Christians still spoke of Saturday as the Sabbath.[9] Not until the fourth century did John Chrysostom and Ambrose openly equate

---

8. Around AD 115, Ignatius of Antioch wrote that Christians changed their observation of the Sabbath to the Lord's Day as it is the day when our lives arose due to his death. Ign. *Magn.* 9. From same period, *Didache* 14 may instruct that on the Lord's Day believers should "come together, break bread and hold Eucharist, after confessing your transgressions that your offering may be pure." Justin Martyr also states that Christians assembled on Sunday because it was the day upon which God created the world and upon which Christ rose from the grave. *1 Apol.* 67.

9. The *Apostolic Tradition*, usually accepted as the work of Hippolytus in the early third century, states that those who are to be baptized should bathe on the fifth day of the week, fast on the preparation for the Sabbath (i.e., Friday), pray and be exorcized by the bishop on the Sabbath (Saturday), and then receive their baptism beginning at dawn on a Sunday. *Trad. ap.* 20:7; 21:1. Baldovin rejects the standard interpretation that Hippolytus wrote the *Apostolic Tradition* and discusses some implications of this conclusion. Baldovin, "Hippolytus and the *Apostolic Tradition*."

Sunday and the Sabbath. This idea was formalized politically when Constantine decreed that certain kinds of labor should not be performed on that day. The theological and social concepts laid down in the fourth century paved the way that has been followed by many believers throughout church history who have celebrated Sunday as the Christian Sabbath.

This is not to say that Christians have been unanimous in their understanding of how the Sabbath and Sunday should be connected. The first generation of Reformers, for instance, tended to spiritualize the Sabbath, arguing that any day was suitable for worship and rest. Many of their heirs, however, returned to the strong sabbatarian position that was common throughout much of church history, identifying Sunday as the Sabbath. Following this tradition, the Westminster Confession, written around 1646 by English and Scottish Puritans, says,

> As it is of the law of nature, that, in general, a due proportion of time be set apart for the worship of God; so, in his word, by a positive, moral, and perpetual commandment, binding all men in all ages, he hath particularly appointed one day in seven for a sabbath, to be kept holy unto him: which from the beginning of the world to the resurrection of Christ, was the last day of the week; and, from the resurrection of Christ, was changed into the first day of the week, which in Scripture is called the Lord's Day, and is to be continued to the end of the world, as the Christian Sabbath.[10]

Even though this gained wide support among many Protestant Christians, the early Anabaptists argued that the Bible did not explicitly state that the first day of the week should be celebrated as the Sabbath. Ever since, seventh day sabbatarians have argued that since the Sabbath and seventh day were connected from the time of the creation accounts, God's commands should still be followed.[11]

As this overview has shown, God intended the Sabbath to provide his people with physical, religious, and social benefits. Any theology of Sabbath keeping today should center on these principles. The Sabbath reminded Israel that all of life, and particularly their work, was to be lived in recognition that God cared about what they did and that he provided for all their needs. It also gave them an opportunity to refocus their lives in relation to their Creator and his creation, teaching them to live according to God's timetable, with regular intervals of work and rest. It reminded them that though work

---

10. The Confession of Faith, 21.7.

11. A seventh day Sabbath is practiced by modern day Seventh Day Baptists, Seventh Day Adventists, and some others.

was a good part of God's creation, everyone needed rest. The Sabbath thus demonstrated God's desire for justice in the land he gave to the people he redeemed from slavery. Furthermore, it spoke of the covenant relationship they shared with God that should not be broken.

At the beginning of the New Testament era, the Sabbath was understood to be a special day upon which to worship God by reading his word and praying and was celebrated in this way by the earliest Christian communities. Even so, the coming of Jesus heralded the dawning of a new age in which the old covenant was fulfilled and a new one established. The covenant signs of the Sabbath and circumcision were recognized as potential stumbling blocks for some who wished to worship the Father. Jesus proclaimed that the day was created to benefit people by freeing them from bondage. The Sabbath thus looked forward to the eternal rest that believers would receive by recognizing the defeated powers of sin, death, and the evil one through Christ's work on the cross.

FEASTS AND FESTIVALS

The Sabbath gave Israel a tangible way to live out each week, remembering that their covenant God cared for them as their Creator and Redeemer. In a similar manner, Israel's worship revolved around a number of feasts and festivals celebrated through the months and seasons of the year.[12] By examining these different holy days, we can learn something about how Israel lived before God in time and discover ways that we can live our lives before him too.

New Moon Festival

On the first day of the lunar calendar when the crescent moon first became visible, Israel celebrated the New Moon Festival.[13] Like other festivals, this was to be a time for rejoicing marked by the blowing of trumpets at the time sacrifices were offered (Num 10:10; Ps 81:3).[14] Often mentioned in associa-

---

12. Much work has been done to discover how Israel's festivals developed historically. For a brief overview and bibliography, see Armerding, "Festivals and Feasts," 300–313.

13. In Hebrew, the new moon is *ḥōdeš*. Although the word is often used for "month," its use for the new moon, the first day of the month, is common. The new moon is only explicitly called a festival in Psalm 81:3.

14. While Numbers 10:10 indicates a silver trumpet, Psalm 81:3 calls for a *shophar* (ram's horn). Whether this is due to a development or variation in practice is not clear.

tion with the Sabbath, it was a day when people were to rest from their work. Its distinguishing feature was the addition of several sacrifices beyond the daily requirement: two young bulls, seven lambs, and a male goat, along with a variety of grain, flour, oil, and wine (Num 28:11–15). With these additions, some believe that the New Moon was considered more important than the Sabbath.[15]

Though the festival was celebrated throughout Israel's history, nothing is said about what people should do on the day, except for offering additional sacrifices. During the monarchy, it was considered an occasion for a special meal which may have been held on the first and second day of the lunar month (1 Sam 20:5–26). At this time, it was expected that a person who was ceremonially unclean would not take part. Some may have used this festival or a Sabbath as an occasion to visit a prophet (2 Kgs 4:23).[16] God sometimes chose the New Moon to reveal himself to the people (Ezek 26:1; 29:17; 31:1; 32:1; Hag 1:1). It may be that they were more prepared to hear him speak as it was a holiday and they were not distracted by work.

Although the New Moon was intended to provide people with rest and an opportunity to express joy, some Israelites during the late monarchy period viewed the day as an unwelcomed interruption of commerce (Amos 8:5). The general disregard of the day led some prophets to announce that Yahweh hated the New Moon Festival and would bring it to an end (Isa 1:13–14; Hos 2:11). Evidently, many thought their participation in religious festivals was enough to keep them in right standing with God, even though they neglected his requirement for a just society and had adopted syncretistic religious practices. Despite God's rejection of the way Israel celebrated the new moon, prophets looking toward the end times foresaw a renewal of the festival that would attract people from many lands who would come to Jerusalem and worship Yahweh on that day (Isa 66:23). Ezekiel envisioned the prince leading the people in worship during the New Moon Festival and Sabbath (Ezek 45:17; 46:1–7).

In postexilic times, the New Moon Festival regained its former status. After Zerubbabel led a group of Jews back to Jerusalem, they celebrated this festival before the foundation of the temple was laid (Ezra 3:1–6). On this

---

Trumpets may have been blown to alert people that the moon had appeared again so they would know when to celebrate, as part of the celebration, or perhaps both.

15. Hartley, "New Moon," 527.

16. The reason for this is not clear. As the passage in question mentions a woman visiting Elijah, it may be that Elijah only received visitors on the Sabbath or New Moon Festival, that the woman mentioned in the passage regularly saw him at that time, or that she was free from work on those days and thus had time to see him. See Hobbs, 2 Kings, 51–52.

day, Ezra later read the law to the people who assembled to hear what God had to say to them (Neh 8:2).

The New Moon Festival is mentioned in only one New Testament passage. Responding to some people who taught the church in Colossae that Christians should keep the Jewish festivals, Paul told his readers that they should "not let anyone judge you by what you eat or drink, or with regard to a religious festival, a New Moon celebration or a Sabbath day" (Col 2:16). Paul's conclusion that these days are only a shadow that is completed in the reality found in Jesus Christ indicates that Christians are free not to celebrate the day since observing the day will not bring them closer to God.

Passover

Israel began their year by commemorating the Passover—*pesaḥ*—in remembrance of God's greatest redemptive act in their history. The festival was celebrated on the fourteenth day of the first month of their calendar and was immediately followed by the week-long Feast of Unleavened Bread that began on the fifteenth. This second feast was such an integral part of the first that at times the two were combined under the heading of Passover.[17] Passover and the Feast of Unleavened bread were always tied to God's redemption of Israel and establishment of his covenant with them. Celebrants thus looked to Yahweh as Creator and Redeemer. The connection with the spring harvest added another element to their celebration, as it reminded them that God was their provider. Since he gave them what they needed, they were to bring gifts according to the blessings they had received from the Lord so that they could pass on his blessings to those in need (Deut 16:17).

In preparation for the first Passover, God had Moses tell each family to select a year-old male lamb or kid on the tenth of the month and sacrifice it at twilight on the Passover night. Using hyssop, they daubed some of the blood on the doorframes so that when God's angel went through Egypt to strike down the firstborn sons of the Egyptians, he would pass over every house where he saw the blood.[18] The sacrificed lamb would be roasted without

---

17. "Passover" was used to refer to the historical event, the festival celebrated in remembrance of the event, and the festival including the Feast of Unleavened Bread. It could also refer to the sacrificial victim (Exod 12:21; while the Hebrew text has only the word for Passover, many English versions translate it "Passover lamb"). Paul applies this nomenclature to Jesus in 1 Corinthians 5:7 (where many English versions add "lamb" though the Greek has only Passover).

18. Although other interpretations have been put forward for the Hebrew word *pesaḥ*, its use in Exodus 12 provides the best interpretation of its meaning. When God comes to bring judgment on the Egyptians and their gods, he will "pass over" the

having any of its bones broken and eaten with bitter herbs and unleavened bread. The Israelites were to eat the meal in haste, dressed for travel.

This sacrifice was unusual in that it was carried out by the head of each family without priestly intervention. Indeed, the first Passover was celebrated before the Levitical priesthood was consecrated. By the time Israel had entered the land of Canaan, the celebration was more centralized. The rules given in Deuteronomy stated that Passover animals were to be sacrificed and eaten "at the place the LORD will choose as a dwelling for his Name" (Deut 16:2, 5–7). The feast was then celebrated as one of the three pilgrim festivals to be attended by all male Israelites (Exod 23:14–17; Deut 16:16). The centralization of the festival was completed with the building of the temple in Jerusalem, at which time the sacrifice of Passover animals was given over to the priests (2 Chr 8:12–13).

While the Passover began with the sacrificial meal and flight from Egypt, the day was reenacted yearly throughout Israel's history as "a lasting ordinance" (Exod 12:14). On this day, Fathers would instruct their children about the history and meaning of the Passover (Exod 12:26–27; 13:8). Their explanation came to be known as *haggadah*, from the Hebrew for "telling" or "explanation," because of Moses' words to the people, "On that day tell your son, 'I do this because of what the LORD did for me when I came out of Egypt'" (Exod 13:8). The stories of the Passover were at first oral instructions based upon memory of the event and the text of Exodus. During rabbinic times, the Passover *haggadah* was formalized and scribal explanations enhanced the simple recounting of the event.

During the first century, Jews made an annual pilgrimage to Jerusalem to celebrate the Passover. However, after the temple was destroyed, the Passover regained its earlier status as a family celebration. Although we expect that Jesus and his disciples regularly made the trip to Jerusalem to join the Passover festivities, the Synoptic Gospels mention only one Passover feast—Jesus' last one, during which he officiated in his Last Supper.[19] The Gospel of John apparently mentions three Passover feasts that were celebrated during

---

Israelites when he sees the blood upon their doorframes. It is therefore a sign of his protective care of the people who recognize him as God and obey his commands. Note that the Hebrew word lies behind the English adjective "paschal." For a summary of various views, see Kraus, *Worship in Israel*, 45–46.

19. Scholars have often discussed whether the Last Supper corresponded with the Passover meal as indicated in the Synoptic Gospels (Mark 14:12), or whether Jesus' final meal with his disciples was actually a day earlier. This is because John's Gospel can be interpreted to place Jesus' crucifixion at the time when the Passover lambs were slaughtered. For a brief account of the issues involved, see Martin, "Lord's Supper," 912–13. For a deeper examination, see Marshall, *Last Supper and Lord's Supper*, 57–75.

Jesus' earthly ministry (John 2:13; 6:4; 12:1).[20] Even so, John says little about how Jesus and his disciples celebrated the day except where he joins the synoptic accounts in relating his final meal before the crucifixion. Acting as the head of the house, Jesus served his disciples and lead in the liturgy of the *haggadah*.

Before giving thanks for the bread and wine, Jesus informed the disciples that he would not eat the Passover again until it was fulfilled in the kingdom of God (Luke 22:16). While this reference probably looks forward to the eschatological banquet in God's kingdom, it may point to the Lord's Supper, which the disciples would be charged to do "in remembrance of me" (Luke 22:19) but which also maintains a view toward the future. Significantly, the Passover takes on new meaning as Jesus' followers share the bread and wine in remembrance of his sacrifice for them. No longer would they solely recall God's redemption from Egypt that led to the Sinaitic covenant. From now on, they would think of the new sacrificial Lamb whose blood established a new covenant for the people of God and who redeemed them from their sins.[21]

At the end of their Passover meal, Jesus and his disciples "sang a hymn" and went out to the Mount of Olives (Matt 26:30). It is likely that they sang Psalms 115–118 or a portion thereof, as the Hallel (Psalms 113–118) had become part of the Jewish Passover tradition.

The apostolic church instinctively recognized that Jesus' sacrifice corresponded with the sacrifice of the Passover lamb. Even before the beginning of his formal earthly ministry, John the Baptist had introduced him as "the lamb of God" (John 1:29, 36). John's Gospel later equated Jesus' death with the sacrifice of the Passover lamb by highlighting its prophetic significance: "These things happened so that the scripture would be fulfilled: 'Not one of his bones will be broken'" (John 19:36; cf. Exod 12:46; Num 9:12; Ps 34:20). Writing to the believers in Corinth some two decades after the crucifixion, Paul made use of paschal imagery when he exhorted them to clean out the old leaven of evil behavior because "Christ, our Passover lamb, has been sacrificed" (1 Cor 5:7). Christians should become a new lump of unleavened dough, separating themselves from evil and rejoicing in Jesus' accomplishment on the cross. Paschal purity is to be maintained in spiritual and moral terms so that they experience joy in the context of "sincerity and truth" rather than "malice and wickedness" (1 Cor 5:8). Similarly, Peter

---

20. John's reference to three Passovers is the primary indication we have that Jesus' ministry spanned two or three years. Some lengthen his ministry by another year by assuming the unnamed feast mentioned in John 5:1 was the Passover.

21. Jesus refers to the new covenant to show that his work fulfils the prophecy of Jeremiah 31:31–34.

reminds his readers that they should be holy as God is holy and live lives of purity since they were redeemed "with the precious blood of Christ, a lamb without blemish or defect" (1 Pet 1:15–19). Jesus is also portrayed as the Lamb of God in Revelation, where he joins God on the throne because he is worthy of worship as the one who purchased men for God from all peoples through his death (Rev 5:6–13). In addition, Revelation looks forward to the wedding banquet of the Lamb (Rev 19:7–9), a meal that he would share with his bride—the people he has purified.

It seems clear that the early Christians replaced the Passover festival with a celebration of the Lord's Supper due to its connection with Jesus' Last Supper. To share in the body and blood of Christ gave Christians an opportunity to remember God's redemption, not on a yearly basis, but every time they shared the elements with one another. And though it seems likely that Jewish Christians would have continued to celebrate the Passover for many years, the exodus was overshadowed by the sacrifice of Jesus, God's greatest act of redemption, performed for all. Another reason the Passover became less important for Christians is related to the spread of the faith to the Gentile world. Gentiles were not taught to keep the Jewish festivals. And even Jewish Christians who lived in Palestine would have found it impossible to celebrate Passover in the way they had been used to after the temple was destroyed in 70 AD.

By the beginning of the second century, another change in Christian practice influenced the way Passover was approached. As more and more believers in Jesus recognized that his resurrection day was appropriate for celebrating his life and work, Sunday became known as the Lord's Day—a day for worshipping the risen Lord Jesus. For the same reason, the Passover season took on new meaning for those who wished to remember the great work God accomplished through Jesus' death and resurrection. As a result, a new festival—Resurrection Day or Pascha—soon surpassed Passover in the Christian calendar. In many languages, this festival came to be known as Easter.

Feast of Unleavened Bread

The Feast of Unleavened Bread—*ḥag hammaṣṣôṯ*—was celebrated immediately after the Passover, beginning on the fifteenth day of the first month and lasting for seven days. On the first day of the feast, all leavening agents were to be removed and all bread made and consumed during the period was to be free of leaven.[22] In later times, the Passover *haggadah* required each

---

22. Although many Bible versions use the word yeast, there is no evidence that

family to go through the house and sweep up every crumb of bread with a feather and then burn it. Eating bread without leaven signified that the people of God left Egypt in such haste that there was not enough time for bread to rise. Remembrance of their slavery in Egypt led to this bread being called the "bread of affliction" (Deut 16:3).

On the first and seventh day of the feast, the Israelites were to hold "sacred assemblies" or "holy convocations." This term, which is also used of the Sabbath, New Moon Festival, and each of the five annual feasts, indicated that Israel was to gather for worship on those days. Although no instructions were given as to the nature of the assemblies or how lay people should worship, priests offered special sacrifices. Like the Sabbath, all regular work was to stop on the first and seventh days of the Feast (Num 28:18, 25).

In the Gospels, the Feast of Unleavened Bread is only mentioned in conjunction with the Passover when Jesus was crucified (Matt 26:17; Mark 14:1, 12; Luke 22:1, 7). In Acts, it marks the time when Herod seized Peter, intending to kill him as he had James (Acts 12:3), and the time when Paul's co-workers sailed from Philippi to Troas toward the end of the third missionary journey. The connection between leaven and evil that needed to be rooted out is mentioned by Paul when he warned the church in Corinth to be rid of a person whose sin was worse than that committed by unbelievers (1 Cor 5:6–9). According to Paul, since Christ is our Passover, we should keep the festival (jointly the Passover and Unleavened Bread) by removing the old leaven and living a life of purity. Nothing in the New Testament says whether or how early Christians celebrated the day.

Feast of Weeks

The Feast of Weeks—*ḥag šābuʿôt*—was the second major feast of the year and the second of the three annual festivals that all males were to celebrate. The festival receives its name from its scheduling seven weeks after Passover, when the barley harvest was at its end and the wheat harvest was just beginning. Its purpose was to remind Israel of their dependence upon the Lord and of their need to thank him for a good harvest. As it was held fifty days after Passover, it was often referred to as Pentecost[23] and its association with

---

ancient Israel was familiar with the substance. The rising agent used in biblical Israel for making bread was undoubtedly a fermented lump of dough like sourdough starter retained after a batch had risen and added to a new batch of dough.

23. Pentecost comes from the Septuagint translation of *yôm ḥămiššîm*—*pentēkonta hēmeras*—"fifty days" (Lev 23:16). In New Testament Greek, it is known simply as *pentēkostē* (Acts 2:1; 20:16; 1 Cor 16:8).

the wheat harvest led to it being called the Feast of Harvest—*ḥag haqqāṣîr* (Exod 23:16)—or the Day of Firstfruits—*yôm habbikkûrîm* (Num 28:26).

The feast was to be celebrated with a joyful sacred assembly. Like the Sabbath, all regular work stopped. The expressions of joy and freedom from work were a reminder that Israel had been freed from slavery in Egypt (Deut 16:12). On the first day of the festival, celebrants brought an offering of the firstfruits of their new grain baked into two leavened loaves and waved by the priest. Bringing firstfruits was significant as it gave Israel the opportunity to acknowledge that Yahweh, as Creator, owns all things and has the right to them.[24] The generation that prepared to enter the land was also instructed to bring "a freewill offering in proportion to the blessing the LORD your God has given you" (Deut 16:10). As the Lord had promised to bless them in the land, they should have plenty for themselves and enough to share with others. This promise of God's blessing with its associated requirement to bless others is strengthened by the command attached to this festival that they were not to reap to the edges of the field, but provide for the needs of others and leave the gleanings for the poor (Lev 23:22). As they rejoiced over God's provision for their needs, they should make it possible for the poorest in society to rejoice as well.

While the common citizen brought an offering of new grain, priests offered a series of sacrifices, including seven year-old male lambs, one young bull, and two rams as a burnt offering, one male goat for a sin offering, and two year-old lambs for a peace offering. That the number of animals offered far surpassed those brought for the Feast of Unleavened Bread probably indicates that a celebration after the harvest should be more lavish as an expression of gratitude and as a means of helping the poor.

Sometime during the Second Temple period, Jewish rabbis linked the Feast of Weeks with the giving of the law and promoted the day as a time to renew the Mosaic covenant.[25] This connection between the law and Pentecost has given many Christians reason to believe that Luke's description of the first Christian Pentecost in Acts 2 reveals his view that there was both continuity and discontinuity in the giving of the law and the giving of the Spirit. Both come from God to benefit his covenant people. Even so, the gift

---

24. Israel was to bring their firstborn sons and animals, and the first of their harvest to the Lord. Whereas firstborn sons and some animals could be redeemed, produce was to be given to God as an offering for the upkeep of the priests and Levites whom God accepted as substitutes for the firstborn sons of Israel (Num 3:12–16).

25. Although the Bible never explicitly states that the law was given on Pentecost, rabbis came to this conclusion by noting that the Passover was on the fifteenth of the first month, the arrival at Sinai on the third month (or the third new moon), and that a number of days passed before Moses received the law on Mt. Sinai. They used this information to demonstrate that fifty days elapsed between Passover and the giving of the law.

connected with the ancient Pentecost centered on the Torah, while the gift given on the latter Pentecost centered on Jesus Christ and the Holy Spirit who reveals him.[26]

Whatever connection Luke would have drawn between the giving of the Holy Spirit and the law, he is clear that God sent his Spirit to fulfill John the Baptist's prophecy that the one who came after him would baptize with the Holy Spirit and fire (Luke 3:16). The parallels with Jesus' baptism are similarly of great importance in his exposition. Just as the Holy Spirit came upon Jesus with power after his baptism so that he could minister to those around him, he also empowered the church on Pentecost for their ministry. Thus, the 120 disciples who met in the upper room were baptized and immediately went out to preach the gospel so that another 3000 people were added to their number by the end of the day. Since these people came together as a new community united under a new covenant, there is good reason for considering Pentecost the birthday of the church.

Although Luke makes no explicit reference to firstfruits in Acts 2, there was a promise that more believers would be added to the church as the gospel spread. Other New Testament writers follow their Old Testament counterparts. When Paul wrote that "we have the firstfruits of the Spirit," he indicated that Christians still look forward to something more, something greater (Rom 8:23). The gift of the Holy Spirit is a promise, not for a more abundant harvest, but that our adoption as children of God will be made complete and that we will be fully redeemed as our bodies are raised to newness of life. "Christ has indeed been raised from the dead, the firstfruits of those who have fallen asleep" is similarly used to encourage Christians that as Christ was raised so would others be raised along with him (1 Cor 15:20). But each will come in turn. Christ is the first to be raised, then those who belong to him will also be raised (1 Cor 15:23).

James explained that those who are born through the word of truth are the firstfruits of creation (Jas 1:18). Christians are the first part of the created order to become a new creation; one day the whole of creation will be renewed.[27] The eschatological significance of this passage is developed in the book of Revelation, which identifies the 144,000 who follow the Lamb as the firstfruits who were offered to God and the Lamb (Rev 14:1–4). The 144,000 serve as firstfruits in the sense of being an offering made to God

---

26. See Longenecker, *Acts*, 65. But note the caution urged by John Stott who says that since Luke does not develop the symbolism pertaining to harvest or the giving of the law that many Christians have found here, we cannot be sure of its importance to him. Stott, *The Spirit, the Church and the World*, 62.

27. Davids, *James*, 90.

that looks forward to the promise of more to come.[28] The interpretive problem is whether this is a promise of more believers (whether Jews or from all humankind) or if it, like James (and Romans 8), points to God's redemption reaching a larger part of creation.

Feast of Trumpets

The Feast of Trumpets[29] was held on the first day of the seventh month (Tishri)[30] and heralded the month of three major festivals: Trumpets, the Day of Atonement, and Tabernacles. Although the term is not used in the Bible, the festival is called Trumpets due to the trumpet blasts that resounded on the day. Though critical scholarship of an earlier age frequently linked the Feast of Trumpets to an autumnal New Year's Day, it seems more likely that the festival concluded the agricultural year and that it has special significance simply because it opens the seventh month with its other important festivals.[31]

During the Feast of Trumpets, all regular work was suspended and a sacred assembly, punctuated with trumpet blasts, held. Though nothing is said about what most Israelites should do during the assembly, priests were to sacrifice burnt offerings and sin offerings to Yahweh. In addition to the regular daily sacrifices and New Moon sacrifices, these would consist of "one young bull, one ram and seven male lambs a year old, all without defect" along with their accompanying grain offerings and a goat as a sin offering to make atonement (Num 29:2–5). It was these additional offerings, and perhaps a more prolonged period of trumpet blasts, that distinguished the day from a standard New Moon Festival.

Day of Atonement

The Day of Atonement—*yôm hakkippurîm*—often referred to as Yom Kippur, was celebrated on the tenth day of the seventh month. Considered the

---

28. For various theories as to the makeup of the 144,000 and the meaning of their being firstfruits, see Beale, *Revelation*, 416–23, 732–44.

29. In Numbers 29:1, the festival is simply referred to as *yôm tĕrû'â*, which the NIV interprets, "a day . . . to sound the trumpets," though "a day of alarm" or "a day of [trumpet] blast" is more literal since the term does not explicitly indicate a trumpet sound and can even be used of a shout. Even so, the timing of the festival with the new moon makes it likely that the blowing of trumpets is in view.

30. The seventh month corresponds to September/October on our calendars.

31. For a brief discussion of the relevant issues, see Garrett, "Feasts and Festivals of Israel," 251–52.

most solemn day of the year, this was a day to cease all regular work and hold a sacred assembly.[32] On the Day of Atonement, the Israelites were told to "deny yourselves," which probably refers to fasting, lest they be cut off from their people (Lev 23:29). It was also the day for the Jubilee year to begin. This made it of special importance for those who had lost their land or entered servitude as it pointed to freedom, not only from their sins, but also from their loss of property or liberty.

On the Day of Atonement, Yahweh forgave the sin his people had committed during the previous year so that he could remain with them and bless them. The rituals performed on that day ensured the sins of the priests and the people were covered, the sanctuary was cleansed from the sin that stained it from a year's worth of sacrifices, and the sin was removed from the community when the scapegoat was led away from the camp.

Three men shared responsibilities for the main activities of this day: the high priest, a man who released the scapegoat in a solitary place, and another man who burned the remainder of the sin offering. The high priest began the day by bathing his entire body and dressing himself in his priestly linen clothes. Evidently, the solemnity of the occasion made wearing the special high priestly garments inappropriate. Whereas his special clothes befitted his high position as mediator before the people and God, when he came into the closest proximity to the Holy One, his glorious garments needed to be replaced by simple robes. On the Day of Atonement, no man could be exalted—even the high priest was simply the servant of Yahweh. The priest washed himself before and after the ritual to signify that he would bring no uncleanness into the holy of holies or carry any that had been cleansed from the sanctuary back into the camp.

Due to the seriousness of sin, the high priest entered the tabernacle with a young bull and a ram for himself and two goats and a ram for the community of Israel. The high priest first sacrificed a bull to atone for his own sin and the sin of his family. Only when he was physically clean and cleansed from sin could he dare approach God with the blood that would atone for the people's sin. After slaughtering the bull, he took a censer of burning coals, placed incense upon it, and carried it behind the curtain so that the smoke would obscure the atonement cover[33] of the ark of the covenant. The smoke

---

32. Philip Jenson reminds us that even though we consider the Day of Atonement a festival, "strictly speaking it is not a festival, for on this day the Israelites were commanded to 'afflict themselves' (Lv. 16:29; 23:27–32; Nu. 29:7)." Jenson, "The Levitical Sacrificial System," 36.

33. Many Bible versions refer to the atonement cover—*kappōret*—as the mercy seat. While scholars debate the meaning of the word, it seems likely that *kappōret* is derived from the Hebrew word for "to atone." Its position on the ark set it apart as the place

evidently prevented him from seeing God's throne and being struck dead by directly encountering God's holiness. When the holy of holies was filled with smoke from the incense, the high priest took some of the blood of the sacrificed bull and sprinkled it in front of the atonement cover.

After this ritual, two goats—which had previously been selected by lots, one to be sacrificed to Yahweh and the other one to be released as the scapegoat[34]—would be brought forward and the one chosen for Yahweh slaughtered. The high priest sprinkled the blood of this goat on and in front of the atonement cover seven times to cleanse the community from sin.

After atonement was made for the high priest and the people, the tent of meeting and the bronze altar of the tabernacle were cleansed by being sprinkled with blood (Lev 16:16, 18–20). As Wenham describes it, "These atonement-day rituals make the impossible possible. By cleansing the sanctuary, they permit the holy God to dwell among an unholy people."[35]

The ceremonies were completed when the remaining goat was brought forward so that the priest could lay his hands on its head, confess the sins of his people, and transfer their sin to the goat. The scapegoat thus carried their sins away to a solitary place where it was released. To mark the end of the rituals, the high priest washed himself and put on his normal priestly apparel. Similarly, the man who led the goat away washed himself and his clothes before returning to camp. Finally, the remains of the bull and goat sacrificed for the sin offering were carried outside of the camp and burned. The man who performed this task washed his clothes and himself before returning.

Although the Day of Atonement rites are performed by only a few people, the fact that everyone was to observe a Sabbath rest, refrain from work, and fast indicates its importance for the nation. The day ensured that the nation could remain holy as they lived in the presence of their holy God. Not even the holiest man in society was permitted to approach God and live unless he had first been made holy. And even though the Israelites were not permitted to witness the acts of atonement that went on in the holy of holies, they could watch the scapegoat being led away and know that their sins had been removed from the camp and God would continue to dwell among them.

Few New Testament passages mention the Day of Atonement. One of them simply calls it "the Fast" and uses it to indicate that Paul's shipboard

---

where atonement was made so that God could forgive his people's sin and allow them to remain in covenant relationship with him.

34. See the commentaries for the different interpretations that have developed over the meaning of the scapegoat or "goat to Azazel."

35. Wenham, *Leviticus*, 233.

journey to Rome took place late in the year (Acts 27:9). In the only passage where it features prominently, the festival is not mentioned by name but can be recognized by the work of the high priest who brought sacrifices for himself and for the people into the "inner room" once a year (Heb 9:6–10). The lack of specific reference to the festival, however, does not imply that it was unimportant for New Testament theology. In fact, the concept of atonement is foundational for an understanding of what Jesus accomplished on the cross. According to the author of Hebrews, the atonement rituals performed by the high priest were only a preparation for the coming of Jesus, who opened access to the holy of holies so that all of God's people could enter.

As Hebrews views it, the old covenant sacrifices made it possible for people to approach God and be forgiven, though not perfectly. Regular sacrifices were required for people to remain in relationship with God, but since only the high priest could enter the holy of holies once a year, it was impossible for people to draw near to God any time they had need. This, Hebrews announces, was reversed by Jesus. When Jesus offered himself as a sacrifice, the veil separating the holy place from the holy of holies was torn asunder, giving all believers instant access to God's throne room (Heb 10:19–22; cf. Matt 27:51; Mark 15:38; Luke 23:45). Since Jesus died once for all, there is no need for further sacrifices for sin or to celebrate a Day of Atonement (Heb 9:12, 26). Instead, Christians look to the events of Good Friday and Easter as decisive in providing atonement for all who have faith.

The writer of Hebrews demonstrates several ways in which Christ's work was greater than that which was performed under the Old Testament law and that it was sufficient for everyone no matter when they lived. First, the high priest sinned and needed to offer a sacrifice for himself before he made atonement for the people, but since Jesus never sinned, he did not have to bring a sacrifice for himself (Heb 7:26–28). Second, whereas the high priest was required to make regular sacrifices, Jesus presented himself as the perfect sacrifice that did not need to be repeated (Heb 9:6–14, 24–26).[36] Third, the high priest's ministry only gave him access to the earthly sanctuary once a year, while Jesus' ministry allowed him (and his followers) to enter the heavenly sanctuary where he remains in the presence of God and intercedes for his people who are free to boldly approach God's throne (Heb 9:7, 11–12, 24).[37] Fourth, the sacrifices offered by the priests were a

---

36. Hebrews makes a further comparison between Jesus' sacrifice and the one performed on the Day of Atonement by stating that as the remains of the bull and goat were burned outside the camp, so Jesus suffered outside the city wall (Heb 13:11–13).

37. It may be significant that the New Testament continues the idea introduced during the time of Israel's wanderings that "there is one God and one mediator between God and men" (1 Tim 2:5). But instead of the Levitical high priest, "the man Christ

constant reminder that sin was not to be taken lightly and that the blood of bulls and goats could not remove it permanently, but Jesus' one-time sacrifice makes those who follow him perfect (Heb 10:1–18). Surpassing the goat sacrificed for the sins of the people and the one that carried away their sin, Jesus perfectly atoned for his people as he both bore their sin and destroyed its power over them.

This leads to a somewhat ironic conclusion. Jesus' death on the cross makes celebration of the Day of Atonement irrelevant for Christians who have experienced a once-and-for-all forgiveness through the work of the perfect high priest and the offering of the perfect sacrifice. Even so, it makes it even more important that we understand the theological purpose behind the festival, without which the meaning and extent of Jesus' sacrifice cannot be grasped.

Feast of Tabernacles

The third great pilgrim festival was Tabernacles—*ḥag hassukkôt*—or the Feast of Booths. It is also known as Sukkoth (*sukkôt*) and the Feast of Ingathering (*ḥag hā 'āsîp*). This festival began on the fifteenth day of the seventh month and lasted until the twenty-second. The first and eighth days of Tabernacles were set aside for sacred assemblies; no work was allowed on either day. Held during the grape harvest at the end of the agricultural year, it was to be a seven-day period of rejoicing before Yahweh because he supplied his people with all their food and, particularly, their summer fruit and wine.[38] Since the festival was held at the end of the year, celebrants looked forward to the new year and what Yahweh would provide in the future.

But the festival did not focus merely on God's present or future provision for his people; it looked back to his preservation while they were in the wilderness. Thus, everyone was required to leave their homes and build a tabernacle or booth out of tree branches in which they would live for the full seven days (Lev 23:42–43). Living in booths reminded them of what their ancestors experienced during their wilderness sojourn when God provided them with food.

The Feast of Tabernacles featured the most complex order of sacrifices, with a different set of offerings to be presented on each day of the week. On the first day, thirteen bulls, two rams, and fourteen male lambs

---

Jesus" serves as the mediator of the new covenant.

38. Its association with the grape harvest and drinking wine may indicate that this was the festival which Elkanah celebrated with his wives when Eli mistakenly concluded that Hannah was drunk. See Rowley, *Worship in Ancient Israel*, 89–90.

were sacrificed as burnt offerings, along with one goat as a sin offering, and the associated grain and drink offerings. During the rest of the festival, the number of sacrificial victims remained the same except for the bulls, which decreased by one for each day until the seventh when seven bulls were offered. On the eight day, only one bull was sacrificed along with the other offerings. The sacrifices of this week—17 bulls, 15 rams, 105 lambs, and 8 goats—were wholly consumed as burnt offerings. The extravagance of incinerating all these animals reminded Israel of their need to depend upon God to live in the land.

Tabernacles was celebrated during the monarchy and after the restoration (2 Chr 8:13; Ezra 3:4; Neh 8:14–18). It appears that it was the first feast celebrated after the Jews returned to Jerusalem from exile in Babylon. The book of Nehemiah records that the day was celebrated after Ezra read from the law that Israel was to live in booths for a week during the seventh month. While he was reading, the people expressed great joy because they could learn from and live by God's requirements. After the exile, the feast came to symbolize a future hope, not only for Israel, but for the other nations that would join in the celebration of the Feast of Tabernacles (Zech 14:16–19). This prophecy looked forward to a time when Jerusalem would be safe from all its enemies and God would fulfil his promise of blessing all the nations through the descendants of Abraham. Those who refused to worship Yahweh would be deprived of rain.

In the New Testament, the Feast of Tabernacles is mentioned directly only in John 7. This passage begins with Jesus ministering in Galilee because the Jewish leaders in Judea wanted to kill him (cf. John 5:18). His brothers, however, encouraged him to go up to Judea during the Feast so that his disciples could see his miracles. Jesus went up secretly, and, half way through the week, began preaching in the temple courts: "If anyone is thirsty, let him come to me and drink. Whoever believes in me, as the Scripture has said, streams of living water will flow from within him" (John 7:37–38). This phrase, which linked streams of water with the outpouring of the Holy Spirit, reflects concepts that were closely associated with Tabernacles. Sometime during the second temple period, a water-pouring ritual was added to the festivities as a reminder that the God who had provided water from the rock in the wilderness also sent rain for crops to grow. During this rite, the high priest drew water from the pool of Siloam, carried it to the Temple in a procession, and poured it out to God at the time of the morning sacrifices. When Jesus invited the thirsty to drink of the water that he gives, he makes use of this Tabernacles theme in order to compare himself with the rock through which God gives water to his people.[39] However, whereas the water-pouring rite needed to be repeated every year, Jesus' gift of the Holy Spirit would go on and on. The feast is thus completed in him. Those who do not accept his life-giving water will become like the nations that Zechariah prophesied would experience drought for not worshipping the Lord.

Purim

In addition to the festivals that were celebrated from the beginning of Israel's history, two other feast days were later added to remind God's people how he had worked in their history. Purim (*pûrîm*) was celebrated from the time of Esther when Israel was rescued from Haman, the enemy of the Jews.[40] The name of the festival comes from the Persian word *pûr*, "lot," because Haman cast lots to select a day and month for the Jews to be destroyed (Esth 3:7; 9:24, 26). Haman's plans were overturned as Mordecai pleaded with Esther to appeal to the King to intervene for her people and the Jews fasted and prayed. Instead of being a day of destruction, the thirteenth and fourteenth of Adar[41] became days of celebration as the Jews remembered God's saving hand moving in their midst. During modern festivities, the book of Esther is read aloud while the audience cheers Esther and Mordecai and jeers Haman whenever their names are read.

Purim is not mentioned in the New Testament. Just as Christians use other holidays to commemorate God's deliverance, we could also use Purim in this way.

Hanukkah

The festival of Hanukkah, often called the Feast of Dedication, is celebrated for eight days beginning on the twenty-fifth of the ninth month (Kislev).[42] It was inaugurated in order to celebrate the cleansing and rededication of the Jerusalem temple in 165 BC after Judah Maccabeus led an army of Jews against the Greek Seleucids under Antiochus IV, who had captured Jerusalem three years earlier and desecrated the temple by offering sacrifices to Zeus there. Each year, the festival is celebrated by lighting a menorah in remembrance of the golden menorah in the temple that was re-lit on

---

39. Jeremias, "λίθος," 277–78.
40. For more about this festival, see Mack, "Purim."
41. This would be in February or March in our calendar.
42. As 25 Kislev occurs near the winter solstice, the festival is held in December.

the same day and time that the temple was desecrated. The lighting of the menorah leads to the festival being called the Feast of Lights.

This feast is mentioned in John 10:22–39, which tells how Jesus gave proof that he was the Messiah to a group of Jews who asked about his credentials. While it is a fitting day for Christians to remember that Jesus is the light of the world and that he brought a great deliverance from the tyranny of Satan and sin, Hanukkah has not been considered a holy day for the church. In part, this may be due to its proximity to Christmas.

CONCLUSION

As this overview of the biblical holy days has shown, Israel's worship was anchored to the weeks, months, and seasons of the year to remind them that all of life was to be lived before God. Frequently, the days were tied to great salvific events from their history and had covenantal implications. As they had been redeemed from slavery in Egypt, the wiles of a Persian prince, and the plans of a Seleucid king, Israel celebrated Yahweh's mighty acts of liberation. Since he was the one who provided the land and the rain, Israel could rejoice in God's goodness during the three main harvest festivals.

Celebrating Yahweh's lavish gifts of salvation and produce in their "land of milk and honey" reminded Israel that these things did not come by chance, their own ingenuity, or the help of other deities. It further freed them from participating in the fertility rites associated with Baal worship. As Yahweh provided all his people's needs, he alone should be worshipped in purity.

In addition to their focus on God's redemption and provision, the holy days of Israel served as regular reminders that he had established his covenant with them. As they celebrated the weekly Sabbath, the covenant stipulations associated with the day laid out in the Ten Commandments were impressed upon them anew. The Passover and the Feast of Unleavened Bread brought the exodus to mind, and with it the Sinaitic covenant. The covenantal focus of this festival is enhanced for Christians since Jesus established the new covenant through his blood by sharing his last meal with his disciples at Passover. Pentecost also centered on covenantal themes as Israel celebrated it as the anniversary of God giving the law and a day for renewing the covenant. Similarly, the covenant was a major focus of the Day of Atonement.

Many of Israel's holy days either took on new meaning or became superfluous for the early church. Some festivals were reinterpreted as Christians reflected on Jesus' earthly ministry, especially his death on the cross.

Once the church spread beyond Judea, some of the festivals were deemed unnecessary for Gentile Christians to follow. Several festivals underwent change due to the destruction of the temple in AD 70.

While the holy days set out in the Old Testament underwent substantive changes in the New Testament age, God's new covenant people still need to remember his work in creation, redemption, and continued provision. As we still need to live out our days, seasons, and years before God, new meanings were given to some of the old festivals and a whole new set of holy days were developed throughout church history. The church's application of its biblical theology of worshipping God in time by developing holy days and festivals after the canon of Scripture was completed goes beyond this book's aim of providing a biblical theology of worship. However, since it has a lot to say about how the historic church lived out its faith through the year, an overview of the church year can be found in the appendix.

8

Worship and Praise

From Genesis to Revelation, praise characterizes the people of God. Christians, from the first to the twenty-first century, have rightly praised God as individuals and in groups, for as the psalmist says, "it is fitting for the upright to praise him" (Ps 33:1; cf. Ps 147:1). Responding to the many psalms that urge God's people to "Praise the Lord" for who he is and for what he has done, Christian praise has resounded throughout the earth as God's people have raised their voices to recount his works for the sake of others, shouting out his glories, and singing and playing songs that magnify his greatness. These vocal and instrumental expressions of praise have, at times, been supplemented by physical actions such as raising hands, waving palm branches, and dancing. But like other forms of worship, simply engaging in an activity associated with praise is insufficient if one's heart is not in it (Pss 9:1; 86:12; 111:1).

Earlier we saw that people have different concepts about what worship is. This is equally true about praise. Like worship, some people associate praise with a particular type of song. Indeed, a veritable industry has grown up around "worship and praise." Short songs, frequently based upon a verse from the Psalms[1] or another biblical book, have been set to catchy tunes that can be easily learned and sung, released on various media, and published in a wide assortment of books. While these songs provide material that can lead us into praise, equating them with praise myopically narrows the means

---

1. The Psalms have been the source of more than 3,500 songs that have been copyrighted and are administered by the CCLI licensing company. Witvliet, *Biblical Psalms,* 118.

by which we can extol God and blurs the panorama that is available to those whose eyes are clear and hearts are open to respond to the wonders of God.

While some have reduced praise to a shadow of what it should be, others virtually black it out, questioning why we should praise God and why he would demand it. In a reflection titled "A Word about Praising," C. S. Lewis explains his initial resistance to the idea of praising God and how he overcame it.[2] At first, Lewis equated God's requirement of praise with the need certain people have to be assured that they are great. He further likened the vocal acclamation of a congregation to the crowds that clamor in the presence of a dictator, millionaire, or celebrity. If we despise the one who seeks his own praise and the many who cry out for the attention of the powerful, how could we possibly admire the praise of God? As Lewis reconsidered the issue, he produced a simple, yet thought-provoking, meditation on the nature of praise and concluded that it is our natural desire to tell others about something wonderful we have experienced. No matter whether we enjoy a book, a sport, the weather, or a tasty meal, we want to share it with others so that they can enjoy it too. Lewis thus suggests that a person who knows God will genuinely want to tell others about their experience of God and solicit their response. This is praise. And this explains why the psalmists continually exhort others to praise the Lord. They are moved by their encounter with God and want others to join them in their experience and proclamation of it.

BIBLICAL WORDS FOR PRAISE

As with worship, our understanding of praise must begin with a study of the words Scripture uses for the concept. In the Old Testament, the major verb for praise is *hālal*, "to praise, extol." The noun for praise—*těhillâ*—is noteworthy in that its plural form—*těhillîm*—is the Hebrew title of Psalms, the book of praises. The Psalms are so centered on praise that around two-thirds of the verbal and nominal uses of this word in the Bible are found in that one book. Much of our examination of praise thus rightly centers on the Psalter in which the verbal form usually comes as an imperative, commanding God's people to praise him—"Hallelujah."[3] The verb *hālal* is

---

2. Lewis, *Reflections on the Psalms*, 77–83.
3. Westermann, "הלל *hll*," 371. Though the Hebrew phrase *halělû-yāh* or *halělû yāh*—transliterated "hallelujah" and translated "Praise the Lord"—first appears as the last word in Psalm 104:35 (or the first verse of the following chapter in the Septuagint), it is found a total of twenty-three times in the Psalter, along with the variants *halělû 'et* Yhwh, "Praise the Lord" (Pss 117:1; 148:1, 7; cf. Jer 20:13) and *halělû 'et šēm* Yhwh, "Praise the name of the Lord" (Pss 113:1; 135:1). In other psalms, God's people, angels,

regularly used when one praises God for who he is, for his attributes, or for his all-encompassing might. Since the psalms that speak of God as the object of praise focus on his being and attributes, they have been termed psalms of descriptive praise.[4]

Another important word is the verb is *yādâ*, which in the hiphil means "to praise, confess, give thanks," and is used in the Bible almost exclusively of praise for God. Its associated noun, *tôdâ*, "thanksgiving," can be used of a thank offering or of the joyful song that might accompany that offering or be given at any other time.[5] Invariably, the psalmist offers his thanksgiving as a response to something God has done (Pss 9:4; 108:4; 118:21).[6] Psalms that use the verb *yādâ* when bringing praise to God and focus on his specific acts of salvation can rightly be called psalms of declarative praise.[7] As the author considers a specific act of God, he may express his desire to give thanks to or praise the Lord (Pss 9:1; 108:3; 118:21) or encourage others to thank or praise God (Pss 30:4; 97:12; 136:1–3). The fact that *yādâ* is variously translated "thanks" and "praise" indicates that the concepts are fairly synonymous to the Hebrew mind. It has been argued that Hebrew doesn't have a word for thanks as such and that thanksgiving is simply one type of praise.[8] If we are to differentiate between the concepts, we might say that thanksgiving is our private response to God, while praise is our response to God as expressed before others. A further difference is that thanksgiving addresses the object of praise, while praise informs others about what was done. It should be clear that when we bring our thanks to God in the presence of others and encourage them to consider God's works and thank him with us, the two activities meld into one.

Psalms of Thanksgiving are related to Psalms of Lament (see the next chapter), as they provide the response that one brings to God after he has responded to the prayer of lamentation. Biblical laments usually end with the speaker expressing his desire to praise God. When this happens, the word

---

or the physical creation are commanded to *halĕlûhû*, "praise him" (Pss 22:24; 148:2, 3, 4; 150:1, 2, 3, 4, 5).

4. Westermann, *Praise and Lament*, 31–32.

5. The singing of a song of thanksgiving is such an important aspect of worship that it is considered greater than the sacrifice of an ox or young bull (Ps 69:30–31).

6. In Hebrew, this motivation clause begins with *kî*, which is usually translated "for" or "because" in English.

7. Westermann, *Praise and Lament*, 31–32.

8. Westermann, *Praise and Lament*, 25–30. See also, Miller, "Enthroned on the Praises of Israel," 10–11. I have heard people attempt to distinguish between praise and thanksgiving by saying the first is what we do in response to who God is and the second is our response for what he does. Biblical texts praise and thank God both for who he is and what he has done.

yādâ is normally present even though it is not discernable in translation. Thus, Psalm 7 ends "I will give thanks to the Lord because of his righteousness and will sing praise to the name of the Lord Most High" (Ps 7:17).[9]

The parallelism of the second phrase of Psalm 7:17 identifies another word that points to a means of praising God—singing. The verb *zāmar*, means "to make music, to sing with or without instrumental accompaniment." Though there is no reason the word could not be used for secular songs, in the Bible it is found almost exclusively in the Psalms and always with God as its object.[10] Like *hālal*, *zāmar* frequently occurs as an imperative—"Sing praises to the Lord" (Pss 12:11; 30:5; 98:5; Isa 12:5), "Sing praises to (our) God/Lord" (Pss 47:6; 68:33; 147:7), or "Sing praise to him/(the glory of) his name" (1 Chr 16:9; Pss 33:2; 66:2; 68:5; 105:2; 135:3). It is thus used to exhort God's people to render him the praise that is his due, particularly when they are gathered to worship him. The use of the word in context and its rendering as *psallō* in the Septuagint indicates that it usually signifies singing to the accompaniment of stringed instruments, though this is not essential. Nouns derived from this word include *zāmîr* and *zimrâ*, both of which mean "a song." Another noun form, *mizmôr*, "song," inexplicably appears in the titles of fifty-seven psalms and nowhere else. Singing songs of praise was obviously a key part of the worship of God in Israel.

The New Testament writers also made use of different words for praise. One of the major words used is *doxazō*, which means "to glorify, praise, honor, magnify." Jesus exhorted his listeners to live in such a way that people will glorify or praise God (Matt 5:16). He then performed miracles that gave others reason to glorify his Father (Matt 9:8; 15:31). Whereas its associated noun, *doxa*, usually denotes glory, honor, magnificence, or splendor, *doxazō* sometimes takes on the concept of praise in the sense of one's reputation (John 5:41, 44; 8:50, 54).

The word *aineō*, "to praise, extol," is used six times in Luke and Acts (Luke 2:13, 20; 19:37; Acts 2:47; 3:8–9), and once each in Romans and Revelation (Rom 15:11; Rev 19:5). Its corresponding noun, *ainos*, is found twice with the meaning of "praise" (Matt 21:16; Luke 18:43). Derived from this word, *epaineō* also means "to praise," and its noun form *epainos*, means "praise, approval, fame." In the New Testament, it can indicate God's approval of his righteous ones, particularly at the time of judgment (Rom 2:29;

---

9. The range in meaning of *yādâ* in this type of construct is indicated by the various translations which read, "I will praise the Lord" (KJV) and "I will give thanks to the Lord" or similar (CSB, ESV, NASB, NIV, NLT, NRSV, RSV).

10. Only four of forty-five occurrences of this word are outside the Psalms, and even they are found in contexts that can be considered psalmic (Judg 5:3; 2 Sam 22:50; 1 Chr 16:9; Isa 12:5). Barth, "זמר," 93.

1 Cor 4:5; 1 Pet 1:7). It also refers to the community's praise offered to God in response to his salvation.[11]

Associated with the Hebrew words for praising God through singing or otherwise making music is *hymneō*, "to sing, sing praise" (only in Matt 26:30; Mark 14:26; Acts 16:25; Heb 2:12) and its nominal form *hymnos* (only in Eph 5:19; Col 3:16).[12] All four of these words are used in the Septuagint to translate *tĕhillâ*. The other word for singing is *psallō*, "to play a stringed instrument, make melody, sing praises" and its nominal, *psalmos*, "a psalm" (1 Cor 14:26; Eph 5:19; Col 3:16).[13]

Biblically, praise is a verbalization of approval or admiration due to the inherent qualities of a person or thing, or resulting from what the person or thing does or has accomplished. When God is the subject, we praise him by telling others about his greatness and our desire that they join us in exalting him. Praise is characterized by joy and frequently marked by song, music, and dancing. Those who know God and have experienced his saving works cannot contain this information, but are compelled to tell others about him so that they can join in too. By calling others to acknowledge God's actions, worshippers gain even more because "praise not merely expresses but completes the enjoyment; it is its appointed consummation."[14]

Though God is the primary object of praise in the Bible, humans and even cities receive praise.[15] On the visual level, Sarah is praised for her beauty (Gen 12:15), as is Absalom (2 Sam 14:25). According to Proverbs, a man who is wise will be praised (Prov 12:8), though this should not come from his own mouth but be acknowledged by others (Prov 27:2). Similarly, a woman of virtue will be praised by her husband and her works (Prov 31:28, 31), principally because she fears the Lord (Prov 31:30). All this suggests that it is good for people to receive praise from others if offered rightly.[16] Even so, the praise that God gives is more desirable than human praise (Rom 2:29; 1 Cor 4:5). This truth is spotlighted by John who records that

---

11. Preisker, "ἔπαινος," 588.

12. The English word "hymn" is derived from this word. For a deeper study of the Greek word, see Delling, "ὕμνος."

13. The noun is used by Luke exclusively for the book of Psalms (Luke 20:42; 24:44; Acts 1:20; 13:33).

14. Lewis, *Reflections on the Psalms*, 81.

15. Though called cities "of renown" (NIV; literally "of praise"), the prophecies of the fall of Damascus and Tyre indicate that they will no longer be considered praiseworthy (Jer 49:25; Ezek 26:17). The only time the Old Testament reports that a deity other than Yahweh is praised is when the Philistines praised their god after subduing Samson (Judg 16:24). Ringgren, "הלל *hll*," 406.

16. Since only "Those who forsake the law praise the wicked," the praise they receive is invalid (Prov 28:4).

certain Jewish leaders believed in Jesus but would not openly confess their faith since they were afraid of being thrown out of the synagogue. Their motivation for hiding their belief is clear: "they loved praise from men more than praise from God" (John 12:43). The rebuke of those with inverted values is cutting and should remind us that even though our lifestyle should give people reason to praise us, we should be more concerned about what God thinks of us.

Beyond their sparse recognition that people can, and indeed should, be praised, the biblical authors are mainly concerned with the praise of God. As Israel engaged the God who called them into relationship with himself, their regular response was to praise him with song. Most of these songs reflected their experience of God in history, their contemplation of his power in creation, and their recognition of his personal greatness.

PRAISE OF GOD FOR HISTORICAL DELIVERANCE FROM ENEMIES

Israel's consideration of God's acts in history is linked to their experience of deliverance from their enemies. This is clearly seen in the earliest songs recorded in the Bible. The Song of Miriam exalts Yahweh for saving Israel from the waters of the sea in which Pharaoh's army was destroyed (Exod 15:1–18). As the song opens by recounting God's glorious triumph over his enemies, it sets the stage for what is to come and reminds Israel that they should respond to God with songs of praise since he protects and delivers them.

> Then Moses and the Israelites sang this song to the LORD:
> "I will sing to the LORD, for he is highly exalted.
> The horse and its rider he has hurled into the sea.
> The LORD is my strength and my song;
> he has become my salvation.
> He is my God, and I will praise him,
> my father's God, and I will exalt him.
> The LORD is a warrior; the LORD is his name. (Exod 15:1–3)

Though God delivered Israel from the Egyptians, they faced other enemies once they entered the land of Canaan. In the book of Judges, the Song of Deborah praises Yahweh for delivering his people from their enemies as they fight under his lead (Judg 5:2–31).

> On that day Deborah and Barak son of Abinoam sang this song:
> "When the princes in Israel take the lead,

> when the people willingly offer themselves—
> praise the Lord!
> "Hear this, you kings!
> Listen, you rulers!
> I will sing to the Lord, I will sing;
> I will make music to the Lord, the God of Israel.
> "O Lord, when you went out from Seir,
> when you marched from the land of Edom,
> the earth shook,
> the heavens poured,
> the clouds poured down water.
> The mountains quaked before the Lord, the One of Sinai,
> before the Lord, the God of Israel. (Judg 5:1–5)

The song recalls Israel's battle against Sisera, the commander of the Canaanite king Jabin. During this fight, Deborah and Barak led out the troops of Israel under the Lord's command and routed their enemies. The response to God's deliverance was to sing his praise. Throughout Israel's history, more songs that recognized the need of God's protection were recorded in the Psalms. However, in contrast to the examples from Exodus and Judges that are tied to concrete historical situations, most psalms that speak of deliverance are adaptable to suit a variety of times and needs due to their lack of historical specificity. These psalms make it clear that God fights for Israel and against their numerous enemies, which Kraus categorizes as "enemies of the nation," "enemies of the individual," and "mythical powers."[17]

The royal psalms best demonstrate that God fights the enemies of Israel. By focusing on the king as Yahweh's representative, they proclaim that the enemies of the king and the nation are God's enemies. When attacked by foreign chariots and horses, Israel responds by pleading that God would fight for them. At times, the foreign powers are named (Pss 60:10–11; 83:6–11; 137); usually they are not. Since many of the psalms are not historically anchored, they can be applied to multiple situations by modern worshippers—even when facing spiritual enemies. While God's people pray for deliverance, they rejoice because Yahweh promises to make the king's enemies a footstool for his feet (Ps 110:1) and assures them that David will not pay tribute to foreign powers but that God will strike down all foes in his wrath (Pss 89:22–23; 110:5). Even though Israel is usually God's tool to punish the nations that do not recognize him (Ps 79:6), when they turn from following the Lord, he uses the nations to chastise them. Israel's context reminds us that praise of God is not entirely celebratory, as though God's people never lose. God is praised by people who live in the real world where

---

17. Kraus, *Theology of the Psalms*, 126–36.

sin and conflict abound. Even when they do not feel God's presence due to personal sin or the attacks of others, they recall his actions in history and his power in creation and praise him for those great works. In times of distress caused by national or spiritual enemies, the psalms of praise may take on an eschatological bent as those who sing them look forward to the relief God will give in the future.

In addition to rescuing his chosen nation from foreign enemies, God delivers individuals from personal enemies. Many psalms relate the experience of one who has faced physical, social, or psychological danger. By crying to the Lord, he expresses hope that God will save him so that he will again praise the Lord in the assembly (Ps 56:10–13). Like the nations that surrounded Israel, these enemies are characterized by their rejection of God. Their attacks are compared to hostile armies (Pss 55:20–21; 56:1; 59:1–4), hunters who set traps for their prey (Pss 7:15; 9:15; 31:4), and wild animals ready to strike (Pss 7:2; 59:6, 14).[18] Although they may have wealth or a powerful position in society, they set themselves against the righteous, the weak, and the poor. They particularly focus their taunts on those who are sick, claiming the illness proves that God has forsaken them. Psalms written for individuals to confront their enemies allow them to call out to God in their weakness and wait with assurance that he will hear and respond. Frequently, they encourage the one who is in difficulty so that he can persevere until deliverance comes (Pss 3, 91). They also serve as a reminder that God is the judge who will hold evil people to account (Pss 7:6–9; 96:10–13). These psalms thus give a person who might easily be distracted by life's problems an opportunity to turn to the Lord for help. On many occasions, the simple remembrance that the Lord is near leads directly to praise, or at least provides hope that praise will be raised in the future.

A number of psalms indicate that God delivers his people from the mythical powers that are associated in some way with one's human enemies. In most cases, these give metaphorical descriptions of the power wielded by the psalmist's enemies but which are counted as nothing when compared with Yahweh's might. Thus, the enemy's desire to destroy the psalmist is likened to death, Sheol, and the pit (Pss 18:4–5; 30:3; 86:13). When faced with the prospect of being cut off from God, prayer for deliverance is offered. This may include statements of trust that God will truly save. After the anticipated rescue comes, prayers of thanksgiving form the appropriate response. Israel's historical experience included times when their enemies overcame them and destroyed their land. In a psalm that laments the destruction of the temple by invaders, the psalmist recalls God's creative

18. Kraus, *Theology of the Psalms*, 130–31.

power which overcame the sea monster and Leviathan—two mythological creatures associated with primeval chaos (Ps 74:13–17). These creatures find their way into the psalm, not because Israel believed the ancient myths, but because their remembrance that Yahweh could easily overcome creatures of legendary strength gave them confidence when facing enemies so powerful that they had put an end to their way of life in the land. Such a remembrance is a motivation for praise, even when situations seem grim.

PRAISE OF GOD FOR HIS POWER IN CREATION

Deliverance from enemies frequently moved Israel to exult in the Lord. It was not, however, their only reason for praising him. On many occasions, they sang out his glories because of his power displayed in creation as illustrated by Psalm 33.

> Sing joyfully to the Lord, you righteous;
> it is fitting for the upright to praise him.
> Praise the Lord with the harp;
> make music to him on the ten-stringed lyre.
> Sing to him a new song;
> play skillfully, and shout for joy.
> For the word of the Lord is right and true;
> he is faithful in all he does.
> The Lord loves righteousness and justice;
> the earth is full of his unfailing love.
> By the word of the Lord were the heavens made,
> their starry host by the breath of his mouth.
> He gathers the waters of the sea into jars;
> he puts the deep into storehouses.
> Let all the earth fear the Lord;
> let all the people of the world revere him.
> For he spoke, and it came to be;
> he commanded, and it stood firm. (Ps 33:1–9)

This psalm is grounded in an exhortation to praise God with voice, musical instruments, and new compositions because of his work as Creator. The one who speaks the stars into existence deserves to be extolled with songs that are creatively written and skillfully played. The one who stores up the rain so that the sea might be refilled and the ground refreshed should be heralded with a shout of joy that is continually renewed. The Lord should be feared—worshipped—by everyone in the world because it came into existence when he said the word. For his creative power and for his faithfulness, Israel responds to God with praise.

Psalm 33 is only one of the many psalms that direct God's people to praise him for creating the cosmos. This theme is so pervasive that von Rad says, "The creation and preservation of the world by Jahweh was certainly one of the principle subjects of the hymns of the Old Testament."[19] The psalmists describe God's power in creation in a number of ways. Sometimes they make use of imagery. The creation of the heavens is thus said to be the work of God's hands (Pss 8:3; 19:1). "Hands" or "fingers" speak of the creative power of God molding things into existence. After completing this work, God sits enthroned in glory over the earth (Ps 29:10). Indeed, God is so mighty that all creation—the mighty waters, the desert wastes, the mighty cedars, oaks, and forests—hears and is affected by his thundering voice (Ps 29:3-9). Even the most majestic and awesome parts of nature are as nothing when compared to the power of the Lord. As his people consider his greatness and might, they rightly respond with praise.

Praise should also emerge from one's reflection that God has created everything that exists. He made the heavens (Pss 8:3; 19:3; 33:6; 96:5; 146:6), the sun and moon (Ps 74:16), the stars (Ps 33:6), the earth (Pss 24:1-2; 74:17; 95:5; 146:6), the sea (Pss 95:5; 146:6), the north and the south (Ps 89:12),[20] the day and night (Ps 74:16), the seasons (Ps 74:17), all the animals (Ps 8:6-8), and humankind (Ps 8:5). As Creator, God reigns as the great king of creation. From the psalmists' perspective, "Creation and kingship are inseparably connected."[21] This is expressed magnificently in Psalm 24: "The earth is the LORD's, and the fullness thereof, the world, and those who dwell therein" (cf. Ps 89:11). Five times this psalm calls Yahweh the "King of glory" (Ps 24:7-10). The entire Psalter resounds with the idea that God made the world, it belongs to him, and he rules over it as king. The Lord rules in heaven (Pss 11:4; 103:19). The Lord rules over the sea (Ps 89:9). He rules over the earth (Ps 47:2, 7). He rules over the nations (Pss 22:28; 47:8; 72:11). Indeed, he rules over everything (Ps 103:19) as king forever (Pss 9:7; 10:16; 29:10; 45:6; 145:13). Yahweh's rule over creation is reflected in Israel's recognition that he was their king. The potentate of all that exists must also

---

19. Rad, *Old Testament Theology*, 361.

20. That is, he created Zaphon and Yamin. Zaphon is the name of a mountain to the north of Palestine and therefore connected with the north. Yamin means "right hand." It takes on the connotation "south" because that is the hand that is toward the south when a person faces the rising sun in the east. The verse indicates that since Yahweh created the far north and the south, his reign is universal.

21. Mays, *Psalms*, 284.

reign over his chosen people who respond to him with praise. How can one not respond by crying, "Hallelujah!"?

PRAISE OF GOD FOR HIS PERSONAL GREATNESS

Praise flows from God's people as they consider his historical works of redemption and his powerful acts of creation. In addition, God is extolled simply because of who he is. Thus, David praises him for his greatness and majesty.

> Praise be to you, O Lord,
> God of our father Israel,
> from everlasting to everlasting.
> Yours, O Lord, is the greatness and the power
> and the glory and the majesty and the splendor,
> for everything in heaven and earth is yours.
> Yours, O Lord, is the kingdom;
> you are exalted as head over all.
> Wealth and honor come from you;
> you are the ruler of all things.
> In your hands are strength and power
> to exalt and give strength to all.
> Now, our God, we give you thanks,
> and praise your glorious name. (1 Chr 29:10–13)

This psalm, sung towards the end of the king's life, exalts Yahweh as the king of all who permits others to rule under him. Earthly kings must, therefore, acknowledge that they are merely his servants who should thank and praise him for being the source of all.

PRAISE OF GOD IN THE PSALMS

Even though songs of praise, or fragments thereof, can be found throughout the Bible, the major collection is the Psalms, the book of praises. Even though many of the songs in the collection are not classified as psalms of praise, the overall direction of the book leads its readers to praise and worship the God of Israel.[22] No matter what season one faces in life, the Psalms provide words for encountering God through expressing praise, trust, or delight, confessing sins, and voicing deep-seated pain. Even lament usually

---

22. Westermann, *Praise and Lament*, 250–58.

leads to praise as the psalmists charge their readers to praise God and continually announce their personal intention to do so.

The frequency of the command to praise God in the Psalms is striking.[23] Whether we read "praise the LORD" (*halĕlû-yāh*[24] or *hôdû YHWH*), "Blessed be the LORD" (*bārûk YHWH*; in NIV "Praise be to the LORD"), "sing/sing praise to the LORD" (*zamrû YHWH*), or something similar, the verbs are imperative.[25] In most cases, they occur with a plural subject, indicating that praise is a congregational activity. As a body, God's people are charged to praise him because he deserves praise and because it provides them with a means of expressing their joy in his presence.

God's praise is not limited to people. According to the Psalms, creation and all its parts should praise the Lord (Pss 69:34; 89:5; 96:11–12; 98:7–8; 103:20–21; 148:1–12). The Psalter's consistent instruction about praise is summed up in its final verse: "Let everything that has breath praise the LORD. Praise the LORD" (Ps 150:6).[26]

The Psalms provide many reasons why creation and all its parts should praise God. The simplest reason is that he is exalted in splendor above creation. God is also to be praised because of his righteous judgment of the nations (Pss 96:13; 98:9). Creation should praise him because he provided salvation for his people (Ps 148:14). The psalmists even encourage creation to praise God because he will save his people and rebuild their land (Ps 69:35–36). Deliverance is a major motive for praise.

Praise, in the Psalms, is closely related to life. All that has breath—and some things lacking breath—is commanded to praise God. This is no theoretical concept. The psalmist is aware that praise of God is an essential part of his own life. He thus prays, "Let me live that I may praise you" (Ps 119:175). From this perspective, praise should be considered "the purpose of life."[27] To live is to praise God and to praise God is to truly live. The truth of this is felt so deeply that some psalms recall that "It is not the dead who praise the LORD" (Ps 115:17) and "No one remembers you when he is dead. Who praises you from the grave?"[28] (Ps 6:5; cf. Isa 38:18). Praise is for the living and the living should praise. The dead are unable to join the earthly

---

23. According to Westermann, the words for praise occur in the imperative more frequently than any other verb in the Bible. Westermann, *Praise and Lament*, 15.

24. Or *halĕlû yāh*.

25. Westermann provides a list of parallel terms for praise found in the imperative. Westermann, "הלל *hll*," 372.

26. P. D. Miller sees this statement as the climax of the book. Miller, "'Enthroned on the Praises of Israel,'" 8.

27. Allen, *Psalms 101–150*, 144.

28. "Grave" is literally Sheol.

assembly of God's people where they can praise God before others. This explains why the psalmists frequently ask God to preserve them from their enemies. Life is lived in Yahweh's presence and results in his praise.

Since praise was such an essential part of life lived before Yahweh, it is not surprising that Israel formed institutions to promote God's praise. David established a guild of musicians from among the Levites who continually sang, played various musical instruments, and raised sounds of joy (1 Chr 15:16–24).[29] Whether led by the Levitical musicians or others, worship in ancient Israel was frequently accompanied by instruments such as the harp, lyre, ram's horn, trumpet, flute, drum,[30] cymbal, bells, and others.[31] In some instances, these instruments may have been used together to form an orchestra or small ensemble. At other times, they may have been played alone. Musical instruments were an integral part Israel's expression of praise (Pss 33:1; 81:2–3; 98:5–6; 149:3; 150:3–5).

As Israel expressed their praise in word and song, they also engaged in physical activities including clapping hands (Ps 41:7), raising hands in prayer (Pss 63:4; 134:2), and dancing (Exod 15:20; 2 Sam 6:12–14; Pss 149:3; 150:4). Worship without kneeling or other bodily movements may not have been recognized. This is seen in the exhortation of Psalm 95:6–7:

> Come, let us bow down in worship,
> let us kneel before the LORD our Maker;
> for he is our God and we are the people of his pasture,
> the flock under his care.

Praise was a most important part of community life in ancient Israel. The covenant relationship they shared with Yahweh gave them many reasons to praise him with exuberant joy and to urge others to praise him as well.

---

29. First Chronicles 25:1 records that David set apart some of the sons of Asaph, Heman, and Jeduthun "for the ministry of prophesying, accompanied by harps, lyres and cymbals." The nature of their prophecy is not clear. It may have been understood as direct messages from God like the classical prophets except for the uncommon accompaniment by music (cf. 2 Chr 20:14–17). Another possibility is that their songs of praise were considered prophecy because the songs proclaimed God's authoritative word. Selman, *1 Chronicles*, 235. Allen Ross apparently combines these ideas as he identifies the prophesying as the writing of the psalms that would be incorporated into Scripture. Ross, *Recalling the Hope of Glory*, 257–58.

30. The instrument translated "tambourine" in the NIV and other translations was a small, shallow, round drum. It was similar to a modern tambourine without the metal "jingles."

31. For a recent examination of the musical instruments referred to in the Bible, see Braun, *Music in Ancient Israel*, 12–45.

PRAISE IN THE NEW TESTAMENT

As the New Testament shows, early Christians continued to praise God in many ways. Praise was offered by people who recognized God's work that led to the birth of Christ and by people who acknowledged that God was working through Jesus. Jesus praised the Father and encouraged his disciples to do the same. In this section, we will consider some of the examples of praise found in the New Testament.

Luke's Gospel begins with the announcement of the birth of John the Baptist. Though Zechariah returned from his temple ministry unable to speak, his faith and joy grew during the months of silence while the baby developed in his wife's womb. Once the promised son was born and named, Zechariah erupted into such exuberant praise that all his neighbors and those living in the surrounding hills heard how God would use the child to announce salvation for his people. His subsequent prophecy echoes words frequently used in the Old Testament by those who praised God for his acts of redemption. "Praise be to the Lord, the God of Israel, because he has come and has redeemed his people" (Luke 1:68; cf. 1 Kgs 1:48; Pss 41:13; 72:18; 106:48).[32] The complete prophecy (Luke 1:68–79) is commonly known as the *Benedictus* (from the Latin for "blessed"), and is one of three songs or canticles found at the beginning of Luke which are read or sung as part of the liturgy in multiple church traditions.[33]

If the birth of John resulted in God's praise, even more so the birth of Jesus. First, the angels praised God, saying, "Glory to God in the highest, and on earth peace to men on whom his favor rests" (Luke 2:14). This paean of joy was echoed by the shepherds who heard the angelic tidings about Mary and Joseph and found the baby Jesus laying in a manger. The men returned from the stable "glorifying and praising God for all the things they had heard and seen, which were just as they had been told" (Luke 2:20). Everyone who heard the shepherds' story about the birth of Jesus were similarly amazed and undoubtedly joined them in praising God for what he had done (Luke 2:18).

Not long afterwards, when Jesus was taken to Jerusalem to be circumcised and Mary presented a purification offering, two elderly people met

---

32. Note that *eulogētos* is used in the Septuagint to translate *bārûk Yhwh*, which can be translated either "bless the Lord" or "praise the Lord." Either way, it reflects Old Testament terminology for praise.

33. The other canticles recorded in Luke include the *Magnificat* (from its first word in Latin which means "magnify")—Mary's song anticipating the birth of her son (Luke 1:46–55), and the *Nunc dimittis* (from the Latin for "Now dismiss" [your servant]), the song based on Simeon's praise to God upon seeing the baby Jesus (Luke 2:29–32).

them at the temple and spoke words of praise. The first, Simeon, took the baby in his arms and praised God for the child in words that caused his parents to marvel (Luke 2:29–33). Then the prophetess Anna gave thanks to God and spoke out about Jesus to all who were awaiting the redemption of Jerusalem. Her praise indicated her desire that others share her joy for seeing Jesus (Luke 2:36–38).

Throughout Jesus' ministry, people regularly praised God for what he did. On most occasions, those who were healed praised God for his miraculous works (Luke 13:13; 17:15, 18; 18:43). Others who witnessed the miracles similarly praised God (Matt 9:8 [= Mark 2:12; Luke 5:25–26]; 15:31; Luke 7:16; 18:43; 19:37). Jesus' works of power were recognized as signs that pointed to God's deliverance from both disease and demons. Jesus was praised for his ability to teach when he visited the synagogues of Galilee (Luke 4:15). He opened God's word to the people in an exciting, new way that caused amazement and led to praise. At his triumphal entry into Jerusalem, crowds swarmed around Jesus with palm branches in hand and shouted, "'Hosanna to the Son of David!' 'Blessed is he who comes in the name of the Lord!' 'Hosanna in the highest!'" (Matt 21:9). The term "hosanna" comes from the Hebrew of Psalm 118:25, where the psalmist asks the Lord to "save us." This was a cry of praise to God as the crowd identified Jesus as the Son of David—the source of salvation. Their use of "blessed" is another sign of praise, this time directed to Jesus who is the means of God's salvation. Finally, the centurion who witnessed Jesus' death praised God (Luke 23:47). While it is likely that he saw in Jesus the sacrifice of a martyr,[34] as used by Luke, it is the final recognition by a Gentile that God should be praised for Jesus' work on the cross. Luke's final word on God being praised for the work of Jesus comes in the last verse of the book when the disciples, after the ascension, gathered in the temple for praise (Luke 24:53).

Luke 10 records one of the few explicit accounts of Jesus praising the Father when he sends out the seventy-two to visit the towns he was preparing to visit.[35] When the disciples returned from healing the sick and preaching the kingdom of God, they informed Jesus, "Lord, even the demons submit to us in your name" (Luke 10:17). Jesus responded that he had given them power to overcome the enemy, but warned that they should not rejoice because the demons obey but because their names are recorded in

---

34. Marshall, *Gospel of Luke*, 876.

35. Another version of this prayer is found in Matthew 11:25–27, where the context is the sending out of the twelve apostles and where it appears Jesus thanks God that he has hidden his gospel message from the towns in which he performed his miracles but revealed it to the disciples who accepted it. A third statement that Jesus brought praise to God is recorded in Hebrews 2:12.

heaven (Luke 10:19–20). He then expressed his own joy as he turned to his Father with a prayer that follows the form of a psalm of thanksgiving praising God for something he has done.[36] Jesus thus praises the Father that[37] he had hidden the gospel message and its power over demonic forces from the wise but revealed it to those he has chosen. From Jesus' perspective, the fact that God reveals the mysteries of salvation, not to the wise but to the simple, is a reason for joy and for encouraging others to rejoice with him.

In addition to the praise recorded in the Gospels, the authors of the Epistles praise God for his salvation and encourage others to praise him too. As in the Old Testament, praise often grows from one's recollection of God's works of deliverance. Thus, Paul wrote to the church in Rome recalling that believers were justified and reconciled with God through the blood of Jesus. Just thinking about this great salvation moved him to add, "Not only is this so, but we also rejoice in God through our Lord Jesus Christ" (Rom 5:11). Sharing his joy with others elicits praise.

Immediately after the greeting in his epistle to the church in Ephesus, Paul writes an extended section praising God for all the spiritual blessings that are ours in Christ. In one long, complex Greek sentence that encompasses all of Ephesians 1:3–14, Paul praises God—Father, Son, and Holy Spirit[38]—reflecting Old Testament forms of praise for God's creational power and historical actions in bringing salvation to his people. The structure of the blessing follows the Old Testament in giving reasons for praising God.[39] At the same time, it adopts a uniquely Christian recognition of God as the "Father of our Lord Jesus Christ."[40] God the Father is to be praised for choosing us to be holy and blameless in his sight, for predestining us to be adopted as his sons, for giving us redemption through Jesus' blood, and for letting us know the mystery of his will (Eph 1:3–10). God's main reason for choosing us is that our existence might be to the praise of his glory. Praise

---

36. Marshall, *Gospel of Luke*, 433. Jesus' use of *exomologeō*, could be influenced by its common use in the Septuagint for *yādâ*, which features prominently in psalms of thanksgiving.

37. The *hoti* in Greek parallels the Hebrew *kî* which introduces the motivation clause of a psalm of thanksgiving.

38. For an examination of the Trinitarian content of this passage, see Stott, *Ephesians*, 32–36.

39. Lincoln rightly says that it fits Westermann's category of declarative praise. Lincoln, *Ephesians*, 11.

40. The phrase, "Praise be to the God and Father of our Lord Jesus Christ," may have been a common liturgical expression in the early church, like "Praise be to the LORD, the God of Israel" was in Old Testament times (1 Sam 25:32; 1 Kgs 1:48; 8:15; Pss 40:14; 71:18; 105:48; cf. Luke 1:64). The exact wording of Ephesians 1:3 is also replicated in 2 Corinthians 1:3 and 1 Peter 1:3 (cf. 2 Cor 11:31).

is not only an aspect of our private and corporate worship, but an essential part of who we are as people chosen by God.[41] When people hear that we have been saved, God receives praise. Paul concludes the section by writing that those who have heard and believed the gospel were sealed with the Holy Spirit who guarantees our inheritance in Christ. This again is to the praise of God's glory (Eph 1:12–14).

A similar prayer launches Peter's first epistle. In words that match Paul's in Ephesians 1:3, Peter revels in God's great mercy that provides us with a new birth and a living hope through Jesus' resurrection from the dead. He delights in knowing that an imperishable inheritance is reserved in heaven for those who are protected by God's power through faith and that this inheritance will be revealed in the last time. He is also pleased that his readers share his joy in spite of the difficulties they face in life. The grief and trials they bear prove that their faith is genuine and results "in praise, glory and honor when Jesus Christ is revealed" (1 Pet 1:7; cf. 4:16). It should be noticed that the praise, glory, and honor come to those who, like their Savior, persevere through the cares of this world and enter into the presence of God. Those who praise God for what he has done will be praised by God for what they have done.

Other New Testament passages closely connect the praise God receives for his work in us and the way this becomes apparent as we live it out. Thus, Paul prays that Philippian believers may grow in love so that they can discern what is best and become pure and blameless in Jesus Christ (Phil 1:9–11). When the "fruit of righteousness that comes through Jesus Christ" fills our lives, God receives glory and praise. Viewing things from a slightly different perspective, the author of Hebrews exhorts his readers to continually "offer to God a sacrifice of praise," and informs them that this is performed whenever they do good and share with those who are in need (Heb 13:15–16). James similarly examines the connection between the praise of God and our actions toward people when he decries the sad fact that many use the same tongue to praise God and curse humans (Jas 3:9–10). He exclaims that "this should not be," because our praise of God should be reflected in the words we speak regarding people created in his image. Our words toward others should match what we say we believe about God.

The final book in the Bible paints the most vibrant picture of life in heaven where saints join angels and other creatures that fall down before God in worship. Praise here is described according to the categories developed by Old Testament writers. God is praised for what he has done and

---

41. Lincoln, *Ephesians*, 36.

for who he is. God's attributes are frequently a source for praise, but most clearly in the trisagion found in Revelation 4:8.[42] "Holy, holy, holy is the Lord God Almighty, who was, and is, and is to come." The cry of the living creatures in this passage is reminiscent of the praise uttered by the Seraphim in Isaiah 6:3 when they gathered before God's throne to acknowledge him and voice his attributes. It has also become familiar to Christians throughout the ages who have spoken similar words as part of their liturgy or sang them in praise of the most holy one. When used in this manner, believers on earth join with the heavenly beings to praise God for who he is.

Even though the heavenly realms are separated from the physical world, God's work in the latter is not forgotten. The twenty-four elders praised him for his mighty works in creation (Rev 4:11). Though this undoubtedly recognizes God as the creator of the invisible spiritual world, his power in creating the physical universe is not forgotten. He created "all things"—spiritual and physical—according to his own will. Similarly, the heavenly beings recognize God's power in salvation. The great message of Revelation is that Jesus, the Lamb who is "the Lion of the tribe of Judah, the Root of David, has triumphed" (Rev 5:5). Jesus is exalted in a new song "because you were slain, and with your blood you purchased men for God from every tribe and language and people and nation. You have made them to be a kingdom and priests to serve our God, and they will reign on the earth" (Rev 5:9–10). For his being, his creative power, and for deliverance of his people, God—Father and Son, the one who sits upon the throne and the Lamb—is praised. Just as the psalmists insisted that everything that has breath should praise the Lord, we are told that "every creature in heaven and on earth and under the earth and on the sea, and all that is in them" sang their praise to God (Rev 5:13).

PRAISE AND THE CHURCH

Praise has been a very important part of the worship of God as long as people have experienced him and shared their experience with others. Christians praise God during scheduled worship services and at other times when they feel compelled to share their joy about God so that others can enjoy him too. Those who praise God in a biblical manner focus on their personal and/or communal experience of him. As modeled by the biblical writers, praise should be based upon our concrete experiences of God who

---

42. Trisagion comes from the Greek meaning "thrice holy," thus "holy, holy, holy." It is used for the words of the seraphs in Isaiah 6:3, the living creatures in Revelation 4:8, and the Trisagion Prayer of several liturgical traditions. The Latin equivalent is *tersanctus*.

has demonstrated his power by creating the heaven and earth, worked out salvation in history, and revealed his glorious attributes. Only when we have a real encounter with God can we share that with others so that they can praise him too.

Since the book of Psalms is the main biblical collection of praise, it should be one of our main sources in building up our vocabulary and theology of praise. We should be struck by the breadth of its approach, for not only does it teach us how to respond to God when we are happy and assured of God's presence, it also lets us know that when we are sad or our hearts filled with doubt, we can come to God to praise him for what is past and receive encouragement that praise will be part of our future. Not only does the Psalter provide words for praise regardless of our emotions, it also invites us to approach God formally and informally. This is applied to a congregational setting by Ron Allen who suggests that, "the Psalms give us ample reason for both liturgy *and* spontaneity in our worship services. The very *formal nature* of the Psalms would argue for liturgy, for shape and direction to the church at worship. But the *call* of the Psalms is for excitement, for spontaneity, for delight in God and in His deeds today."[43] What is true for the congregation is true for the individual. The Psalms give us words to pray when we don't know what to say and provide us with models to copy when we face issues that they do not address directly. Whether used for public worship or personal piety, the scope of the Psalms encompasses much of life and incorporates ideas and actions that may be considered opposites.

> The Psalms speak of both social justice and personal transformation; they embody hand-clapping exuberance and profound introspection; they express the prayers of both the exalted and the lowly; they are fully alive in the present, but always point to the future on the basis of the past; they highlight both the extravagance of grace and the joy of faithful obedience; they express a restless yearning for change and a profound gratitude for the inheritance of faith; they protest ritualism but embody the richest expression of ritual prayer.[44]

Is there any excuse for failing to use such a treasure house of material that was designed for the praise of God?

As we consider how to use the Psalms today, we need to remember that they were written to be sung. The words of C. S. Lewis on this regard deserve reflection.

---

43. Allen, *And I Will Praise Him*, 241. His italics.
44. Witvliet, *Biblical Psalms*, xviii.

the Psalms are poems, and poems intended to be sung: not doctrinal treatises, nor even sermons. . . . Most emphatically the Psalms must be read as poems; as lyrics, with all the licences and all the formalities, the hyperboles, the emotional rather than logical connection, which are proper of lyric poetry. They must be read as poems if they are to be understood . . . Otherwise we shall miss what is in them and think we see what is not.[45]

Space limits us from beginning a discussion about reading the psalms as poetry.[46] It is, nevertheless, in the best interest of any reader of the Psalms to learn something of the basics of Hebrew poetry in order to read the book more intelligently. This is particularly important for those who use the Psalms as a source for song lyrics. Words should not be wrested from their context with no regard to their place in the overall structure or meaning of a psalm. A better, though perhaps more difficult, approach than simply plucking some words from a psalm and setting them to music, is to render the biblical poem in modern idiom. Throughout history, biblical poetry has often been rendered so that it could be sung in other languages using non-Jewish musical forms. At times, these renderings remained extremely close to the original wording; at other times, they became much freer translations or paraphrases of the ideas in the Psalms.

From very early times, monks translated the psalms and sang them in Latin. By the eleventh century, the chanting of psalms in Benedictine monasteries had become "the most regular part of the office services," so that, in addition to the other prayers offered and Scripture passages read, the monks chanted all the 150 psalms every week.[47] While few modern congregations will take up Latin chants, the Psalms have been translated into many modern languages so that they can be chanted according to Gregorian and other plainsong styles.[48] Though these forms will not appeal to all, another historical tradition renders biblical poetry in various metrical forms with rhyming words to make them easier to sing.[49] Promoted by Martin Luther and John Calvin, the singing of metrical psalms has had a great influence

---

45. Lewis, *Reflections on the Psalms*, 10.

46. For biblical poetry, see Kugel, *The Idea of Biblical Poetry* and Fokkelman, *Reading Biblical Poetry*. For a standard form critical introduction to the Psalms, see Westermann, *Praise and Lament*. For a more basic introduction to the Psalms and biblical poetry, see Longman, *How to Read the Psalms*.

47. Hiley, *Western Plainchant*, 19–21.

48. For a brief introduction to the way chanting can be used in churches today, see Witvliet, *Biblical Psalms*, 94–101, and the resources provided there.

49. For more on metrical psalms, see Witvliet, *Biblical Psalms*, 106–14, and the resources provided there.

on Lutheran and Reformed churches as well as others. So important was the singing of Psalms to the early colonists that the first book printed in America, *The Bay Psalm Book*, was a collection of metrical Psalms.

An example of a metrical psalm based on Psalm 1:1–2 comes from Sternhold and Hopkins's Psalter from 1562.[50]

> 1 The man is blest that hath not lent
> to wicked men his ear,
> Nor led his life as sinners do,
> nor sat in scorner's chair.
> 2 But in the law of God the Lord
> doth set his whole delight,
> And in the same doth exercise
> himself both day and night.

New rhythmic versions of the Psalms continue to be written. Some churches sing them exclusively in corporate worship as the only songs that are inspired.[51] Other groups, particularly from Reformed and Presbyterian traditions, combine the use of the metrical psalms and other songs in worship. Many believers have never sung metrical Psalms. This may be because it is not part of their tradition. It may also be that metrical psalms are considered difficult to sing, written in archaic language, or considered too dull or monotonous.

Whatever reasons one may give for not singing psalms, it remains true that psalm singing connects worshippers to God through God-inspired words and with members of the church who have used them throughout history. It also reminds us that the Psalms, as poetry, were written to arouse our emotions, direct our wills, and stimulate our imaginations.[52] Music does this in a way that surpasses the mere reading of a text, even a poetic text. Since psalms were composed for doxology, we should use them in the way that best enables us to praise God, and in many cases, this will be through song.

There are two basic settings in which we can sing the psalms as prayed poetry: public and private worship. First, since many of the psalms were written for congregational use, we can use them in a congregational setting.[53] Communal laments, communal songs of thanksgiving, and commu-

---

50. Sternhold, Hopkins et al., *The Whole Booke of Psalmes*.

51. The Council of Laodicea (363–364) forbade psalms written by private individuals to be used in the church.

52. Longman, *How to Read the Psalms*, 75.

53. Anderson's statement that the Psalter is referred to as "the hymnbook of the second temple" and "the prayer book of the synagogue" reminds us that since it was originally compiled for congregational use, it should be used for congregations today.

nal songs of praise can greatly enhance our worship. They can also be read as a call to worship by a member of the congregation, or recited responsively or in unison by a small group or entire congregation. Psalms can provide texts for sermons. If preached with sensitivity to the original setting and the needs of the congregation, the Psalms can come alive for a new generation of believers who want to understand and respond to God's ancient revelation and praise him for what he has done in the past, continues to do, and will complete when he fully establishes his kingdom.

Second, we can use the psalms in private worship. Many psalms were clearly written for personal reflection, confession, thanksgiving, and praise. By listening to the psalms and praying them, we can learn how to praise God more effectively and pray with more meaning. But even though the psalms can be used in private worship, we should not think of them as "individualistic poems such as a modern person might compose to express personal thoughts and feelings. Rather, the psalms show that the individual finds his or her identity and vocation in the community that God has created."[54] Without connection to God's people, the individual cannot properly apply the psalms to his or her own situation. Without the community, the individual has no one to invite to join in the praise the Psalms were written to elicit.

Another aspect of how the Psalms were used in ancient worship that should affect their use today pertains to their being written to be accompanied by various instruments. The use of many instruments in Israel's worship should encourage us that we can use many kinds of instruments when we worship God today. This has not always been appreciated. Throughout the ages, some Jewish synagogues and not a few Christian churches have refused to use musical instruments for public worship. Some have argued that, even though instruments were used in Israel's temple, the New Testament does not warrant their use in the church. Some Christians thus only sing songs to God without accompaniment. Even so, the door opened in the Old Testament for using musical instruments was not shut by any New Testament author. Indeed, the frequent command in the Psalms to make music on various instruments firmly closes the door on anyone who rejects their use.

Finally, we should note that the Psalms focus on God: the great Creator of the universe, the one who redeemed Israel from captivity, the one who rules as king over the nations, the one who is magnificent in his being. The Psalms were designed to help Israel consider the person of God and his actions in creation and in history so that they could respond to him with praise. In the same way, the Psalms provide us with an excellent vehicle for

---

Anderson, *Out of the Depths*, 9.
54. Anderson, *Out of the Depths*, 6.

focusing upon God and his mighty acts so that we too can praise him. As we read them, we join the saints of the ages who rejoiced when they considered the great things he has done. We can also join those who are sorrowful by crying out to God in faith that he will deliver us in the same way he has delivered his people in the past. This will be the focus of our next chapter.

9

Worship and Lament[1]

Life does not consist of all warm, sunny days and peaceful ease. At times, we are confronted with difficulties that cause us to cry out in pain or scream that life is unfair. Many things—the loss of a spouse through death, divorce, or dementia, inability to find a marriage partner or conceive a child, failure to find or keep a job, physical pain, psychological or sexual abuse, depression, etc.—rob us of the joy we desire. Equally, they impact our worship of God—particularly if we reduce worship to praise that reflects a joyful heart. But worship is not merely a celebration of good times. It consists of bowing down to God in submission, fearing him for his majesty and power, and serving him in our daily lives. And since life is filled with tough times, it is imperative that we learn how to worship God through them. Thankfully, the Bible tells us stories of people who called out to God in their need and preserves literary forms designed to bring our laments to God when times are difficult.

The Bible nowhere hides the reality that life can be difficult. Adam's sin forced his removal from the blissful garden to face an existence of painful, sweaty toil in order to produce food to eat. His son Cain, after killing his brother, was driven from the land and forced to wander from place to place while the ground refused to yield its crops to him. But trouble is not always the result of one's sin. Righteous Noah was required to build an ark in order to rescue his family and the animals of the world from the depravity of others. Abraham and Sarah lived a nomadic existence and felt the pain

---

1. A different version of this chapter was published as "Worshipping God through Suffering," *Mission Round Table* 12, no. 3 (September–December 2017): 35–39.

and shame of not being able to bear a son until their old age. Their grandson Jacob refused to be comforted when he thought his son Joseph had died. Hannah's inability to bear a child, compounded by the provocation of her rival, prompted her to cry out that God might grant her a son. King David experienced the sting of sin when his adultery with Bathsheba was uncovered and the child she bore died despite his fervent prayers. Many of the writing prophets were caught up in the sin of their people to the extent that they were carried off into exile.

These Old Testament stories are a small sample of the resources the Bible gives to help people facing life's difficulties. They are supplemented by numerous New Testament accounts of broken people seeking Jesus for healing and truth. In the Gospels, Acts, and the Epistles, we read of the apostles, whose testimony that Jesus was the Christ caused them to face pressures that were so far beyond their ability to cope that they despaired of life (2 Cor 1:8; cf. Rom 9:2). Through this, they learned not to rely upon themselves but upon the God who answered both their prayers and the prayers of the churches they founded.

Indeed, Jesus, the "man of sorrows" (Isa 53:3), faced rejection throughout his earthly ministry and ultimately suffered the cruelest of deaths after his agonizing vigil in the Garden of Gethsemane (Mark 14:34). As he hung on the cross, Jesus cried out to the Father with words drawn from one of the lament psalms: "*Eloi, Eloi, lama sabachthani?* . . . My God, my God, why have you forsaken me?" (Matt 27:46; Mark 15:34; cf. Ps 22:1). His final words were likewise drawn from a psalm of lament: "Father, into your hands I commit my spirit" (Luke 23:46; cf. Ps 31:5). The hour in which Jesus performed his greatest act of worship was marked by sorrow, suffering, and prayers of lament.

That both testaments acknowledge that people face pain and distress[2] and that they can bring them before God in open worship contrasts greatly with the way many Christians face grief and disappointment today. The attitude that followers of Jesus should only express joy and praise is deceptive, as it contradicts our personal experience of pain and the biblical testimony of how people (including Jesus) responded to their troubles. As Brueggemann has pointed out about the modern church, the "serious religious use of the lament psalms has been minimal because we have believed that faith does not mean to acknowledge and embrace negativity."[3] What is true about the psalms of lament is true about the use of any form of lament in worship.

---

2. For an argument that distress is a dominant motif in Psalms, see Johnston, "The Psalms and Distress," 63–84.

3. Brueggemann, *The Message of the Psalms*, 52.

Our reticence to use them may stem from an inordinate influence by a success-driven and forward-looking culture that thinks all negatives can and should be overcome.[4] It may also be due to our misunderstanding of what God provides for us in Christ. The reality of pain, shame, and grief does not go away in this life. For this reason, this chapter draws upon biblical teaching about the place of lament in worship in order to help individuals and churches become aware of and begin to draw upon these resources when they encounter pain, loss, or disappointment.

PSALMS OF LAMENT

Undoubtedly, the most accessible biblical resource for those facing difficulties is the psalms of lament.[5] The psalmists experienced all the seasons of life. Whether they faced joy or grief, they recognized that the proper response is to turn to God, let him know how they felt, and ask him to help them through. Although suffering was sometimes the result of personal or communal sin, the psalmists readily admitted that life can be extremely difficult and that it is proper for believers to bring their pain, confusion, and frustration to God. The psalms of lament provide models of the right way to complain to God. Around sixty of the 150 psalms in the total collection are laments, making it the largest grouping of psalms by genre.[6] Moberly states,

> Such predominance of laments at the very heart of Israel's prayers means that the problems that give rise to lament are not something marginal or unusual but rather are central to the life of faith. . . . Moreover they show that the experience of anguish and puzzlement in the life of faith is not a sign of deficient faith, something to be outgrown or put behind one, but rather is intrinsic to the very nature of faith.[7]

It is important for worshippers to appreciate that, "The lament itself is a form of worship."[8]

---

4. Brueggemann, *The Message of the Psalms*, 53.

5. In addition to the lament psalms, other biblical examples of lament include various passages in Job (especially 29–31), Jeremiah (11:18—12:6; 15:10–21; 17:12–18; 18:18–23; 20:7–18), Lamentations, and Habakkuk (1:2–4).

6. Bernhard Anderson lists forty-eight individual laments, thirteen communal laments (with two more questionable), and several psalms of mixed genre that include lament. Anderson, *Out of the Depths*, 219–23.

7. Moberly, "Lament," *NIDOTTE*, 4:879.

8. Murphy, "The Psalms and Worship," 25. See also Jinkins, *In the House of the Lord*, 33.

From an emotional point of view, the psalms of lament are the opposite of a hymn of praise, as they are experienced as "psalms in a minor key" that provide words for raising complaints and petitions to God.[9] Though commonly divided into individual and corporate psalms of lament, there is an additional distinction in this genre. Some of these songs locate the source of difficulty in one's circumstances and seek God's deliverance, while others identify God as the one who brings the trouble and entreat him to withhold his hand. No matter what circumstances prompted their composition, these psalms are primarily intended to help people present their needs to God, ask him to resolve their difficulties, and bring them back to praise.

Scholars have identified a number of distinguishing characteristics of these psalms. Although none of the following elements is present in every psalm of lament, and they may come in a different order, most of them will be identifiable.

1. Address to God (invocation).

2. A petition to God for help. This may include a cry for help taking the form, "How long . . ." or "How long, O Lord . . ." (Pss 6:3; 13:1-2; 35:17; 74:10; 79:5; 80:4; 89:46; 90:13; 94:3).

3. A description of suffering (complaints). This is the main part of the psalm that states the psalmist's motivation for prayer. Reference is often made of the activities of three subjects: the psalmist (or the people), the psalmist's foes, and God ("thou" or "you"). Various psalms emphasize one of these subjects over the others.

4. A confession of sin or assertion of innocence. This depends upon whether the psalmist believed he was suffering due to his own sin or in spite of his innocence.

5. A curse on one's enemies. Also known as imprecation.

6. A statement of confidence in God that is frequently based upon the psalmist's experience of God's deliverance in the past.

7. A statement that praise or blessing will follow deliverance.

The different parts of the psalms of lament help us identify their genre and give us an entry as we use them in our personal and corporate worship. They are primarily prayers that lead us from lament to praise. Since God understands our difficulties, we entreat him to intervene. By praying lament

---

9. Though generally categorized as psalms of lament, some scholars refer to them as psalms of complaint or psalms of petition. They can also be categorized as psalms of prayer. See Broyles, "Lament," 386–87. Since all these motifs are present in some but not all psalms of the genre, the use of one label does not negate the importance of the others.

psalms, we are directed to identify the source of pain and to look beyond it, in expectation that God will restore us and lead us to praise him in the future. These psalms become models to follow, guides that lead us from pain to praise, from fear to faith. Indeed, as the believing community acknowledges that life is fraught with danger and disorder, these prayers become *"an act of bold faith."*[10] No matter what brings disorder and difficulty, these prayers give us the opportunity to express tremendous confidence in the God who cares enough to see us through so that we can praise him again. This return to praise anchors the laments in the context of communal worship, for it is only in the presence of others that we can rightly praise God. Though most modern Christian worship is bereft of lamentation, we would benefit from its rediscovery.

Psalms of lament acknowledge that pain and difficulties come from many sources. Enemies, whether military or political, threaten (Pss 13:2; 22:6–8, 12–13, 16–18, 20–21; 44:10–16), rulers abuse their authority (Ps 58:1–2), illness weakens, and death seems imminent (Pss 38; 41; 88). Even so, lament psalms rarely identify the enemies or illnesses in any detail. In this, they contrast greatly from laments found in the historical books of the Bible that expressly state the circumstances in which they were uttered (e.g., Josh 7:7–9; Judg 21:3). This lack of specificity aids modern worshippers who can adopt the psalms to suit the circumstances they face as they bring them to God in prayer.

The psalms of lament, particularly the communal laments, also help by showing us that the psalmists frequently experienced God's absence and expressed their pain and confusion because they felt God had rejected (Pss 43:2; 44:9), abandoned (Lam 2:7), or forgotten (Ps 42:9) them. At times, it seems that he had hidden his face (Pss 13:1; 44:24) or fallen asleep (Ps 44:23). God's perceived failure to help prompts them to ask the questions "Why?" and "How long?" "Why, O Lord, do you stand far off? Why do you hide yourself in times of trouble?" (Ps 10:1). "Why have you rejected us forever, O God? Why does your anger smolder against the sheep of your pasture?" (Ps 74:1). By asking "Why?" the psalmist demonstrates his feelings that God is in some way responsible for the trouble. Could it be that God does not care about his plight? Is he impotent to deal with the problem? Or is he punishing the lamenter for some reason?

A similar thing happens when the psalmist asks "How long?" The difference is that this question "implies distress of some duration."[11] The problem that produced the difficulties just keeps going on and on. Despite the

---

10. Brueggemann, *The Message of the Psalms*, 52. His italics.
11. Westermann, *Praise and Lament*, 177.

passing of time, it seems that God will do nothing to deal with the problems his people face. "How long, O Lord? Will you forget me forever? How long will you hide your face from me? How long must I wrestle with my thoughts and every day have sorrow in my heart? How long will my enemy triumph over me?" (Ps 13:1–2). When trouble and grief continue without end, it is imperative that one confesses his feelings of abandonment and unease to God and then expresses his trust that, despite his circumstances or feelings, God will surely intervene (Ps 13:5–6).

The place of lament in the Psalter indicates that God is interested in our pain as much as he is in our joy. This should give us hope as we approach him for help during times of difficulty. Even more, it should encourage us that even as God has helped people in the past, he will help us. The words written by the psalmists encourage us that we too can dare to approach God in anger, fear, and doubt because that is how we feel even if it does not reflect our reasoned theological beliefs. One who comes to God in grief or pain does not have to pretend everything is all right or come up with the "right words" that God will accept. Rather, they can trust God to accept their feelings even when they don't know what to say. And even though we may not receive a speedy answer to our questions, the fact that we address God as the one who hears and answers indicates that the light of faith has already begun to penetrate the clouds of despair.

Simply praying a psalm of lament does not ensure an instant solution to all problems so that God's people will only experience praise. Those who have lost a loved one cannot, simply by praying, bring them back or be rid of the grief or guilt that will forever pursue them. Raising a lament to God does not release a person experiencing the early stages of Alzheimer's from facing a future of fear and forgetfulness. A woman who cries, "How long, O Lord?" as she agonizes over an abusive relationship may not be instantly freed from her assailant. It is, therefore, essential that we never consider laments psalms to be magical formulas that ensure praise will immediately fill the lives of those who pray them. As the crisis that leads to the lament may last for a long period of time before it is resolved, we may need to pray the psalms of lament repeatedly as we face our trials.[12] But as the form of biblical lament indicates, those in trouble need to be steered in the direction of hope. God hears our prayers, cares about our situation, and will come to our aid. Since God will certainly intervene, we can be sure that in time praise will follow.

---

12. Witvliet, *Worship Seeking Understanding*, 46–47.

LAMENT AND THE CHURCH

Lament is rarely given a substantial place in the church, as worship is usually equated with joy and celebration. Expressions of pain, fear, or grief are regularly viewed as symptoms of unbelief or treated as embarrassing abnormalities that should be politely ignored. Strangely, this sidelining of the one hurting is similarly present in many modern funerals that have replaced ministry to the grieving and proclaiming the gospel message that death has been overcome in Jesus Christ with a simple recounting of what made the deceased special. This situation is unacceptable because it marginalizes suffering and ignores a great body of biblical material that was written to help people through difficult times.[13] When we leave no room for lament in our worship, we may well give the impression that people struggling with grief, trauma, and abandonment are either substandard Christians or that they have been left to plough through their difficulties on their own.

Few modern Christians have experienced relief from grief or pain through a liturgical use of biblical lament. The closest that most Christians come to experiencing relief from grief or pain through lament is found in prayers of confession and absolution. Positively, these prayers provide us with release from the guilt of sin and enable us to praise God for his goodness. While some in the congregation may simply mouth the words and fail to experience any change, the prayers are designed to lead us from despair to joy as we acknowledge that we have sinned against God and receive assurance that he has pardoned us through Jesus Christ. In many settings, the prayer of absolution is followed by a hymn of praise to emphasize the joy that one should feel after being forgiven.

Although the words used in these prayers are often taken from the New Testament, they reflect themes that reverberate throughout the psalms but are most closely related to the seven psalms of penitence that have been recognized from the early Christian centuries—Psalms 6; 32; 38; 51; 102; 130; and 143.[14] Although the early church often reserved these psalms for those who were sick or dying, they quickly became an integral part of personal piety as individuals sought deliverance from sin and guilt. Modern Christians who are burdened by sin can similarly respond by adopting this ancient biblical pattern. If one of these psalms was read and commented on during confession, the congregation could more intelligently adopt the words of the lament while bringing their needs to God. Similarly, a sermon

---

13. Verhey, *Reading the Bible in the Strange World of Medicine*, 123.

14. Of these, Psalm 32 is usually categorized as a psalm of thanksgiving rather than a psalm of lament. According to Broyles, only Psalms 32; 51; and 130 are chiefly concerned with sin and forgiveness. Broyles, "Lament," 389.

based on one of these psalms could help a congregation understand its purpose in ancient Israel and how to use it today when confessing sins.

In addition to serving as an aid in confession, modern worshippers can use psalms of lament in other ways. Churches from many traditions recognize that since God is the great physician, prayers for the sick can be meaningfully incorporated into worship. Individuals who are ailing can come forward so that hands can be laid on them and prayer offered for their healing. As many lament psalms were written for people experiencing physical illness, there is great pastoral value in making them part of our prayers. Not only do they provide the suffering with words to express their feelings and fears to God in faith, they also point them to the hope that God will hear their prayer, intervene for them, and give them reason to praise his name again. Learned in public worship, these inspired words can be taken home so that a person can address God again when praying for herself or someone else.

But psalms of lament should not merely be added to the prayers for the sick. To limit the invitation for prayer to those with physical ailments implies that suffering from other problems is less significant. Along with Jesus, we should welcome everyone in need to come for prayer just as he embraced the world of his day, saying "Come to me, all you who are weary and burdened, and I will give you rest" (Matt 11:28). The weary, the burdened, the abused, the ignored, the unemployed, all need Jesus and all can be strengthened when they pray the psalms of lament, searching for the hope that God gives as an integral part of the prayers.

Psalms that can be prayed for the sick include Psalms 20; 38; and 41. One should be careful in the use of these psalms as some of them relate illness to personal sin. Such a psalm should be used in a case where sin is present but perhaps exchanged for another when sin is not an issue. Another caution in the use of these psalms is that the words uttered should never be considered a magical formula for physical healing. Long ago, Jewish Rabbis warned that the Torah and Psalms were for spiritual healing and that those who used them for physical healing were guilty of sorcery and should be considered heretics.[15] While they may overstate the case, their warning should be heeded to keep us from descending into sub-Christian practice.

Reaching beyond the individual, when a church, nation, or the world is facing a crisis of some sort, services of lament are in order. People throughout the world suffer for a wide variety of reasons—natural or manmade. Earthquakes, typhoons, tsunamis, wildfires, volcanic eruptions, and pandemics strike without regard for one's religious orientation. The same

---

15. *Shevuot* 15b; Rambam, *Hilchot Avodat Kochavim* 11.12.

is true when it comes to war, social disorder, and ethnic strife. At the same time, Christians can be singled out for direct attack by governments and other members of society so that their continued existence in some countries is threatened. When such disasters hit, it is only right to call out to God, "Why?" When evil is constantly perpetrated, how can one not ask the judge of heaven, "How long?" and then plead that he put them in their place and destroy their works? When trouble or disaster hits a large body of believers, the appropriate response is to bring a corporate lament to God, whether during the main weekly service of the church or a special service.

Services of lament are particularly needed for individuals and groups facing severe difficulties who find it impossible to take part in a service of praise as it conflicts with their feelings and experience. At such times, bringing heartache and confusion to God may be the only thing that makes worship possible. Joining their brothers and sisters in lament gives sufferers an opportunity to take hold of the faith of others who are grieving along with them or have grieved in the past. When the group has worked through the time of trouble by bringing it to the Lord of all mercy and receiving his answers, they find it possible to return to God with words of praise.

The use of lament in worship need not be reserved for exceptional times of tragedy. It can, and arguably should, become part of our regular worship of God as we traverse the seasons of the year. One of the best ways to do this is to integrate lament into the celebration of the Christian Year. As this cycle of feasts developed in early church history, two penitential seasons—Advent and Lent—took prominent place. Sadly, for many churches today, the penitential longing of Advent and Lent has been eclipsed by the glory of Christmas and Easter (and often obliterated by the glitter of commercialism). Even so, our desire to experience the joy of Christ's birth and resurrection should not deprive us of time to consider the wonder of the incarnation that brought on our Savior's suffering. By becoming man, the Creator faced obscurity, the Almighty experienced rejection and ridicule, the Righteous One endured temptation without giving in to sin, the eternal Lord died for the sins of others. These sober realities require somber reflection. As the seasons of Advent and Lent were designed to give us time to consider these themes, we should avail ourselves of this opportunity.

This does not mean that the seasons should only focus on fasting and solemn thoughts. Advent and Lent, while not designed to follow the structure of the psalms of lament, work in a similar direction since they begin by focusing on sin, suffering, and weakness, and end with celebrations of hope and joy on Christmas and Easter. Like the laments, both seasons are imbued with eschatological hope. As the Old Testament saints remembered God's past salvation while awaiting deliverance from their times of trouble, those who celebrate Christmas and Easter remember what God accomplished through the first Advent of Jesus as they await the second Advent when Christ will fully establish his kingdom, judge the world of sin, and allow us to experience the resurrection life in its fullness.

A church can introduce lament into Advent services in several ways. One of the easiest is to plan a service around Psalm 80, which has been associated with Advent and makes use of vineyard metaphors that are echoed in John 15:1–7.[16] In the psalm, and throughout the Old Testament, the vine is used to symbolize Israel, particularly as it comes under judgment for failing to produce good fruit (cf. Isa 5:1–7; Jer 2:21; Ezek 15:1–8). In contrast to the picture of Israel as a corrupt vine, the Johannine image presents Jesus as the *true* vine who fulfills his calling by bearing good fruit for his Father. Believers in Jesus, as the branches that are grafted into the vine, bear good fruit because his Spirit works through them. As part of our Advent worship, Psalm 80 reminds us that we, like Israel, need to call on the Lord God Almighty to "Make your face shine upon us, that we may be saved" (Ps 80:7, 19). Even though we deserve to be trampled like the vine in the psalm, we can be sure that salvation comes to us through Jesus, "the son of man you have raised up for yourself" (Ps 80:17). The lament helps us acknowledge our sin and the one who brings forgiveness and gives us the hope to move forward as people who are wholly restored in Jesus.

Lent was long held to be a season to contemplate one's mortality in the light of the temptations, suffering, and death of Christ. During this period, prayers of penitence accompany fasting as people express sorrow for sin and strive to be more like Jesus. Christians who have never fasted during Lent can discover that the discipline forces them to acknowledge their physical and spiritual weakness and shows them their need for God's mercy and strength. Churches can provide instruction for those who have never observed Lent and correct mistaken ideas about what the fast is for, so that everyone can benefit from the season. At the end of Lent, congregations can discover that Good Friday may be the most fitting day of the year for lamentation as it memorializes Jesus' death. Services held on that day should be solemn and thoughtful as the crucifixion is recalled. In recent years, many churches have discovered that a Tenebrae Service, with its series of readings and hymns that concludes in darkness, can be a moving way to worship God through lament rather than praise.

---

16. The Revised Common Lectionary includes Psalm 80 in the Advent readings for all three years of the lectionary cycle. However, the Lectionary shortens the reading so that much of the lament is omitted. Isaiah 64:1–9, the only other lament text found in the Advent readings of the Revised Common Lectionary, is similarly shortened.

Restoring lament to our worship clearly benefits the church in numerous ways. When we acknowledge that life is not always joyful, lament allows us to move through the difficult times in God's presence. This is true whether the difficulty is the result of a natural disaster, traumatic experience, or chronic illness. The inclusion of lament may similarly make it possible for those who have felt marginalized by their problems to worship in a new way. It can help us come to a new perspective about sin and the hope we have that Christ has sufficiently dealt with it on the cross. As we follow the pattern set out in the psalms of lament, we learn that we can boldly bring all our troubles before the Lord who will hear us, intervene for us, and give us the hope that we will praise him again in this world and be freed from trouble in the next.

10

Worship and Sacrifice

Few Christians have ever witnessed an animal sacrifice. Neither sheep nor goats are ever slaughtered during our worship services. We have no priests who burn flesh, blood, and fat so that God can forgive sin and restore our right standing before him and the community. The Bible's repeated references to sacrifice frequently comes across as baffling, if not repugnant, so that most of us simply ignore it as irrelevant to our world. Even so, God had reasons for establishing the sacrificial system that played such an important part in Israel's worship. Indeed, as we will see, a firm grasp of the theology behind the Old Testament sacrificial system is essential if we are to understand what Jesus did to make ongoing sacrifices unnecessary. This chapter will thus examine biblical sacrifice to show us what it accomplished in the history of Israel and the church. We will also look at New Testament teaching about sacrifice in general and in the atoning work of Jesus.

Sacrifices have been part of the religious experience of people from the beginning. In the Old Testament, sacrifices included animals (or their parts, such as blood and fat), grains (whether whole, ground into flour, or mixed with other substances), and liquids (usually wine), and could be presented as sin and guilt offerings or shared as fellowship meals. The earliest offerings mentioned in the Old Testament were those brought by Cain and Abel.[1] Upon emerging from the ark, Noah presented burnt offerings

---

1. Contrary to a common interpretation, it is unlikely that Cain's offering was rejected for not including blood. The Hebrew word for the gifts the brothers brought to God usually denotes grain offerings. Cain's offering was probably rejected due to his attitude and the fact that he only brought *some* rather than the *firstfruits* of his produce. This is contrasted with his brother who brought the best he could bring—the

to the Lord. Abram built a series of altars to Yahweh as he moved about Canaan. Though it mentions their sacrifices, the Old Testament is silent about how these worshippers knew that they should bring gifts to God or in what way. Neither does it inform us how people who worshipped other deities determined to bring them gifts in a similar fashion. Though scholars have tried to establish connections between the sacrificial terminology and practices of Israel and the surrounding nations, their conclusions often run in different directions.[2] Our path will be to illuminate what the Bible says about the sacrifices made to Yahweh by his people Israel.

GENERAL CONCEPTS ABOUT SACRIFICE

In English, the terms offering and sacrifice are often used interchangeably. It should be recognized, however, that offering is the broader term that carries the general sense of a gift while sacrifice suggests a particular kind of offering that is presented to a deity. This understanding of the words is similar to their use in biblical Hebrew, though the Old Testament term for sacrifice (*zebaḥ*) is much narrower, as it is almost always equated with what is frequently called the peace offering. All other "sacrifices" are termed offerings (*qorbān*). Even so, the term sacrifice can be loosely applied to all the offerings that the Israelites brought to God.

Atonement

One of the most important concepts pertaining to Old Testament sacrifices is that they atone for sins. Though specifically associated with the sacrifices performed on the Day of Atonement, most of the biblical sacrifices are said to "make atonement" for sin.[3] The English word points to an "at one(ment)," a concept that highlights what is accomplished at the end of the process—sinners are restored to communion with God and the community. Scholars debate the basic meaning of the Hebrew word for atonement (*kpr*), but agree that it focuses on the *process* by which atonement is made, not its end result. Those who trace it to an Arabic root that means "to cover" (*kafara*),

---

fatty portions from the firstborn of his flocks. See Waltke, "Cain and his Offering."

2. See Rowley, *Worship in Ancient Israel*, 111–12 and the bibliographic information footnoted there for different approaches to the beginnings of sacrifice and its original significance.

3. Thus, the burnt offering (Lev 1:4), the sin offering (Lev 4:20), the peace offering (Lev 4:26), and the guilt offering (Lev 6:7) are said to make atonement. Grain offerings, when accompanying other sacrifices, are also said to atone (Lev 14:19–20).

understand that the blood of the sacrifice covers sin so that God does not see it.[4] If it derived from an Akkadian root meaning "to wipe away" (*kuppuru*), atonement purges people or things of sin so that God can associate with them. This interpretation is best supported by the fact that atonement is made for the tabernacle and its furnishings, which are cleansed of the sin they have accumulated over time. The word can also be understood as "to ransom by substitution" based on the cognate Hebrew noun *kōper*, which regularly means "ransom." According to this interpretation, the animal sacrificed is a ransom for the life of the person who deserved to die for his sin.

Whatever the source of the word, it seems that the Israelites understood atonement both in the sense of purifying things and functioning as a ransom for people.[5] But no matter how they would have understood the process of atonement, it is clear they applied it to a wide range of situations. As Wenham summarizes Kiuchi's conclusions, atonement "is a broad idea involving several subsidiary ones."

> Altars and priests are 'sanctified' (Ex. 29:33, 36, 37) i.e., made fit to officiate in worship. 'Lepers' and others are cleansed (Lv. 12:7, 8; 14:20). Sinners are forgiven (Lv. 4:20) and guilt is carried (Lv. 10:17). Sin and uncleanness lead a person from the realm of life into the realm of death. Sacrifice stops this process, indeed reverses it. It gives life to those doomed to die.[6]

All atoning sacrifices dealt with sin and uncleanness. Whereas sin upset the fellowship God desired to have with people and kindled his wrath, sacrifice restored the relationship. But it was essential to bring the sacrifices God assigned in line with the design he communicated. For God to accept an offering, the ritual needed to be performed in the right way by the right person—a priest. For atonement to be made, blood needed to be spilt, the life of a creature had to be given for the sinner (Lev 17:11).

A Pleasing Aroma

In addition to making atonement, sacrifices are often said to be received by Yahweh as a "pleasing aroma." While the Bible never explains how the Lord might find the smell of burning flesh to be pleasant, the term is used to refer

---

4. Though this interpretation finds support in the fact that the cover of the ark is called the *kappōret*, the verb never means "cover" in the Old Testament.

5. Wenham, *Leviticus*, 28. For a deeper examination of the word, see Averbeck, "כָּפַר," 689–710.

6. Wenham, "The Theology of Old Testament Sacrifice," 81–82, summarizing Kiuchi, *The Purification Offering*, 87–109.

to a wide range of sacrifices, some of which may not have been burned on the altar.[7] That the Lord accepts a sacrifice as a pleasing aroma probably means that he accepts the individual who sacrifices along with the sacrifice presented. As the word translated "pleasing" can be rendered "quieting" or "soothing," it can be argued that sacrifice appeases God's wrath.[8] This seems to be the point in Genesis 8:21:

> The LORD smelled the pleasing aroma and said in his heart: "Never again will I curse the ground because of man, even though every inclination of his heart is evil from childhood. And never again will I destroy all living creatures, as I have done."

By presenting a burnt offering, Noah appeased God's wrath. Though human wickedness had precipitated the flood (Gen 6:5), God would not destroy all living creatures again (Gen 8:21). God's anger was soothed by what amounts to a propitiatory sacrifice so that he does not treat sinners as they deserve. When he receives the pleasing aroma of sacrifice, he forgives sin. However, God's heart is not turned by the mere performance of ritual. As he warned Israel when giving them the law, if they refused to listen to his instructions, he would "take no delight in the pleasing aroma of your offerings" (Lev 26:31) and punish them by sending them into exile (Lev 26:32–33).

Parties Involved in Sacrifice

Three parties were involved in Old Testament sacrifices—God, the worshipper(s), and the priest(s). From the time the first couple sinned, God demonstrated his grace to sinners by seeking them out and making it possible for their fellowship with him to be restored. The sacrificial system given through Moses was thus an expression of God's grace to his covenant community by which they could be reconciled to a holy God after becoming defiled by personal or societal sins. By revealing his will about the way sacrifices could be offered, God showed that he was approachable and that he desired to be their God. And lest people think that the mere performance of some rituals would magically secure his pardon, God informed them that reconciliation could not happen without his acceptance of the rituals and personal offer of forgiveness. The stress on properly offering the required

---

7. Sacrifices said to be a pleasing aroma include the burnt offering (Exod 29:18), the peace offering (Lev 3:5), and the grain offering (Lev 2:2). It is also used in connection with a drink offering or libation (Num 15:7).

8. This is rejected by Milgrom, *Leviticus 1–16*, 162. Nevertheless, he admits that the idea may be present in Genesis 8:21 and Leviticus 26:31 and provides some grammatical and historical support for the interpretation.

sacrifices should not detract from the reality that God, being holy, is not as interested in sacrifice as he is in having his people obey his will (1 Sam 15:13–22; Jer 7:21–28). Whereas sin defiles a person, sacrifice makes God's people holy.

The second essential party in sacrifice was the worshipper—the person who had sinned or become unclean. To be restored to God and/or others, the worshipper was required to bring an offering to God, trusting that God would receive him. Whether acting as his own priest or enlisting the help of the Aaronic priests, he would lay his hand upon the animal to be sacrificed and then slay it before having all or part of it burned upon an altar. Laying hands on the sacrifice apparently signifies that the death of the animal represents the death the worshipper deserves due to his sin or that his sin is transferred to the animal that bears it in his place.

The priest served as a mediator to bring the worshipper's offering to God. In patriarchal times, a family head would serve as priest for his household. After the giving of the Mosaic law, only Aaronic priests were permitted to offer up the blood of the sacrifice at the altar in the tabernacle, though others might bring peace offerings and other sacrifices to solitary altars located in different parts of the land. After the priest sprinkled blood on the altar and burned all or part of the offering as required by the law, God would accept what was presented and forgive the person's sin.

Sacrifice and Covenantal Relationship

The involvement of the various parties in the offering of sacrifices reveals the Old Testament view that sacrifice was an integral part of Israel's covenantal relationship with Yahweh. The link between covenant and sacrifice can be traced to the time of Noah when he built an altar and presented "some of all the clean animals and clean birds" as a burnt offering (Gen 8:20). Immediately thereafter, God made a covenant with Noah, his descendants, and every living creature that was with him and provided the rainbow as the sign of his promise.[9]

The connection between covenant and sacrifice is repeated in the story of Abraham. Right after God called him (Gen 12:1–3), Abraham left his father's home for Canaan where he built a series of altars to Yahweh. Although he is never explicitly said to sacrifice on the altars, it can be surmised that he did so. The connection between covenant and sacrifice was solidified at the time God promised to give Abraham a son from his own body and repeated

---

9. While the covenant was promised in Genesis 6:18, it was not put into effect until Genesis 9:9–17.

his promise to give him the whole land of Canaan (Gen 15:1–20). Abraham was instructed to bring a number of animals, split them in two, lay them out on the ground with the halves opposite each other, and protect them from birds of prey. While Abraham lay in a trance, "a smoking firepot with a blazing torch" passed through the pieces as the Lord accepted the offering (Gen 15:17). That the act of dividing the animals for a sacrifice is clearly tied to the covenant rite is reflected in the Hebrew idiom for covenant making—to *cut* a covenant. As the two parties come together, the dismembered animals remind them that they should suffer the same fate if they break the covenant. The sacrifice is the concluding act that binds the members of the covenant.

As God's covenant with Abraham included his descendants, it laid the foundations upon which the Sinaitic covenant was built. While gathered at Mt. Sinai, Israel received the Ten Commandments and other stipulations of the covenant. These included the sacrificial rites Israel was required to perform, not as a means of entering, but of maintaining covenant relationship with God. The fact that sacrifices could not be separated from God's covenant in Old Testament religion distinguished it from all the other ancient Near Eastern religions.[10]

Sacrifice and Holiness

Many Christians are confused by the details of the sacrifices described in Leviticus. While this is understandable, it is important to realize that the author of the book is more interested that people lived holy lives than in the details of ritual.[11] Words like "holy" (*qādôš*) and "clean" (*ṭāhôr*), and their opposites, "unclean" (*ṭāmēʾ*) and "profane" (*ḥillēl*) fill the book, forming a kind of grid through which all people and things can be evaluated. Since a person's standing as holy, clean, unclean, or profane effects his relationship with God and his need to present sacrifices, a study of these concepts will demonstrate not only how they relate to one another, but also what the sacrificial system is designed to deal with.[12]

---

10. Kraus, *Worship in Israel*, 122.

11. Numerous Old Testament theologians have recognized that holiness is the most important theme in Leviticus. See Longman and Dillard, *Introduction*, 84; Wenham, *Leviticus*, 18. R. K. Harrison identifies it as one of two central themes of the book along with "separation from what was unclean." Harrison, *Numbers*, 2.

12. The following discussion is indebted to Wenham's explanation in *Leviticus*, 18–25.

From the perspective of Leviticus, the normal state of a person is clean. That is, when a priest pronounces a person cured of a skin disease to be "clean" (Lev 13:6, 13, 17), his condition would be what a modern doctor would call "normal" or "healthy." However, while being clean is good, it is not the best possible condition. Those who want to draw near to God must not only be clean, they must be holy. The holiness that Leviticus desires is, as Wenham states, "a state of grace to which men are called by God, and it is attained through obeying the law and carrying out rituals such as sacrifice."[13] A person can, therefore, become holy by obeying the law, by being given to God (e.g., the priests, Levites, and Nazirites), or by performing certain rituals (such as washing oneself and/or offering a proper sacrifice) after becoming contaminated by sin or coming into contact with something unclean. Even though a person may do something to become holy, he can only become holy as God makes him holy. Thus, "I am the LORD, who makes you holy," is a common refrain throughout Leviticus and marks the path to holiness (Lev 20:8; 21:8, 15, 23; 22:9, 16, 32).[14]

Though being clean is normal and being holy is a more desirable condition, Leviticus describes how people enter the abnormal condition of becoming unclean. There are many ways in which a person can become unclean: sin, bodily discharges, childbirth, contact with someone or something dead, eating certain foods, or contracting a skin disease. It can result from personal sin or spring from natural causes. Just living a normal life can make a person unclean. And whereas we should resist concluding that being unclean is necessarily sinful or evil, it remains an undesirable condition. Since being unclean is the opposite of being holy, unclean people who draw near to God run the risk of death. To approach God, an unclean person must perform the ritual that will deal with the particular type of uncleanness experienced. Depending upon the source of uncleanness, this may be as simple as taking a bath, but it may include presenting some type of sacrifice.

The Israelites, their wilderness camp, and the animals they eat all belong to the category of clean. Within Israel and their camp, some people and things are considered holy. The tabernacle (which is God's dwelling place), the priests who work at the tabernacle, and the sacrificial animals are all holy, even though their holiness is not inherent. Only God is intrinsically holy. The tabernacle, priests, and animals must be consecrated before they become holy. And as the story about the death of Nadab and Abihu shows, even those who have been consecrated must act according to Yahweh's

---

13. Wenham, *Leviticus*, 23.
14. This could also be translated, "I am Yahweh who sanctifies you."

directions or they may pay with their lives. Holiness can have no contact with that which is unholy.

Degrees of Holiness				
	Most Holy	Holy	Clean	Unclean
Land	Holy of Holies	Tabernacle	Camp	Outside of Camp
People	High Priest	Priests/ Nazirites	Israelites	The Nations
Animals		Sacrificial animals	Clean animals	Unclean animals

If some things are clean and others are holy, there is also the category of "most holy." The holy of holies (otherwise referred to as the most holy place) is the holiest place in the camp of Israel. Significantly, it is located at the very center of the camp within the holy area of the tabernacle and the clean area of the camp. This placement ensures that it will not be easily defiled by that which is unclean. The only person allowed to enter the holy of holies is the holiest person in Israel—the high priest—and he only goes in once a year—the Day of Atonement—to make atonement for any sins that might have defiled the ark.

On the other end of the scale are people and things that are unclean. Geographically and physically, things that are outside the camp of Israel are unclean. Non-Israelites and Israelites who are affected by sin or certain maladies are also considered unclean. Before they can encounter the holy God, they must become clean. This requires time and/or some sort of ritual cleansing, depending upon the seriousness of the uncleanliness. However, some sins were considered so heinous that it was impossible for a guilty person ever to be made clean again; only the death of the person could remove the pollution caused by their sin.[15] This could, in part, explain why God insisted that the Canaanites be destroyed. They were so unclean (due to their rejection of God and their evil practices) that Israel stood in grave danger of being contaminated by them so that they could not approach God.

FIVE MAIN OLD TESTAMENT SACRIFICES

People live in a dynamic relationship with God that requires being clean or holy. This highlights the need for sacrifice to deal with uncleanness. The Old

---

15. Sins requiring the death penalty included certain kinds of sexual sin (Lev 18:20–30), idolatry (Lev 20:2–5), murder (Num 35:16–21, 31), and profaning the sacred (Lev 7:19–21; 22:3, 9).

Testament recognizes that uncleanness can come from sin or other sources. It also describes various sacrifices that restore those who are unclean so they can relate to God. Many of the requisite sacrifices, the occasions they were to be offered, and what they accomplish are delineated in the first seven chapters of Leviticus. The five main types of sacrifice are the 'ōlâ, the minḥâ, the šĕlāmîm, the ḥaṭṭā' t, and the 'ašam, otherwise known as the burnt offering, the grain offering, the peace (fellowship) offering, the sin (purification) offering, and the guilt (reparation) offering. When the offering focused on uncleanness or sin, the worshipper was not allowed to eat any of it, as it was wholly given to God. Even when priests were allowed to eat part of a sacrifice, their portion was "waved" before God, indicating that it belonged to him.

Five Types of Old Testament Sacrifice					
Name	Purpose	Victim	God's Portion	Priest's Portion	Offerer's Portion
Holah ('ōlâ) Burnt offering, Holocaust	To atone for sin "An aroma pleasing to Yahweh"	Male animal (young bull, sheep, goat, dove, young pigeon) without blemish	Entire offering burned	Nothing	Nothing
Minhah (minḥâ) Grain offering, Meal offering, Cereal offering	Possibly signified the covenant relationship between God and Israel or was reckoned a gift to the sovereign God "An aroma pleasing to Yahweh"	The only sacrifice not involving animals Fine flour, cakes, or wafers with oil, incense, and salt Either cooked or uncooked	A part burned as a "memorial portion"	The rest	Nothing

Offering	Purpose	Animal	Altar/Burning	Priest's Portion	Offerer's Portion
Shelamin (šĕlāmîm) Peace offering, Fellowship offering	To express thanksgiving, result of a vow, or freewill "An aroma pleasing to Yahweh"	Male or female animals (ox, sheep, goat) without blemish	Fatty portions and kidneys burned	Right thigh to officiating priest; Breast to other priests	Remainder to be eaten by those who are clean (if for thanksgiving, to be eaten same day; if for vow or free will, to be eaten within two days; the rest to be burned)
Hattat (ḥaṭṭā't) Sin offering, Purification offering	To cleanse the sacred items in the tabernacle due to sin	Priest or congregation: young bull Leader: he goat Commoner: she goat or lamb Poor: dove or pigeon	Priest: blood sprinkled on veil and incense altar, the rest burned Leader: blood sprinkled on bronze altar	Priest or congregation: nothing (all burned) Leader or commoner: remainder	Nothing
Asham ('āšam) Guilt offering, Reparation offering, Compensation offering	To compensate for sins Damages were set at 6/5 of value	Ram without blemish	Blood sprinkled on altar Fatty portions, kidneys, and liver burned	Remainder	Nothing

Burnt offering[16]

The burnt offering (*'ōlâ*)[17] is one of the main Old Testament sacrifices that atone for sin (Lev 1:4). In tabernacle worship, priests presented a burnt offering every morning and evening. Individuals could also bring a burnt offering to God to thank him for deliverance or to acknowledge that they had fulfilled a vow. The sacrificial animal was a male—young bull, sheep, goat, dove, or young pigeon—without blemish. The priest or individual bringing it would lay his hand(s) upon it and slay it. After a priest sprinkled some of the blood on the altar, the rest would be burned up, signifying that the whole had been given to God.[18] Along with some other sacrifices, when rightly offered, it is considered "an aroma pleasing to Yahweh." If the animal was given as a substitute for the worshipper, the fact that it was wholly given to God indicated that the person gave himself totally to God out of love and in obedience.

Grain offering[19]

While the Hebrew word for the grain offering (*minḥâ*) is frequently used for a gift to another person or tribute to a ruler (1 Sam 10:27; 1 Kgs 4:21), when used of sacrifice, it usually refers specifically to offerings of grain, whether whole, roasted and crushed, or ground into flour. On occasion, a *minḥâ* could include flesh or fat, but this appears to have been unusual (Gen 4:4; Judg 6:18–21). Grain could be presented to God in its raw state, or as fine flour mixed with oil and incense, cooked or uncooked. However it was offered, a "memorial portion" was burned on the altar for the benefit of the giver. This part was called "an aroma pleasing to the LORD" (Lev 1:2). The rest, the "most holy part," was given for the priests to eat within the holy area of the tabernacle (Lev 2:3).[20] Along with the grain offering, wine was regularly poured out on the altar as a drink offering or libation, particularly when the two complemented the morning and evening burnt offerings (Exod 29:38–41; Num 28:1–8) and fellowship offerings (Lev 9:4; Num 6:17).

---

16. Description is found in Leviticus 1:1–17; 6:8–13.

17. The Hebrew *'ōlâ* is related to a verb meaning "to go up." The concept is that the offering "goes up" to God in smoke. It is also called the "whole burned offering" (*kālîl*), signifying that all of it was burned up.

18. If an animal was presented, its skin would not be burned; if a bird, its crop would not be burned.

19. Description is found in Leviticus 2:1–16; 6:14–23.

20. If a priest brought a grain offering, nothing was to be eaten; the whole was to be burned (Lev 6:19–23).

Grain offerings were often presented along with burnt and peace offerings. It is likely that the showbread was considered a type of grain offering.

Peace offering[21]

The third type of sacrifice has traditionally been called the peace offering, though some Bible versions render it "fellowship offering/sacrifice" (CSB, NIV) or "sacrifice of well-being" (NRSV). These differences in translation stem from various ways in which the root of the word *šĕlāmîm*, is understood. Though an exact interpretation is difficult, the fact that the word is related to *shalom*—peace, wholeness, etc.—makes it likely that the sacrifice proclaimed the worshipper to be at peace with God and others because his relationships were made whole.[22] Though not explicitly stated in Scripture, it is likely that this was always the final offering in a series, as it proclaimed that all relationships were well as a result of the sacrifices.[23] The peace offering is the only Old Testament offering that is regularly referred to as a sacrifice (*zebaḥ*).[24]

Leviticus discusses three distinct types of peace offerings: one to express thanksgiving, a second to signify the fulfilment of a vow, and a third to bring a freewill offering to God (Lev 7:11–34). The offering was only required when a vow had been fulfilled; the other forms were optional. The sacrifice commenced when a worshipper brought a male or female animal without blemish (whether ox, sheep, or goat), laid his hand on its head, and slaughtered it. Afterwards, the priest sprinkled the sacrificial blood on the sides of the altar and burned the fat that had surrounded the major organs. When the blood and fat were rightly burned, the sacrifice became "an aroma pleasing to Yahweh."

As noted earlier, biblical sacrifice is inseparable from covenant relationship. The peace offering brings this out in a special way by signifying that all who partook of it shared in the covenant. One's part in the covenant is seen by the extent to which the sacrifice was shared. Yahweh was the most important member of the communion as he received the best parts—the

---

21. Description is found in Leviticus 3:1–17; 7:11–34. For an in-depth study of the word, see Seidl, "שְׁלָמִים, *šĕlāmîm*."

22. For a summary of different views on how the Hebrew *šĕlāmîm* has been understood, see Milgrom, *Leviticus 1–16*, 220–21.

23. Averbeck, "Sacrifices and Offerings," 715.

24. R. J. Thompson indicates that the *zebaḥ* and the *šĕlāmîm* "are sometimes interchangeable (Lv. 7:11–21; 2 Ki. 16:13, 15), sometimes distinguished (Jos. 22:27; *cf.* Ex. 24:5; 1 Sa. 11:15), sometimes independent (2 Sa. 6:17–18; Ex. 32:6), and sometimes combined into a compound expression." Thompson, "Sacrifice and Offering," 1362.

fatty portions. The officiating priest received the right thigh while other priests shared the breast. The remainder was eaten by members of a family, clan, tribe, or other group who shared in the covenant. According to Leviticus, a thanksgiving offering was to be eaten on the day it was offered and a vow or freewill offering could be eaten within two days. Anything not eaten in the prescribed period was to be burned or the offering and the giver would be judged unacceptable by God. As the sacrifice of a peace offering may have marked a rare opportunity for a family to eat meat, it would have been an occasion of great festivity. Peace offerings could be part of the celebration of victory or the installation of a king (1 Sam 11:14–15). The Passover can be understood as a special kind of peace offering.

Sin offering[25]

The sin offering (*ḥaṭṭā' t*) was presented to atone for the sin of individuals or the entire nation and to cleanse the altar and other sacred items which had been corrupted by sin.[26] It is specifically intended to atone for those who have sinned unintentionally (Lev 4:2) and for purifying ceremonial uncleanness. For this reason, women who were unclean through childbirth, and anyone with a skin disease, bodily discharge, or who touched a corpse, were instructed to bring one (Lev 12–15). Sin offerings were also presented on special occasions, such as the ordination of a priest, the dedication of the altar, and on festival days, particularly the Day of Atonement. Since it purified people and things from sin, it is sometimes known as the purification offering.[27]

The animal sacrificed and ritual performed depended upon the nature of the offence and the position of the offender in society. The differentiation in sacrificial practice apparently signified that the sins of the community leaders had more serious consequences than the sins of others. The place where the blood of the sacrifice was sprinkled suggests that sins committed by those who came into the closest contact with the tabernacle contaminated it to a deeper degree so that atonement needed to be made at the appropriate level. The blood of the offerings was used to cleanse the deepest level a particular individual or group could enter into the tabernacle. While

---

25. Described in Leviticus 4:1—5:13; 6:24–30.

26. The Hebrew word *ḥaṭṭā' t* is used for both sin and the sin offering. At times, this results in a bit of ambiguity as to whether sin or its antidote is in view.

27. For an argument that favors "purification offering" for contextual, morphological, and etymological reasons, see Milgrom, *Leviticus 1–16*, 253–54.

the law held priests and leaders more responsible, it also ensured that the poor were not required to bring more than they could afford.

The costliest of sin offerings—a bull—was brought when a priest or the entire congregation sinned. After the bull was sacrificed, some of its blood was sprinkled in the holy place in front of the veil and on the altar of incense and the rest poured out at the base of the bronze altar. Its fat (and kidneys if a priest had sinned) were burned on the altar with the remainder burned outside the camp. Nothing could be eaten. A community leader who sinned was required to bring a male goat as an offering, lay his hands on it, and slay it. Some of the animal's blood was sprinkled on the bronze altar and the rest poured out. The fat was burned and what was left given to the officiating priest. A commoner was required to sacrifice a female goat or female lamb for their sin. The blood of the offering was sprinkled on the horns of the altar, the fat burned for the Lord, and the remainder presented to the priests. A poor person could bring two doves or pigeons and the extremely poor a grain offering. If a sin offering was brought for a leader or commoner, the priest would receive the part that was not burned. In no case would the one who brought the sacrifice receive anything.

Guilt offering[28]

The guilt offering— 'āšam—differs from the sin offering mainly in its requirement that restitution be made for certain sins. Since reparation is a major aspect of this sacrifice, many scholars refer to it as a reparation offering or compensation offering. Two categories of sin fall under the guilt offering: unintentionally sinning "in regard to any of the Lord's holy things" (Lev 5:15) and defrauding, stealing, or otherwise cheating a person out of his personal property (Lev 6:1–5). Though no example illustrates how a person might sin against the holy things, it likely pertains to eating food that had been set aside as the priests' holy portion or perhaps to not paying the full amount promised in a vow.[29] In addition to the two reasons given in Leviticus 5, guilt offerings were required after a person with a skin disease was cleansed (Lev 14:12–28), after a man had sexual intercourse with a slave girl (Lev 19:19–22), and when a Nazirite's vow had been disrupted through contamination by a corpse (Num 6:9–12). No explanation is given as to why the guilt offering was necessary in these cases.

---

28. Described in Leviticus 5:14—6:7; 7:1–7.

29. Note that a guilt offering is brought by a Nazirite who renews his vow after being contaminated by a dead body (Num 6:9–12).

The offering ensured that a misappropriated item was restored and right relationships reestablished. To secure this, the worshipper brought a ram without blemish to the priest and returned the value of the article that was stolen plus one-fifth of its value to the person wronged or the priest (if the sin was against the sacred things). The blood of the sacrifice was sprinkled on the sides of the altar, its fatty portions, kidneys, and liver burned, and the rest given to the priest as his portion; the worshipper receiving nothing.

Later in Israel's history, Isaiah would portray the Servant of the Lord as a guilt offering. Isaiah 53:4–12 identifies the suffering of the Servant as a personal sacrifice on the behalf of others and highlights the substitutionary aspects of atonement that he performs. The Servant not only "took up our infirmities and carried our sorrows" (v 4), he was also "pierced for our transgressions" and "crushed for our iniquities" (v 5). Like a sacrificial animal, he is led away in silence to be slaughtered on our behalf (vv 6–7). The purpose of the sacrifice becomes more explicit in verse 10 where we are told that he becomes (or makes himself) a guilt offering.[30] The sacrifice of the Servant makes reparation for the sins of many so that their relationship with the holy God can be restored. Wenham indicates that since the Servant is Jesus, the need for the guilt offering is negated.

> Christ's death, the perfect reparation offering, has therefore made it obsolete, along with the other sacrifices. It is no longer necessary to attempt to compensate God for our failure by bringing a ram or a lamb to the altar. Our spiritual debts have been written off in the sacrifice of Christ.[31]

As we will see below, what is true of guilt offerings is true for the others as well. Jesus' sacrifice makes them obsolete. Christians should study the Old Testament sacrifices in order to learn what it takes to repair one's damaged relationships with God and others so that they can better understand what Christ has done for them.

---

30. A comparison of the versions attests that translating Isaiah 53:10 is extremely difficult. As no explicit subject is given for the verb "to make," the addition of "the Lord" in the NIV ("though the Lord makes his life a guilt offering") is, as Motyer rightly states, "an interpretive addition which may or may not be correct." Motyer, *Isaiah*, 439. The form of the verb could be either second person masculine singular ("though you make his life a guilt offering," so NIV footnote; cf. CSB, KJV, NRSV) or third person feminine singular which takes "his life/his soul" (the Hebrew for "life" is a feminine noun with a third person masculine singular pronominal suffix) as the subject ("when his soul makes an offering for guilt," ESV; cf. NASB, NLT, RSV). Only if the second person masculine is judged to be correct and interpreted as referring to Yahweh (who was the subject of the first verb in the verse) would it be correct to add "the Lord" here.

31. Wenham, *Leviticus*, 112.

Occasions and Order of Sacrifices

The Mosaic law regulates a number of occasions when sacrifices should be made at the tabernacle. Every day, the priests were to sacrifice two lambs (with an accompanying cereal offering), one in the morning and one in the evening (Exod 29:38–41; Num 28:1–8).[32] On the Sabbath, they would offer two additional lambs, and on the new moon, a burnt offering of two bulls, one ram, and seven male lambs, along with a grain offering. Additional sacrifices were offered on the major festivals of the year.[33] In addition to the required daily and seasonal sacrifices, individuals brought offerings for personal sin, when they received purification after childbirth (Lev 12:1–8), or were cleansed from an infectious skin disease (Lev 14:1–32). In some cases, a sacrifice accompanied the confirmation of a treaty between individuals (Gen 31:54) or was made to celebrate the Lord's goodness to a person and his or her family (1 Sam 1:1–5). Requests for safety or deliverance might initiate sacrifice, as might one's response to the Lord's deliverance. Burnt offerings and peace offerings might thus accompany prayers that the Lord would end a plague (2 Sam 24:18–25) or celebrate the return of the ark after it had been captured by the Philistines (2 Sam 6:1–19).

A special use of sacrifices was to consecrate people and things for a special task. Thus, special offerings were brought for twelve continuous days when the tabernacle was consecrated (Lev 7). Similarly, burnt offerings, sin offerings, and peace offerings highlighted the ordination of priests (Exod 29; Lev 8–9). Upon fulfilling a vow, Nazirites sacrificed to God so they could reenter the congregation as normal citizens (Num 6:9–21). Burnt offerings, grain offerings, and peace offerings were sacrificed in abundance when Solomon's temple was dedicated (1 Kgs 8:62–64). A coronation was often heralded with peace offerings (1 Sam 11:14–15; 1 Kgs 1:9, 25).

On many occasions, different sacrifices were offered together according to a regular order. First came the guilt offering, followed by the sin offering, with a peace offering (along with its associated drink offering) coming last. The order implies that as sinners come to God, restitution must be made for whatever they have done wrong and the sinner purified before they can celebrate their restored relationship with God. But even though the peace offering usually followed the others, on certain occasions, no peace offering is mentioned. On the Day of Atonement, this may be because a celebration meal was inappropriate due to the solemn nature of the ritual

---

32. For other references to the daily offering, see 1 Kings 18:29; 2 Kings 3:20; 16:15; Ezekiel 46:13–14.

33. See chapter 7, "Times and Seasons of Worship," for the sacrifices that were offered for particular days and festivals.

performed. At other times, a peace offering may have been offered purely to celebrate the goodness of the Lord.

SACRIFICE IN THE HISTORIES, PSALMS, WISDOM, AND PROPHETS

Apart from the book of Leviticus, the Old Testament provides very little instruction about sacrificial worship. Only occasional glimpses of Israelites bringing sacrifices to Yahweh are found in the historical books, Psalms, Wisdom, and Prophets.

Following the story of Israel living as slaves in Egypt for four hundred years and wandering in the wilderness for forty more, the book of Joshua narrates Israel's settlement in Canaan. Building upon themes laid down in Deuteronomy, Joshua focuses on rest in the land, God's covenantal relationship with his people, and holy war.[34] Though the book is concerned that God's people express holiness in worship, it says little about Israel's sacrificial practices. The main references to sacrifice are the report of the Passover ceremony held at Gilgal (Josh 5:10–12) and of the burnt offerings and fellowship offerings presented at Mount Ebal when the blessings and curses were read (Josh 8:30–35). After the two-and-a-half tribes returned to their inheritance on the east of the Jordan, they constructed an altar as a memorial of their unity with the other tribes, though it was not intended to be a place to offer sacrifice (Josh 22:21–29). While Judges similarly provides sparse information about sacrificial rites, it records that from an early stage, some Israelites engaged in clearly aberrant practices, such as Jephthah offering his daughter as a burnt offering (Judg 11:30–40) and (even though sacrifice is not explicitly mentioned) Micah making an idol and hiring a Levite to be his priest (Judg 17:1–13).

Though these books rarely mention sacrifice, they provide information about sacrificial rites that paralleled those made at the tabernacle. According to Leviticus, only the Aaronic priests could handle the blood or other parts of an animal sacrificed at the tabernacle. Even so, throughout Israel's history, other sacrificial altars were built. While some of these "solitary altars" were used illicitly for syncretistic practices, others were constructed at God's instruction (Josh 8:30–35; Judg 6:25–26). At times, they were used by priests making rounds to give people from different parts of the land an opportunity to bring their sacrifices to God (1 Sam 7:17). At other times, lay people offered sacrifices to the Lord as part of a communal meal. While

---

34. For more on the concept of holy war, see Longman and Reid, *God is a Warrior*; Lind, *Yahweh is a Warrior*; Rad, *Holy War*; and Miller, *The Divine Warrior*.

solitary altars were mainly used for burnt offerings and peace offerings, grain and drink offerings were also presented upon them. Sin and guilt offerings were reserved for tabernacle or temple worship.

Some of the later historical books center on worship in the temple cult. This is particularly true in Chronicles, which gives primacy of space to the work of David and Solomon who planned for and built the temple and instituted the liturgical service of priests and Levites. David's aim to enhance the worship of Yahweh is seen in his wish to build a house—a temple—for God, but this wish is not fulfilled because he was a man of war. Even so, God promises to build a house—a dynasty—for him and indicates that one of his descendants would build a house for God (1 Chr 17:1-14). David then buys the threshing floor of Ornan the Jebusite to be the site for a future temple and begins to offer up sacrifices there in addition to the ones presented at the tabernacle which was then at Gibeon (1 Chr 21:24-29). After Solomon builds the temple and sets up its furnishings, an incredible number of animals are sacrificed as part of the dedication service (2 Chr 7:1-7). Chronicles sees the temple in Jerusalem as a symbol of God's presence in Israel. From the perspective of its author, Jerusalem is the only place where sacrifice should be offered because Yahweh chose it to house the ark.

However, as Israel's history progressed, temple worship degraded. The people misused the sacrificial rituals designed to restore fellowship between them and God to the point that prophets frequently proclaimed them useless. In the end, the Northern Kingdom was sent into exile for breaking Yahweh's covenant, particularly its instructions on how to worship God (2 Kgs 7-23). And even though Huldah prophesied that King Josiah would not personally see the coming disaster, the Southern Kingdom would also be exiled because they broke God's covenant by offering sacrifices to idols (2 Kgs 22:11-20).

Exilic writers frequently drew attention to the importance of temple worship and its accompanying sacrifices. The book of Ezra begins with Cyrus's proclamation to rebuild the temple in Jerusalem and narrates how worship was reestablished in the city. Led by Zerubbabel the governor and Jeshua the priest, the builders first constructed an altar for burnt offerings, celebrated the Feast of Tabernacles, and made provision to celebrate the new moon and yearly feasts (Ezra 3:2-5). After laying the foundation of the temple, the priests and Levites led the people in praising and giving thanks to the Lord (Ezra 3:10-11). In spite of the temple project being temporarily abandoned due to outside pressure, the job was completed as the prophets Haggai and Zechariah encouraged the builders (Ezra 5:1-2; 6:14). The rededication of the temple produced more celebration and sacrifice, saw priests and Levites reappointed to their orders according to Mosaic instruction, and led to the celebration of the Passover and Feast of Unleavened bread. Starting the journey with fasting and prayer for protection, Ezra the priest led a second group of returnees to Jerusalem who offered more sacrifices to the Lord (Ezra 8:15–36).

Whereas the Psalms played a key role in temple and synagogue worship and in private spirituality, they say little about sacrifice. Kraus laments that even though sacrifice "constituted a special theme in the cultic life of Jerusalem. It is . . . astonishing how little is in fact said in the Psalms on this theme."[35] Only rare psalm titles contain any information about their possible liturgical use in conjunction with sacrifice. The title of Psalm 100, "A psalm of thanksgiving," may indicate that it was to be used by people bringing a thank offering. Similarly, the titles of Psalms 38 and 70 may signify their use in conjunction with a memorial offering (cf. Lev 2:2; 24:7). Only occasional reference to offerings and sacrifices are made in the psalms (Pss 50:5, 8–14, 23; 54:6; 56:12; 66:13–15; 116:17; 118:27). In addition, the payment of vows—an act performed in conjunction with sacrifice—is mentioned (Pss 22:25; 65:1; 116:18). Courtman notes that three motives are given by psalmists for offering sacrifices: "to give thanks, to bring a petition, and to offer worship."[36]

One of the few sustained discussions of sacrifice is found in Psalm 50, which concentrates on its covenant context. As the main speaker in the psalm, God summons all creation so that he can judge the people who have made a covenant with him through sacrifice. Since he is supreme in power and has no needs, he does not even require sacrifice or burnt offerings.[37] Significantly, God's people—his "consecrated ones" (Ps 50:5)—needed the sacrificial system to maintain their relationship with him. Even so, God was not interested in mere ritual performance, but in a thankful heart and properly fulfilled vows.[38] Clearly distinguishing them from the righteous, God asks the wicked, "What right have you to recite my laws or take my covenant on your lips?" (Ps 50:16). Sacrifice, as part of covenant worship, is exclusively for those who are in a right relationship with God or who want to be made right with him. Sinners have no part in it.

---

35. Kraus, *Theology of the Psalms*, 93.

36. Courtman, "Sacrifice in the Psalms," 41.

37. Since the Hebrew word translated "sacrifice" in Psalm 50:5, 8 is *zebaḥ*, a peace offering could be in view. A similar idea is found in Psalm 40:6–8 which also speaks of God not desiring sacrifice and offerings but obedience to his revealed will.

38. Note that the "thank offering(s)" (CSB, NIV) or "sacrifice of thanksgiving" (ESV, NASB, NRSV) mentioned is from the Hebrew *tôdâ*, the same word found in the title of Psalm 100.

Wisdom literature similarly adds little to our understanding of sacrifice. Job sacrificed a burnt offering to God on behalf of his children in case they had sinned, and for his friends after God pointed out their sin (Job 1:5; 42:8-9). Other Wisdom books echo standard biblical teaching that God is not pleased with cultic actions divorced from true piety and that the condition of one's heart is more important than simply engaging in religious activities. Mere religiosity is consistently viewed negatively. Qohelet thus warns his readers to watch their steps when going to God's house, being careful to listen (i.e., obey) rather than offering the sacrifice of fools who do not even realize that their actions are evil (Eccl 5:1). Proverbs informs that, when carried out with wrong motives, any religious act is an abomination, a word with clear cultic significance. Thus, the sacrifice of the wicked and the prayers of those who reject God's instruction (*torah*) are abominations (Prov 15:8; 21:27; 28:9). The rebellious woman in Proverbs 7 becomes a negative example of one who treats her sacrifice with contempt as she seduces an undiscerning youth while boasting that she had presented peace offerings and paid her vows (Prov 7:6-23). Since the meat from a peace offering was to be eaten by the one making the sacrifice, the woman is inviting the youth to share a feast with her. By accepting her offer to partake in this religious meal, the youth joins her rejection of true worship and is himself led off to slaughter. The bed, linens, and spices that serve as a sexual enticement unexpectedly produce the odor of death[39] and lead to Sheol, the place where a person can neither praise nor worship God (Pss 6:5; 115:17) and where wisdom cannot be known (Eccl 9:10).

The prophets, whether speaking in pre-exilic, exilic, or post-exilic times, frequently denounced the sacrificial practices of their listeners (Isa 1:10-17; Jer 7:21-23, 30-31; Hos 8:11-13; Amos 5:21-25).[40] According to some earlier scholars, the prophets dismissed sacrificial religion for a spiritual, inner religion concerned with moral fellowship between God and humans. This perspective described prophetic religion as diametrically opposed to the priestly religion centered on sacrificial rites. While the moral element is indisputably present in prophetic religion, recent scholarship has shown that the formerly held dichotomy was unjustified. It is now recognized that prophets who denounced sacrificial practices at various times in Israel's history were concerned with the misuse of the system, not its existence. Since God gave the people his moral law *and* the sacrificial system, it was wrong for them to bring sacrifices to God while knowingly disobeying his commands. This concept is captured in the answer to Micah's rhetorical

---

39. Clifford, *Proverbs*, 89.
40. For a good introduction to this subject, see Lucas, "Sacrifice in the Prophets."

question of whether he should bring various and numerous offerings (even his firstborn!) to worship the Lord. God has shown what is required: "To act justly and to love mercy and to walk humbly with your God" (Mic 6:6–8). Similarly, Amos reports that after Yahweh denounced the empty worship of his people, he instructed them to "let justice roll on like a river, righteousness like a never-failing stream" (Amos 5:24).

While the prophets often castigated their compatriots for bringing improper sacrifices to God, they did not wholly write off the system. Jeremiah and Ezekiel, who witnessed the destruction of the temple and end of sacrificial rites, anticipated a day when sacrifice would be re-established in its pure form (Jer 17:26; Ezek 43:18–27; 46:1–24). The post-exilic prophets Haggai and Zechariah had a particularly important role in encouraging those who returned to Jerusalem while they rebuilt the temple so that sacrifices could again be presented to God. They further saw Jerusalem as a destination for people from many nations who would come to worship him.

SACRIFICE IN THE NEW TESTAMENT

The Old Testament sacrificial system was familiar to all Jews in the first century AD. This probably influenced the limited references in the New Testament to people presenting offerings at the temple. Of the examples given, Mary's trip to Jerusalem to be purified after childbirth followed instructions from Leviticus (Luke 2:21–24; cf. Lev 12:3, 8). Mary and Joseph joined the huge crowds in the annual pilgrimage to Jerusalem to celebrate the Feast of Passover when they were required to sacrifice and eat a Passover lamb. When Jesus journeyed with them in his twelfth year to celebrate the Passover, he undoubtedly took part in the sacrifices and continued to do so throughout his ministry years when he visited Jerusalem on the great festival days. Though he never denounced the sacrificial system, Jesus clearly maintained the prophetic ideal that sacrifice must reflect a right heart and obedience to God's will (Matt 5:23–24).

The Gospels record that Jesus' disciples accompanied him to Jerusalem to attend a number of different feasts. After his resurrection, they regularly went to pray at the temple at the time sacrifices were offered. On Paul's final trip to Jerusalem, the church leaders convinced him to visit the temple and pay for the purification rites of a group of men who had taken a vow, probably to serve as Nazirites (Acts 21:23–26).[41] Despite the uncer-

---

41. Though no explicit statement is made about this being a Nazirite vow, the fact that the men were prepared to shave their heads indicates that it is likely, as the Old Testament instructs that one who ends a vow as a Nazirite should shave (Num 6:13–20).

tainty surrounding the meaning of this event, Paul testified before Felix that he had returned to Jerusalem after several years' absence in order to bring gifts to the poor and present offerings in the temple (Acts 24:17). Though Gentile believers had been released from these practices (Acts 15:1–29), early Jewish Christians evidently found no contradiction between accepting the gospel of Jesus Christ and taking part in sacrificial rituals. The lack of evidence to the contrary makes it likely that they followed Old Testament practices until the temple was destroyed in AD 70 when all sacrifices ceased.

Even so, Christians soon recognized that the crucifixion was the final sacrifice that both completed the Old Testament system and made temple sacrifices irrelevant. The New Testament thus frequently comments on the nature of Christ's sacrifice and metaphorically relates it to various Old Testament sacrifices. According to John the Baptist, Jesus is "the lamb of God, who takes away the sin of the world" (John 1:29, 36). Peter similarly reminds his readers that they were redeemed by "the precious blood of Christ, a lamb without blemish or defect" (1 Pet 1:19). Likewise, Revelation speaks of Jesus as the Lamb who purchased for God people from every tribe, language, people, and nation, and, by being slain, received power, wealth, wisdom, strength, honor, glory, and praise (Rev 5:6–14). Paul identifies Christ as the Passover whose sacrifice frees us from slavery to sin (1 Cor 5:7), the sin offering brought for sinful humanity (Rom 8:3),[42] the fragrant offering sacrificed to God (Eph 5:2), and as the propitiation for our sins that effectively deals with the wrath of God (Rom 3:25; cf. 1 John 2:2). John uses sacrificial imagery when he says that the blood of Jesus purifies us from sin (1 John 1:7). The author of Hebrews understands the whole sacrificial system to be a mere shadow that pointed to the supreme work performed by Jesus. Whereas the blood of animals could not adequately deal with sins, Jesus' offering of himself did (Heb 10:1–10). And since he, as the priest greater than any from the Aaronic order, entered not only the holy of holies but God's heavenly throne room, he ensures that everything is cleansed and the way into God's presence is eternally secured.

In addition to portraying Christ's crucifixion in sacrificial terms, New Testament writers described their personal ministry in terms regularly used of priests. Thus, Paul describes his "priestly duty of proclaiming the gospel

---

Whereas some have argued that Paul would not have taken part in this kind of temple rite at this point in his career, there is no reason for such a conclusion. As Bruce says, Paul's readiness to do this shows his willingness to be "all things to all men" (1 Cor 9:19–23). Bruce, *Acts*, 392. For a brief summary of different views on why Paul may have been asked to purify himself, see Marshall, *Acts*, 345–46.

42. Second Corinthians 5:21 may also point to Jesus becoming a sin offering for us. See NIV footnote, NLT.

of God, so that the Gentiles might become an offering acceptable to God, sanctified by the Holy Spirit" (Rom 15:16). Gentiles, not sheep, have become the acceptable sacrifice offered by the apostle. At other times, they saw their own lives as sacrificial, as when Paul speaks of his approaching death as a drink offering that is being poured out (Phil 2:17; 2 Tim 4:6). A similar image is found in Paul's exhortation that Christians should "offer your bodies as living sacrifices" (Rom 12:1) and Peter's recognition that believers have replaced the temple as "living stones" who are built upon Jesus and have replaced the Aaronic order as "a holy priesthood, offering spiritual sacrifices" (1 Pet 2:4–5). These concepts especially influence the way we should think about sacrifice today.

SACRIFICE AND THE CHURCH

While Christians are familiar with the biblical story about sacrifice, its practice lies far beyond our personal experience. Since we view it as being attached to an obsolete era—the old covenant—we usually fail to engage the biblical testimony about why God desired his people to come to him through this means. This explains why most readers of the Mosaic law are ignorant that sacrifice primarily addressed issues of holiness and covenant fellowship. Old Testament offerings were presented primarily so that people might become holy and that a series of sacrifices was usually concluded by a fellowship meal uniting the people with God and one another. Perhaps our failure to appreciate the Old Testament sacrificial system stems from our understanding that Jesus' sacrifice made all other sacrifices irrelevant. However, if we fail to grasp the intent of the Old Testament sacrifices, we can never appreciate what was actualized through Christ's death. And if we cannot comprehend what the crucifixion accomplished, we cannot give God the praise that is his due for making a way so that we can be fully reconciled to him and become his holy people.

However, despite our unfamiliarity with the slaughter of animals and related rituals, we continue to use sacrificial terminology. Frequently, we hear challenges to sacrifice our lives, our time, or our money to serve the Lord. In response, many people are persuaded to give up a vocation and enter full-time Christian service as a pastor or missionary. Others are challenged to sacrifice their time for the sake of a cause that will benefit the church. Still more determine to sacrifice their standard of living in order to free up funds for the work of the kingdom. Would the Bible recognize these things as sacrifice? There is a sense in which this approach focuses too much on the individual who gives up something and not enough on the role of

God to whom sacrifice should be made. As C. T. Studd, the great missionary to both China and Africa, famously said, "If Jesus Christ be God and died for me, no sacrifice can be too great for me to make for him." At its roots, offering a sacrifice is not so much about what we give up for God, but about how we respond to the God who gave all for us.

There is no reason to conclude that since Christ's death brought an end to the Old Testament sacrificial system, his followers are exempt from bringing sacrifices to God. In fact, Christians are commanded to offer *spiritual* sacrifices to God (1 Pet 2:5), sacrifices that pertain to the age of the Holy Spirit who empowers God's people for service. And since all believers are the "living stones" who make up the "holy priesthood," all should actively offer such sacrifices. Whatever service we offer to God and others is sacrificial in the sense that we bring our gifts to be used for his service under the power of the Holy Spirit. This includes our practice of spiritual gifts.

Scripture provides us with several examples of the kinds of sacrifices Christ's disciples should bring. The author of Hebrews specifies three that we can offer: praise, good deeds, and sharing with those in need (Heb 13:15–16). The worship of God should abound with praise, offered rightly "through Jesus." Good deeds should be offered to God since we were "created in Christ Jesus to do good works, which God prepared in advance for us to do" (Eph 2:10). We should also give to support the needs of others, because our sharing is received as a fragrant offering that is pleasing to God (Phil 4:18).[43]

Another type of sacrifice we may offer is prayer. The psalmist thus expresses the wish, "May my prayer be set before you like incense; may the lifting up of my hands be like the evening sacrifice" (Ps 141:2). Using similar temple imagery, the book of Revelation likens the prayer of the saints to burning incense (Rev 5:8; 8:3–4). As the prayers of God's people span the ages, so does covenantal fellowship. Whereas the new covenant people do not express their fellowship by sharing a peace offering, they do come together to remember the sacrifice that initiated the covenant. Those who share in the Lord's Supper should experience it as their own sacrifice of praise and thanksgiving to God for his works in creation and salvation. As we partake of the bread and wine, we should praise and thank God for creating them along with the other elements. We also offer praise to God for sending Jesus as an expression of his love so that we, and all creation, can be restored to the Father through Jesus' sacrifice on the cross.

Sacrifice is not just something that we should do. It is something that we should be. Paul instructs his readers to offer their bodies as living

---

43. Paul's terms relate monetary gifts to the Levitical sacrifices that were often said to be an "aroma pleasing to the Lord."

sacrifices (Rom 12:1). It is of critical importance that Paul said to "offer your *bodies*." In an age when Platonic philosophy taught that the body was bad and that only the spirit was good, Paul insisted that the most physical part of us—our bodies—should be wholly devoted to God. Neither sacrifice nor worship should be conceived as essentially a matter of the heart or the mind. As John Stott says, "No worship is pleasing to God which is purely inward, abstract and mystical; it must express itself in concrete acts of service performed by our bodies."[44] Paul refuses to distinguish between one kind of Christian who should sacrifice a career to go into ministry and the rest who are free to do whatever they want. All Christians are to sacrifice themselves and live for the Lord at home, at work, and at play. All Christians are to consider everything they do to be sacrificial, no matter what it is or where they do it. Just as the animals brought to the temple were wholly given to God, followers of Jesus who offer themselves as living sacrifices become "wholly God's property."[45] In addition to belonging to him because he is Creator and Redeemer, the Christian also belongs to him "by virtue of his own free surrender of himself," a surrender which has "to be continually repeated."[46] Like taking up one's cross daily to follow Jesus (Luke 9:23), Christians must continually offer themselves as sacrifices, demonstrating their experience of new life in Christ and making personal holiness transparent to all by living in conformity to God's will.

In this chapter, we have seen that though most Christians have no direct experience of animal sacrifice and that the death of Jesus has effectively brought the Old Testament sacrificial system to a close, we should not ignore biblical instruction about the topic. The Levitical teaching about the power of sacrifice to cleanse from sin, make unclean people holy, and unite them in covenantal relationship with God is essential if we want to understand what Jesus' sacrifice accomplished. Christ is the perfect sacrifice, the perfect priest, and the perfect tabernacle. Jesus' death puts sacrifice in a new perspective so that it becomes a personal giving of oneself and one's gifts to God and his work under the power of the Holy Spirit. Our praise, prayer, thanksgiving, acts of charity, and different forms of ministry should all be recognized as offerings we bring to God in response to who he is and what he has done for us. Let us, therefore, "continually offer to God a sacrifice of praise . . . do good and . . . share with others, for with such sacrifices God is pleased" (Heb 13:15–16).

---

44. Stott, *Romans*, 322.
45. Cranfield, *Romans, Vol. 2*, 599.
46. Cranfield, *Romans, Vol. 2*, 600.

11

Worship and Baptism

Ever since Jesus told his disciples to recall their last supper "in remembrance of me" and instructed them to make disciples by "baptizing them in the name of the Father and of the Son and of the Holy Spirit," Christians have recognized and practiced the two sacraments or ordinances of baptism and the Lord's Supper. These practices quickly became the two most distinctive rituals in Christian worship. This chapter will consider the meaning of sacraments in general and then focus on baptism, the ordinance that initiates Christians to the church. The following chapter will examine the Lord's Supper in Christian worship.

SACRAMENTS

Christians divide on whether to refer to baptism and the Lord's Supper as sacraments or ordinances. Some prefer the second word because "sacrament" is never found in our English Bibles. It comes into English through Latin, and particularly the Vulgate version of the Bible that translates the Greek *mustērion* as *sacramentum* instead of the more common *mysterium*—"mystery." But not even in the Vulgate does *sacramentum* correspond to either baptism or the Lord's Supper, retaining instead its basic meaning of a mystery that was revealed by God.[1] In its original, secular use, *sacra-*

---

1. This can include making known the mystery of God's will that all things are summed up in Christ's redemptive work (Eph 1:9–10; 3:3), the mystery of the marital relationship as considered in the light of Christ and his church (Eph 5:31–32), the mystery of godly living that is connected to the worship of Jesus Christ as proclaimed in

mentum was the money set aside as a pledge payable in the event that a law case was lost or the oath of loyalty taken by a soldier entering service. In the early church, both meanings were combined so that Christians understood the sacraments as swearing an oath of allegiance to God and receiving from him a sign or pledge that he would keep his promises. The sign was often seen as a mystery in the sense of something that was revealed to the church yet hidden from those outside the faith. The term only took on the narrower meaning of a sacred thing or ritual by the church fathers of the third and fourth centuries.

From the time of Augustine (354–430), sacraments have been understood to be outward and visible signs of an internal and spiritual grace conferred by Christ upon those who receive them. While Roman Catholics, Eastern Orthodox, and many Protestants agree on this, their conception of the number of the sacraments and explanations of how the sacraments benefit their recipients differ greatly. Protestants recognize only two sacraments—baptism and the Lord's Supper. These are accepted because they were explicitly instituted by Jesus who commanded his followers to repeat them (Matt 28:19; Luke 22:19; 1 Cor 11:24–25). They are also recognized as signs of the new covenant that parallel the signs of the old covenant—circumcision and Passover. As males (whether babies or adult converts) entered the old covenant community through circumcision, everyone who enters the church is to experience the one-time initiation rite of baptism. Similarly, as the Israelites were to recount God's redemption from Egypt by regularly celebrating a Passover meal, all Christians are to participate in the Lord's Supper "in remembrance" of Christ's great act of redemption on the cross.

Roman Catholics and Orthodox agree that baptism and the Lord's Supper are sacraments, but do not limit them to two. In part, this is because the term *sacramentum* was used throughout church history in a broader sense to refer to any number of signs that God was at work among his people. As a result, medieval scholars could identify up to thirty different sacraments. This number was standardized at seven by Peter Lombard (ca. 1100–1160), who distinguished between sacraments—which both signified and conferred grace—and sacramentals (*sacramentalia*)—which are lesser rites that do not confer grace but incite the believer to faith, acts of devotion,

---

an early Christian hymn (1 Tim 3:16), the mystery of the seven stars and seven golden lampstands that are said to refer to the angels of the seven churches and the seven churches respectively (Rev 1:20), and the mystery of the woman and the beast that the angel would reveal to John (Rev 17:7).

Since the context in which *sacramentum* is found in these six verses regularly finds *mustērion* translated with the parallel term *mysterium* (Eph 3:4, 9; 6:19; 1 Tim 3:9; Rev 10:7; 17:5), there is no reason to assign a special meaning to *sacramentum* in any of them.

sorrow for sin, etc.[2] In addition to baptism and the Eucharist, Lombard's list of sacraments included confirmation, penance, extreme unction (last rites),[3] orders (ordination), and matrimony. Though no earlier explanation of the sacraments had been stated in precisely the same way, Roman Catholics hold that Lombard's account provides a clear and accurate statement of what the church had always believed.[4] Lombard's explanation, found in his *Sentences*, informed many generations of Catholic theologians, was confirmed by the Councils of Florence (1439) and Trent (1547), and continues to be recognized as orthodox Catholic doctrine.[5]

Lombard's conclusions about the sacraments included the idea that they confer saving grace *ex opere operato*—"from the work done." This means that the sacrament brings God's grace to an individual as long as he or she does not resist and the rite is performed by an ordained priest. The doctrine that the sacraments impart grace is known as sacramentalism, an idea that also maintains a person must rightly receive the sacraments in order to attain salvation. The concept that the sacraments must be administered by a priest is connected to the doctrine known as sacerdotalism, which maintains that a special class of priests is necessary to serve as mediators between God and his people.[6]

While the Roman Catholic Church has held to this understanding of the sacraments from the twelfth century, all the Protestant Reformers rejected both the arguments for seven sacraments and the idea that they operate *ex opere operato*. Rather, the Reformers maintained that while the term

---

2. Sacramentals include such rites as making the sign of the cross, folding hands and bowing the head for prayer, celebrating the seasons of the church year, etc. Objects, such as statutes, icons, the rosary, wedding rings, and holy water, were also considered sacramentals.

3. After the Second Vatican Council, this rite was broadened from being administered only when a person approached death to a more general prayer for healing from sickness. The official name of this Catholic sacrament as practiced today is "anointing of the sick."

4. The recent *Catechism of the Catholic Church* quotes the conclusion of the Council of Trent on the origin of the seven sacraments. "'Adhering to the teaching of the Holy Scriptures, to the apostolic tradition and to the consensus . . . of the Fathers', we profess that 'the sacraments of the new law were . . . all instituted by Jesus Christ our Lord.'" *Catechism of the Catholic Church*, 289.

5. Some recent Roman Catholic scholars have voiced their opinion that baptism and the Lord's Supper were the only sacraments instituted by Jesus and that the conclusions made by the Council of Trent on this issue need to be reexamined. Osborne, *Christian Sacraments in a Postmodern World*, 7.

6. The *Catechism of the Catholic Church* allows that "In the case of necessity, anyone, even a non-baptized person, with the required intention, can baptize, as long they use the Trinitarian baptismal formula." *Catechism of the Catholic Church*, 320.

sacramentum can be used in a general sense, there is no scriptural warrant for recognizing any more than baptism and the Lord's Supper, as they were ordained by Christ.[7] The Reformers were similarly adamant in their rejection of the idea that the sacraments effectively communicated grace simply by being performed. Rather, they argued, the sacraments were only effective when they were received by faith.[8] Understanding them in Augustine's sense as "visible words," they placed them alongside the preached word as aids that stimulate faith in those who received them, or simply confirm the faith that the Holy Spirit had already placed in the believer's heart through the proclaimed word. As concrete images, they were understood to speak to the senses in a way the preached word cannot.

The Reformers were united in their belief that the sacraments were not a means of special grace. Even so, Luther and some other Reformers maintained that the sacraments were a special means of grace, even though the grace was given by God and was dependent upon the faith of the recipient. Following Calvin, the Reformed view is that grace is bestowed on a person as Christ blesses them and the Holy Spirit performs his work when they receive the sacraments in faith.[9] While Lutherans agree that faith must be present, they concur with Catholics that the sacraments in some sense confer saving grace. Their disagreement with Catholicism is that instead of finding the source of grace in the elements, they locate it in the power of God's word proclaimed when the sacraments are dispensed.

Other Protestant communities, particularly those who followed Zwingli and the Anabaptist tradition, wholly denied that the sacraments

---

7. Even though Luther at one time considered penance a third sacrament, he ultimately recognized that it could not be placed in the same category as the other two as it had no accompanying sign. Lutheran theology eventually subsumed penance under the sacrament of baptism, seeing it as enabling a person to return to the baptismal promise of regeneration and providing enablement to turn from the power and effect of sin in one's life.

8. C. O. Buchanan suggests that the medieval doctrine and Reformers' view may have been much closer "than either side would have been happy to concede" since the Catholic view always held that the recipient must not erect a barrier to God's grace. Stated another way, a person would not resist the sacrament because of faith. Buchanan, "Sacrament," 607. This is supported by the *Catechism of the Catholic Church*, article 1133, which states, "The Holy Spirit prepares the faithful for the sacraments by the word of God and the faith which welcomes that word in well-disposed hearts. Thus the sacraments strengthen faith and express it." *Catechism of the Catholic Church*, 293.

9. Thus, the Westminster Shorter Catechism, question 91, contains the following question and answer.
Q: How do the sacraments become effectual means of salvation?
A: The sacraments become effectual means of salvation, not from any virtue in them, or in him that doth administer them; but only by the blessing of Christ, and the working of his Spirit in them that by faith receive them.

were instruments of grace. Instead, they maintained that they function purely as a sign and seal of grace already received. From this perspective, the only benefit they give believers is to strengthen their faith and give them an opportunity to obey Jesus' commands. Following in the footsteps of Zwingli and others, some modern denominations and congregations refuse to use the term sacrament. Instead, they prefer to call baptism and the Lord's Supper ordinances since they were *ordained* by Christ. This understanding has been accepted by groups as diverse as Baptists and the Assemblies of God. Even so, it is no more possible to find the word "ordinance" in Scripture than "sacrament." Both terms were applied after the New Testament era and both espouse positive truths. As signified by the Latin *sacramentum*, Christians are baptized and partake of the Lord's Supper to proclaim their loyalty to Jesus Christ. By doing so, they also demonstrate obedience to his commands—his ordinances—and receive from him the pledge that their sins are forgiven and that they will remain united with the church in this age and the next. Thus, despite the frequent concern over the term used, these rites do benefit believers in several ways. They remind us of the work that Jesus performed on our behalf and of our unity with the church that he established. They give us an opportunity to obey his instruction. Through them, faith is strengthened and believers are enabled to experience the grace God freely extends to those he loves.

BAPTISM

Although baptism is a distinctively Christian rite, its roots stretch to a time before the church began and displays similarities to various water purification rites practiced by many ancient Near Eastern people. As Christianity emerged from the faith of ancient Israel, Old Testament teaching may have influenced the practice of sprinkling water upon people and things to make them clean. Jews, from before the time of Christ, immersed themselves in water for purification. Jews also baptized proselytes to the faith after they underwent ceremonial circumcision, the person coming out of the water being considered a Jew in the fullest sense of the word. This initiation ceremony to Judaism was the only occasion baptism was practiced by Jews as a one-time event. Perhaps the most fastidious in their washings were the Essenes—the Jewish sect that lived near Qumran and probably produced the Dead Sea Scrolls. Not only were those who joined their community required to be baptized, every member submitted to a daily washing in water so that they could retain ritual purity.

John's Baptism

Early followers of Jesus were undoubtedly acquainted with ritual cleansing as commonly practiced in the first century AD. Even so, Christian baptismal rites were not modeled on Jewish forms but on the practice of John the Baptist. The forerunner of the Christ prepared the way for Christian baptism by preaching a baptism of repentance and requiring those who confessed their sins to perform acts that demonstrated their sincerity (Mark 1:4; Luke 3:3, 7–14). John's baptism was distinct from Jewish baptism in several respects.[10] It was a one-time washing to demonstrate conversion of heart rather than a repeated purification ritual. It also differed in that it was not reserved for Gentile converts. John insisted that Jews needed this sign of repentance as much as Gentiles did. Although this would have greatly challenged their beliefs about being saved simply because they were God's chosen people, great crowds traveled from the countryside of Judea, from the area around the Jordan, and from Jerusalem to be baptized by John (Matt 3:5; Mark 1:4). Despite widespread acknowledgement that John's ministry was from God, many priests, scribes, and elders rejected him (Mark 11:27–32; Luke 20:1–7).[11]

John's baptism was significant for recognizing that all people—Jews and Gentiles—need to come to God as repentant sinners to restore their relationship and become members of his kingdom. By locating his work in the wilderness along the Jordan River, John may have linked it to other significant events in salvation history, such as Israel's entrance into the land under Joshua, to signify that simply residing in the land was not sufficient. Rather, one must become a member of the kingdom of God. His work similarly recalled the prophetic ministries of Elijah and Elisha as they parted the waters of the Jordan as a sign that God's Spirit empowered them, and Elisha sent the Gentile Naaman to the Jordan to be cleansed of his leprosy.[12]

---

10. For a good summary of the source of John's baptism, arguing that it developed parallel to rather than from either the Jewish proselyte or Essene purification baptism rites, see Johnson, *The Rites of Christian Initiation*, 7–12.

11. While most Jewish leaders rejected John, some Pharisees and Sadducees were likely baptized by him (Matt 3:7).

12. The connection with Elijah is particularly important as Malachi prophesied that the earlier prophet would return before the coming Day of the Lord (Mal 3:1; 4:5–6) and John is identified as a returned Elijah (Matt 11:14; 17:12–13; Luke 1:17). The description of John wearing clothes made of camel's hair and having a leather belt around his waist clearly links him with Elijah's distinctive attire (Matt 3:4; Mark 1:6; cf. 2 Kgs 1:8). And though John denied being Elijah redivivus (John 1:21, 25), it is probably right to conclude that Jesus was more aware than John of his true identity. See Carson, *John*, 143.

John's baptism prepared for the coming of the Messiah and provided the setting in which the Messiah's ministry began. John was the herald, the voice Isaiah prophesied would come from the wilderness to usher in the reign of the Lord (Isa 40:3–5; Matt 3:1–3; Mark 1:2–4; Luke 3:2–6; John 1:23). As John's preaching reminded his hearers of the prophets of old, people questioned whether he might be the promised Messiah or one of the prophets sent to announce his coming. Denying that he was the Messiah, John pronounced that he would be followed by another more powerful than he. In fact, next to the coming one, John felt that he was less than a servant (Matt 3:11; Mark 1:7; Luke 3:16; John 1:27). The one he announced would not merely baptize with water, but with the Holy Spirit and fire. Though the Gospels never define baptism with the Holy Spirit and fire, it seems best to see this as one baptism with two elements. The Messiah would separate between all of humankind, blessing the righteous with the gift of the Holy Spirit and serving a fiery judgment upon the wicked.[13]

Although John anticipated that the Messiah would follow him, he expressed surprise when Jesus came to him to be baptized. "I need to be baptized by you, and do you come to me?" Only when Jesus informed him that "it is proper for us to do this to fulfill all righteousness" was he willing (Matt 3:14–15). It is likely that Jesus wanted either to identify with John's baptism and mark it with his seal of approval or to participate in a corporate confession of the sins of his people, particularly since he would one day atone for their sin.[14]

In all four Gospels, Jesus' baptism marks the formal beginning of his ministry. The Holy Spirit visibly descended upon him "like a dove" and the Father proclaimed that he was pleased with his Son (Matt 3:16–17; Mark 1:10–11; Luke 3:22; John 1:32–33).[15] Immediately thereafter, Jesus was led by the Spirit into the wilderness to face Satan on his own turf. Returning from the wilderness, still led by the Spirit, Jesus begins to take over from his forerunner by exhorting his listeners to "Repent, for the kingdom of heaven is near" (Matt 4:17).

The Synoptic Gospels say nothing about Jesus or his disciples baptizing those who accepted his preaching. What little we learn about this comes

---

13. This interpretation is supported by John's illustration of the threshing floor in which the wheat is gathered into the barn and the chaff burned up. See Ladd, *A Theology of the New Testament*, 33–35.

14. Blomberg, *Jesus and the Gospels*, 221.

15. One should notice the Trinitarian overtones at Jesus' baptism that would later become part of the baptismal liturgy. When the Son of God is baptized, the Father speaks his approval and the Spirit descends upon him to lead him and empower him for ministry.

from the Gospel of John. While John was baptizing in the Jordan, Jesus and his disciples went into the countryside of Judea where they also baptized (John 3:22–23). The Evangelist adds that the disciples, not Jesus, baptized people, and that they baptized greater numbers than John (John 4:1–2). When apprised of this situation, John expressed his pleasure, saying that "He must become greater; I must become less" (John 3:30). This attitude always characterized John's ministry, as his aim was to point people to the one who would follow him.[16]

As Jesus focused his ministry on the Jews and the Twelve baptized in Judea, it is likely that they joined John in baptizing Jews, with a view toward repentance and kingdom membership. Other comparisons are difficult to make due to a lack of evidence. Even so, both should be differentiated from Christian baptism which would be inaugurated after the sending of the Holy Spirit.[17]

Christian Baptism in the New Testament

The Gospels say little about what baptismal practices may have existed before Pentecost or what meaning may have been assigned to them. However, Matthew regards baptism to be a central Christian practice as he records Jesus' final instructions to his disciples that informed them baptism was not an option for his followers. In his Great Commission, Jesus proclaimed:

> "All authority in heaven and on earth has been given to me. Therefore go and make disciples of all nations, baptizing them in the name of the Father and of the Son and of the Holy Spirit, and teaching them to obey everything I have commanded you. And surely I am with you always, to the very end of the age" (Matt 28:18–20).

Since all power has been given to him by the Father, Jesus sends out his disciples to "make disciples." As the imperative verb in the Greek of the passage, "make disciples" is associated with three dependent participles—going, baptizing, and teaching—to which it lends its imperatival force. Baptism, according to Jesus, is so indispensable that he sets it apart as a major aspect of disciple making. Due to their experience with Jesus and John the

---

16. John had already explicitly informed some of his disciples that Jesus was the Lamb of God, with the result that they left him and followed Jesus (John 1:35–37).

17. That John's baptism was not considered a valid form of Christian baptism is clear from Acts 19:1–5 which tells of Paul baptizing a group of John's disciples at Ephesus. As nothing is said about whether the people baptized by the disciples during Jesus' earthly ministry were again baptized after Pentecost, the reader is left to speculate.

Baptist, the apostles would have understood baptism to follow repentance from sin and usher people into fellowship with God. Though their experience of baptism was limited to repentant Jews, Jesus expanded its scope so that "all the nations" should become his disciples and be baptized into the name of the Father, the Son, and the Holy Spirit. That new disciples are baptized *into* God's name indicates that they belong to God as his personal possession. They no longer belong to the world or even to themselves. As God's possession, they should fear him and serve him through their practical worship. And as the Trinitarian formulation informs us, Jesus does not say to baptize into the *names* of the Father, the Son, and the Holy Spirit, but into the (singular) *name*. The God who, in the Old Testament, was known by the name Yahweh should now be known by the name Father, Son, and Holy Spirit. And according to Jesus, allegiance to and "experience of God in these three Persons is the essential basis of discipleship."[18] Only by laying this foundation could the disciples continue the process of making disciples by teaching all that Jesus taught while he was on earth.

From the beginning of the church, baptism was recognized to be an initiation into God's kingdom and was originally performed immediately after confession of faith. Thus, on the day of Pentecost, the disciples baptized 3000 new believers. As they spread out with the gospel, they baptized others almost as soon as they expressed their faith in Christ and repented of their former sins (Acts 2:38, 41; 8:12, 13, 16, 36, 38; 9:18, etc.).[19] No biblical examples can be given of people waiting to be baptized or attending pre-baptismal classes to ensure their faith was sincere or that they understood the basic doctrines.[20] Though the church, by the late second century, often required candidates to recite or respond to baptismal creeds and later church fathers required a probationary period of up to three years before administering baptism, such regulations are unknown in the biblical record. The early church's practice of making disciples through baptism continued even when an occasional person who was baptized later proved not to have faith (Acts 8:13–24).

18. France, *Matthew*, 414–15.

19. Apparently, the Apostolic Church regularly baptized in the name of (the Lord) Jesus rather than the Trinitarian name (Acts 2:38; 8:16; 10:48; 19:5; Rom 6:3; Gal 3:27). F. F. Bruce suggests that, in Acts, the trinitarian formula "was appropriate for Gentiles turning to the true God from idols," while "baptism into the name of the Lord Jesus as Messiah was sufficient in the case of Jews or Samaritans, who had no need to profess monotheism." Bruce, *The Acts of the Apostles*, 187.

20. Only one case can be cited of an individual asking to be baptized: the Ethiopian eunuch, whose question, "Why shouldn't I be baptized?" (Acts 8:36) indicates that he had either learned something about Christian baptism in Jerusalem or Philip's gospel presentation had included an exhortation to be baptized.

Through baptism, early church leaders recognized that God had chosen a person and brought them to faith in Jesus. As it was open to all, it signified that the church welcomed everyone into the fellowship no matter what their background. As Paul explained it, baptism indicates that the walls that divide people are broken down as they are united as members of God's family through faith in Jesus. "There is neither Jew nor Greek, slave nor free, male nor female, for you are all one in Christ Jesus. If you belong to Christ, then you are Abraham's seed, and heirs according to the promise" (Gal 3:28–29).

Symbolism Associated with Baptism

In addition to providing family recognition, baptism was a reminder that everyone who trusts in Christ's crucifixion for salvation is cleansed from their sins and given new life. Thus, Peter recalls the ark in which Noah and his family "were saved through water," which "symbolizes baptism that now saves you also" (1 Pet 3:20–21). Whether the ark was intended as a type of the cross (Justin Martyr) or the church (Tertullian, Cyprian) is not clear.[21] That the flood is a type for baptism is. It symbolizes baptism in two ways. First, as the flood waters brought judgment upon humankind who were drowned for their sins, the immersion of a new believer symbolizes the death they deserved for their sins before they were raised to a new life. Second, as the water of the flood purified the earth from the corruption brought on by humankind and produced a new creation, so baptism metaphorically washes away spiritual corruption and creates a new being. The washing it provides is "not the removal of dirt from the body but the pledge of a good conscience toward God" (1 Pet 3:21). The author of Hebrews considers baptism from a similar angle, exhorting his readers to "draw near to God with a sincere heart in full assurance of faith, having our hearts sprinkled to cleanse us from a guilty conscience and having our bodies washed with pure water" (Heb 10:22). In this way, baptism is compared to the Old Testament purification rites during which people are cleansed by being sprinkled with water, blood, or oil. It also recalls the prophecy of Ezekiel in which Yahweh says he would bring his people back to their own land.

> I will sprinkle clean water on you, and you will be clean; I will cleanse you from all your impurities and from all your idols. I will give you a new heart and put a new spirit in you; I will

---

21. Kelly believes the second is more likely. Kelly, *Peter and Jude*, 158. Grudem links Noah fleeing to the ark with Christians fleeing to Christ, their hope of escape from judgment. Grudem, *1 Peter*, 163.

remove from you your heart of stone and give you a heart of flesh. And I will put my Spirit in you and move you to follow my decrees and be careful to keep my laws. (Ezek 36:25-27)

As God's promise to cleanse his people's hearts ensured that they would have new lives, baptized believers in Christ were assured that they too would be made new. This does not suggest that baptism accomplishes anything *ex opere operato*. The doctrine of baptismal regeneration—the idea that a person is saved though the rite of baptism—should be firmly rejected.[22] No salvific benefit is derived from the ritual, as the outward cleansing is meant to symbolize the purification of one's conscience that comes through faith in the work of Christ. Since baptism reflects Old Testament themes of cleansing, many Christians through the ages have sprinkled water upon the head of the baptismal candidate to symbolize the cleansing they have received.

Another symbol associated with baptism is the death of a person to his or her old life and the beginning of a new life for those who believe in Jesus (Rom 6:3-4; Col 2:12). As argued by Paul, "We were therefore buried with him through baptism into death in order that, just as Christ was raised from the dead through the glory of the Father, we too may live a new life" (Rom 6:4). The death and resurrection of a believer is dramatically acted out through immersion that symbolically portrays a believer dying to sin by being buried under water before rising up from the water as a new creation.[23]

The death and resurrection of the believer signified by baptism has important implications for one's life of faith. On the one hand, it has a moral aspect, indicating that baptized people should consider themselves to be "dead to sin" (Rom 6:11). Just as sin has no hold over Jesus, it has no hold on those who are baptized in his name. They should, therefore, cease living as slaves to sin and demonstrate that they are now slaves to righteousness, living in obedience to God's will as those who are "alive to God in Jesus Christ" (Rom 6:11). On the other hand, the symbols of death and resurrection that are part of baptism are not limited to new life on earth but have an eschatological thrust. They indicate that a believer is in this life recognized by God as being in Christ and that they will attain to the final resurrection when they will be united with Christ forever (Rom 6:5; Titus 3:7).

---

22. This understanding of baptism as a somewhat magical rite that washed away sins developed toward the end of the second century and has influenced different sections of the church ever since.

23. Putting off the old life and taking on a new one can be symbolized by the removal of old clothes before baptism and putting on new ones after coming up out of the water. In the early church, baptismal candidates frequently entered the water naked to symbolize complete washing and a new life.

BAPTISMAL PRACTICES AND THE CHURCH TODAY

An examination of what the Bible teaches about baptism must be related to the various baptismal practices that developed throughout church history and are practiced today.[24] The summary of some of the major baptismal traditions that follows is not to promote one mode of baptism that should be adopted by all, but to inform readers about variant positions within the church.

The New Testament gives no explicit instruction as to how baptism should be administered. Even so, three basic modes of baptism have been practiced throughout church history—immersion (sometimes called "infusion"), pouring ("affusion"), and sprinkling ("aspersion"). Many Christian traditions maintain that any of the modes are permissible, while some (mainly of the Baptist tradition) greatly prefer one over the others. Immersion reflects what is regularly acknowledged to be the basic meaning of the Greek words for baptism and was apparently the method originally practiced by the church. At the time the *Didache* was written, baptism by immersion "in living water," that is, "running water," was considered normal. This book's discussion of the ritual adds, "But if you have no living water, baptize into other water; and if you cannot do so in cold water, do so in warm. But if you have neither, pour out water three times upon the head into the name of Father and Son and Holy Spirit."[25] Thus, by the beginning of the second century, pouring water over the head of the candidate was permissible when necessary. Though sprinkling was not officially sanctioned until 1311 when the Council of Ravenna placed it alongside immersion as a proper mode of baptism, it was an ancient practice though it is impossible to determine when it was first used. By some counts, pouring and sprinkling are virtually interchangeable.[26]

As Jesus instructed his disciples to baptize "in the name of the Father and of the Son and of the Holy Spirit," Christians from very early times practiced what is known as "trine baptism." This requires the candidate to be baptized three times, whether by immersion, sprinkling, or pouring water. The quote previously given from the *Didache*, along with instructions from *Apostolic Tradition* 21.14–18, indicates trine baptism was a standard practice in the second and third centuries. Trine baptism is still commonly practiced

---

24. For a brief overview of the way various Christian traditions view baptism, see Crawford, "Baptism: Baptist View." Dau, "Baptism: Lutheran View," Lindsay, "Baptism: Reformed View," and Robertson, "Baptism: Baptist View."

25. *Did.* 7.

26. Translations of ancient documents are not consistent in which word is used for baptism.

by some traditions (e.g., Eastern Orthodoxy and the Church of the Brethren). While the symbolism vividly highlights the Trinity, most churches find it unnecessary as the threefold name of God used in conjunction with a single baptism similarly speaks of the Trinitarian nature of the rite.

Believers frequently divide over their understanding of the baptism of infants and children. The basic issue is whether a person needs to express personal faith to be baptized or if one's parents or guardians, as members of the community of faith, may express faith for their children until they are old enough to articulate their own faith. Another way of looking at it is to say that infant baptism focuses more on "the priority of grace to faith," while believer's baptism focuses more on "the believer's response to grace."[27] The problem is not easily settled as the New Testament neither expressly commands nor forbids the baptism of the children of believing parents. The passages that are taken to support the practice refer to the baptism of a "household" as in the case of Lydia, the Philippian jailer, and Stephanus (Acts 16:15, 31; 1 Cor 1:16), though they are open to various interpretations. In many ways, infant baptism becomes a problem for the second and subsequent generations of believers as they consider how their children relate to the church.

The major argument for believer's baptism is that the Bible assumes faith and repentance before baptism. Those who hold this position insist that infants should be excluded as they are not capable of exhibiting faith.[28] Support for paedo-baptism is usually tied to a covenantal theology that connects baptism with circumcision as the sign that one has become part of the people of God (Col 2:11-12). As Israelite children who were circumcised have a part in the old covenant, the children of Christians who are baptized are believed to have a part in the new covenant. Many who espouse infant baptism maintain that no one should consider the act to be a right, but that it should be reserved for children whose parents are committed Christians who, as active members of a community of faith, are prepared to raise them in the ways of Christ and the church. The existence of faith remains an integral part of infant baptism.

---

27. Oden, *Pastoral Theology*, 113. Supporters of infant baptism include Calvin, *Institutes* 4.14–16; Jeremias, *Infant Baptism in the First Four Centuries*; Jeremias, *The Origins of Infant Baptism*; and Bromiley, *Children of Promise*. Supporters of believer's baptism include Aland, *Did the Early Church Baptize Infants?*; Beasley-Murray, *Baptism in the New Testament*; Barth, *Teaching of the Church Regarding Baptism*; and White, *Biblical Doctrine of Initiation*.

28. Although some suggest children could have incipient faith, this cannot be tested, and it is admitted by most Protestants that the baptism of children does not ensure that they will one day exercise their own faith. By the same measure, the baptism of older people does not guarantee that they will remain in the faith.

The differences we find today have existed since the third century when infant baptism was widely practiced in both the East and West.[29] Even so, differences of opinion and practice were clear. While children as young as one year old are known to have been baptized on the day of their death,[30] some prominent church leaders from Christian families were not baptized until adulthood.[31] Tertullian felt that it is best to delay baptizing young children until "they have become able to know Christ" (*De baptismo* 18). Taking a completely different view, *Apostolic Tradition* 21.4 makes allowance for parents of "children who cannot answer for themselves" to answer for them when they are baptized. Origen understood that the tradition of baptizing very young children came from the apostles (*In Romanos commentaria* 5).

Another issue associated with baptism concerns the people who are allowed to perform the rite. When he gave the Great Commission, Jesus instructed his disciples to make disciples by baptizing and teaching. Nothing in this passage or the rest of the New Testament limits this instruction to the apostles or other church leaders or outlines qualifications for those who baptize others. While the apostles baptized new believers in Christ, so did others. Philip the evangelist, one of the seven appointed to serve widows, baptized the Ethiopian eunuch (Acts 8:38). Ananias, the disciple from Damascus, apparently baptized the Pharisee Saul who later became known as Paul (Acts 9:18). Even so, most early baptisms were apparently performed by a church leader, such as a pastor or bishop.[32] Although the Bible never states that lay people cannot baptize others, since baptism is the responsibility of the church, leaders usually perform the rite as the appointed representatives of the church.

CONCLUSION

Christians have historically recognized the sacraments or ordinances of baptism and the Lord's Supper to be vehicles of God's grace and expressions of personal faith. When combined with faith and God's word, the Holy Spirit uses them to build our faith and to enable us to experience God's love. Baptism and the Lord's Supper are to be incorporated into the worship of the church as they were ordained by Christ and serve as means for us to proclaim our loyalty and obedience to him. They also serve as signs that our

---

29. As was infant communion.
30. Cabié et al., *The Sacraments*, 62.
31. The most outstanding of these were probably Basil the Great, his brother Gregory of Nyssa, and their friend Gregory of Nazianzus (whose father was a bishop).
32. It should be noted that these roles were not separated before the fourth century.

sins are forgiven, we are accepted as members of the one true church, and we have a future in God's eternal kingdom.

Baptism is the sacrament through which we are ushered into the church, testifying to the faith we have in the redemption brought about by Jesus and the new life breathed into us by the Holy Spirit. It speaks of the cleansing we receive through the blood of Jesus, of our death in his death that delivers us from the power of sin and death, and of our new life in the Spirit that we gain through his resurrection.

The Bible's teaching about baptism should impact our practice in a number of ways. Christians who have not been baptized for whatever reason should respond to Jesus' command that new disciples be baptized by submitting themselves to the water. Although the onus is often put upon the believer to seek baptism if they so desire, biblical precedent should move church leadership to be as proactive in leading people to baptism as they are in bringing them to confession of faith and discipleship.

Biblical teaching could also influence another modern practice—"rebaptism." Many Christians who were baptized as infants feel moved or are strongly encouraged to submit themselves to the water again after they have publically professed their faith. Others are baptized again after joining a denomination or local church that requires a particular form of baptism for membership, partaking of communion, or active service. Though the reasons for repeating baptism are often understandable, biblical and theological reasons exist that render such actions questionable. Baptism should be as unrepeatable as justification and adoption.[33] Paul's proclamation that there is "one Lord, one faith, one baptism" (Eph 4:5) must be taken seriously. Though one's baptism might be remembered or reenacted, it cannot really be repeated.

Even though the Bible provides no baptismal liturgy and no description of baptism as part of a service of worship, it can play a significant role in the public worship of God. Baptisms recognize that someone has come to faith in Christ and thus announce the growth of the church. But even if baptism does not follow immediately upon a person's confession of faith, services featuring the rite provide an excellent opportunity to welcome new members to the church, allow them to testify of God's grace in their lives, and proclaim that anyone who trusts in the power of Christ's blood can be cleansed from sin and brought into relationship with God and his people.

When baptisms are incorporated into the worship of the church, members are given an opportunity to express joy for Christ's work in the lives of the individuals. They also provide an occasion to remind people

---

33. Stevens and Green, *Living the Story*, 133.

of the meaning of their own baptism and the need for faith if it is to be effective. Furthermore, they make it possible to repeat the message of the gospel and show that those who respond are incorporated into God's family. Churches that baptize infants should be careful to explain what the rite does and does not do for the child. They should also remind parents and others present that the child should be brought up to know Christ and express personal faith in him.

As with other aspects of worship, it is important that Christians understand the position their own church holds concerning baptism and learn to appreciate why other traditions differ in their theology and practice. Until we can attain unity on these matters, we should be careful to express charity toward others and recall the biblical instruction that the Holy Spirit who brings us into the church through baptism is the same Spirit who regenerates those who have adopted or inherited other baptismal practices.

12

Worship and the Lord's Supper

In the previous chapter, we examined the meaning of the term sacrament and introduced the Christian sacrament of initiation—baptism. This chapter will examine the second ordinance that has been practiced since the beginning of the church—the Lord's Supper. Different Christian groups variously refer to it as the Lord's Table, the breaking of bread, Communion, Eucharist, and the Mass. We will look at these terms and discuss different aspects of the sacrament these terms bring out.[1] We will then consider the implications of the way the Lord's Supper is discussed in the Bible and make suggestions about how the Lord's Supper can be used in modern corporate worship.

TERMS FOR THE LORD'S SUPPER

The Lord's Supper recalls the Last Supper Jesus shared with his disciples before being led away to trial and crucifixion. Although the words are not found in any of the Gospel accounts of the Last Supper, Paul referred to the Lord's Table in 1 Corinthians 10:21 and to the Lord's Supper in 1 Corinthians 11:20. The connection with the Last Supper reminds us that Christians in the first century often shared meals together and that during these meals, they remembered Jesus' sacrifice by sharing bread and wine.[2] This meal was

---

1. Eastern Orthodoxy calls this sacrament the Holy Liturgy or simply the Offering.
2. Though many modern churches use grape juice instead of wine, this practice only began after 1869 when Thomas B. Welch discovered how to pasteurize grape juice to prevent fermentation. See White, *Christian Worship and Technological Change*, 81–86. "Wine" is used in this chapter to refer to the contents of the communion cup

called the *agapē* or "love feast," a term only found in the Bible in Jude 12 but commonly used in first-century writings.³ Were it not for the abuse of this meal by believers in Corinth, it is probable that Paul would not have produced his major teaching on the Lord's Supper, which was written to correct their errors and provides us with words that are used in many liturgies (1 Cor 11:20–22, 33–34). By the middle of the second century, the Western church no longer celebrated the Lord's Supper and *agapē* together. While they were associated for a while longer in the Eastern church, the *agapē* was soon abandoned as a meal for the whole church and, where it remained, served only as a charity meal for the poor.

The term "communion" or "holy communion" reminds us that this simple ritual highlights the means by which those who partake are brought into fellowship with God and with one another. Jesus' sacrifice, signified by the broken bread and wine, opens the way for people to become members of God's family. The connection between Christ's action on the cross and the memorial meal is reflected in the KJV translation of 1 Corinthians 10:16, where the Greek word *koinōnia* is translated "communion."⁴ "The cup of blessing which we bless, is it not the communion of the blood of Christ? The bread which we break, is it not the communion of the body of Christ?" Paul seems to indicate that sharing in the cup points to the vertical relationship we have with Jesus, while the bread points to the horizontal relationship we have with other Christians who compose the body of Christ on earth.⁵ Although the main purpose of 1 Corinthians 10 is to warn believers that sharing the Lord's Supper is incompatible with participation in pagan meals, it supports the idea that the bread and wine speak of our communion with Christ through his blood and with one another as members of his body who partake of the same bread.⁶

As the meal was known for the characteristic blessing and breaking of bread, it is also referred to as the Eucharist or the "breaking of bread." Eucharist is derived from the Greek verb *eucharisteō*, which means "to be

---

whether fermented or not.

3. See Blue, "Love Feast," 578–79. While the meal is also found in some manuscripts of 2 Peter 2:13, most scholars consider it a scribal assimilation to Jude 12. See Metzger, *Textual Commentary*, 704.

4. Most modern English versions translate the word "participation" (ESV, NIV, RSV) or "sharing" (CSB, NASB, NRSV).

5. Fee, *First Corinthians*, 467.

6. It is, therefore, right that Christians partake of the Lord's Supper with others and not alone. Many churches thus take leftover elements to those who are sick or otherwise unable to attend a service. Those who cannot otherwise join the larger assembly are unified with the body as they partake of the same bread and wine.

thankful, give thanks," or its associated noun *eucharistia*, "thankfulness, gratitude, thanksgiving." The word is used for the sacrament because Jesus gave thanks before he shared the bread and wine with his disciples (Matt 26:27; Mark 14:23; Luke 22:17, 19). It is also used because during the meal, we express our thanks to God that Jesus came to earth to die as a sacrifice for us. That Eucharist was the technical term for the sacrament at the beginning of the second century is clear by its use in the *Didache*. It remains the most common term for the Lord's Supper in many churches today.

The phrase "to break bread" was used to speak of the action performed by the head of the house at the beginning of a meal (Jer 16:7; Lam 4:4; Mark 6:41; 8:6). It was thus a common expression for sharing a meal. Since early Christians frequently ate meals together in conjunction with partaking of the Lord's Supper, they quickly adopted "breaking of bread" in reference to the sacred meal.[7] Since "breaking of bread" is occasionally used without reference to wine, some have argued that at its earliest stages, the sacrament was celebrated with the sharing of only one element. Contrary to this position, the biblical record indicates that both bread and wine were shared from the beginning. Breaking of bread was used to refer to the whole meal, both elements subsumed under one head, *pars pro toto*.

The term Mass comes from the Latin word *missa*, which means "dismissed." The sacrament may have received this title because, in the early church, non-communicants who attended the first part of a service were dismissed before the eucharistic service began. It may also have come from the closing words of the service in Latin, "*Ite, missa est*," "Go, you are dismissed." Seen in this light, it encourages those who are united in Christ as symbolized by the supper to enter the world to serve God in their daily lives.

THE LORD'S SUPPER IN THE NEW TESTAMENT

The celebration of the Lord's Supper springs from the Last Supper Jesus shared with his disciples. Earlier, we saw that this supper was almost certainly

---

7. It is not always clear which New Testament references to breaking of bread refer to common meals, which refer to the Lord's Supper, and which unite the Lord's Supper with an *agapē*. Behm says that Acts 2:42, 46 "refers to the daily fellowship of the first Christians in Jerusalem and has nothing to do with liturgical celebration of the Lord's Supper." Behm, "κλάω," 731. Bruce follows the conclusion of Rudolf Otto that in these verses, the Lord's Supper, in conjunction with a meal, is in view. Bruce, *The Acts of the Apostles*, 100, referring to Otto, *The Kingdom of God and the Son of Man*, 312–14. Longenecker sees the breaking of bread as an ordinary meal in Luke 24:30, 35; Acts 20:11; 27:35 and probably Acts 2:46. He does, however, believe that its placement between "the fellowship" and "prayer" in Acts 2:42, takes it out of the realm of ordinary meals and connects it with Christ's passion. Longenecker, *Acts*, 85–86.

a Passover meal that was hosted by Jesus who intended that it should parallel and supplant the Passover feast. While Jesus served the meal, "he took bread, gave thanks and broke it, and gave it to them, saying, 'This is my body given for you; do this in remembrance of me'" (Luke 22:19). Similarly, after the supper, "he took the cup, saying, 'This cup is the new covenant in my blood, which is poured out for you'" (Luke 22:20).[8] Instead of remembering the bread of affliction eaten at the time of the exodus, Jesus' disciples were to remember his body given as a redemptive sacrifice. Instead of linking wine to the blood of the animals sacrificed and smeared on doorframes, they were to remember his blood that stained the cross so that they could be spared from God's wrath. As the cup ushered in the new covenant, God's new covenant community uses the symbols to commemorate the salvific sacrifice that was offered once even as the exodus was a once-for-all event. Thus, in the same way that each generation of Jews was to relive the exodus experience when they shared the Passover meal, each generation of Jesus' disciples is to relive his passion by sharing the meal he established that night.

Though rarely mentioned outside of the Gospels, the breaking of bread appears in several significant passages in the book of Acts and in 1 Corinthians where Paul corrects its abnormal practice in the church he founded. The first probable reference comes in Acts 2:42, which records that the early church "devoted themselves to the apostles' teaching and to the fellowship, to the breaking of bread and to prayer."[9] As the breaking of bread is listed with the teaching of the apostles, fellowship, and prayer, it more likely refers to the Lord's Supper than to a common meal and should be counted among the characteristic worship practices of the early church.[10] As the church spread from Jerusalem, the practice spread so that by the late fifties, Gentile believers as far away as Troas joined the apostles in celebrating Christ's death (Acts 20:7).[11]

---

8. These words of institution were so significant for the early church that Paul repeated them almost word for word when he instructed the Corinthian church how they were to celebrate the meal (1 Cor 11:23–26).

9. Note that "fellowship" (*koinōnia*) in this verse likely refers to the early believers' common sharing in God through Jesus Christ and their mutual enjoyment through meeting together and sharing with those in need rather than participating in the Eucharist. The following clause, however, probably has the Communion in view (cf. Acts 2:44–45).

10. A century later, Justin Martyr's description of Christian worship parallels Luke's. Justin says Christians gathered on a Sunday to read the memoirs of the apostles and writings of the prophets, hear an exhortation to live out these teachings, offer up various kinds of prayer and thanksgiving to which the congregation responded "Amen," receive bread and wine, and take up an offering for the needs of orphans, widows, and others. Justin, *1 Apol.* 67.

11. The account of Paul breaking bread in Troas is the earliest unambiguous

Undoubtedly, the most important biblical passage on the Lord's Supper is 1 Corinthians 11:20–34. Given in the context of Paul's correction of the Corinthian church for numerous misunderstandings of how the Christian life should be lived, this passage underscores his contention that their practice of the sacrament had strayed so far from his original teaching that what they shared could no longer be called the Lord's Supper (1 Cor 11:20). In Corinth, a distinction was made between social groups—the wealthy ate sumptuously and drank heavily, while the poor were left with little. As was common in Corinth, divisions separated believers that the meal should have united. Rather than humiliating the poor by their eating habits, Paul instructed the rich to eat at home or perhaps to share all food equally.

The habits and attitudes of certain Corinthian believers forced Paul to repeat some of the lessons he had taught them when he founded the church and further explain the effects of their actions. He begins by reminding them that during his eighteen months in Corinth, he had passed on instruction from the Lord that they were to do the same in remembrance of him.[12] By informing them that the bread was "my body, which is for you," Jesus indicated that his death was for their benefit and for the benefit of others. By informing them that the cup was "the new covenant in my blood," he let them know that they were part of a new covenant community. If Jesus had given himself in this way, the Corinthians should not abuse his meal or each other, but give themselves to those who were members of the same community of faith.

The divisions they were causing were so serious that Paul was impelled to insist that all who participate in the Lord's Table should examine themselves to ensure they receive it in a worthy manner rather than being "guilty of sinning against the body and blood of the Lord" (1 Cor 11:27). To show that their improper celebration of the Supper had already made them guilty, Paul reminds them that some of them had become sick and others had died.

PRACTICAL OUTWORKING OF THE BIBLICAL TEACHING ON THE LORD'S SUPPER

Paul's teaching about the Lord's Supper reminds us to examine our hearts' condition when partaking of the bread and wine and to consider the past,

---

statement that Christians met on a Sunday for worship.

12. Discussions about whether Paul received this instruction by direct revelation from Christ or indirectly through receiving the authoritative tradition passed on through the apostles, while frequent, are inconclusive as we possess inadequate evidence to provide unequivocal support for either position. They are furthermore somewhat irrelevant, as the same Lord is the source no matter how he gives instructions.

present, and future orientation of the Eucharist. We find this expressed in 1 Corinthians 11:23–27.

> For I received from the Lord what I also passed on to you: The Lord Jesus, on the night he was betrayed, took bread, and when he had given thanks, he broke it and said, "This is my body, which is for you; do this in remembrance of me." In the same way, after supper he took the cup, saying, "This cup is the new covenant in my blood; do this, whenever you drink it, in remembrance of me." For whenever you eat this bread and drink this cup, you proclaim the Lord's death until he comes. Therefore, whoever eats the bread or drinks the cup of the Lord in an unworthy manner will be guilty of sinning against the body and blood of the Lord.

As Paul understands it, celebrants of the Lord's Supper should remember Christ's historical work of distributing the elements to his disciples that pointed to his imminent death on the cross. They should also realize that when they receive the bread and wine in the present, they appropriate God's grace for living and proclaim the gospel of his death. In addition, they look forward to the future reality that Jesus will one day come again to unite his followers in his kingdom where they will partake of the eschatological marriage supper of the Lamb.

The Lord's Supper Looks Back to the Cross

By twice reiterating that the Lord's Supper was to be celebrated "in remembrance of me," Paul firmly connects the Lord's Supper with the Last Supper and Jesus' death on the cross. Celebrants should, therefore, see the Eucharist as an opportunity to recall the events of the night when Jesus was betrayed and his ensuing crucifixion. The night began with Jesus washing his disciples' feet. He then taught them about heaven, the Holy Spirit, and his relationship with them. He later prayed for himself, for his closest disciples, and for all who would believe because of their testimony. During the meal, he shared bread and wine with those he had called to be his own, informing them that the elements symbolized his body and blood that would be offered as a sacrifice so that sins could be forgiven.

When we celebrate the Lord's Supper, we should recall how Jesus came to be the Lamb of God who takes away the sin of the world. As we partake of the bread, we should contemplate his body, both in life and in death. We should remember the sacred mystery that Jesus was God become man. In Jesus, the transcendent Creator became immanent, entering his creation as

Immanuel. The one who had always existed entered a womb and was born. The Word became flesh. The God who is spirit took on flesh and bones. The God who is free from the confines of time became tied to an existence within time and space. The designer of the elements revealed himself as living water. The maker of wheat became the bread of life. The Holy One interacted with sinful humans and ultimately bore their sins on his own body. The source of animal life surrendered himself as a sacrificial lamb. And though we will not meditate on each one of these ideas every time we partake of the bread, we should fill our minds with them. We should simultaneously remember that Jesus knows us intimately, empathizes with our situations as he shared this life with us, and he sets us free from the bondage of sin through his self-giving sacrifice.

As we drink the fruit of the vine, we should recall the new covenant God established with his people. In Jeremiah 31:31–34, the prophet reminded Israel that the old covenant needed to be replaced since they had broken it. But in spite of their sin and rebellion, God would not forget them. Instead, he would "put my law in their minds and write it on their hearts. I will be their God, and they will be my people" (Jer 31:33). That the new covenant is established by the blood of Jesus reminds us that when the first covenant was established, "Moses then took the blood, sprinkled it on the people and said, 'This is the blood of the covenant that the LORD has made with you'" (Exod 24:8). In the same way the sprinkling associated with the first covenant was understood to have atoning significance, Jesus made sure that his disciples understood that his blood of the covenant "is poured out for many for the forgiveness of sins" (Matt 26:28). As we receive the cup, we should remember that Jesus was the Lamb of God who came into the world to save sinners. Though he was sinless, he became a sin offering so that rebels could become righteous (2 Cor 5:21). By dying on the cross, he made it possible for everyone who comes to him to be reconciled to God.

A central part of our celebration of the Lord's Supper looks back in remembrance of the life and death of Jesus Christ. It is not, however, merely a remembrance service, as a sacrament is a sign or pledge of more to come. The Lord's Supper thus gives us an opportunity to look forward with anticipation to what the Lord has yet to give us.

The Lord's Supper Looks Forward to the Kingdom

All the Gospel accounts of the Last Supper and Paul's teaching about the Lord's Supper agree that the feast looks to the future. Even so, they address the future orientation of the meal in somewhat different ways. When Jesus passes out the wine, he tells his disciples, "I will not drink of this fruit of the vine from now on until the day when I drink it anew with you in my Father's kingdom" (Matt 26:29; cf. Mark 14:25; Luke 22:16). This statement clearly looks forward to the eschatological messianic banquet prophesied in the Old Testament and Revelation (Isa 25:6–9; Rev 19:9). By saying that he would again drink the cup with his disciples, Jesus lets them know that they have a future with him in the kingdom of God. Christ's death, far from being the end of his ministry, was the apex of his ministry and the way by which God's kingdom would come. His disciples should, therefore, be encouraged that they would both see him again and share in his glory. When Jesus said that he would not share in the Passover again, he "implies that the disciples will."[13] They will continue to celebrate the Passover in the way he has redefined it for them even though he will not be present in the same way.

Though he did not quote Jesus' statement about sharing wine in the kingdom, Paul adds his own admonition about the future. "For whenever you eat this bread and drink this cup, you proclaim the Lord's death until he comes" (1 Cor 11:26). Paul here points to Jesus' future return, demonstrating his understanding that the Supper points to the eschaton. The Eucharist thus reminds us that God has more to give to those who unite in the name of Jesus. Everyone who partakes of the bread and wine in faith can be assured that they have a future with Christ. They should also recognize that their participation in the meal unites them not only with those who share in the distribution, but also with those who now worship Jesus in heaven and with those who will yet join them in the kingdom.[14] Furthermore, since the meal is a proclamation of the Lord's death—a gospel presentation—it anticipates that others will believe in him.

From the earliest times, the eucharistic liturgy referred to the return of the Lord and the end of this age. A eucharistic prayer found in *Didache* 10 reads, "Let grace come, and let this world pass away. Hosanna to the God (Son) of David! If any one is holy, let him come; if any one is not so, let him repent. Maranatha." The use of *maranatha* in this setting has led some to conclude that it was a common phrase in early Christian liturgies. Some have suggested that its use in 1 Corinthians 16:22 indicates that the book was originally written to be read in conjunction with a Communion service. Though it is doubtful that the letter was written for this purpose,

---

13. Behm, "κλάω," 735.

14. The understanding that Christians worship with those in heaven is reflected in the Proper Preface found in the *Book of Common Prayer*. "Therefore, with angels and archangels and with all the company of heaven, we laud and magnify thy glorious name; evermore praising thee and saying, Holy, holy, holy, Lord God of hosts, heaven and earth are full of thy glory: Glory be to thee, O Lord most High. Amen."

there is good reason to believe that *maranatha* was used in both Aramaic- and Greek-speaking churches where it may have served as a confession of the Lord's presence ("the Lord is come"), a prayer for him to be present at their worship ("O Lord, come"), or a prayer for his speedy return ("O Lord, come"; cf. Rev 22:20).[15]

Our participation in the Lord's Supper faces the future as we await the return of Christ when he will reign over all creation as King of kings and Lord of lords. It also orients our hearts toward the great wedding supper of the Lamb when people from every tribe and nation and people and tongue will gather as the bride of Christ. By looking forward, we discover the need to spread the gospel to the whole world, expecting that others will join us in the kingdom. But even this is not enough. Our celebration of the Eucharist turns us to the past and the future to inform us how we should live today.

The Lord's Supper Affects Us in the Present

When Jesus broke bread and shared wine with his disciples, he instructed them to "Do this in remembrance of me." Each generation of Christians that responds to his words and partakes of the elements receives God's grace and demonstrates their obedience to their Lord. They recognize that Communion signifies the fellowship shared by all believers in Christ. And while the Eucharist is not a new sacrifice, it allows God's people to offer their own sacrifice of thanksgiving and praise for what the Lord has done for them. It also requires that they examine themselves to be sure they partake worthily. Finally, as Paul explains, the meal is a proclamation of the Lord's death to the community of the faith and to the world.

Not everyone agrees as to how or whether the meal transmits God's grace to those who receive it. But whether the Lord's Supper is a direct instrument of grace or simply signifies grace that has already been received, recipients experience the elements, in Augustine's term, as "visible words" that accompany the preached word to stimulate faith and obedience. The bread and wine signify Christ's body and blood that were given as a sacrifice that those who believe might receive forgiveness of sin and live for God. By rightly partaking of them we are reminded of our current relationship with God through his Son Jesus Christ and encouraged to remain in fellowship with him through faith.

Those who eat the Lord's Supper identify themselves with their Lord and with his people. As Paul declared to the divided Corinthian church, "Is not the cup of thanksgiving for which we give thanks a participation

---

15. Kuhn, "μαραναθά," 472; Hurtado, *Lord Jesus Christ*, 141.

(*koinōnia*) in the blood of Christ? And is not the bread that we break a participation (*koinōnia*) in the body of Christ? Because there is one loaf, we, who are many, are one body, for we all partake of the one loaf" (1 Cor 10:16–17). There is a real sense in which those who share in the one loaf—he who is the Bread of Life—become one body—the body of Christ. And whether one only experiences the Communion with a single local body or has the privilege of sharing it with a large assembly of believers who come from numerous ethnic, national, and denominational backgrounds, the sacrament points to the real unity Christians share due to our faith in the work of Christ.

Since the Lord's Supper was intended to unite Christ's followers, we should be concerned when we find it difficult or impossible to share the Lord's Supper with others due to racial, doctrinal, denominational, or other differences. Though valid reasons may exist for not sharing the Eucharist with some who are identified with Christianity,[16] it is possible to set up divisions like the ones Paul castigated when he informed the church in Corinth that they were not celebrating the Lord's Supper. And though it may not be as serious as disunity, the physical setting in which we share the Eucharist may obscure the communion we share. Sitting in rows or kneeling at a rail with our eyes fixed to the front can give us little connection with those around us. Even in traditions that incorporate the "sharing of the peace" into the liturgy, there may be little interaction between those who share the meal.

Many local assemblies should reassess whether their communion services truly unify their membership in the wider church. The size of congregation, physical layout of the church building, and other issues may influence what can be done, but fellowship should be actively pursued. It may be that a local church could implement a modern day *agapē* that incorporates sharing bread and wine in the context of a congregational meal during which people can interact on a closer level. Introducing a time for prayer into the Lord's Supper service, whether leaders pray for individual congregants or members pray for each other, can also bring people together. When I was a youth, our communion service ended with the singing of "Blest be the Tie that Binds," as the congregation held hands in a circle and

---

16. Due to different theological understandings about its meaning, many Protestants find it impossible to share the Lord's Supper with Roman Catholics (and *vice versa*). And though many willingly invite others who express faith in Jesus and have been baptized to join them in the sacrament, some find themselves unable to share with anyone outside their denomination or group. Almost all who trace their roots to the great ecumenical councils of the first four centuries are unwilling to share the Lord's Supper with any who do not hold to a Nicene understanding of the faith.

were encouraged to pray for each other until we met again. Cell groups of some traditions could add a celebration with the bread and wine that unites to their study of God's word and prayer.

The possibility of divisions and the presence of other types of sin makes it imperative that those who wish to receive the Lord's Supper worthily examine themselves. Though the Bible never mentions the possibility, some may need to examine themselves to determine whether they are true believers in the Lord. Others may need to excuse themselves due to sin that needs to be addressed. As has been recognized from sub-apostolic times, only those who believe the gospel, have been baptized, and are living as in accordance with Christian truth should be allowed to partake.[17]

Paul's warning to the Corinthian church about receiving Communion in an unworthy manner mainly concerns living out the faith, particularly in one's relationship with other believers. As is clear from the context of his discourse, one should express the self-giving love of Christ rather than being consumed with personal interests. Similarly, one should not be part of divisions in the church, be they erected over sociological, theological, denominational, or other issues. To be worthy to partake, a person might need to seek out a Christian brother or sister (or even a family member) and deal with misunderstandings or sins that have hurt the relationship.[18] Though not easy, examining one's relationships and ensuring that they are right make it possible to partake of the Lord's body and blood in a worthy manner. As Paul warned, failure to do this could result in sickness or death (1 Cor 11:28–30).

Many Communion liturgies contain an announcement for everyone to examine themselves to see if they have unconfessed sins. While this should be applauded, examination should not be put off until the last few moments before the bread and wine are distributed. Rather, we should continually prepare ourselves during the days, weeks, and possibly even months before we share the bread and wine. Unless the Eucharist is served weekly, it would be wise to announce an upcoming celebration and encourage congregational members to prepare themselves. Special times could be set aside during the week preceding the service for prayer and restoration. In this

---

17. *Did.* 9; Justin Martyr, *1 Apol.* 66.

18. Though confession is an important part of Christian living, Donald Bloesch wisely warns that confessing secret sins may cause more problems than keeping them concealed from all but God. "We would do well to keep in mind that some sins should be confessed only to God because of the disruption that an open confession might cause in the community. Some sins should be hidden even from those closest and dearest to us—for their sake, not necessarily for ours. We do not confess in order to add burdens to another but to receive renewed confidence that God is with us and for us." Bloesch, *The Church*, 171.

way, some who might not have been willing to partake due to personal sin would be given time to confess their sins to God, receive absolution, and be reconciled to other believers.

A final thing to learn about the present experience of the Lord's Supper is that it is a proclamation of the Lord's death (1 Cor 11:26). The gospel is preached every time we share Communion, though not through the action of breaking bread and distributing it along with wine. Rather, it is through the words that are proclaimed when the elements are shared.[19] While the symbols point to Jesus' atoning sacrifice on the cross, without the words of institution that explain the bread is his body that was given for us and the cup is the new covenant in his blood, their meaning remains hidden. But when the gospel explanation is preached, the symbols take on added significance so that those who partake of the bread and wine can relate them to the Lord's death and the salvation that comes to those who believe in him.

The way the Eucharist speaks of the preaching of the gospel for the salvation of the world is beautifully worded in a prayer found in the *Didache*. "As this broken bread was scattered upon the mountains and being gathered together became one, so may Your Church be gathered together from the ends of the earth into Your kingdom."[20] These words, which demonstrate the evangelistic burden early Christians felt as they considered the Communion they shared with Christ and his church, should impel us to think deeply about the effects of the body and blood of Jesus upon a world that he came to save and our part in spreading that message.

By looking to the past and the future when we share the Eucharist in the present, we receive a proper perspective of our lives as Christians. We are reminded that we are part of the church because of what Christ has done for us in history. As members of the church, we are to relate to our brothers and sisters as equals in Christ and recognize our role in reaching others with the gospel and bringing them to full discipleship until Christ's kingdom is fulfilled and we all take part in the marriage supper of the Lamb.

DISAGREEMENTS ABOUT THE MEAL INSTITUTED TO BRING UNITY

It is a sad fact that the meal intended to unite the followers of Christ has often been a source of division. In some cases, illustrated by the church in Corinth, already existing factions can result in a failure to rightly celebrate the Lord's Supper. Other Christians refuse to share bread and wine with

---

19. Schniewind, "ἀγγελία," 72; Fee, *First Corinthians*, 557.
20. *Did.* 9.

anyone who proclaims to be a follower of Jesus but hold different theological understandings of the ordinance. While all Christians acknowledge that the bread and wine symbolize the body and blood of Christ, major differences arise when we attempt to explain the connection between the symbol and the reality, particularly when it relates to the way Christ is present in the meal. Is it merely a memorial of Christ's death as Zwingli, the Anabaptists, and their followers have held? Or is Christ actually present when believers partake of the elements as believed by many other Christians? And if Christ is present, is he present in a physical, spiritual, or some other way?

The explanation that unites the bread and wine with Christ's body and blood in the closest manner is known as transubstantiation. According to this doctrine, which developed during Medieval times and was pronounced an article of faith by the Fourth Lateran Council (1215) and upheld by the Council of Trent, when the words of consecration are spoken during the Mass, the bread and wine substantially become the body and blood of Christ even though their appearance remains unchanged. Although it is sometimes maintained that the approach originated before Western Christianity was influenced by Aristotelian thought, the major arguments in its favor use Aristotle's distinction between "substance" and "accident" to show that the essential nature of the elements changes so that they become Christ's body and blood even though their outward appearance remains the same.

The Reformers consistently argued that the philosophical basis for transubstantiation was incompatible with historic Christian teaching. Nevertheless, they varied in their understandings of how Christ was present in the Lord's Supper. Luther's view, known as consubstantiation, denied that the bread and wine become the body and blood of Jesus by undergoing a change in substance. Even so, Luther described Christ's presence in physical terms, explaining that the elements are simultaneously bread and wine and the body and blood of Christ. Calvin rejected all notions that Christ was physically present in the meal since he ascended to heaven bodily. He did, however, argue for the spiritual presence of the Lord when his followers partook of the Eucharist. Zwingli and the Anabaptists argued that Jesus is no more present in the sacrament than he is at any other time or space. From their perspective, even as the apostles would not have taken the words "this is my body" literally since Jesus personally gave them the bread, those who have received the apostles' message about Jesus should not think that he is physically present in the elements.

As none of the explanations is explicitly stated in the Bible, one must ask whether it is right to refuse to share that which our Lord instructed his followers to do in remembrance of him with others who interpret the command in a different way. The churches that rightly announce before

Communion that all who believe in Jesus as Savior and have been baptized are welcome to join in the meal set a good example for others to follow.

Another area of division over the Eucharist is whether it should be considered a sacrifice, and if so, what kind of a sacrifice. From early in church history, the language of sacrifice was clearly used in the context of the Lord's Supper. Even so, it usually pointed to bringing a sacrifice of thanksgiving and praise to God or of sacrificing oneself to the Lord. Not until the fourth century was it linked to a propitiatory offering of the body and blood of Jesus. And it was only after the Reformers took issue with the idea that the Eucharist should be considered a sacrifice that the Council of Trent proclaimed it a doctrine of the church. From the Reformers' standpoint, the idea must be rejected since Jesus never said that his suffering would be repeated each time his disciples ate bread and drank wine in his memory. They believed that the book of Hebrews sealed the case since it spoke of Christ's sacrifice as being once for all and its argument that his performance as the great high priest who entered heaven and sat down ensured that he would never have to offer himself or suffer again. As with the different interpretations of the presence of Christ in the elements, differences here have made it virtually impossible for Protestants and Catholics to share the Lord's Supper.

Another cause for division has to do with the people who are permitted to lead a service and/or dispense the elements. Although there is no biblical evidence to support the practice, many denominations require that an ordained minister be present when the Lord's Supper is celebrated and personally administer the elements. In Catholic tradition, the presence of a priest is considered essential for transubstantiation to take place.[21] Although other traditions may not accept transubstantiation, they often require an ordained pastor, elected elders, or other recognized leaders to serve. This may be in order to give the service more dignity, to ensure that "everything should be done in a fitting and orderly way" (1 Cor 14:40) by properly trained leaders, or simply due to tradition. However, as we saw with baptism, there is no biblical reason why this should be considered essential even though it may be the preferred method.

CONCLUSION

Baptism and the Lord's Supper are two important aspects of our worship of God that were commanded by our Lord and have been practiced

---

21. Roman Catholics find it impossible to share the Eucharist with Protestants due to their rejection of transubstantiation and "especially because of the absence of the sacrament of Holy Orders." *Catechism of the Catholic Church*, 353.

throughout church history. As we work to enhance our understanding and practice of worship we should strive to strengthen our understanding and use of these sacraments or ordinances so that we can better worship our Lord as we remember his work for us in the past and of the time we will be together with him in the future.

13

Worship and the Word

Throughout this book, we have seen that worship is our right response to who God is and what he has done in creation and redemption. Worship can only be performed by those who relate to God spiritually and are sanctified so that they can obey his will. And it is only through reading and studying the Bible as God's revelation to us that we can learn who he really is and discover what he wants his worshippers to do. The Bible gives us glimpses into the lives of individuals and communities engaged in the worship of God that reveal proper and improper worship practices and expose issues that were of concern to earlier believers as they interacted with God. At the same time, the Bible demonstrates that God's word spoken and read can transform the lives of those who encounter him. As we draw near to God, listen to his word, and allow the Spirit to convict us of sin and instruct us in righteousness, our hearts are transformed so that we can worship him rightly.

The Bible should be so central to our understanding and practice of worship that we should question whether any ritual or form that is not based upon biblical revelation is actually an expression of true Christian worship. Since God has revealed the way he wants his people to worship him, ignorance is inexcusable and rejection of this revelation is sin. We must, therefore, be careful whenever we consider adopting methods or forms of worship that are not clearly mentioned in Scripture. At best, they are human inventions and, at worst, demonic substitutes. If our worship practice omits elements that God intended to be included or adds items that he disallows, any appeal to relevance is irrelevant, all claims to intellectual depth are the product of deluded minds, and attempts to promote emotional uplift expose airy sentimentality.

If we are to worship in a way that pleases God, we should follow the example of the Westminster Divines who identified a number of acts the Bible specifically instructed Christians to perform in their worship that they believed should be scrupulously followed and further ascertained that many other practices should be rejected as they have no scriptural warrant. As laid out in *The Larger Catechism*, the Bible required the following in worship: (1) reading God's word, (2) preaching God's word, (3) diligently listening to God's word preached, (4) properly observing the sacraments of baptism and the Lord's Supper, and (5) prayer to God in the name of Christ by the help of the Holy Spirit.[1] To these, the Westminster Confession of Faith adds, (1) the singing of psalms, (2) "religious oaths and vows," (3) fasting, (4) giving of thanks on special occasions, and (5) keeping the Sabbath.[2] As all of these were identified as having biblical warrant, they were considered essential parts of Christian worship.[3]

Believers today need to consider these conclusions carefully and humbly. If the Puritan fathers were correct that the Bible requires these expressions of worship, we need to examine our practice to see if we do them. If we do not, we need to amend our ways to reflect biblical teaching. This is not to say that we must adhere to the Westminster Confession or adopt every Puritan practice. Though they were diligent Bible scholars, the Westminster Divines were not infallible. Neither did they agree on every theological detail or every matter of biblical interpretation. Even so, any imperfections they may have had, far from being a reason for dismissing their conclusions, should motivate us to reexamine the Bible to see if what they said is so. At the same time, it should move us to consider to what extent we have based our worship practices upon Scripture and to what extent we have based them on tradition or something else.[4]

MINISTRY OF THE WORD

The Westminster Confession recognized that God's word was to have a central place in worship by being read, preached, and listened to. This was

1. The Larger Catechism, Questions 156–96, 248–83.
2. The Confession of Faith, 21.
3. Though the early Protestant theologians correctly asserted that our worship should be based upon biblical revelation, their worship included practices that are not specifically mentioned in the Bible. Events such as weddings and funerals, and the celebration of Christ's birth and resurrection, while unknown in the New Testament, nevertheless provide wonderful occasions and themes for worship.
4. For an introduction to the way the Puritans' theology and practice of worship can positively influence ours, see my article, "Facing New Paradigms in Worship."

no seventeenth-century invention. From the earliest days of the church, Christians valued the Old Testament as God's word of truth, given to testify of God's acts and will. The importance of reading and/or listening to God's word read is patent in the question Jesus frequently asked, "Have you never read . . . ?" (Matt 12:3, 5; 19:4; 21:16, 42; 22:31). Jesus expressed his frustration with the Jewish leaders because those who read the Scriptures should comprehend its meaning and understand God's ways and will. The fact that they did not grasp what God intended indicated that they did not read it properly. A further indication that they failed to comprehend God's truth is their inability to see Christ in its pages. Paul would later write that one reason they found it difficult to comprehend the meaning of Scripture was that a veil covered their hearts, a veil that could only be taken away by Christ (2 Cor 3:14–16). Even those who were nearest to Jesus were often slow to comprehend what he said. For this reason, after Jesus rose from the grave, he opened their minds to understand how the Scriptures pointed to him (Luke 24:45).

The Hearing and Reading of God's Word

But even though spiritual blindness or dullness of mind can erect barriers that prevent people from grasping God's written revelation, reading and hearing God's word is still essential both for believers and those who are not. Since it is through hearing "the word of Christ" that people come to faith (Rom 10:17), the contents of this word must be made known. Succinctly stated, the word of Christ is the good news that God has entered history in the person of Jesus Christ who was crucified, died, and rose again to forgive our sins, reconcile us with God during this age, and prepare us to spend eternity with him.[5] But the word is more than the gospel uttered; it is also the written word transmitted by Old Testament prophets, poets, and sages. The Old Testament complements the preaching of the gospel as the word which is "able to make you wise for salvation through faith in Christ Jesus" (2 Tim 3:15). But whether preached or read, the word is concerned with more than conversion. Paul identified the texts of the Old Covenant as "God-breathed and . . . useful for teaching, rebuking, correcting and training in righteousness, so that the man of God may be thoroughly equipped for every good work" (2 Tim 3:16–17).

The early church thus clung to the Old Testament as God's word that brings salvation and helps people grow in faith so that they can do all that

---

5. For the kerygmatic-pneumatic character of the gospel being the word of God, see Ladd, *A Theology of the New Testament*, 429.

pleases God. However, as the books of the New Testament were written, they added this new revelation to the Old and read it in church as Scripture. Though Paul never explicitly likened his letters to Old Testament Scripture, he encouraged various churches to pass on his letters and to read the letters he wrote to other churches (Col 4:16; 1 Thess 5:27). Clearly, he believed their authority reached beyond the original addressees.[6] That some of Paul's letters were widely circulated toward the end of the first century is evidenced by 2 Peter, which puts them in the same category as "the other Scriptures" (2 Pet 3:15–16). By the beginning of the second century, most of the Pauline epistles were distributed as a collection rather than as individual letters, further demonstrating that the early church recognized they were universally applicable and should be read by all. Though the Gospels were written after Paul's letters, they were also gathered and circulated together from the early second century. Not only could believers read one account of the life, death, and resurrection of Jesus, they could read four that viewed the history from slightly different perspectives. Other books were gradually recognized as belonging to the collections of New Testament writings until the church proclaimed the twenty-seven books to be authoritative at the Councils of Hippo in 393 and Carthage in 397.

These gathered books were always considered God's words in the sense that he moved men to write what he wanted and that whenever it is read or preached, God speaks through it still. As Packer says, "Holy Scripture should be thought of as *God preaching*—God preaching to me every time I read or hear any part of it—God the Father preaching God the Son in the power of God the Holy Ghost."[7] Whenever Scripture is read, God speaks to those who listen. But since the listeners may not be sensitive to his word, it needs to be preached, to be expounded, so that the hearers may best understand what God is saying and thus enabled to apply it to their lives.

The Preaching of God's Word

Divine revelation needs to be explained anew to each generation as they live in a new context. Deuteronomy is the Mosaic restatement of the law for the generation that was preparing to settle in the land of Canaan after surviving their wilderness wanderings. The book of Nehemiah explains how Ezra read from the law of Moses so that those who had returned to the land after the exile might know God's will for them and obey it (Neh 8–10). As the reading of Scripture was accompanied by an explanation of what it meant, simply

---

6. Meye, "Canon of the NT," 602.
7. Packer, *God has Spoken*, 97. His italics.

reciting the words was clearly not enough. The nascent church similarly realized that the word of God needed to be read and explained. Jesus' final instructions to his apostles required them to make disciples by "teaching them to obey everything I have commanded you" (Matt 28:20). The apostolic message was based upon his example and backed by his authority. From the day of Pentecost, the preaching of the apostles was recognized as bringing salvation to many and included as one of the foundational acts of worship (Acts 2:42). The importance of preaching was highlighted when the church in Jerusalem faced the possibility of division over who would care for Hellenistic Jewish widows. The apostolic response was that though this ministry was important, it was not under their purview. Instructing the Hellenists to choose seven men who were full of the Holy Spirit and wisdom to perform this task, the apostles declared that their job was to "give our attention to prayer and the ministry of the word" (Acts 6:4).[8]

Since the apostles identified God's word as the focus of their ministry, it is imperative that we understand what they meant by the term. This is particularly important since we often use "word of God" as a synonym for the Bible. Though the New Testament occasionally uses "the word" or "the word of God" to refer to the Old Testament (Matt 15:6; Mark 7:13; John 10:35), the apostles could not have used the term for the whole Bible since it did not exist in their time. What then, would they understand the "word of God" to be? In one passage, it is used to designate direct prophetic revelation from God (Luke 3:2). More frequently, it points to the words spoken by Jesus or to the message about Jesus that was preached by the apostles and others in the church. The word of God is thus "a common designation in primitive Christianity for the gospel," a term that "is used to indicate the continuity between the message of Jesus and that of his disciples."[9] Jesus, the living Word, speaks the word that is true and provides the basis for eternal life (John 5:24). Both before his crucifixion and after his resurrection, Jesus speaks to his disciples, giving them his words so that they can take the gospel message to others.

From their earliest days of preaching the kingdom, Jesus was both the source and the content of the apostolic message. After the ascension, the message preached by the apostles was frequently referred to as "the word of God," "the word of Christ," or something similar (Acts 6:2; 1 Cor 14:36; cf. Acts 8:25; 17:11; Gal 6:6; 1 Thess 1:8). Only when people hear this message

---

8. Note that the seven and the apostles were involved in ministry (*diakonia*). The first group had a social ministry to widows, the second a teaching and pastoral ministry to a wider group. The translation, "daily *distribution* of food" in Acts 6:1 of the NIV, disguises the fact that it is the same word as in "ministry of the word" in v 4.

9. Marshall, *Luke: Historian and Theologian*, 160.

can they receive the faith necessary for salvation (Rom 10:17). Since the good news about the living Word is the "word of life," those who receive it receive new life (Phil 2:16; 1 John 1:1–2). Since it is the "word of the cross," it centers on the atoning sacrifice of Jesus who died as the suffering servant of Yahweh in order to demonstrate God's power over sin and death (1 Cor 1:18). Thus Paul, knowing that false teachers would distort the truth of the gospel, could commit his listeners to "the word of his grace, which can build you up and give you an inheritance among all those who are sanctified" (Acts 20:29–32). Since this word was the only means of salvation and sanctification, the proclamation of Jesus as the Messiah was such an imperative that all of Christ's disciples were urged to preach to everyone who was willing to hear. Paul thus exhorted Timothy, "Preach the Word; be prepared in season and out of season; correct, rebuke and encourage—with great patience and careful instruction" (2 Tim 4:2).

It seems clear that the apostles understood the word of God to refer to the preached message about Jesus. That was not, however, the extent of the referent. Both the Old and New Testaments are clear that God's word can be rendered into written form by the leading of the Holy Spirit. When God spoke at Sinai, his words were written down. When they were read, the Israelites responded as though God was again speaking. As a written account of God's work in creation and history, and particularly of his self-revelation through Jesus Christ, the Scriptures remained God's word for people to read, hear, and obey. The apostles thus frequently cited Old Testament passages when they preached Jesus. Since God's written word pointed to the coming of God's living Word, it provided the context and content of their proclamation. When the canon of Scripture was completed, the whole became recognized as "God's word written" that should be read and preached in the church.[10]

THE WORD IN THE CHURCH TODAY

The Bible's place in worship should be understood by the church today as it continues to provide the context and content of the Christian faith as well as the foundational truths about the worship of God. The Bible teaches us about the God who created us and made a way of salvation through Jesus Christ. It informs us that God desires certain things from those who worship him and that those who ignore this teaching run the peril of falling into sub-Christian forms of worship that God rejects. The Bible should, therefore, be our main source for learning about worship and provide us with the main content of

10. "Thirty-Nine Articles of Religion," 20.

the teaching without which worship will be vacuous or idolatrous. The centrality of the Bible in Christian worship was recognized by Justin Martyr who wrote that, "on the day called Sunday, all who live in cities or in the country gather together to one place, and the memoirs of the apostles or the writings of the prophets are read, as long as time permits; then, when the reader has ceased, the president verbally instructs, and exhorts to the imitation of these good things."[11] Followed by prayers, the Lord's Supper, and a collection for the poor, the reading and teaching of God's word typified the weekly gathering of God's people. There was no conception that worship could take place without the Bible being read and interpreted.

The Bible's key role in worship highlights the false distinction many churches make between the *worship* part of a service (when we sing and pray) and the *teaching* part (when we listen to Bible readings and a sermon). As R. T. Kendall notes, the early church knew no such division. "In the book of Acts, which is the earliest historical account of the Church, the emphasis is not on singing. It is not even on the Lord's Supper. On every page—almost, it seems, on every other line—the emphasis is on preaching."[12] As he sees it, worship should be defined as "the response to, and/or preparation for, the preached word."[13] This view matches the outlook of the early Reformers, who considered the reading, hearing, and preaching of the Bible to be the climax of worship because it is here we encounter God most directly. When God's word is read and preached, the Holy Spirit can edify or rebuke us as needed. Only when people actively listen to God's word can they receive the message that brings salvation, healing, and spiritual sustenance for the coming week. As worship is our right response to God and he reveals himself through the Bible, we need to hear it read and explained or we will not be able to respond to him with other forms of worship, such as praise, prayer, and living lives of worship before him.

Though the apostles who were commissioned to engage in the ministry of the word are no longer present, the same Spirit who empowered them has gifted other individuals to follow in their footsteps as mouthpieces for God. Pastors and other church leaders should, therefore, make certain that the Bible is read as the word of God revealed through his prophets and apostles and that it is explained so that today's hearers can understand what it means for them and respond to it in a way that pleases him. This is true worship.

In a bygone age when most people were illiterate or unable to afford a personal Bible, the only time they heard the word of God read was when

---

11. Justin Martyr, *1 Apol.* 67.
12. Kendall, *Worshipping God*, 46.
13. Kendall, *Worshipping God*, 16.

they gathered with other believers at church. In order to enable believers to hear and learn God's word, early church leaders devised a series of regular readings from the Old Testament, the Gospels, and the Epistles that gave them an opportunity to hear the whole counsel of God on a regular basis. These systematically arranged lessons or lectionaries from each part of the Bible were scheduled to be read on assigned days so that all the major passages of the Bible would be covered over time. In most services, one of the lessons would serve as the text for preaching. The other lessons for a particular day might provide background for the passage that would be taught or reinforce biblical teaching that went beyond the text preached on.

Whereas poverty and illiteracy remain barriers that prevent some from hearing the Bible regularly, many Christians today possess numerous Bible translations and yet rarely read it for themselves. Far too often, the only scriptural input that many receive is what is read or preached during a weekly worship service. And since many churches have not maintained the practice of reading from different passages of Scripture, biblical intake may be reduced to a few verses read before the sermon. This leaves those who do not read their Bibles during the week as biblically starved as the illiterate who have no one to read the Bible to them.

Some churches give little time to reading the Bible during a service simply because they have never really considered these issues. Other churches may have determined to limit Scripture readings to save time for other things or because they believe that some in the congregation might become bored by listening to someone read the Bible. In a computerized world where people are programmed to have exciting things pass before their eyes in rapid succession, listening to a reading that lasts for five or ten minutes might seem like a huge burden. But since the Bible brings us into contact with God as does nothing else, we need to develop the habit of listening to his voice. This is far more important than providing more time to hear some human reveal his or her mind to us. In many cases, we need to discover ways to make the Bible, which Hebrews 4:12 tells us is "living and active," come alive. The fact that our congregation might be insensitive to God's word, easily distracted, or inadequately prepared, does not negate their need of scriptural input and may be an indication of their true need of spiritual food.

Whenever possible, the Bible should be read by those who can read well.[14] Training sessions in how to read the Bible aloud could help prepare some for this task. To help listeners who may be distracted, one could

---

14. For a relatively short introduction on how to read Scripture aloud, see Dombek, "Reading the Word of God Aloud," 419–44.

provide some background information on the assigned passage and/or point out some issues in the text that they should take note of. If members have a flair for the theatrical, some type of dramatic reading could be attempted. This can add to interest and involve more people in the service. Another way to involve the whole congregation in the reading is to read certain passages responsively.[15] Whatever method we use, we should be sure that those who read the Bible in church are well-prepared to read clearly and with feeling. They should be prepared to read in the same way a church musician is prepared to play and a preacher is prepared to give the sermon.

When reading the Bible in church, it is best to announce the reading, whether formally or informally, to prepare the congregation to listen to God's word. The passage to be read should be announced clearly so that the listeners can find the text in their Bibles and follow along.[16] The text should be announced at least twice to give people adequate time to locate the reference. The ancient liturgies and many modern worship manuals introduce the readings with a phrase like the following.

> Hear the word of God as recorded in the book of Genesis chapter one verse one through chapter two verse three.

or

> The gospel of our Lord Jesus Christ as recorded in John's Gospel chapter six verses one through fifteen.

or

> Let us listen to the word of the Lord for us today.

At the conclusion of the reading, a closing sentence might be used such as one of the following.

> Thanks be to God.

or

> Here ends the reading of the lesson.

---

15. Responsive readings work very well with many psalms because each verse contains an individual thought. They often do not work well with Pauline epistles because Paul's sentences often extend to several verses and the change in voices breaks up his thought in a way that is most unnatural.

16. Whereas many churches have adopted the practice of projecting the text of Scripture onto a screen, presumably to help those who are unfamiliar with the Bible, I find it ultimately unhelpful, as those who never look up anything in the Bible will never overcome their unfamiliarity.

or

> Let us pray: Gracious Father, by your Holy Spirit, cause these words which have been read to us become for us the very word of life. Amen.

These phrases are suggestive and may be substituted by others. Introductions and conclusions to the readings remind us that reading Scripture is a serious task that brings us into contact with God as his written word becomes his spoken words to us. One pastor I knew frequently introduced the reading of Scripture in a way calculated to help people consider the nature of the Bible, how we should respond to it, and how it should affect our lives. Since it is in the form of a creed, he would ask everyone to hold up their Bibles and say it along with him. "I believe the Bible. It is the word of God. Every word of God is true. I will therefore gladly accept it today. Wherever my thinking or practice differs from the word of God, I will change, with God's help."

When we read God's word, God speaks to us. We therefore need to read it widely, deeply, and frequently. If we want to know God's will, we must know his word. If we want our congregations to grow in their knowledge of God and his ways, we must give them the opportunity to hear him speak to us. But in addition to the reading of God's word, we need to hear God's word preached to us so that we can better understand how the ancient text relates to our modern world. As John Stott explains, we preach the Bible due to three basic beliefs. (1) "Scripture is God's Word written," (2) "God still speaks through what he has spoken," and (3) "God's Word is powerful."[17] As our worship focuses on our relationship with God, we need to hear his voice and allow him to work in our lives.

Both the reading of the Bible and the preaching of the sermon are integral parts of our worship. By listening to God's word read and positively responding, we humbly submit ourselves to his will. By listening to a sermon preached, we allow the text of Scripture to search our hearts and minds so that we can be changed into the likeness of Jesus Christ. And as worship is our proper response to God, when we listen to God's word read and preached, we learn how to respond to him properly. Sermons that are designed to lead us into worship will inform us about what God has said in his word about who he is and about our relationship with him. They will prompt us to respond to God's greatness and majesty. They will assure us that God has entered into history not only in times past but also in the present in order to make a difference in the lives of men and women, boys

---

17. Stott, *Between Two Worlds*, 96–109.

and girls, of both the Israelites and all other cultures. They will turn our attention to what is called the *kerygma*—the proclamation of the gospel of Jesus Christ—and the *didache*—the teaching of the doctrines and practices of the faith.

Sermons that lead us to worship are not necessarily those that make us feel good or address popular themes. The duty of the prophet in ancient Israel, it is often said, was to afflict the comfortable and comfort the afflicted. Preaching should challenge us to reject the way of the world that we find so easy to follow. Often, it is only when the word of God confronts us with sin that we are shaken out of our complacency and pride and learn that we need to fall down before our holy God, confess our sins to him, and change our lifestyles so that we can more resemble a true child of God. Thus, it is often through the more difficult and challenging sermons that we really learn how to worship. Others of us need to be comforted that God is there to help us and protect us from the world, the flesh, and the devil. A good preacher will learn how to do this so that the right word will be delivered to his congregation at the right time. In this way, he will ensure that the people entrusted to him by God will be prepared for a life of worship on this earth in anticipation of an eternity of worship in the presence of the living God.

Since the reading and preaching of the word of God is necessary for us to respond to him in worship, it is sad that many of our services end almost directly after the sermon has ended. Once the pastor puts away his notes and closes his Bible, we quickly find ourselves outside the door and into the world without having adequate time to reflect and make an adequate response. Not even when the sermon is followed by a "hymn of response," an offering, and a closing prayer do we have ample time to consider how to respond to that which should be God's word for us today. This is perhaps one of the reasons the early church followed the liturgy of the word with the liturgy of the upper room. After listening to God speak through his word, they responded by sharing the elements of the Lord's Supper. The ancient Christians understood that more time was needed in order to respond to what God was saying to them. Slowing down instead of rushing away after the ministry of the word may have given them more opportunity to consider what was said and how it applied to them.

14

Worship and Prayer

The God we worship is the God who speaks. He speaks creation into existence. He speaks life into human beings. He speaks to the people he has chosen—through theophanies, visions, and prophetic revelations, through his Son Jesus Christ, and through the Holy Spirit's inspired word. Since God has spoken to us, we can know who he is. Though he spoke in many ways in the past, God's primary means of communicating with us now is through his word. As we saw in the last chapter, reading, preaching, and listening to God's word is an essential part of our spiritual lives and our proper response to God in worship. While the Bible is God's most important means of communicating with us, prayer is our most important means of communicating with him. Through prayer, we inform him what we think, how we feel, and, particularly, what we desire him, our sovereign God, to grant us or someone else. As God speaks to us through the Bible, his words fill our thoughts and provide us with the vocabulary for prayer, the words that enable us to express things that are important to him and reflect his desires. Thus, while prayer is our response to God using our own words, these words ultimately come from him, as he is the originator of language and the one who, through the Bible, teaches us what to say.

While prayer is talking to God, it takes on many forms. Some people, like Adam in the garden, Abraham in the wilderness, and Moses at the burning bush and Mt. Sinai, were privileged to converse with God face to face. Most, however, never speak to God so directly. The simplest form of prayer may comprise an invocation of the Lord's name (Gen 4:26). More frequently, it is made up of the petitions one brings to God in time of need, whether they be short (Matt 14:30) or long, for oneself or others.¹ As in the psalms, prayer can be expressed through highly developed poetic forms designed to help people praise God for good things, express sorrow in bad times, and thank God for his mercies and other blessings. When words fail, prayer requires that the Holy Spirit intercede "with groans that words cannot express" (Rom 8:26). When sins come between a believer and the Lord, prayer becomes an ardent cry for forgiveness and restoration.

All Christian prayer is based on the belief that God is immanently available and desires to listen to his people and help them with their needs. Though he does not need to, he allows himself to be influenced by our petitions and gives us what we ask for.² This comes through clearly when Abraham prays for Lot and Sodom (Gen 18:20–33), when Moses prays for the Israelites (Num 11:2; 21:7; Deut 9:20, 26–29), and in many other passages. Prayer is not so much a way for God's people to inform him of their needs (which he knows already) but to allow them to align their wills with his. As we respond to God's word and will, prayer "becomes one of the ways in which the creature cooperates with God in order to bring about God's plan."³ Through prayer, we join God's work in our lives and in the world. As we see how God answered the prayers of the Old and New Testament saints, we gain courage to expect that God will answer our requests as well.

We learn even more from Jesus' teaching that lets us know we can approach God boldly, with expectancy, and honestly believe that God will give us what we need. Jesus explained that the heavenly Father is greater than human fathers who give their children the things they need. For this reason, God's children should continually ask, seek, and knock so that they can receive his good gifts (Matt 7:7–11). God, unlike the unjust judge who only responded to the widow's need because she was wearing him out with her incessant pleas for justice, will not put off his chosen ones who come to him but will give them what they need (Luke 18:2–8). As Jesus brought his requests to the Father at any time of the day, so can we, for Jesus is with us, interceding for us while we pray (Rom 8:34; Heb 7:25).

---

1. Bloesch says that "The essence of true prayer is heartfelt supplication, bringing before God one's innermost needs and requests in the confident expectation that God will hear and answer." Bloesch, *The Struggle of Prayer*, 67.

2. This is not an absolute. God is free to grant our requests or withhold them from us. It should be remembered that he did not assent to Jesus' thrice given request that the cup pass from him (Matt 26:29–44) or release Paul from his thorn in the flesh (2 Cor 12:7–9).

3. Okholm, "Prayer," 623.

THE LORD'S PRAYER

Jesus provides the biblical model for prayer that complements the Psalms. The Lord's Prayer appears in two places in the Bible. In Matthew's Gospel, it is part of the Sermon on the Mount where it complements alms-giving and fasting as one of the proper ways to perform acts of righteousness (Matt 6:9–13). Here, Jesus distinguishes a true child of God from the "hypocrites" who desire that people recognize them for their ability to pray and the pagans who think they will be heard due to their many words (Matt 6:5–8). In Luke's Gospel, Jesus teaches this prayer to his disciples when they specifically ask him how they should pray (Luke 11:2–4). In this context, there are four brief teachings that encourage people not to give up in prayer but to continue to ask because God desires to give good gifts (including the Holy Spirit) to his children (Luke 11:2–11). The model prayer of Jesus has been recited regularly wherever Christians meet. While congregations can benefit by praying this prayer liturgically, it is rightly reported that "The familiar invitation to 'repeat the Lord's Prayer' more often than not keeps us from entering into its meaning."[4] Overfamiliarity with the words can keep us from praying them rightly.[5] As Jesus' instructions in Matthew remind us, prayer is to be between an individual and God and in remembrance that God already knows our needs.

The address to God—"Our Father"—and the series of requests found in the Lord's Prayer remind us that prayer has an object and that it is mainly petitionary. When told to pray to "Our Father," Jesus' followers are reminded that this prayer is only for those who are God's children. These are those who Lohmeyer calls "the eschatological community of the disciples," which includes all past, present, and future members of the church.[6] Those who have been baptized into Christ can join Jesus by referring to God as "Abba," the intimate Aramaic term for father (Mark 14:36).[7] This address, which characterized Jesus' prayers, was almost unknown in Jewish prayers. Even so, the early church quickly picked it up. Paul encouraged believers in both Rome and Galatia to follow Jesus' lead and the urgings of the Spirit by praying to God as "Abba, Father" (Rom 8:15; Gal 4:6). Prayer should thus be as natural as a child talking to his or her father, expressing a childlike love and

---

4. Laymon, *The Lord's Prayer*, 11.

5. I have particularly noted this when the Lord's Prayer is sung, as choir members and congregation alike focus on the music at the expense of the words.

6. Lohmeyer, *The Lord's Prayer*, 21.

7. As Aramaic was Jesus' native tongue, he likely used "Abba" in all his prayers even when the Greek has *pater*, or something similar. Kittel, "ἀββᾶ," 6; Jeremias, *The Lord's Prayer*, 18–19.

trust in the God who always hears and answers us. Jesus' disciples should exhibit the same close relationship with God as he did. God is our Father because Jesus is our brother. As adopted children of the heavenly Father, we will always be accepted and loved.

The address also indicates that prayer is made to *our* Father. Since God is our Father, Christians are all brothers and sisters who pray with and for each other. Throughout his model prayer, Jesus repeatedly uses first-person plural pronouns. This reminds us that it is not a prayer for *me* to pray, but for the whole church to pray. An individual only prays the prayer as a representative of the whole church and brings the petitions with the whole church in mind.[8] To pray this prayer as an individual who is only concerned about her own needs is to misuse it. As those who pray to "our Father," we acknowledge that we are not self-sufficient but are bound to our brothers and sisters in Christ.

The Lord's Prayer begins with God and centers on his holiness, his sovereign reign, and his will to be done in our lives. After the address comes a series of petitions, three of which pertain to God, the other four to us.[9] The first request is not that God's name be *made* holy, as it is holy from eternity to eternity. Rather, it is that his name be *recognized* as holy by his church and the world. Since we are naturally unholy people, we can only approach God in humility as we ask him to make us holy like himself. The prayer also reminds us that God is establishing his kingdom on earth, a kingdom that is both a present reality and a future expectation that Christ will consummate in the coming age. As citizens of the kingdom, we must be sure to know and obey God's will, including his desire that we proclaim God's kingdom to others so that they too can submit themselves to do his will and experience his goodness.

Only after we focus on the one who is worshipped do we respond by bringing him issues that pertain to our human condition—our basic diet and material needs, a request for personal forgiveness and our need to forgive others, deliverance from temptation, and protection from evil. The request for bread clearly goes beyond food to encompass all our material needs. And since Jesus is the bread of life, the petition includes our spiritual

---

8. Karl Barth is probably correct to say that there is an extent to which we pray this prayer in solidarity with the world, particularly the part of the world that has not yet heard the gospel or come to faith in Christ. Barth, *Prayer and Preaching*, 44.

9. Barth notes that "the arrangement of these petitions is, in a sense, analogous to that of the ten Commandments." The first three petitions correspond to the first four commandments and the last ones to the last six commandments. Barth, *Prayer and Preaching*, 28.

needs as well (John 6:33, 35).[10] God's holiness sets off our sins in a great contrast, reminding us to confess our sins, believe wholeheartedly that God has forgiven and will forgive, and that we need to forgive as we have been forgiven. The prayer similarly reminds us that we need God to protect us from the sins that are most likely to tempt us. As only God can protect us from the evil that is present in our world, in our society, and in our own lives, only he can protect us from the evil one and his forces.[11]

The Lord's Prayer as given in the book of Matthew is clearly a prayer to be imitated, not so much at the level of the words themselves, but as a pattern, a model that moves us to pray the petitions mentioned by Jesus and goes beyond them to bring other requests to our heavenly Father. The Lucan version, which is prefaced by "When you pray, say," authorizes Christians to pray the very words of the prayer. It is for this reason that the prayer has a rightful place in our liturgical worship of God. The difference in wording between the Evangelists can either be traced to their reproducing different forms of a prayer that Jesus taught on multiple occasions,[12] to the form of the prayer that was used by different communities of Christians in the later first century when the Gospels were written,[13] or to both.[14]

---

10. Augustine discerned that the petition for bread could refer to one or all of three things: physical provisions, the sacrament, or spiritual food. Augustine, "Our Lord's Sermon on the Mount," 25. We should probably remove the idea of the sacrament from this list, as the Eucharist had not been instituted when Jesus taught the prayer to the disciples. Evely, *We Dare to Say "Our Father,"* 93–94.

11. The adjective *ponēros* used in Matthew 6:13 can be used as a substantive "the evil one," whether for an evil person (Matt 5:39, 45) or of the devil (Matt 13:19; John 17:15). While Matthew 6:13 could be rightly translated "deliver us from evil" or "deliver us from the evil one," there is not much difference in the interpretations as deliverance from the first would include the evil one who seeks to harm us and deliverance from the second would include the evil acts he desires to bring our way.

12. Geldenhuys and Bruce, "Lord's Prayer," 910; Lohmeyer, *The Lord's Prayer*, 30.

13. Jeremias, *The Lord's Prayer*, 9–10. Jeremias admits it is possible "that Jesus himself spoke the 'Our Father' on different occasions in a slightly differing form, a shorter one and a longer one." *The Lord's Prayer*, 12.

14. As recognized in most modern translations, the words "for yours is the kingdom and the power and the glory forever. Amen." do not appear in the earliest Greek manuscripts, versions, or patristic citations but became a standard liturgical ending for the prayer that was added to later manuscripts.

CORRECTING ERRONEOUS THOUGHTS ABOUT PRAYER

Although Christians should expect to receive what they ask for in prayer, true prayer is not a matter of coercing God to do our bidding. The Bible denounces the idea common in folk religions that prayer is a magical means of moving the divine to intervene in life. Followers of folk religions believe that a deity is required to act if the right words are spoken or the proper ritual is performed. Similarly, some Christians have concluded that if they pray the right words in the right way, God must give them what they want. Rote prayers, such as the Lord's Prayer, the Jesus prayer,[15] the "prayer of Jabez,"[16] or the Hail Mary, can become stumbling blocks to those who believe that saying the prayer will make God more inclined to do what they want. A similar error is seen in the common belief that since Jesus promises that "the Father will give you whatever you ask in my name" (John 15:16), every prayer should conclude, ". . . in Jesus' name, amen," or something similar. The error of this teaching is easily identified when we notice that no biblical prayers end with these words. If the words were an essential part of prayer, they would regularly be found in biblical prayers. But if praying in Jesus' name does not refer to using these words to signify that a prayer is completed, what does it mean? According to Bloesch,

> To pray in the name of Christ means to pray in the awareness that our prayers have no worthiness or efficacy apart from his atoning sacrifice and redemptive mediation. It means to appeal to the blood of Christ as the source of power for the life of prayer. It means to acknowledge our complete helplessness apart from his mediation and intercession. To pray in his name means that we recognize that our prayers cannot penetrate the tribunal of God unless they are presented to the Father by the Son, our one Savior and Redeemer.[17]

Another error many commit when they pray is thinking that God should provide them with signs to indicate his will. At times, this is set in terms of "casting a fleece" in imitation of Gideon (Judg 6:36–40). The problem is that Gideon was guilty of testing God because he did not want to do

---

15. This prayer, "Lord Jesus Christ, Son of God, have mercy on me, a sinner," comes from the words of the publican in Jesus' parable of the Pharisee and the publican and has been used by the Orthodox church from ancient times.

16. The prayer of Jabez is found in 1 Chronicles 4:10. It has been popularized in recent years by Bruce Wilkinson.

17. Bloesch, *The Struggle of Prayer*, 36–37. See also, Grenz, *Prayer*, 16–17.

what God had clearly told him to do. So, to free himself from God's demand, he made an impossible request for dew to fall only on the fleece and not on the ground. The text is clear that Gideon knew he was wrong, as he begs God not to be angry before asking for a second impossible sign. Gideon's lack of faith and his desire to escape responsibility motivated his request. The same motivations regularly drive people to look for signs today. "To seek for signs is to try to dictate the way in which God answers. It is asking God to go contrary to his Word."[18] It is for these reasons that the apostles never asked God for signs about what he wanted them to do. Since they had his word, his Spirit, and his presence in the church, they did not need to request miracles to indicate his will.

PRAYER IN THE CHURCH TODAY

Prayer played an important part in both Old Testament and New Testament worship and in the worship of the early church. It is equally essential that we learn how to pray for the benefit of our personal devotions, times of group prayer, and congregational meetings. As we grow in one, we will grow in the others. While much of what follows focuses upon congregational prayer, it can also be applied to private prayer. Christian prayer should be practiced at home and in *ekklesia*, by individuals who make up the church and by the church that is composed of individuals.[19]

Several important comments should be made about public prayer. First, prayer is made to God, not to the congregation. It is not proper to try to teach others through our prayer, or to use prayer to make announcements. Doing so cheapens prayer. To pray is to converse with God. When we pray, we should ensure we are talking to him. Second, congregational prayers should use a "we" mode. As in the Lord's Prayer, the one who prays is praying on behalf of the whole congregation and represents the whole congregation before God. In some churches, the person leading prayer turns to join the congregation by facing in the direction they are facing. This physical gesture symbolizes that the one praying is part of the whole body of Christ that corporately approaches God as a group.

Third, those who pray in public should use simple language that everyone can understand. If we study the prayers recorded in the Bible, we will be surprised by their simplicity. Biblical prayer rejects putting on a special voice or adopting a distinctive prayer vocabulary with its own grammatical rules. Jesus might well group those who pray in such a fashion along with

18. Bloesch, *The Struggle of Prayer*, 82.
19. Barth, *Prayer and Preaching*, 11.

the hypocrites who want to be seen praying or the Gentiles who think their many words will give them a hearing. If God does not accept those who show off in prayer or who use an abundance of words, we should not be deceived into thinking that he will hear us because we use a special vocabulary, grammar, or pronunciation when we pray.

Fourth, a review of biblical prayers and historical prayers reminds us that the word "Amen," was frequently said by others at the conclusion of a prayer to indicate their agreement with what was prayed. Although there is good historical and biblical evidence to support the use of this word along with prayers, we should understand that it is not something that we should just say automatically. Saying "amen" indicates agreement with what has been said. If someone does not pray clearly or uses words that are not within our vocabulary, the "amen" should remain unsaid, just as it should if someone prayed for something that is ridiculous or blasphemous. The "amen" is good and right if we use it correctly, to indicate that we hear, understand, and agree with what has been prayed for or preached on, but should not be used simply to indicate that we are present or that we acknowledge a pause in a prayer. Saying "amen" signifies that we have joined the prayer of another so that their prayer becomes our prayer.

Types of Prayer for Public Worship

The issues mentioned above are intended to improve our practice of prayer in public worship. The following discussion briefly examines some of the kinds of prayer that are frequently used in congregational settings. The intention is not to insist that each type of prayer mentioned should be used in every service, but to introduce readers to prayers that may enhance corporate worship. All the types of prayer mentioned here have biblical precedents.

Invocation

An invocation is an opening prayer. Since the word "invoke" means to appeal or petition, this prayer usually appeals to God to be present and lead us into worship. Frequently, it also expresses our adoration for God and helps us focus on his greatness. For example:

> Almighty God, before whom all hearts be open, all desires known, and from whom no secrets are hid: cleanse the thoughts of our hearts by the inspiration of thy Holy Spirit, that we

may perfectly love thee, and worthily magnify thy holy name; through Jesus Christ our Lord. Amen.[20]

A biblical example can be found in Psalm 86.

> 1 Hear, O LORD, and answer me, for I am poor and needy.
> 2 Guard my life, for I am devoted to you. You are my God; save your servant who trusts in you.
> 3 Have mercy on me, O Lord, for I call to you all day long.
> 4 Bring joy to your servant, for to you, O Lord, I lift up my soul.
> 5 You are forgiving and good, O Lord, abounding in love to all who call to you.
> 6 Hear my prayer, O LORD; listen to my cry for mercy.
> 7 In the day of my trouble I will call to you, for you will answer me.

Collect and Litany

A collect[21] is a short prayer that brings one basic petition to God. In medieval times, a collect—introduced by a general call for the congregation to bring their individual requests to God—was used to "collect" the prayers into a unified petition to ask God for his grace, peace, etc. Collects are common in Catholic, Anglican, and Lutheran liturgies, and rarely found in others, though there is no reason why they could not be used by all churches. The form has influenced prayers from most Christian traditions, as they express common requests in a succinct and memorable manner.[22] In addition to some general collects and collects for special occasions, *The Book of Common Prayer* includes a collect for each Sunday of the church year to help worshippers focus on the meaning of each day lived out before God.[23]

An example of a collect that may be prayed on the second Sunday after Epiphany is:

> Almighty God, in Christ you make all things new: Transform the poverty of our nature by the riches of your grace, and in the renewal of our lives make known your heavenly glory; through Jesus Christ our Lord. Amen.

---

20. Skoglund, *A Manual of Worship*, 90.
21. This word should be stressed on the first syllable.
22. The invocation given in the previous section is in the form of a collect.
23. Though *The Book of Common Prayer* contains many collects, not every Anglican church uses them all.

As can be discerned in the above prayer, all collects follow the same general form though the words vary.

- Address/Invocation ("Almighty God," "Father in heaven," "Eternal God," etc.)
- Attribute of God that relates to the following petition
- Petition
- Statement expressing the purpose or anticipated result of the petition
- Statement expressing mediation ("through Christ our Lord")
- General affirmation ("Amen")

It should be clear that a collect is centered on God from beginning to end. He is called upon to hear the request because of his power to meet our needs through Jesus Christ. He is asked to respond to our needs because he has shown himself to respond to such needs in the past. And as he meets our needs now, we expect to become more like him or more pleasing to him. It is, therefore, a prayer designed to make us think more about God than about ourselves. It helps us focus on his attributes and ability more than on our wants and desires. While neither the form nor the collects used historically have direct scriptural warrant (though see Acts 4:24–30), they are a useful means of bringing our requests to God in a way that recognizes his sovereignty and ability to answer. We can thus prepare our own collects as we pray for the needs of our various congregations.

A similar type of prayer is a litany,[24] which consists of a series of petitions or thanksgivings (whether short or long) to which the congregation responds with a fixed reply. Though the form is not based upon a biblical model, it is similar to what is found in Psalm 136.

> Give thanks to the LORD, for he is good.
> His love endures forever.
> Give thanks to the God of gods.
> His love endures forever.
> Give thanks to the LORD of lords:
> His love endures forever.

Here, the people respond to the statements made by the leader and thus make his prayers their own. In other forms, the leader may say a phrase that cues the people to respond with a known phrase. For example, after bringing a petition to God, the leader may say, "Lord, in your mercy . . ."

---

24. The word litany is derived from the Greek *litaneía*, "supplication."

to which the congregation replies, "hear our prayer."[25] In a standard litany, each petition focuses on a single item or concern. This gives the people an opportunity to hear and give verbal assent to each request in turn. One litany from *The Book of Common Prayer* addresses the triune God in each of his persons and requests his mercy upon his people.

> God the Father, creator of heaven and earth,
> have mercy upon us.
> God the Son, Redeemer of the world
> have mercy upon us.
> God the Holy Spirit, giver of life,
> have mercy upon us.
> Holy, blessed, and glorious Trinity, three Persons in one God,
> have mercy upon us.[26]

The phrase "have mercy" reflects the words of what was perhaps the first litany regularly used in early liturgies: *Kyrie eleison*, "Lord, have mercy."

Confession, Prayer for Forgiveness, and Absolution or Assurance of Forgiveness

When we worship the God who is most holy and demands that we should also become holy, we instantly realize that we are not holy people, but sinners who can only enter his presence due to his grace. As we humbly face our predicament, we should respond by confessing our sin and asking God to make us holy. To help us in this direction, many churches include a prayer of confession toward the beginning of a worship service. During a confession, the congregation may be prompted to acknowledge their sins silently before God, to ask for his forgiveness, and to call upon God to make them worthy to worship him. Following this prayer comes an acknowledgement that forgiveness comes to those who trust in the grace of God and the power of Jesus Christ who overcame sin by his death on the cross. This may be through one of the general confessions and declarations of absolution found in prayer books or by quoting 1 John 1:9 along with other appropriate words.

A general confession and declaration of absolution that has been commonly used throughout the English-speaking world is found in the *Book of Common Prayer*. Traditionally, the first paragraph of this would be prayed

---

25. It is usually best for the one leading prayer to announce the phrase to be repeated or to have the litany written in a prayer book or order of service, or projected so that everyone knows what they are to say and when.

26. General Synod of the Church of Ireland, *The Book of Common Prayer*, 175.

by the whole congregation, the second by the minister, with everyone joining in the final amen.

> Almighty and most merciful Father, we have erred, and strayed from thy ways like lost sheep. We have followed too much the devices and desires of our own hearts. We have offended against thy holy laws. We have left undone those things which we ought to have done; and we have done those things which we ought not to have done; and there is no health in us. But thou, O Lord, have mercy upon us, miserable offenders. Spare thou them, O God, which confess their faults. Restore thou them that are penitent; according to thy promises declared unto mankind in Christ Jesus our Lord. And grant, O most merciful Father, for his sake, that we may hereafter live a godly, righteous, and sober life, to the glory of thy holy name. Amen.
>
> Almighty God, the Father of our Lord Jesus Christ, who desireth not the death of a sinner, but rather that he may turn from his wickedness and live; and hath given power, and commandment, to his ministers to declare and pronounce to his people, being penitent, the absolution and remission of their sins: he pardoneth and absolveth all them that truly repent and unfeignedly believe his holy gospel. Wherefore let us beseech him to grant us true repentance, and his Holy Spirit, that those things may please him which we do at this present; and that the rest of our life hereafter may be pure and holy; so that at the last we may come to his eternal joy; through Jesus Christ our Lord.
> Amen.

As the language here is antiquated, other words can be used while praying for forgiveness and acknowledging pardon.[27] Even so, these clearly express the idea that sinners need to and can draw near to God through Jesus Christ, be forgiven, restored to a right relationship with God, and go on to live a godly life as empowered by the Holy Spirit. They are, therefore, useful in private and public prayer. And though no minister is present during private prayer, the God who forgives sin is, so the remembrance that he pardons and absolves those who believe the gospel is still appropriate and beneficial for the one who prays.

---

27. More recent editions of the *Book of Common Prayer* and other service manuals provide briefer and linguistically more up-to-date confessions and absolutions.

Pastoral Prayer

In many traditions, the pastoral prayer is the main prayer of the service and may contain petitions for the needs of the world, the nation, the local church and its officers, the individuals in the church, those who have yet to come to faith in Christ, and much more. While some churches require that only the pastor of the church, a bishop, or other churchman be allowed to say this prayer, others permit various lay people to pray. Indeed, in some churches, the pastor never prays this prayer. Whether the prayer is read or extemporaneous, the person praying should be aware of the needs faced by the congregation and be prepared to bring them to the Lord. As the needs of the congregation and of the world constantly change, the contents of this prayer should continually change. The needs brought out in this prayer can be expanded upon by a wider section of the congregation who join together for a regularly scheduled or special prayer meeting. They can also be raised up before God by members of the congregation when they return home.

Prayer for Healing

People who are sick, regardless of the severity of their illness, desire to be made whole. James 5:13–15 instructs those who are sick to "call the elders of the church to pray over him" and that the elders are to pray and anoint them with oil. Although the context appears to indicate that the person is so ill he cannot make it to the assembly meeting but needs to call the elders to where he is,[28] there is no reason to limit this kind of prayer to a private house or hospital room. As Jesus healed sick people during synagogue services, we can pray for sick people during church services.

Praying and anointing with oil is not a magical rite that will insure that a sick person will be healed.[29] Neither is it something that must be performed by a person with a particular spiritual gift, as James indicates that elders should be involved and the New Testament never includes healing as a qualification for eldership. Rather, praying for the sick is both a biblical and Christian response to our brothers and sisters in need. As James indicates, the effectiveness of the prayer is related to the faith of the one who prays, not the one for whom prayer is made (Jas 5:15). But even when the

---

28. Davids, *James*, 192.

29. In the ancient world, oil was commonly thought to have curative powers. While this concept may be present in James 5:14, of more importance is the symbolism of oil as an outward sign of the prayer that is prayed or of the presence of the Holy Spirit who is the divine giver of life. It is not oil but the prayer offered in faith that brings healing (Jas 5:15). Davids, *James*, 193; Balchin, "Oil," 586.

prayer of faith is offered, it is the Lord who will raise up the infirm person. Praying for the sick may be offered as part of the pastoral prayer or another portion of the service may be wholly given over to prayers for healing and/or other personal needs. Following the instructions in James more closely, this prayer can be made at the home or hospital bed of an unwell person.

Prayer for Offering

In many churches, a prayer is said before and/or after the collection of the offering. This prayer reminds us that we bring our money (or other offerings) to God as part of our worship and allows us to acknowledge that we are dependent upon God for everything we have and that we dedicate our gifts to the one who owns all things and to whom we owe everything. Praying about the gifts we bring to the Lord should not be limited to corporate prayer. Individual Christians should seek the Lord's guidance about the gifts they should bring and how they can forward God's kingdom. Prayer can be offered concerning the amount of money or other gifts that should be given to a local church, denomination, missionary society, parachurch organization, etc.

Benediction

A benediction is a closing blessing. In many ways, it is not really a prayer as it is directed toward the congregation and expresses the wish that God would make himself known to everyone in a special way. Common benedictions include the Aaronic blessing from Numbers 6:24–26 and the Grace from 2 Corinthians 13:14.[30]

> The LORD bless you and keep you;
> the LORD make his face shine upon you and be gracious to you;
> the LORD turn his face toward you and give you peace.
>
> May the grace of the Lord Jesus Christ,
> and the love of God,
> and the fellowship of the Holy Spirit be with you all.

Some common blessings have been adopted from Scripture for use as a closing benediction for a church service.

---

30. For a brief introduction to benedictions in worship along with examples and bibliography, see Chapell, *Christ-Centered Worship*, 252–62.

> The peace of God, which passes all understanding, keep your hearts and minds in the knowledge and love of God, and of his Son Jesus Christ our Lord; and the blessing of God almighty, the Father, the Son, and the Holy Spirit, be with you, and remain with you always. Amen.[31]
>
> The God of all grace, who called you to his eternal glory in Christ Jesus, establish, strengthen and settle you in the faith; and the blessing of God almighty, the Father, the Son, and the Holy Spirit, be among you and remain with you always. Amen.[32]

It should be appreciated that the benediction is not merely a final statement at the close of a service. It is a reminder that the God who called us to be his people and who joins us as we worship him is the one who goes with us as we face another week in the world where we live for him and serve him. It is thus an opportunity to receive strength for what lies ahead. Since God blesses us, we can be sure that he will provide for all our needs. We can take courage that his kingdom will come and his will be done. As people who receive God's blessing, it is fitting that we are sent out into the world to live in the grace of Christ and the power of the Holy Spirit. For this reason, the benediction will be followed by a dismissal that includes a charge to serve the Lord or to live for him.

> Go in peace to love and serve the Lord.

or

> Let us go forth into the world, rejoicing in the power of the Spirit.

CONCLUSION

Our worship of God is built upon the relationship we have developed with him through mutual communication. God speaks to us through his word. We respond to him through prayer. As we read the Bible, we discover what God desires of us. As we pray, we align our wills with his. This may come about through the admission that we are sinful people in need of forgiveness. It may prove itself through our petitions on the behalf of ourselves or others. But no matter what type of prayer we offer to God, he accepts it

---

31. General Synod of the Church of Ireland, *Book of Common Prayer*, 221.
32. General Synod of the Church of Ireland, *Book of Common Prayer*, 367.

as a sweet fragrance like that of the incense offered by the priests who did his bidding (Ps 141:2; Rev 5:8; 8:3–4). When we pray, we join God in his work. In many cases, God only works through his people when they pray. We therefore need to respond to him as our sovereign and allow him to do his work in and through us. As our service rendered to the King of kings, it is a most vital part of our worship of God.

15

Worship and Spiritual Gifts

Throughout my lifetime, spiritual gifts has been one of the hottest topics for Christians. The church where I grew up and the Christian university I attended both regularly taught about the gifts and encouraged everyone to seek or discover the gift that the Spirit had for them. A seminary class I took required all students to take a spiritual gifts inventory that resembled tests designed to identify personality types.[1] One friend took the instruction to discover his gift so seriously that he claimed to have tried them all so he could eliminate those he didn't have. Another friend expressed concern that the Holy Spirit might give her a gift she didn't want. For many of us, spiritual gifts greatly impacted our experience as Christians, whether positively or negatively.

With time, I learned that many believers, following ideas developed by Augustine and built upon by B. B. Warfield,[2] were convinced spiritual gifts were only for the apostolic church, being foundational in nature, and that they had ceased with the completion of the canon of Scripture. At the same time, I was informed that interest in the gifts of the Spirit was renewed by Pentecostal and Charismatic believers who were mainly interested in the sensational gifts, such as healing and speaking in tongues.[3] Another group of Christians were happy to practice the majority of the gifts, but considered

---

1. Interestingly, the test I took identified one of my primary gifts to be "martyrdom," which an acquaintance quipped was a gift that could only be used once. Subsequent editions of the test dropped martyr from the list of gifts.

2. Warfield, *Counterfeit Miracles*.

3. I have since learned that Pentecostal and Charismatic interest in spiritual gifts is much broader than that.

the "sign gifts" (e.g., tongues, interpretation of tongues, prophecy, healing, discerning of spirits) to have ceased. Among those who agreed that the gifts are for today, differences emerged about whether a person could have only one gift or more than one and whether the gifts number nine, somewhat more than that, or have no definite number.

While various understandings of spiritual gifts are often attached to different theological backgrounds, it is important to understand that they can be traced to ambiguity in the texts of Scripture.[4] Though modern Christians regularly speak of "the gifts of the Spirit," the phrase is never found in the Bible. Even "spiritual gift" (with the adjective *pneumatikon* modifying *charisma*) is only found in Romans 1:11, where it likely refers to the blessing God will give to the Romans by allowing Paul to visit them.[5] And as the terms used in Romans 12:6–8; 1 Corinthians 12–14; and Ephesians 4:11 are also used elsewhere to refer to other things, they are not technical terms equivalent to "spiritual gifts."[6]

In addition to recognizing that the Bible does not provide an overarching term to refer to the way God empowers his people for ministry, we may also need to adjust our thinking that they are gifts of the *Spirit*. Though we might identify the Holy Spirit as the one who gives gifts, the Bible occasionally cites the Father and the Son as the source. In 1 Corinthians 12:4–6, Paul writes, "There are different kinds of gifts, but the same Spirit. There are different kinds of service, but the same Lord. There are different kinds of working, but the same God works all of them in all men." The parallelism in the passage implies that the gifts, service, and working all refer to the same thing. The Trinitarian language informs us that the whole Godhead dispenses the gifts. This can also be seen in Ephesians 4:11–13, where Christ gave gifted individuals to the church to build it up. Though Romans 12:6–8 is not as clear, Jesus may also be the source of the gifts mentioned there, as the context connects them with the body that is unified in Christ and says the gifts come in accordance with grace, a term that Romans regularly says comes through Jesus (Rom 1:5, 7; 5:2; 16:20).

As popular as talk about spiritual gifts is in many church traditions, the terminology used does not arise directly from biblical revelation. Even

---

4. See Fee, "Gifts of the Spirit," 339–47.

5. Though "spiritual gift(s)" is found in the NIV and some other versions in 1 Corinthians 1:7 and 14:1, in both places they are idiomatic translations of the single Greek words *charismati*—"gift"—and *pneumatika*—"spirituals" or "spiritual things."

6. These terms include: "gifts" (*charismata*, Rom 12:6; 1 Cor 12:4, 31), "spiritual gifts" (lit. "spiritual things," *pneumatika*, 1 Cor 12:1; 14:1), "workings" of God (*energēma*, 1 Cor 12:6), "manifestestations" of the Spirit (*phanerōsis*, 1 Cor 12:7), and "services" (*diakoniōn*, 1 Cor 12:5). Turner, "Spiritual Gifts," 792.

so, the phrase "gifts of the Spirit" remains a useful way to refer to the lists of ministries and phenomena that God has graciously given his church so that everyone can be built up in the faith and play a part in the building up of others. Spiritual gifts are said to include the nine manifestations of the Spirit related in 1 Corinthians 12:8–10 (word of wisdom, word of knowledge, faith, gifts of healing, miracles, prophecy, distinguishing between spirits, speaking in tongues, and interpretation of tongues), the further gifts mentioned in Romans 12:6–8 (prophecy, service, teaching, encouragement, contributing to the needs of others, leadership, and showing mercy), and the leaders that Ephesians 4:11 says are given to the church (apostles, prophets, evangelists, and pastors and teachers).

Observant readers will notice that while these lists overlap in some areas, they mainly point to different gifts. Significantly, the lists highlight various phenomena, ministries, and gifted individuals that are clearly not part of matching categories. These differences, along with the diverse terms used to refer to them, should alert us that the frequent attempt to systematize them is probably misguided. Similarly, identifying the exact nature of each gift—though common in books on the subject—is often impossible since the Bible never defines many of the terms used. For instance, though many books and articles have attempted to provide a clear distinction between "word of wisdom" and "word of knowledge," the pursuit is fruitless as the Bible gives no clue as to what either encompasses. Providing definitions for terms that the Bible leaves undefined usually reveals much more the mind of a human author than the mind of God. A similar thing can be said regarding the frequent attempt to identify a precise number of gifts. The variation and overlap between biblical lists of gifts suggest they are indefinite in number and are related more to give examples of how the Spirit operates than to provide an exhaustive list of his manifestations. Thus, 1 Corinthians 12–14, far from being Paul's treatise on spiritual gifts, was written to correct the Corinthians' over-emphasis on the gift of tongues by demonstrating that the Spirit works in a variety of ways that bring different results.[7] As the passage shows, the Spirit can work through a person's natural abilities, learned abilities, or through more supernatural activities; the decision is his.

As we fine-tune our understanding of spiritual gifts, we should notice that the phenomena, ministries, and gifted people mentioned in these texts are directly related to the church's worship of God. This is indicated by the context of the passages that speak of the gifts, the nature of some gifts that are explicitly said to be used during worship services, and the fact that all the gifts are used to serve God and his church. In Romans 12, Paul prefaces his

---

7. Fee, "Gifts of the Spirit," 342–43.

discussion of the gifts God has given to individual members of the church by urging them "to offer your bodies as living sacrifices, holy and pleasing to God—this is your spiritual act of worship" (Rom 12:1). With these remarks, Paul introduces the major division of the epistle running from 12:1—15:13 and demonstrates that worship should be reckoned a continual offering of our whole selves to God.[8] The worship Paul envisions includes transforming one's mind so that it conforms to God's will rather than the world and developing a proper estimation of one's self in relation to the rest of the body of Christ. Rather than thinking of oneself as superior, a disciple of Jesus is to serve others to the best of his or her abilities with the gifts God has given. As members of the body, we are to understand how we fit and humbly perform the function for which we were made.

The body metaphor is repeated in 1 Corinthians 12, where Paul uses it to demonstrate that a multiplicity of gifts is essential for the church to function properly. He introduces the subject with a reminder that although the Corinthians had originally been "pagans" who worshipped "mute idols" (1 Cor 12:2), the Holy Spirit gave them a new object of worship when he enabled them to recognize that "Jesus is Lord" (1 Cor 12:3). In addition, the Spirit gave them gifts that can also be described as "different kinds of service" or "different kinds of working" (1 Cor 12:4-6). As the Holy Spirit works through his people, they serve and edify each other in any number of ways as part of their worship of God. A properly functioning body will—in contrast to the Corinthian fixation on one gift and much contemporary practice that limits those who can participate—manifest multi-member ministry as the Holy Spirit empowers each to serve in various ways. While a hierarchy of gifts is recognized, freedom must be given so that all can serve (1 Cor 12:28–31). Similarly, room should be given for all to be edified and built up by the gifts of others.

From a biblical perspective, the main arena for practicing spiritual gifts is the communal worship service. This comes through in 1 Corinthians 14, which explains that the church in Corinth, in their excitement over speaking in tongues, downplayed the other gifts. Paul felt that this caused confusion during worship and hindered the congregation from being edified. While he does not outlaw tongues, he limits its use in public worship and insists that prophecy is more important.[9] According to the apostle, tongues has value

---

8. Cranfield, *Romans, Vol. 2*, 595, 601. Note that the word translated "worship" is *latreia*, which is almost always used in the Septuagint for the cultic worship of God.

9. Prophecy should be taken in the sense of exhortation and exposition rather than prediction. Barrett, *First Corinthians*, 316. Though some limit the prophetic gift to preaching, the context reports that Paul commends it to all in the same way he instructs everyone to "Follow the way of love and eagerly desire spiritual gifts" (1 Cor 14:1). As

in that the speaker is edified through his personal communion with God. However, prophecy has greater value as it edifies the whole church by speaking to everyone "for their strengthening, encouragement and comfort" (1 Cor 14:3). Paul's point is that the church can demonstrate that they "eagerly desire the greater gifts" (1 Cor 12:31) by promoting and using the gifts that best edify the worshipping community.[10] When the growth of the community is elevated above the desires of the individuals, not even prophecy will eclipse the practice of other gifts.[11] Various people are allowed, indeed expected, to take part in the worship of God as long as it is done in an orderly fashion (1 Cor 14:26; 40).

God's desire that the church grows as a body that serves is explained in Ephesians 4:11–16, where we read that Jesus gives leaders to the church so that everyone can be built up in the faith and perform the ministry God wants them to do. Apostles, prophets, evangelists, and pastors and teachers are part of Jesus' plan to train people in the church to serve God and each other. Paul implies that unity in the faith and maturity in Christ will only be accomplished when church leaders equip and set people free to serve the body of Christ. The training envisioned could come during a time of worship or on some other occasion and will result in Christians serving during organized worship and as part of one's lifestyle of worship.

SPIRITUAL GIFTS AND WORSHIP IN THE CHURCH TODAY

Since service and worship are closely related, spiritual gifts should be reckoned a God-given means for us to worship by serving him and one another. Much as the Aaronic priests and Levites worshipped through serving the congregation, the Messianic kingdom of priests should worship God by acting out spiritual rituals and performing practical deeds for each other. As noted above, each gift is a specific ministry with a particular effect. In many cases, there is a connection between one's spiritual gifts and abilities. A person could be a "natural teacher" or learn how to preach well through taking a course at a theological college. But if this person gets up in the pulpit and delivers what is otherwise a technically sound sermon and yet no one benefits spiritually, we should conclude that the gift of teaching was

---

not all will preach, other verbal means of building others up must be understood.

10. Fee, *First Corinthians*, 654.

11. Paul thus limits the number of people who can prophesy in a service, instructs that all prophecy must be subject to the examination of others (1 Cor 14:29), and encourages others to participate in other ways.

not exercised. Natural and learned abilities become spiritual gifts only when the Spirit enables a person to use them to build up the body of Christ. In addition to using natural abilities or learned skills, people at times manifest a more spontaneous movement of the Spirit, perhaps through a miraculous gift or by performing a task that goes beyond their normal capabilities but is used by the Spirit to help the church grow.

My study of the Pauline passages that speak of spiritual gifts leaves me unconvinced by arguments that they have ceased. Even so, I believe that the emphasis many churches and parachurch groups have placed upon gifts may not be wholly beneficial. While we should desire gifts, especially "the greater gifts," Paul's emphasis on mutual service and edification should be the primary guide of our thoughts and practice. It is not as important that I find *my* gift, as that I discover how I can serve in the church so that others are built up. Instead of worrying about what spiritual gifts I might have, or being intimidated by them since they are "mysterious," I should simply look for ways to serve. Someone who is ignorant of spiritual gifts but helps the church grow is far more valuable than those who have "discovered" their gifts but do not use them, as if such is even possible. Since spiritual gifts only exist as they are used, it is impossible for someone to know what their gift is and not use it.

The emphasis that is sometimes placed on finding and practicing one's own gift(s) may also obscure the reality that the gifts belong to the Holy Spirit, not to us. They are *his*. He gives them out "just as he determines" to empower people for service (1 Cor 12:11). And even though the text doesn't explicitly say so, the Spirit can take them away as and when he determines. We do not have to pick and choose between the gifts or be concerned about what we might be given, for God is the giver of good gifts. All we need to do is trust that the Lord who knows our abilities, needs, and what he wants us to do for his kingdom will give us what we need to do that.

The Bible is clear that spiritual gifts are granted as an outpouring of God's grace. For this reason, they are frequently referred to as grace gifts. As extensions of God's grace, we do not deserve them any more than we deserve salvation. They are, like the property entrusted to the men in the parable of the talents, something that should be used to the best of our ability as we serve our Master who will reward us if we use them wisely and with effect (Matt 25:14–30). And just as we have no room to boast because of our salvation, God's gifts for service should neither give us reason to boast or to feel spiritually inferior.

The same is true for the ability to identify one's spiritual gifts. Knowing one's gift does not make one a better Christian. The more important question that we need to ask is whether we can see the Spirit working through us. Does the Spirit empower you to serve others? Do others benefit from what you do for the Lord? If you can answer "yes" to these questions, you are practicing a spiritual gift whether you know what to call it or not. As the repeated imagery about the human body indicates, a person who does not have one particular gift should not feel he is less a part of the body. A foot is not a hand and a hand is not a foot, but both are needed. An eye is not an ear and an ear is not a nose, but the body would not function as well if it lacked any of them. In the same way, every member is needed in the body of Christ to serve in some unique capacity. The question wise church leaders must ask is how they can equip and mobilize each member, setting them free to serve. Only when we do this will we be able to worship God in the way he desires.

CONCLUSION

Much recent teaching on spiritual gifts has rightly emphasized the need to practice the gifts. Perhaps a slightly better way to state this would be that we need to allow the Spirit to work through us so that the church will be built up and develop as he desires. For the kingdom of God to come in its fullness, many jobs need to be done. Some serve by teaching, some by giving. Others serve by passing out service sheets, running the sound board, leading music, singing with joy, preparing tea, locking doors, ringing bells, reading Scripture, praying for the needs of the world, taking part in youth ministry, joining summer mission projects, or searching for a new pastor. The list is endless.

No matter what way we serve, whether we can link it to one of the gifts in a biblical list or not, if we are ministering to others in the power of the Spirit so that they are built up in Christ, we are practicing a spiritual gift. May he take delight as we serve his church to his glory.

16

Conclusion: A Life of Worship

This book began by asking the question, "What is worship?" We then acknowledged that even though Christians concur that worship is essential to the faith, they do not always agree on what it is or how it should be done. Often the differences stem from our personal, cultural, ecclesiastical, and educational backgrounds. Even so, we largely agree that people who worship the one true God should be more united in their understandings and practices of such a central part of the faith. This far from satisfactory situation has motivated our study of the biblical teaching about worship so that we can better know God, further understand his will, and more rightly conform our thinking and practice to his desire for us. As we have seen, although Scripture never defines the term, its use of the major words for worship and its witness to the many ways in which ancient Israel and the New Testament church engaged God have much to teach us about how Christians today can and should draw near to God—Father, Son, and Holy Spirit.

As we bring this study to a close, we will review some of the questions asked at the beginning and reflect on what we have learned about different understandings of Christian worship, even as we consider the future of worship.

Is it correct to say that we should worship God because he is worthy of worship? Certainly. Even though God's worthiness is a minor theme in Scripture, it is there. But simply worshipping God because he is *worthy* isn't enough. We worship him because he is the Creator and Sustainer of people and the cosmos. We worship God because he is our Deliverer, our Savior, our King, and our Lord. We worship him because he delights in our worship and we delight in worshipping him whether on our own or with others. We worship him through our joy and grief, our clarity and confusion, and our wholeness and pain. We worship him because he heals us of our diseases and forgives our sins. We worship him because he is worthy, and we worship him for many reasons that are not directly connected with worth.

Is worship something that happens during a special service? Yes. Services are wonderful settings for worship, whether they are formal or informal, planned or spontaneous, indoor or outdoor, attended by many or by "two or three." But since "to serve" is one of the major words of worship, worship does not end just because a service—in the sense of a meeting—ends. The sign placed above the exit door of a church building that reads "Servants' Entrance" highlights our responsibility to worship God by serving him in the world until we return for another service of gathered worship. There is good reason to say that one aim of gathered worship is to equip and empower God's people to enter the world for service. This, of course, raises the question about whether our services are designed toward that end and how we might redesign them so that they are. As we have seen, our service in the world should be expressed through our use of the gifts that God's Holy Spirit graciously allocates to us so that we can minister to one another for mutual upbuilding and so that people who do not yet know God will become worshippers too. How well do our gathered services equip us for this lifestyle of worship? How well do we live out this lifestyle of worship in our day-to-day activities in the world?

Are we right to say that we worship God through singing and praying? Absolutely. Scripture abounds with examples of people worshipping through songs and prayers and it frequently exhorts us to do the same. But as we have seen, if we reduce worship to singing, we miss out on the grandeur that God wants us to experience. Would we be content to say that one rock strata *was* the Grand Canyon? By limiting our focus to a significant and exciting geological formation, we would miss out on the magnitude of the glories surrounding us. As in the natural world, the larger sets the context for the lesser and clarifies its significance. Singing and praying must take their significance from the broader perspective of worship. And for this reason, we need to be careful that our speech does not perpetuate the common idea that worship is all about singing. In addition to singing, communal worship rightly includes such things as reading Scripture, listening to biblical teaching, bringing our offerings and other sacrifices to God, and serving one another in practical ways so that we can all be built up in the faith. It also is demonstrated when we receive others into our fellowship through baptism and as we unite as God's people to celebrate the Lord's Supper. Let us worship God through singing. But let us also be sure that our singing follows the biblical examples of having songs that allow us to approach God in joy and pain with words that are theologically deep and personally releasing. And as we sing, let us keep in mind that the worship of God includes many other activities as well and make sure we verbalize the reality that these too are acts of worship.

Worship, the Bible tells us, is a God-centered and life-encompassing act. It focuses on the God who reveals himself as Father, Son, and Holy Spirit, who instructs us how to worship him, and who gives us the ability to do so. As we have seen, worship is an activity of the heart and mind, the emotion and will, that brings us before God in his majesty, causes us to bow before him as our Lord and Master, moves us to express an attitude of reverence and fear because of his power and love, and impels us to obey his commands in daily and seasonal acts of service that embrace both the sacred and the secular. And for these reasons, we need to move beyond simply learning about worship and make it our goal to worship God in the church and in the world.

Moving from knowledge to practice, particularly when we gather with others, will strike many as an impossible dream. It's not that we are unable to worship. Our problem often stems from the fact that while the Bible identifies many worship practices, it does not provide a prescribed form or order for worship. This is true both for corporate meetings and personal devotions. Those who believe that the worship practices of the church worldwide should demonstrate visible unity will undoubtedly find this a supreme frustration. It will similarly annoy anyone who is hoping for an easy-to-follow pattern to learn and pass on. But the Bible doesn't provide us with a liturgy for every possible event in life or lay out "ten steps for worshipping God." It appears that God is more interested in the content of worship than the style or pattern. He is more concerned about the heart of the worshipper than his routine. What the Bible says about worship is thus much more descriptive than prescriptive. For this reason, it is possible for Christians from various traditions, cultures, and times in history to worship God in different ways—providing that the object and content remain the same.

This is what we find at the end of our Bibles. Though many consider Revelation to be a book that is cram-packed with strange creatures and even stranger prophecies, there are good reasons to see it as the supreme book of worship. The main question it asks of its readers is whether they will worship the God of creation who revealed himself through Jesus Christ or worship someone or something else. The book similarly makes it clear that, in spite of the other beings that can be worshipped and all the religious, ideological, and political systems that can be embraced, there is only one proper object of worship and that is the One who sits on the throne and the Lamb. As the book and its visions unfold, it becomes clear that everything and everyone that is worshipped is judged for attempting to usurp the place that belongs to God alone. In the end, the serpent, the beast, the false prophet, and the great prostitute are defeated by the Lamb and come to nothing. No longer will they be worshipped and no longer will their worshippers be found, as they will all be judged and sent to destruction for rejecting God.

A different end awaits those who worship in spirit and in truth. The scenes described in Revelation 4, 5, and 7 reveal a riot of sights and sounds as God's worshippers joyfully encircle the heavenly throne to proclaim his eternal praise. The angels, living creatures, twenty-four elders, and the redeemed who come from every tribe and nation and people and tongue worship the One who sits on the throne and the Lamb by their words and actions. Their cry, "You are worthy, our Lord and God, to receive glory and honor and power, for you created all things, and by your will they were created and have their being" (Rev 4:11; cf. 5:9, 12), is the clearest biblical statement that God's worth and creaturely worship come together. But acknowledging God's worth isn't enough. The groups that gather before the throne each in turn cry out in awe because of his holiness, fall to the ground to proclaim his praises, wave palm branches to magnify their movement, and shout to acknowledge his salvific power. The sounds, sights, and actions fill God's throne room where he is served day and night, without a prescribed liturgy. Each group worships God in unique ways that enhance everyone's experience. And when one group exhausts itself with praise, another steps up to worship God in a totally different way. Significantly, when it comes to humankind, cultural and linguistic distinctions can be readily discerned. If this is how worship is done in heaven, should we be overly concerned about variations in style or language on earth? Could we not combine a few when we come to meet God? Should we not learn from the worship of others and join them so that we can multiply their praise and ours? When we pray that God's "will be done on earth as it is in heaven," should we not consider how our worship on earth can be done like it is in heaven? If, as the Puritan David Clarkson said, "worship is the nearest resemblance of heaven,"[1] shouldn't our worship mirror the patterns evidenced there?

Revelation declares that believing people from every tribe and nation and people and tongue will become the bride of Christ and worship him forever in the new heavens and the new earth. This is what we were created for, and this is what we were redeemed for. When my 102-year-old father felt that his time on earth was drawing to a close, he told us he had something he wanted to say. His concluding thought after living a long and

---

1. Clarkson, *Works*, Vol. 3, 194.

faithful life was that he was "a sinner on his way home," solely because he was traveling the way of the cross. Though these were not his final words, they were significant in that they recognize that everyone who comes to know God through Jesus Christ—no matter their tribe, nation, ethnicity, or language—comes as a sinner in need of grace and mercy and responds to God's salvific act by worshiping him in this world as they prepare for their eternal home where they will worship him forever.

This is the future for all who come to know the God who sits upon the throne and the Lamb who takes away the sin of the world. As it proclaims this future, the book of Revelation returns us full circle to the Garden of Eden and shows us that in the new creation, humans have direct fellowship with God, the tree of life brings healing to all, and there is no curse because there is no sin. What's more, God's people take up their creational status as the image of God by reigning with him forever. Like Jesus, their rule demonstrates their service to their Father God. Ruling over creation is thus an important aspect of their eternal worship that should also be earthed out in this sphere.

Curiously, the recognition that worship will be perfected in heaven glosses the reality that there is one earthly act of worship that is essential here so that sinners, like my father, can find their way home, but will have no place there. This is the preaching of the gospel. In this life, people can only come to know and worship God as we tell them what God has done for them through his Son and the Holy Spirit moves their hearts so that they believe. By accepting the good news that "God so loved the world that he gave his one and only Son, that whoever believes in him shall not perish but have eternal life" (John 3:16), we are transformed from being rebels to worshippers, from sinners to saints. The worship act of preaching the gospel is needed as long as there are people in the world who do not worship the God of creation and salvation. But as soon as all of God's people are gathered for the wedding feast of the Lamb, it will have no more use.

But even though the preaching of the gospel will one day end, the centrality of the good news that we can be redeemed through Jesus Christ frequently moves me to say that worship is the beginning and the end of mission.[2] Only worshippers invite others to join them in worshiping God. We see this again and again in the Bible. On the morning of the resurrection, some women, led by Mary Magdalene, went to Jesus' grave to anoint

---

2. John Piper has famously said: "Missions exists because worship doesn't. Worship is ultimate, not missions, because God is ultimate, not man. When this age is over, and the countless millions of the redeemed fall on their faces before the throne of God, missions will be no more." Piper, *Let the Nations be Glad*, 15. My concept expands upon this by seeing worship as the motivation for mission as well as being its goal, its *telos*.

his body but were alarmed to find that he wasn't there. The possibility that the tomb might be empty had never crossed their minds. So, when the angel told them that Jesus was risen from the dead, they were dumbfounded. The text tells us they went away feeling a strange mixture of fear and joy (Matt 28:8). They could not fathom how a dead man might come alive again. But could it be true? And then, as they were heading back to Jerusalem, they bumped into Jesus. Undoubtedly, their feelings of joy, fear, and bewilderment continued. But when they came into contact with the living Lord, they fell at his feet to worship him. They had seen Jesus. They had touched him. He had spoken to them. And they had worshipped him, because worship is the right response of anyone who encounters the living Lord. And then, they did the next right thing. They returned to Jerusalem to tell his disciples what they had seen and heard, and to let them know that Jesus was alive. In this story, the early morning worshippers became the later morning missionaries who informed others that they too could worship the living Christ. Worship was the beginning of mission.

This theme is repeated later in the chapter when the disciples gathered in Galilee to meet Jesus on the mountain he had appointed. Matthew reports that "When they saw him, they worshipped him" (Matt 28:17). Their encounter with the living Jesus resulted in worship. And shortly thereafter, Jesus gave them the Great Commission and sent them out to make disciples. The rest of the New Testament recounts how the mountain-top worshippers became world-wide disciple makers. Again, only worshippers can lead others into worship and only disciples can make disciples. Worship is the beginning and end of mission.

The same message comes through when the Holy Spirit revealed his will to the church in Antioch about Barnabas and Saul being set aside for a new ministry at a time when they were "worshipping the Lord and fasting" (Acts 13:2).[3] Whether or not this was a formal worship service, a time of prayer for the needs of the church and the world, or taking part in a ministry like caring for the poor or providing food for widows—and the Greek word used here for ministering can include any of these—worship opened this church up to the Spirit's direction about sending away two of their most gifted leaders. Significantly, after hearing from God in the context of worship and fasting, the church took more time to pray and fast (Acts 13:3). This added period of prayer and fasting undoubtedly gave them assurance that the instruction they had received really came from God and strength to obey the Spirit's instruction so that they could send off Saul and Barnabas,

---

3. For a longer exposition of this passage, see my article, "A Meditation on the Church in Antioch and Mission."

who similarly needed assurance and strength if they were to go away. The church's worship resulted in the sending out of Spirit-filled missionaries who opened the door so that many more could also worship the Lord.

Clearly, the Bible sees worship as the beginning and the end of mission. And the gospel is the means toward that end. Worshippers are moved to share the gospel so that others might know Jesus. Sharing the good news about Jesus is thus an important part of our worship. And those who hear and believe the gospel are enabled to truly worship for the first time and for all time. Worship and mission are inextricably linked as those who have experienced Jesus share their experience with others and invite them to get to know him too.

CONCLUSION

We have covered a lot of material in this book, but we have still only begun to learn about worship. Our biblical theology of worship makes it crystal clear that God has not designed one form and style of worship that is required of everyone throughout the ages. Even so, we should be deeply concerned to learn what the living God desires of his worshippers, to strive to please him by doing that, and to help others do the same. Whether we actively lead worship in our local congregation, teach courses on the subject, sing as a member of a congregation, share the gospel with a neighbor, or worship God in some other way, the Bible's teaching on the subject can greatly enhance our experience of God, in public gatherings and in private. The biblical pattern informs us that to worship God, we must discover how to bow down before him in submission; to express our fear as we recognize his power as creator, judge, and defender, and live out his moral demands; and to serve him through acts of devotion and in our earthly vocations.

And as we learn from Revelation, worship is a practice that begins on earth but can only be perfected in eternity. Even so, it is one that we can enjoy right now as it comes as a betrothal gift from our God and Father and his Son Jesus Christ our Lord. This wonderful gift is extended to us by the Holy Spirit who unites us with others in God's family by opening our eyes to understand what he has revealed in his word and giving us all that we need to live it out in this world and in the coming new creation. Worship is one betrothal gift that is best shared with others so that together we can enjoy God as his people of praise and love. This is perhaps why the book of Revelation ends with an announcement that Jesus—"the Alpha and the Omega, the First and the Last, the Beginning and the End"—is "coming soon" (Rev 22:7, 12–13) and follows this up with an invitation to "come."

> The Spirit and the bride say, "Come!" And let him who hears say, "Come!" Whoever is thirsty, let him come; and whoever wishes, let him take the free gift of the water of life.

By taking the gift of the water of life, people are made new and become worshippers of God and the Lamb. As his people and bride, they will reign with him forever and ever. Day in and day out, throughout eternity, they will worship God as they fall before him, sing his praises, and rule over creation in accordance with his eternal design. This will be a life of worship in all its fullness and security and joy. And it is a life that we can begin in this world as we learn to worship our matchless God in all that we do.

It is my sincere hope and prayer that this book has helped you to grow in your understanding of worship. I similarly hope that it has given you reason to reassess your private and public worship of God with the end of bringing them more into line with God's word and will. But even more, I hope that the time you have spent reading these words has enhanced your relationship with God, because that is the ultimate end of worship, and without that, our *acts* of worship are nothing more than a hollow shell. As my final act of worship in writing this book, may I ask you to join me in John's prayer as we anticipate the return of our Lord when he will make all things new and our experience of worship will be perfected. "Come, Lord Jesus" (Rev 22:20). And as we need God's grace to bring us to worship him and sustain us in our worship, let us also minister to one another with John's closing blessing. "The grace of the Lord Jesus be with God's people. Amen" (Rev 22:21).

Appendix

Times and Seasons of Worship: The Church Year

Earlier in this book, we saw that life in this world is situated in space and measured by time. Accordingly, ancient Israel ordered their lives and worship in physical locations and in line with the weeks, months, and seasons of the year. While the first-century Jews who believed that Jesus was the promised Messiah began to rethink their religion, they continued meeting at the temple and synagogues for prayer, celebrating the Sabbath, and taking part in the historical festivals. To the worship traditions they inherited from the Old Covenant religion, Jewish Christians added distinctively Christian worship practices, such as baptism, the Lord's Supper, and attending to the teaching of the apostles. This participation in traditional and new practices indicates that the earliest worshippers of Jesus engaged in what has been called a "liturgical dualism."[1] It did not take long, however, for Christians to develop a different rhythm in their worship of God. This happened as outside pressure forced them to distance themselves from Jewish worship and especially as the faith spread to people who had never experienced the Old Testament worship cycle. Though these developments greatly impacted the way Christians worshipped God through the seasons, they were not directly the result of biblical revelation. For this reason, this appendix was written to acknowledge that the rise of the church year was a post-biblical phenomenon and, therefore, not directly an outgrowth of biblical theology. It does, however, show how Christians applied what they knew about worshipping

---

1. Schmemann, *Introduction to Liturgical Theology*, 59.

God through the times and seasons of the year to their new historical situation. The inclusion of this discussion will prove beneficial to many readers who encounter many of these practices in their regular worship of God and to others who may only be vaguely aware of their existence but would like to know more about them.

The first disciples were all Jews who lived among their Jewish compatriots. It did not take them long to discover that their belief in Jesus as the promised Messiah was unacceptable to many. Jesus had informed them that the time would come when people "will lay hands on you and persecute you. They will deliver you to synagogues and prisons, and you will be brought before kings and governors, and all on account of my name" (Luke 21:12). The disciples could count on the same reception that was given to their Lord (John 15:18–21). Their first evangelistic outreaches in Jerusalem on the day of Pentecost made this obvious. While some hearers expressed their amazement and asked, "What does this mean?" others responded that the evangelists "have had too much wine" (Acts 2:12–13). Soon the apostles faced threats and imprisonment for preaching in the name of Jesus (Acts 4:1–22). Their early practice of joining their brethren at the temple during the time of prayer (Acts 3:1), proclaiming that Jesus was the Christ "in the temple courts and from house to house" (Acts 5:42), and demonstrating to synagogue worshipers that the coming of Jesus fulfilled Old Testament prophecy (Acts 13:14–44) resulted in a combination of acceptance and rejection. Imprisonment, beating, and even martyrdom followed.

After the Jewish revolt that began in AD 66 and the destruction of the temple in AD 70, Judean Christians were almost completely cut off from their roots. Many of them fled to the eastern side of the Jordan and to Asia Minor to escape persecution.[2] And as non-Christian Jews were forced to reformulate their practices in the light of a new political reality, Christian participation in the synagogue was made more difficult, if not impossible. At some time during the early centuries of the modern era, the twelfth of the Eighteen Benedictions—the *Birkat ha-Minim* "the heretic benediction"—was reworded to pronounce a curse on "Nazarenes" and heretics.[3] Believers in Jesus who recited this prayer with their fellow Jews would have been conspicuous for not reciting this part of the benedictions. Unable to worship God following their traditional practices and seasons, Jewish Christians

---

2. Bruce, *New Testament History*, 375–77.

3. The Eighteen Benedictions (*Shemoneh Esreh*), the main liturgical prayer of Judaism, is recited three times a day by observant Jews. For a good of summary of the link between the twelfth benediction and the separation of Judaism from Christianity, see Wilson, *Our Father Abraham*, 64–69.

were left to integrate with the larger Gentile Christian population, dissolve into sects, or return to Judaism.[4]

While the interaction between Christian and non-Christian Jews and the Roman destruction of the temple led to great changes in worship practices, the proclamation of the faith to the Gentile world produced even more changes. Many Gentile believers had little knowledge of the Jewish faith and even less knowledge of their calendar as they lived far removed from Palestine. From an early date, it was recognized that Gentiles need not adopt traditional Jewish practice to become Christians. This is seen from the proclamation of the Council of Jerusalem (Acts 15) and the way the Epistles lack directions on how to observe Jewish holy days.

In the Pauline Epistles, the absence of instructions on the observation of Jewish festivals is conspicuous, as the apostle addresses issues such as division over baptism (1 Cor 1:13–17), misuse of the Lord's Supper (1 Cor 11:17–34), women wearing head coverings in public worship (1 Cor 11:2–16), the role of spiritual gifts (1 Cor 12:1–31; 14:1–25), and orderliness in public worship (1 Cor 14:26–40). Since Paul never shrank from correcting the worship practice of churches he planted, the apostolic church would have expected him to comment on the necessity of keeping Old Testament feasts if they were a Christian's duty.

Claims are, at times, made that some New Testament books were written to follow ancient liturgies or that they allude to liturgical practices of the early church. These all fall short as they tend to read later liturgical practices back into the text, harmonize statements from different books as though they reflected the practice of the whole church, or confuse literary metaphor with liturgical practice.[5] It is in this light that Paul's reference to Jesus as our Passover Lamb and his following exhortation, "Therefore let us keep the festival" (1 Cor 5:7–8) should be read. It should never have been cited as the "oldest evidence of a primitive church year."[6] Far from instructing Christians about the observance of Passover or any other seasonal feast, the text arises in an argument against immoral behavior that Paul likens to leaven that must be removed if the whole batch of dough—the church—is to remain sincere and truthful. Since Christ died as the Passover Lamb, the

---

4. Within a couple of centuries, at least some Christians found it easier to interact with Jews. Thus, John Chrysostom, in a series of sermons preached in Antioch in 386–387, complained about Christians who attended both church and synagogue services. While these sermons, recorded as *Adversus Judaeos*, eventually flamed anti-Semitic flames, his purpose in preaching them was more to convince Judaizing Christians to return to the church.

5. Bradshaw, *Origins of Christian Worship*, 47–59.

6. Webber, *Worship Old and New*, 223.

church should keep itself pure from spiritual adultery. According to Gordon Fee, Paul uses the imagery of the Feast in order to broaden "the application of the death of Christ to Christian life as a whole."[7] The present tense of the verb translated "let us keep the Festival" is significant in that it implies "the continual celebration of the feast."[8] Paul, in other words, is not teaching that Christ's sacrifice should be celebrated yearly by the church, but that it should impact one's life and ethics each and every day. This is an important truth for anyone who celebrates specific dates on the Church Calendar to remember. The core issue is not commemorating the day, but living the life of faith.

Though the New Testament says little about regulating worship according to the seasons and extra-canonical Christian literature from the first two centuries is sparse, a number of distinctly Christian holidays were being celebrated during the second century. By the third century, various groups of Christians ordered their worship around the seasons. The changes permeating the church and the empire in the fourth and fifth centuries were so extensive that it could be concluded that, "A Christian reshaping of time and space enabled people throughout the empire to orient themselves to a new religious imagination, one that was very much geared to each particular culture, its martyrs and local history, as well as the broader drama of Christian salvation."[9]

Many celebrations of salvation began as worship traditions of individual congregations or regional groups of churches. Only with the introduction of a universal liturgy in the fourth century was the way paved for what is known as the Church Year, Christian Year, or Liturgical Calendar to be used for living out the year before God. According to Bradshaw, "The drive towards greater precision in the formulation of doctrine played a significant part in reshaping liturgical practice in a more uniform direction in the Constantinian age."[10] Standardization ensued for two reasons. First, the appearance of heretical sects prompted church leaders to take a stand on important issues and codify orthodox doctrine. Thus, set prayers and catechetical instruction were developed to hold aberrant practices in check. Second, the recognition of Christianity as the religion of the empire ushered in an age when Christians were free to travel around the Roman world and interact with fellow believers from different lands. This, in turn, opened the door for them to be introduced to worship practices previously unknown. As church leaders discussed varieties of practice, they evidently determined

---

7. Fee, *First Corinthians*, 218. See also Barrett, *First Corinthians*, 128–30.
8. Fee, *First Corinthians*, 218, n 18.
9. Baldovin, "The Empire Baptized," 117.
10. Bradshaw, *Origins of Christian Worship*, 222.

to select those which could be used meaningfully by a wider church audience and to set others aside.

The Christian calendar that emerged after the Council of Nicea has remained, to a large extent, unchanged to this day. The following examination provides a brief account of the way the early church's worship of God developed with respect to seasonal holidays. It should be appreciated that the Christian Year had a different intention than Israel's seasonal festivals that were tied to the agricultural seasons or major historical events. The major festivals of the Christian Year all relate to the advent of Jesus and the work of salvation he performed. The change in the calendar further parallels a change in the nature of the time celebrated.

As Jesus' early followers reckoned time, daily hours of prayer, the weekly celebration of the Lord's Day, and some festivals spread throughout the year played significant roles in their worship of God. Modern Christians who similarly worship God on a daily, weekly, monthly, and annual basis—whether individually, as families, or in local congregations—can benefit from learning about the practices of their ancient spiritual kin. Apart from the Sabbath/Lord's Day celebration, we will consider the regular worship practices of the early church, beginning with the daily habit of prayer and then turn to the church year.

DAILY PRAYER

First generation Jewish Christians apparently followed their ancestral traditions of praying to God daily. Immediately after Jesus' ascension, the apostles and others "all joined together constantly in prayer" (Acts 1:14).[11] The book of Acts reports other occasions when prayer was made at specific times of the day. Peter and John are thus said to go "up to the temple at the time of prayer—at three in the afternoon," the time for afternoon sacrifices (Acts 3:1).[12] The centurion Cornelius similarly prayed at this time of the day when he received the vision telling him to send for Peter (Acts 10:3, 30). A few days later, Peter went up on a rooftop at noon to pray when he received a vision letting him know that God accepted Gentiles (Acts 10:9). While it is possible that the times mentioned by Luke corresponded to the hours of

---

11. It is possible, but not certain, that the article in the Greek *tē proseuchē*, "prayer," indicates that all who gathered in the upper room regularly took part in a scheduled prayer service. See Longenecker, *Acts*, 57.

12. While the Greek literally says, "the hour of prayer, the ninth," the NIV renders the idea well. In Luke's Gospel, this was the time people gathered for prayer and incense was burned (Luke 1:10).

prayer practiced by contemporary Jews, there is little evidence that first-century Judaism had either an established liturgy or regulated prayers.[13] Even so, it is likely that the first Christians followed the practices of their Jewish kin. Only later did those attempting to find support for their prayer routines read these hours of prayer back into Scripture as regulated times.

While the New Testament gives no firm instruction about times for prayer, some early church fathers did. Beginning with the *Didache*, Christians were encouraged to offer prayers to God three times a day.[14] This instruction was likely related to the prayer habits of certain Old Testament characters (Ps 55:17; Dan 6:10). Some fathers promoted thrice daily prayer using Trinitarian reasoning. In the early third century, Hippolytus gave Christological reasons for praying three times a day: Christians should pray during the third hour (9:00 AM) since it was the time of the crucifixion, at the sixth hour (noon) because the sky went dark, and at the ninth hour (3:00 PM) as it was the time Christ's side was pierced.[15] He did not limit prayer to these three occasions, specifically adding prayer after rising from sleep, before undertaking any work, before going to bed, at midnight, and at cock-crow.

Along with Hippolytus, many who suggested prayer at the third, sixth, and ninth hour found support in the psalmist's claim to cry out to God in the evening, morning, and at noon (Ps 55:17). Others grounded their prayer times on the patterns of the day, bringing their requests and praise to God in the morning, afternoon, and evening. Eventually, the third, sixth, and ninth hours became known as the apostolic hours of prayer, due in part to the statements made in Acts about the apostles praying at these times (Acts 2:15; 3:1; 10:9).

While praying three times a day was common in the early church, other practices were known. Frequently, twice daily prayer, morning and evening, was suggested, based upon the twice daily sacrifices offered by Old Testament Israel. This became so popular that by the fourth century, Eusebius recorded that morning and evening prayers were universally practiced.[16] Some fathers determined that prayer should also be made at midnight in view of the psalmist's cry, "At midnight I rise to give you thanks for your righteous laws" (Ps 119:62). Others found that the psalmist's words, "Seven times a day I praise you for your righteous laws" gave them reason to pray more frequently (Ps 119:164). Some desert monastics went even farther as

---

13. See Bradshaw, *Origins of Christian Worship*, 36–42.
14. *Did.* 8.
15. Hippolytus, *The Apostolic Tradition* 41.
16. Eusebius, *Commentary on Psalm 64*, quoted in Johnson, "The Apostolic Tradition," 60.

they attempted to follow Paul's advice in 1 Thessalonians 5:17 to "pray continually" literally, by doing away with everything else.

While regular times of prayer have proved to be of great spiritual benefit to Christians throughout the ages, they are nowhere legislated in Scripture. Nor did any one set pattern of prayer practiced in the early church become a model for all times. Modern believers are, therefore, free to pray two times a day, three times a day, or more frequently, as they find it helpful. Many will adopt the established hours of prayer, while others will pray at other regular times, be that upon waking, at meals, before work, at bedtime, or whenever. What is more important than following specific prayer times is daily prayer that acknowledges one's dependence on God for salvation and the ability to live for him, and that demonstrates consciousness of his personal presence, desire to do his will, and reliance upon his help. Prayer should thus be made to express joy, sorrow, thanksgiving, and repentance. It should be raised for both spiritual and mundane matters. While Paul's imperative to "pray continually" has been understood to require unceasing words of prayer, its placement in a book (and in the whole Pauline corpus) that frequently exhorts its readers to be involved in the daily affairs of life makes an overliteral interpretation impossible. Paul's desire is that our lives should be punctuated by prayer. Whether one uses an ancient system of prayer—and if so, which one—or a more modern method is not as relevant as it is to bring one's prayers to the Lord.

ADVENT

Although most modern celebrations of the Christian Year begin with Advent, this season was historically added to the end of the liturgical year that began with Epiphany on 6 January.[17] Advent, which comes from the Latin, *adventus*—"coming"—is celebrated during the period marked by the four Sundays preceding Christmas. It therefore begins on 27 November or the first Sunday after that date. Advent is the season of preparing for the coming of Christ into the world, with the focus placed on the entire incarnation rather than just the nativity. Similarly, Advent is intended to move us beyond Jesus' first coming to remember that he is coming again to reign in his fully established kingdom, gather all his people together, and judge the world.

Traditionally, Advent was considered a fast and churches were decorated with violet or purple colors to symbolize the mourning associated with fasting, though some connect it with royalty in view of Jesus being the

---

17. From the fourth century, the church's liturgical readings began on Epiphany with Matthew's Gospel.

King of kings. Some churches have replaced the violet with a deep blue, to symbolize the night sky on the day Jesus was born. In more modern times, the colors red and green have received a special place at Christmas. Though several explanations have been given regarding the origin of these colors, one common explanation is that the red symbolizes Christ's blood while the green of an evergreen tree symbolizes eternal life.

CHRISTMAS

As it is the day we celebrate the birth of Jesus, many Christians consider Christmas the most important day of the year. Even so, Christmas did not develop as a popular holiday until the fourth century. Early on, churches in various parts of the world celebrated Christ's birth on different dates. In part, this is because neither the Bible nor history records the date when Jesus was born. It is similarly unclear why certain dates were selected as Jesus' birth day. According to one common explanation, the roots of Christmas lie in the decision made by early church leaders to Christianize pagan holidays by infusing them with new meaning. Thus, the Roman feast day *Natalis Solis Invicti*—the birthday of the Unconquered Sun—which had been introduced by Aurelian in AD 274, is said to have prompted church leaders to promote the birth of Jesus on 25 December so that the true Light would be worshipped on that day instead of the sun. Another explanation is that early Christians borrowed from Jewish traditions that equated the death days of the Patriarchs with their conception. This reckoning places Jesus' birth date nine months after his death date on 14 Nisan, which would work out to either 25 December or 6 January, depending on the calendar used.[18] Christmas was thus celebrated by the Western Church on the earlier date and by the Eastern Church on the latter.[19] It was not long, however, before the Greek- and Latin-speaking churches unified their practice, recognizing 25 December as the birth of the Savior and 6 January as the anniversary of the visit of the wise men to Bethlehem—commonly referred to as Epiphany.

In the Christian year, the birth of the Savior is celebrated on Christmas Day, Christmas Sunday, and the second Sunday after Christmas. This festive season continues for twelve days—thus the twelve days of Christmas—ending

---

18. Johnson, "The Apostolic Tradition," 65. Many Orthodox churches celebrate Christmas on 25 December of the Julian calendar, which is the same day as 7 January on the Gregorian calendar.

19. The first certain reference to Jesus being born on 25 December is found in a calendar of martyr's death days dated to AD 354. Baldovin, "The Empire Baptized," 112–13.

on Epiphany. The liturgical color for the Christmas season is white, representing purity and joy. Gold (or yellow) is used in some churches.

EPIPHANY

Epiphany comes from the Greek *epiphaneia*, which means "appearance" or "manifestation." The Greek word was commonly used in religious settings to refer to a divinity that appeared on the earth either in physical form or through a powerful act. Paul used the term with both nuances when he wrote that Jesus appeared on earth as a man who destroyed death and brought immortality to those who believe the good news about him (2 Tim 1:10). As Epiphany comes twelve days after Christmas, it is also referred to as Twelfth Day. The previous evening—Twelfth Night—marks the end of the Christmas season. In memory of the visit of the Magi, it is sometimes called Three Kings' Day. The Eastern Church labels it Theophany—the appearance of God.

From early in church history, Epiphany was celebrated in two different ways, each of which was understood to be an appearance of Jesus as God. By the fourth century, the Western Church assigned 6 January as the date upon which the baby Jesus was made manifest to the Magi who came to worship him and present their gifts. This appearance of Jesus to the Magi speaks of the Gentiles—the nations—coming to worship the one God who made himself known to the entire world through this child. The Eastern Church placed more emphasis on the tradition that Epiphany marked Jesus' baptism by John, which was then followed by the descent of the Holy Spirit upon him (Matt 3:16–17).[20] This manifestation to humankind is understood to be a revelation of the Trinitarian nature of the Godhead. Orthodox Christians who follow the Gregorian calendar celebrate Epiphany on 6 January with most other Christians. Those who follow the Julian calendar celebrate on 19 January.

Epiphany is also celebrated as a season of the church year. The length of the season after Epiphany varies by tradition. Historically, the season began with the Epiphany vigil mass on 5 January and ended with Septuagesima,[21] nine weeks before Easter. The Catholic Church currently considers the

---

20. It has been suggested that the Western Church did not celebrate Epiphany as the day of Jesus' baptism because "Too much attention on the baptism of Jesus might lend credibility to a more adoptionist version of christology." Baldovin, "The Empire Baptized," 118. Adoptionism is the belief that Jesus was born as a human and became divine when the Holy Spirit descended upon him at his baptism or through his resurrection. From the second century, this teaching was recognized as unorthodox.

21. Septuagesima will be discussed in the following section.

season following Epiphany to be "ordinary time."[22] The Anglican communion similarly considers Epiphany to begin with evening prayers on the previous day, but currently ends the season after the festival of The Presentation of Christ, which is observed on 2 February or the Sunday that falls between 28 January and 3 February. The weeks that fall between that date and Shrove Tuesday are considered ordinary time, with each of the Sundays during this period ordered as they precede Lent. Protestant denominations that follow the Revised Common Lectionary celebrate Epiphany from 6 January through Shrove Tuesday. The exact length of the season is determined by the beginning of Lent, the date of which is set by the date for Easter during that year.

As Epiphany is a day to remember the appearance of Jesus in the world, those who have recognized him as Savior could mark the season by determining to show Jesus to others. Individual Christians could find ways to share the gospel with friends and family members or otherwise show Jesus to the world. Churches can similarly ask what they can do as bodies of believers to help their society seek and worship Jesus as the Magi did.

As it is the twelfth day of the Christmas season, Epiphany takes the color white (or gold). The liturgical color for the period of Ordinary Time beginning after Epiphany is green, which is normally related to growth in Christ.

LENT

Lent[23] is the period before Easter that serves as a time of preparation for celebrating the Passion and Resurrection of Christ. It begins on Ash Wednesday and lasts for six weeks. Forty days are traditionally set aside for fasting. The Sundays during this season, including Passion Sunday and Palm Sunday, are all celebrated as feast days when fasting should be broken.[24] Other important days during Lent include Maundy Thursday and Good Friday. Lent is preceded by the three Sundays Septuagesima, Sexagesima, and Quinquagesima, which come from the Latin words for seventieth, sixtieth, and fiftieth since they are approximately seventy, sixty, and

---

22. It is called ordinary time because the Sundays of the season are "ordered," that is numbered, as in "the third Sunday before Lent."

23. The word Lent evidently comes from an old German word for "spring," as this pre-Easter season occurs during the early spring in the northern hemisphere.

24. Some traditions equate Palm Sunday with Passion Sunday and place both on the Sunday before Easter. Other traditions say that Passion Sunday is the fifth Sunday in Lent and that Palm Sunday is the sixth Sunday in Lent, coming the week before Easter.

fifty days before Easter. From the sixth century, these days were treated as a preparation for Lent.[25]

From the early fourth century, Christians recognized Lent as a season of fasting, even though there is no prior record of its existence.[26] Apparently, a forty-day fasting period following Epiphany that was observed by the church of Alexandria was merged with a shorter pre-Easter period of preparation for baptism that was kept by the Western Church.[27] The forty days are understood to correspond to the forty days Jesus fasted in the wilderness. Even after the various parts of the church agreed that a fasting season should precede Easter, the way it was observed differed from place to place.

The day before Lent begins is commonly known as Shrove Tuesday, Pancake Tuesday, or Mardi Gras (Fat Tuesday). Many people celebrate the day with a festival before the fast of Lent begins.[28] For some, it is a day to eat pancakes in order to use up ingredients, like fat and eggs, which were not to be eaten during Lent. On Ash Wednesday, many Christians put ashes on their foreheads as a reminder that their lives are temporary and that their bodies will one day return to dust and ashes.[29] The remembrance of one's mortality, along with the memory of the suffering and death of Christ, serves as a motivation for believers to examine themselves during Lent. While recalling Christ's death, one should determine to mortify one's own flesh, doing away with the sin that Jesus died to forgive. Black—symbolizing death—is the color for Ash Wednesday.

The last week of Lent is known in the Western Church as Holy Week and in the Eastern Church as Great Week. It begins with Palm Sunday (the day of Jesus' triumphal entry into Jerusalem) and concludes on the Saturday before Easter. Christians have celebrated the final week before the crucifixion by reenacting the events that were believed to have transpired each day. Palm Sunday is a time for somber celebration. Many services held

---

25. During the Second Vatican Council in 1969, Septuagesima, Sexagesima, and Quinquagesima were dropped from the Roman Catholic calendar.

26. For a brief overview of the issues involved, see Bradshaw, *Origins of Christian Worship*, 183–85.

27. Evidence exists that at one time, the church in Rome celebrated Lent for three weeks as a period for training catechumens.

28. The most famous celebrations of Mardi Gras take place in New Orleans, Louisiana and Rio de Janeiro, Brazil where it is called Carnival. Despite the abundant news coverage of these celebrations, they are a poor reflection of Christian feasting. The majority who gather for these festivities take little notice of God, choosing instead to indulge their own pleasures.

29. In some traditions, the ash is made by burning palm leaves left over from the previous year's Palm Sunday service.

on that day begin with a procession of people carrying palm branches and crying out, "Hosanna! Blessed is he that comes in the name of the Lord!" in imitation of the crowds who welcomed Jesus to Jerusalem. This joyous announcement must not disguise the reality that the crowd would demand his death within the week.

Thursday of Holy Week is commonly known as Holy Thursday or Maundy Thursday. "Maundy" comes from the Latin *mandatum novum*—"new mandate" or "new commandment." Maundy Thursday commemorates the day when Jesus held his Last Supper with his disciples, washed their feet, and announced he was giving them a new commandment to love one another (John 13:34). Some churches, as an expression of their love for Christ and to follow his example, practice foot washing on this day. Others, to reenact the Last Supper, hold a special *agape* meal that includes foot washing and concludes with Communion. After the service ends, many churches remove all decorations from the church building to prepare for the Good Friday service. Some churches leave their doors open all night for prayer in remembrance that Jesus prayed in the Garden of Gethsemane on the night before his crucifixion.

Good Friday is the most solemn day of the church year as it is the day we remember the death of Jesus on the cross. Services held on the day do not end with joy and celebration, but rather with quietness and sobriety to highlight the horrors of the crucifixion. Joy will follow, but not until Easter morning. It is customary to hold a Good Friday service at noon to mark the time of the crucifixion. Some churches schedule this service to last for three hours to match the time the Lord hung on the cross. These services may include readings from the book of Lamentations and from the Gospel records about the death of Christ. Reflections on the "seven last words of Christ" are also common.[30]

A wide range of liturgical colors are used during the Lenten season. As Lent is a penitential season, the main color is purple. Palm Sunday is celebrated with red. The color for Holy Thursday is white. The liturgical color for Good Friday is black or red (for Christ's passion).

---

30. The "seven last words" are harmonized from the four Gospels in the order it is assumed they would have been said as Jesus hung on the cross. (1) "Father forgive them, for they do not know what they are doing" (Luke 23:34). (2) "I tell you the truth, today you will be with me in paradise" (Luke 23:43). (3) "Dear woman, here is your son" ... "Here is your mother" (John 19:26–27). (4) "*Eloi, Eloi, lama sabachthani?*" ... "My God, my God, why have you forsaken me?" (Matt 27:46; Mark 15:34). (5) "I am thirsty" (John 19:28). (6) "It is finished" (John 19:30). (7) "Father, into your hands I commit my spirit" (Luke 23:46).

EASTER

Easter[31] is the festival celebrating the resurrection of Jesus from the dead and is probably the Christian holiday that was observed from the earliest period. Also known as Resurrection Day or Pascha,[32] it is the most important festival of the church year. Even though the New Testament mentions no celebration of Christ's resurrection on a yearly basis, the designation "the Lord's Day" (Rev 1:10), which referred to "the first day of the week" on which Jesus arose (Acts 20:7), was quickly adopted as the main day for Christian worship in remembrance of the resurrection.

By the second century, several different traditions had developed concerning the proper day to celebrate the resurrection. The differences centered on the relationship of the day to Passover. Many of the Eastern churches used the Hebrew calendar to set the date as the first Sunday after 14 Nisan, while the Western churches, borrowing from Alexandria, settled for the first Sunday after the full moon following the vernal equinox. Churches in Asia Minor and elsewhere connected the resurrection more closely with the crucifixion and celebrated on 14 Nisan, the Jewish Passover day.[33] The variations in dating were discussed at the Council of Nicea (325) which determined that the Western system should be adopted.

The imagery of death and resurrection that was associated with baptism (Rom 6:3–4) made Easter a popular day for baptisms, a practice that probably began in North Africa and Rome, and then spread throughout the church after the middle of the fourth century.[34] In the early church, candidates who had prepared themselves during Lent and who, on the night before Easter, listened to instruction from Scripture about the life of faith were baptized at dawn on Easter morning. They thus symbolically entered into

31. The word Easter comes from the name of an old Anglo-Saxon goddess—Eostre—whose name was associated with a month at the beginning of spring. Early European Christians changed the pagan spring festival honoring her into a Christian festival.

32. This term comes from the Greek word *pascha*, which was used for the Hebrew *pesaḥ*, or Aramaic *pasḥāh*—"Passover." In later Christian usage, it was commonly used for the holiday we call Easter and gave many European languages their word for the Resurrection Day festival. Thus, Latin *pascha*, Italian *pasqua*, Spanish *la Pascua*, Portuguese *Páscoa*, Dutch *pasen*, and French *pâcques*. Pascha is now frequently found in liturgical literature, perhaps to re-appropriate the ancient term for modern English speakers.

33. Those who celebrated the resurrection on 14 Nisan are referred to as Quartodecimans, a term derived from the Latin word for fourteen. Modern scholars believe that this was likely the earliest celebration of the resurrection. See Talley, *Liturgical Year*, 1–32.

34. Bradshaw, *Origins of Christian Worship*, 223.

Christ's death and resurrection as they began their new lives as members of his church.

Eastertide—the Easter season—begins on Easter Sunday. Originally, it lasted for forty days, concluding with Ascension Day, but is now usually counted for fifty days, ending with Pentecost. The church fathers considered the Easter season to be so joyful that they forbade fasting during the period and instructed believers to stand while praying. Churches that had removed all their decorations before Good Friday replaced them to ensure the building looked especially festive when the Lord's victory over the grave was recounted. The somber expressions that accompanied the remembrance of Christ's death were replaced by expressions of great joy. The standard liturgical declaration for the whole congregation to articulate the joy of the resurrection became, "Christ has risen!" answered by, "He has risen indeed!"

Traditionally, the celebration of Easter began on Saturday night with the Easter Vigil. This service that began in darkness was pierced by the lighting of a paschal candle representing Christ as the light of the world. Scripture readings, the singing of the *Gloria*,[35] and a sermon followed. Dawn on Easter Sunday was set aside for baptism, and some churches practiced confirmation or renewal of baptismal vows at that time. An early Easter service ended with the celebration of the Lord's Supper. In more recent times, Protestant congregations and groups have scheduled Sunrise Services in the early hours of Easter morning. As this was the time the women mentioned in the Gospels found the tomb empty, it is considered an appropriate hour to sing about the Savior who rose from the dead and to read and exposit Scripture portions that speak of his resurrection. The liturgical color of the Easter season is white or gold.

ASCENSION

According to the New Testament, Jesus ascended to heaven forty days after he rose from the dead (Acts 1:3). For this reason, the church has celebrated the sixth Thursday after Easter as Ascension Day,[36] in remembrance that Jesus returned to heaven to reign with his Father and intercede for his church. By celebrating Jesus' ascension, Christians proclaim their belief that

---

35. The *Gloria* is an ancient hymn based on Luke 2:14, "Glory to God in the highest, and on earth peace to men on whom his favor rests." It takes its name from the first word of the Latin version, which dates to the middle of the fourth century. The hymn was a basic part of the Latin liturgy from the fifth century. As Lent is a penitential season, the *Gloria* is excluded (as it is in some traditions during Advent). This makes its reappearance on Easter even more significant.

36. In the Eastern Church, it is called *Analepsis*, the "taking up."

the one who ascended will one day return (Acts 1:11). Until that time, they acknowledge that the risen and ascended Lord will be with them through his Holy Spirit, a belief that is remembered in the next Christian feast—Pentecost. From very early times, churches celebrated the Sunday following Ascension Day (the sixth Sunday after Easter) as Ascension Sunday. It takes place one week before Pentecost. White (or gold) is the liturgical color for the day.

PENTECOST

While its roots lie in the Israelite Feast of Weeks, which was celebrated fifty days after the Passover, by the end of the second century, Christians in the West had come to celebrate the day as a festival commemorating the sending of the Holy Spirit. The fifty days between Passover and Pentecost cover the period between the death of Jesus and the gift of the Holy Spirit, whose coming marked the birth of the church. Services held on this day should be occasions of great joy, as the congregation remembers that Jesus has not left us alone but has sent another Comforter who unites us with him and empowers us for ministry in the world.

Sometimes Pentecost is called Whit Sunday ("White" Sunday) as it was often a day for baptisms and the people being baptized wore white. The day is certainly appropriate for baptisms, as the book of Acts tells us that about 3000 people believed and were baptized after Peter preached on the first Christian Pentecost. In some parts of the world, Christians use Pentecost as an opportunity to walk through their communities to share the gospel with people they meet. Such "Whitsun walks" are conscious imitations of the disciples' movements through Jerusalem on Pentecost as they talked to people about Jesus.

We earlier noted that Jewish tradition celebrated Pentecost as the day on which God gave the *Torah* to his people. Christians can similarly remember God's gift of his word on this day. Since the New Testament sees one of the roles of the Holy Spirit as providing inspiration for the writers of Scripture, the day is an appropriate time to give God thanks for the Spirit of inspiration and for his inspired word.

The color for Pentecost is red—the color of flame—to represent the coming of the Holy Spirit, signaled by the tongues of fire that appeared above the heads of the disciples. Green is used for Ordinary Time that follows either Pentecost or Trinity Sunday, depending upon the way the Christian year is reckoned.

TRINITY

The Sunday after Pentecost is known as Trinity Sunday, a festival to celebrate our triune God—Father, Son, and Holy Spirit. Though its roots are obscure, Trinity Sunday may be traced back to the Arian conflict of the fourth century. To counter the Arian denial that God is three persons in one, the church composed prayers to the three persons of the Godhead to be used in Sunday worship. Popular celebration of Trinity Sunday as the first Sunday after Pentecost may not have developed until the appointment of Thomas à Becket as Archbishop of Canterbury on that date in 1162, after which it was mainly observed in England. In 1334, Pope John XXII approved the date as feast day for the entire Western Church.

Some traditions (e.g., Anglican and Lutheran) have referred to the weeks following this festival as Kingdomtide, Ordinary Time, or the Trinity Season. The season includes Trinity Sunday and about twenty-five other Sundays. Other traditions (including the revised Roman rite and the Episcopal Church) recognize the day, but begin Ordinary Time on the Monday after Pentecost. The liturgical colors for the Trinity Season are white for the first and last Sundays, and green for the rest.

SAINTS' DAYS

Before Christianity was recognized as the Roman state religion by the Emperor Constantine, believers were frequently exposed to great danger simply for believing that Jesus was the Messiah and the only way to know the one God. At first, the persecution came mainly from Jews who viewed believers in Jesus as a heretical sect that should be eradicated. The Bible thus mentions Stephen, James, and others as martyrs (Acts 7:57—8:2; 12:1–3; Rev 2:13; 17:6). The church rightly held Christian martyrs in high esteem for their steadfast witness to the faith and willingness to die for the cause of Christ. From the middle of the second century, many congregations that had lost a member due to martyrdom celebrated the anniversary of the death in order to remember their lives and witness and to recall the day the martyr entered eternal life.[37] These celebrations, referred to as *dies natalis*—"day of birth" (into heaven)—formed the beginning of the saints' days.

Saints' days were at first local celebrations held in the memory of a martyr from a specific church. At a time when large gatherings were liable to attract attention from unsympathetic authorities, remembrances were

---

37. Polycarp of Smyrna (d. 155) is considered the first martyr commemorated in this way. Kunzler, *The Church's Liturgy*, 430.

low-keyed affairs that might include a celebration of the Lord's Supper at the martyr's grave. As the fear of persecution faded, saints' days became more widely celebrated. Over time, what began as a remembrance of the death of local martyrs developed into a cult of saints, as relics of the martyrs were bought and traded by various churches. In the Eastern Church, this process was underway by the fourth century. It was slowed in the West until the seventh century, as, before that time, Roman law forbade the opening of graves.

Sometime in the fifth century, after state persecution of Christianity ended, other notable Christian leaders were designated saints even though they weren't martyrs. These were frequently called "confessors," as they faithfully confessed Christ until death. During medieval times, the Christian calendar was filled with saints' days, as various locales and groups vied to have their own saints recognized. By this period, the calendar was also studded with other festivals—such as All Saints' Day, All Souls' Day, the Assumption of the Blessed Virgin Mary, and Corpus Christi—that commemorated doctrines that had developed during those centuries.[38] The cult of the saints and other festivals eventually took over the Christian year so that its original function of reminding the church of Christ's work of redemption was shrouded. As a result, church leaders at various times cried out for the calendar to be reformed so that it would serve its original purpose. Throughout Europe during the sixteenth century, all the Protestant Reformers included the calendar in their list of liturgical and theological abuses that needed to be rectified. While most of the Reformers greatly simplified the liturgical calendar, the major festivals—including Christmas, Good Friday, Easter, Ascension, and Pentecost—remained. Some groups, including the Anabaptists and Scottish Reformers, did away with the Christian year apart from the Lord's Day.

MODERN CELEBRATIONS

In recent years, many churches that had not traditionally followed the Christian year have discovered value in adopting these ancient Christian practices as they celebrate Christ's redemptive labors through the cycle of the years. Many scholars have thus spoken of a "convergence" in worship that crosses

---

38. All Saints' Day (1 November in the Western Church and on the Sunday after Pentecost in the Eastern Church) is used to remember all the saints of the church who were believed to have gone directly to heaven after death. All Souls Day (2 November in the West) was celebrated to remember faithful believers residing in purgatory. Corpus Christi developed to celebrate the Eucharist, particularly the physical presence of Christ as understood in the doctrine of transubstantiation. The assumption of Mary celebrates a tradition that Mary physically ascended into heaven at the end of her life.

denominational lines and draws from Roman Catholic and Protestant, mainline and free church, traditional liturgical and charismatic traditions.[39] While absolute unanimity in practice cannot be found in convergence churches, they often exhibit a strong desire to blend the essential elements of what they consider the "three streams" of Christian thought and practice—Liturgical/Sacramental, Evangelical/Reformed, and Charismatic/Pentecostal. Most fellowships that are impacted by this movement have returned to many ancient church practices, including celebrating the church year.

Another change witnessed in many modern churches is the adoption of some non-biblical holidays of recent origin. These include, among others, New Year's Day, Mother's Day/Mothering Sunday, Father's Day, Grandparents' Day, Clergy Appreciation Day, Labor Day, Memorial Day, Armed Forces Day/Veterans Day/Remembrance Day, Thanksgiving/Harvest Festival, Reformation Day, and the celebration of one's country's national day. Positively, some of these holidays serve as markers of seasons that should be lived out before God. Other holidays remind us that God has placed special people in our personal lives and that he is present in the communal experience of our countries. Such holidays can give churches an opportunity to interact with the larger society. Even so, many of these holidays could lead us down a path that parallels the one laid in medieval times when saints' days steered the church away from the work of Christ by its devotion to individuals and issues of personal, local, or national interest. Some of the new holidays, it can be argued, do more to advance secular or political agendas than they do the cause of Christ. While it may be hasty to reject all these newer holidays as incompatible with a Christian use of time, critical thought should be applied before allowing them to dictate the shape and content of our worship.

CONCLUSION

We have seen that while the first Jewish Christians maintained the rituals and seasons observed by their forefathers, they immediately added new traditions that reflected their understanding that Jesus was the promised Messiah who had both entered time and changed the nature of time. In many cases, internal and external pressures worked together to shape new Christian practices as the church worshipped God through the days, months, and years. The old Jewish traditions that celebrated God's creative and preserving presence through the agricultural seasons and his redemptive acts

---

39. See Sly and Boosahda, "The Convergence Movement," 134–41; Wainwright, "Ecumenical Convergences," 721–54; and Webber, *Signs of Wonder*.

experienced at various times in Israel's history were, to a large extent, left behind. In their place arose a number of different local worship traditions. The existence of a variety of worship traditions in the second and third centuries makes it clear that the liturgies of the fourth century are neither traceable back to apostolic times nor the product of a continual development from the first century. Rather, they are the product of the amalgamation and elimination of various traditions that had been practiced in different parts of the world.[40] The lack of a unified liturgy until the fourth century should not be overlooked by those who look to the early church as a model for contemporary practice. As this book shows, the teaching of Scripture should take first place in providing models that shape our worship.

The fact that fourth-century Christians evaluated some earlier practices, accepting some while rejecting others for doctrinal and/or practical reasons, makes it incumbent upon churches today to submit both ancient and modern rites to critical examination before taking them on. We must similarly weigh the benefits and drawbacks of adopting early worship traditions for modern church use. The same should be said with regards to adding modern holidays to our church calendar. If these days can help us live out our relationship with God through the year, we may want to adopt them. If they erect barriers to our worship, we should reject them. Our adoption or rejection of certain days should be guided by a firm desire to worship God according to the principles he has revealed in his word through all the times and seasons of life. May we be wise in discerning the best way to do this for his glory and our benefit.

---

40. Bradshaw, *Origins of Christian Worship*, 229–30.

Bibliography

Aland, Kurt. *Did the Early Church Baptize Infants?* London: SCM, 1962.
Allen, Leslie C. *Psalms 101–150.* WBC. Waco, TX: Word, 1983.
Allen, Ronald B. *And I Will Praise Him: A Guide to Worship in the Psalms.* Grand Rapids: Kregel, 1992.
Anderson, Bernhard W. *From Creation to New Creation: Old Testament Perspectives.* Overtures to Biblical Theology. Minneapolis: Fortress, 1994.
———. *Out of the Depths: The Psalms Speak for Us Today.* 3rd ed. Louisville: Westminster John Knox, 2000.
Armerding, Carl A. "Festivals and Feasts." *DOTP* 300–313.
Augustine of Hippo. "Our Lord's Sermon on the Mount." In *A Select Library of the Nicene and Post-Nicene Fathers of the Christian Church.* Vol. 6:3–63. Grand Rapids: Eerdmans, 1974.
Aune, David E. *Revelation 1–5.* WBC. Dallas: Word, 1997.
Averbeck, Richard E. "Sacrifices and Offerings." *DOTP* 706–32.
———. "Tabernacle." *DOTP* 807–27.
———. "כָּפַר." *NIDOTTE* 2:689–710.
Balchin, J. A. "Oil." *ISBE* 3:585–86.
Baldovin, John F. "The Empire Baptized." In *The Oxford History of Christian Worship*, edited by Geoffrey Wainwright and Karen B. Westerfield Tucker, 77–130. Oxford: Oxford University Press, 2006.
———. "Hippolytus and the *Apostolic Tradition*: Recent Research and Commentary," *Theological Studies* 64 (2003) 520–42.
Ball, Edward. "Horns of the Altar." *ISBE* 2:758.
Barrett, C. K. *The First Epistle to the Corinthians.* 2nd ed. BNTC. London: Adam and Charles Black, 1971.
Barth, C. "זמר." *TDOT* 4:91–8.
Barth, Karl. *Prayer and Preaching.* London: SCM, 1964.
———. *Teaching of the Church Regarding Baptism.* London: SCM, 1948.
Beale, Gregory K. *The Book of Revelation.* NIGTC. Grand Rapids: Eerdmans, 1999.
Beasley-Murray, George R. *Baptism in the New Testament.* New York: St. Martin's, 1962.
Beckwith, Roger T. *Calendar, Chronology and Worship: Studies in Ancient Judaism and Early Christianity.* Leiden: Brill, 2005.
———. *Daily and Weekly Worship: From Jewish to Christian.* Alcuin/GROW Liturgical Study 1. Bramcote: Grove, 1989.

———. "The Jewish Background of Christian Worship." In *The Study of Liturgy*, edited by C. Jones, G. Wainwright, and E. Yarnold, 39–51. London: SPCK, 1978.
Beckwith, Roger T. and Martin J. Selman, eds. *Sacrifice in the Bible*. Grand Rapids: Baker, 1995.
Begbie, Jeremy. "Worship." *DTIB* 856–58.
Behm, Johannes. "κλάω, κτλ." *TDNT* 3:726–43.
Beyer, Hermann W. "διακονέω, κτλ." *TDNT* 2:81–93.
Blocher, Henri. *In the Beginning: The Opening Chapters of Genesis*. Leicester: IVP, 1984.
Bloesch, Donald G. *The Church: Sacraments, Worship, Ministry, Mission*. Downers Grove: IVP, 2002.
———. *Holy Scripture: Revelation, Inspiration and Interpretation*. Downers Grove: IVP, 1994.
———. *The Struggle of Prayer*. San Francisco: Harper & Row, 1980.
Blomberg, Craig L. *Jesus and the Gospels: An Introduction and Survey*. Nashville: B&H, 1997.
Blue, B. B. "Love Feast." *DPL* 578–79.
Boling, Andrew. "יָרֵא (*yārē'*)." *TWOT* 1:399–401.
Bradshaw, Paul F. *The Search for the Origins of Christian Worship*. 2nd ed. New York: Oxford University Press, 2002.
Braun, Joachim. *Music in Ancient Israel/Palestine: Archaeological, Written, and Comparative Sources*. Grand Rapids: Eerdmans, 2002.
Bromiley, Geoffrey W. *Children of Promise*. Edinburgh: T & T Clark, 1979.
Broyles, Craig C. "Lament, Psalms of." *DOTWPW* 384–99.
Bruce, F. F. *The Acts of the Apostles*. 2nd ed. Grand Rapids: Eerdmans, 1952.
———. *New Testament History*. Garden City, NY: Doubleday-Galilee, 1980.
———. "Paul and Jerusalem." *TynBul* 19 (1968) 3–25.
Brueggemann, Walter. *The Message of the Psalms: A Theological Commentary*. Minneapolis: Augsburg, 1984.
———. *Theology of the Old Testament*. Minneapolis: Fortress, 1997.
Buchanan, C. O. "Sacrament." *NDT* 606–8.
Cabié, Robert, Jean Evenou, P. M. Gy, Pierre Jounel, A. G. Martimort, Adrien Nocent, and Damien Sicard. *The Church at Prayer—Volume III: The Sacraments*. Collegeville, MN: Liturgical, 1988.
Calvin, John. *Institutes of the Christian Religion*, edited by John T. McNeill. Library of Christian Classics. Philadelphia: Westminster, 1960.
Carson, D. A. *The Gospel According to John*. Leicester: IVP, 1991.
Catechism of the Catholic Church, 2nd ed. Washington, DC: United States Conference of Catholic Bishops, 2019.
Chapell, Bryan. *Christ-Centered Worship: Letting the Gospel Shape Our Practice*. Grand Rapids: Baker Academic, 2009.
Childs, Brevard S. *The Book of Exodus*. OTL. Louisville: Westminster, 1974.
———. *Old Testament Theology in a Canonical Context*. Fortress: Philadelphia, 1986.
Clarkson, David. *The Works of David Clarkson, Vol. 3*. Edinburgh: James Nichol, 1865.
Clifford, Richard J. *Creation Accounts in the Ancient Near East and the Bible*. Washington, D.C.: Catholic Biblical Association, 1994.
———. *Proverbs*. OTL. Louisville: Westminster John Knox, 1999.
Consultation on Common Texts, *Revised Common Lectionary Daily Readings*. Minneapolis: Augsburg Fortress, 2005.

Courtman, Nigel B. "Sacrifice in the Psalms." In *Sacrifice in the Bible*, edited by Roger T. Beckwith and Martin J. Selman, 41–58. Grand Rapids: Baker, 1995.
Craigie, Peter C. *Psalms 1–50*. WBC. Waco, TX: Word, 1983.
Cranfield, C. E. B. *The Epistle to the Romans*. Vol. 2. ICC. Edinburgh: T&T Clark, 1979.
Crawford, A. G. "Baptism: Baptist View." *ISBE* 1:415–417.
Dau, W. H. T. "Baptism: Lutheran View." *ISBE* 1:423–426.
Davids, Peter. *Commentary on James*. NIGTC. Grand Rapids: Eerdmans, 1982.
Delling, Gerhard. "ὕμνος, κτλ." *TDNT* 8:489–503.
Dillard, Raymond B. *2 Chronicles*. WBC. Waco, TX: Word, 1987.
Dombek, David A. "Reading the Word of God Aloud." In *Preaching: The Preacher and Preaching in the Twentieth Century*, edited by Samuel T. Logan Jr., 419–44. Phillipsburg, NJ: Presbyterian and Reformed, 1982.
Dumbrell, William J. *Covenant and Creation: A Theology of the Old Testament Covenants*. BTCL. Carlisle: Paternoster, 1997.
———. "Worship and Isaiah 6." In *Covenant and Kingdom: A Collection of Old Testament Essays*, edited by Gregory R. Goswell and Allan M. Harman. RTRSupSer 2. Doncaster, Vic.: Reformed Theological Review, 2007.
Durham, John I. *Exodus*. WBC. Waco, TX: Word, 1987.
Eichrodt, Walter. *Theology of the Old Testament*. Vol. 1. OTL. London: SCM, 1961.
Evely, Louis. *We Dare to Say "Our Father."* Translated by John Bowden. Freiburg: Herder, 1965.
Fee, Gordon D. *The First Epistle to the Corinthians*. NICNT. Grand Rapids: Eerdmans, 1987.
———. "Gifts of the Spirit." *DPL* 339–47.
Fokkelman, J. P. *Reading Biblical Poetry: An Introductory Guide*. Louisville: Westminster John Knox, 2001.
France, R. T. *The Gospel According to Matthew: An Introduction and Commentary*. TNTC. Leicester: IVP, 1985.
———. *The Gospel of Mark: A Commentary on the Greek Text*. NIGTC. Grand Rapids: Eerdmans, 2002.
———. "The Worship of Jesus—A Neglected Factor In Christological Debate?" *Vox Evangelica* 12 (1981) 19–33.
Fretheim, Terence E. *God and World in the Old Testament: A Relational Theology of Creation*. Nashville: Abingdon, 2005.
Garrett, Duane A. "Feasts and Festivals of Israel." *BTDB* 249–55.
Geldenhuys, J. N. and F. F. Bruce, "Lord's Prayer, The." *IBD* 2:910–12.
General Synod of the Church of Ireland. *The Book of Common Prayer*. Blackrock: Columba, 2004.
Green, Michael. *Evangelism in the Early Church*. Revised. Eastbourne: Kingsway, 2003.
Greeven, Heinrich. "προσκυνέω." *TDNT* 6:758–66.
Grenz, Stanley J. *Prayer: The Cry for the Kingdom*. Peabody, MA: Hendrickson, 1988.
Grudem, Wayne. *1 Peter*. TNTC. Grand Rapids: Eerdmans, 1988.
Gunkel, Herman. *The Legends of Genesis: The Biblical Saga and History*. Eugene, OR: Wipf & Stock, 2003.
Gunton, Colin. *The Promise of Trinitarian Theology*. Edinburgh: T & T Clark, 1991.
Harakas, Stanley S. "The Integrity of Creation and Ethics." *St. Vladimir's Theological Quarterly* 32 (1988) 27–42.

Harrell, Daniel. "The 30-Day Leviticus Challenge." *Christianity Today* 52 (August 2008) 30–33.

Harrison, R. K. *Numbers: An Exegetical Commentary*. Grand Rapids: Baker, 1992.

Hartley, John E. "Holy and Holiness, Clean and Unclean." *DOTP* 420–431.

———. "New Moon." *ISBE* 3:527–28.

Hasel, Gerhard. "The Polemic Nature of the Genesis Cosmology." *EQ* 46 (1974) 81–102.

Heidel, Alexander. *The Gilgamesh Epic and Old Testament Parallels*. 3rd ed. Chicago: Chicago University Press, 1963.

Hess, Richard S. and David Toshio Tsumura, eds. *I Studied Inscriptions from Before the Flood*. Winona Lake, IN: Eisenbrauns, 1994.

Hiley, David. *Western Plainchant: A Handbook*. Oxford: Oxford University Press, 1993.

Hippolytus and Burton Scott Easton, *The Apostolic Tradition of Hippolytus*. Cambridge: Cambridge University Press, 1934.

Hobbs, T. R. *2 Kings*. WBC. Waco, TX: Word, 1985.

Hurowitz, Victor A. "Yhwh's Exalted House—Aspects of the Design and Symbolism of Solomon's Temple." In *Temple and Worship in Biblical Israel*, edited by John Day, 63–110. London: T&T Clark, 2005.

Hurtado, Larry W. *Lord Jesus Christ: Devotion to Jesus in Earliest Christianity*. Grand Rapids: Eerdmans, 2003.

Jenson, Philip P. "The Levitical Sacrificial System." In *Sacrifice in the Bible*, edited by Roger T. Beckwith and Martin J. Selman, 25–40. Grand Rapids: Baker, 1995.

Jeremias, Joachim. *Infant Baptism in the First Four Centuries*. London: SCM, 1960.

———. *The Lord's Prayer*. Philadelphia: Fortress, 1964.

———. *The Origins of Infant Baptism*. London: SCM, 1963.

———. "λίθος." *TDNT* 4:268–280.

Jinkins, Michael. *In the House of the Lord: Inhabiting the Psalms of Lament*. Collegeville, MN: Liturgical, 1998.

Johnson, Maxwell E. "The Apostolic Tradition." In *The Oxford History of Christian Worship*, edited by Geoffrey Wainwright and Karen B. Westerfield Tucker, 32–75. Oxford: Oxford University Press, 2006.

———. *The Rites of Christian Initiation*. Revised ed. Collegeville, MN: Liturgical, 2007.

Johnston, Philip S. "The Psalms and Distress." In *Interpreting the Psalms: Issues and Approaches*, edited by David Firth and Philip S. Johnston, 63–84. Downers Grove: IVP Academic, 2005.

Kelly, J. N. D. *A Commentary on the Epistles of Peter and Jude*. Thornapple Commentaries. Grand Rapids: Baker, 1981.

Kendall, R. T. *Worshipping God: Rediscovering the Full Dimension of Worship*. London: Hodder & Stoughton, 1989.

Kittel, Gerhard. "ἀββᾶ." *TDNT* 1:5–6.

Kiuchi, N. *The Purification Offering in the Priestly Literature*. JSOTSup. Sheffield: JSOT, 1987.

Knierim, Rolf. "The Task of Old Testament Theology." *HBT* 6 (1984) 25–57.

Kraus, Hans-Joachim. *Theology of the Psalms*. Minneapolis: Fortress, 1992.

———. *Worship in Israel: A Cultic History of the Old Testament*. Translated by Geoffrey Buswell. Richmond, VA: John Knox, 1965.

Kugel, James L. *The Idea of Biblical Poetry: Parallelism and Its History*. Baltimore: John Hopkins University, 1981.

Kuhn, K. G. "μαραναθά." *TDNT* 4:466–72.

Kunzler, Michael. *The Church's Liturgy*. Amateca. Münster: Lit, 2001.
Ladd, George Eldon. *A Theology of the New Testament*. Revised ed. Grand Rapids: Eerdmans, 1993.
Laymon, Charles M. *The Lord's Prayer in Its Biblical Setting*. Nashville: Abingdon, 1968.
Lewis, C. S. *Reflections on the Psalms*. London: Fontana, 1961.
Lincoln, Andrew T. *Ephesians*. WBC. Dallas: Word, 1990.
Lind, Millard C. *Yahweh is a Warrior: The Theology of Warfare in Ancient Israel*. Ontario: Herald, 1980.
Lindsay, T. M. "Baptism: Reformed View." *ISBE* 1:418–23.
Lohmeyer, Ernst. *The Lord's Prayer*. Translated by John Reumann. London: Collins, 1965.
Lohse, Eduard. "σάββατον, κτλ." *TDNT* 7:1–35.
Longman, Tremper, III. *How to Read the Psalms*. Downers Grove: IVP, 1988.
Longman, Tremper, III and Raymond B. Dillard. *An Introduction to the Old Testament*. 2nd ed. Grand Rapids: Zondervan, 2006.
Longman, Tremper, III and Daniel G. Reid. *God is a Warrior*. Studies in Old Testament Biblical Theology. Grand Rapids: Zondervan, 1994.
Longenecker, Richard N. *Acts*. EBC. Grand Rapids: Zondervan, 1995.
Lucas, Ernest C. "Sacrifice in the Prophets." In *Sacrifice in the Bible*, edited by Roger T. Beckwith and Martin J. Selman, 59–74. Grand Rapids: Baker, 1995.
Mack, Edward. "Purim." *ISBE* 3:1056–1057.
Marshall, I. Howard. *Acts: An Introduction and Commentary*. TNTC. Leicester: IVP, 1980.
———. *The Gospel of Luke: A Commentary on the Greek Text*. NIGTC. Exeter: Paternoster, 1978.
———. *Last Supper and Lord's Supper*. Exeter: Paternoster, 1980.
———. *Luke: Historian and Theologian*. Grand Rapids: Zondervan, 1971.
Martin, Ralph P. "Lord's Supper." *IBD* 912–15.
Mays, James L. *Psalms*. Interpretation. Louisville: John Knox, 1994.
McComiskey, Thomas Edward. "Hosea." In *The Minor Prophets, Volume 1*, edited by Thomas Edward McComiskey, 1–237. Grand Rapids: Baker, 1992.
McConnell, Walter Leslie, III, "An Explication of Ecological Ethics in the Light of the Biblical Creation Accounts." PhD diss., Queen's University of Belfast, 2000.
———. "Facing New Paradigms in Worship: Learning New Lessons from Old Masters." *ERT* 29 (October 2005) 331–46.
———. "A Meditation on the Church in Antioch and Mission: Acts 12:25—13:5." *Mission Round Table* 13, no. 3 (September–December 2018) 32–35.
———. "Worship." *DOTWPW* 929–35.
———. "Worshipping God through Suffering." *Mission Round Table* 12, no. 3 (September–December 2017) 35–39.
———. "'You Shall Have No Other Gods Before Me': God and the Gods in the Pentateuch." *JAET* 13 (June 2005) 19–46.
McGrath, Alister. *Christian Theology: An Introduction*. Oxford: Blackwell, 1994.
McKelvey, R. J. "Temple." *NDBT* 806–811.
Metzger, Bruce M. *A Textual Commentary on the Greek New Testament*. Corrected edition. London: UBS, 1975.
Meye, R. P. "Canon of the NT." *ISBE* 1:601–6.
Michaelis, Wilhelm. "σκηνή, κτλ." *TDNT* 7:368–94.

Milgrom, Jacob. *Leviticus 1–16*. AB. New York: Doubleday, 1991.
Miller, Patrick D. *The Divine Warrior in Early Israel*. Cambridge, MA: Harvard University Press, 1973.
———. "'Enthroned on the Praises of Israel': The Praise of God in Old Testament Theology." *Interpretation* 39 (1985) 5–19.
———. "The Human Sabbath: A Study in Deuteronomic Theology." *PTSB* 6 (1985) 81–97.
Moberly, R. W. L. "Lament." *NIDOTTE* 4:866–84.
Morris, Leon. *Jesus is the Christ: Studies in the Theology of John*. Grand Rapids: Eerdmans, 1989.
———. *New Testament Theology*. Grand Rapids: Academie, 1986.
———. *Revelation: An Introduction and Commentary*. TNTC. Leicester: IVP, 1969.
Motyer, J. Alec. *The Message of Philippians: Jesus our Joy*. BST. Leicester: IVP, 1984.
———. *The Prophecy of Isaiah*. Downers Grove: IVP, 1993.
Murphy, Roland. "The Psalms and Worship." *Ex Auditu* 8 (1992) 23–31.
Nolland, John. *The Gospel of Matthew: A Commentary on the Greek Text*. NIGTC. Grand Rapids: Eerdmans, 2005.
North, R. "חָדָשׁ *chādhāsh*; חֹדֶשׁ *chōdhesh*." *TDOT* 4:225–44.
O'Brien, Peter T. *The Epistle to the Philippians: A Commentary on the Greek Text*. NIGTC. Grand Rapids: Eerdmans, 1991.
Oden, Thomas C. *Pastoral Theology: Essentials of Ministry*. San Francisco: Harper & Row, 1983.
Okholm, Dennis L. "Prayer." *BTDB* 621–26.
Osborne, Kenan B. *Christian Sacraments in a Postmodern World*. Mahwah, NJ: Paulist, 1999.
Otto, Rudolf. *The Kingdom of God and the Son of Man*. 2nd ed. Translated by F. V. Filson and B. L. Woolf. London: Lutterworth, 1943.
Packer, J. I. *God has Spoken*. Revised. London: Hodder and Stoughton, 1979.
Peterson, David. *Engaging with God: A Biblical Theology of Worship*. Leicester: Apollos, 1992.
Piper, John. *Let the Nations be Glad! The Supremacy of God in Mission*. 3rd ed. Grand Rapids: Baker Academic, 2010.
Preisker, Herbert. "ἔπαινος." *TDNT* 2:586–88.
Preuss, Horst Dietrich. "חוה *ḥwh*." *TDOT* 4:248–56.
Procksch, Otto. "ἅγιος." *TDNT* 1:88–115.
Prokurat, Michael. "Orthodox Perspectives on Creation." *St. Vladimir's Theological Quarterly* 33 (1989) 331–49.
Provan, Ian W. *1 and 2 Kings*. NIBC. Peabody, MA: Hendrickson, 1995.
Rad, Gerhard von. *Genesis: A Commentary*. OTL. Philadelphia: Westminster, 1961.
———. *Holy War in Ancient Israel*. Grand Rapids: Eerdmans, 1991.
———. *Old Testament Theology*. Vol. 1. London: SCM, 1975.
Ringgren, H. "הלל *hll*." *TDOT* 3:404–10.
Robertson, A. T. "Baptism: Baptist View." *ISBE* 1:415–17.
Ross, Allen P. *Recalling the Hope of Glory: Biblical Worship from the Garden to the New Creation*. Grand Rapids: Kregel, 2006.
Rowley, H. H. *Worship in Ancient Israel: Its Forms and Meaning*. Philadelphia: Fortress, 1967.
Sanders, J. Oswald. *The Holy Spirit and His Gifts*. Grand Rapids: Zondervan, 1970.

Schaff, Philip. *The Creeds of Christendom. Vol. 1. The History of Creeds*. New York: Harper & Brothers, 1877.
Schmemann, Alexander. *Introduction to Liturgical Theology*. Crestwood, NY: St. Vladimir's Seminary Press, 1975.
Schniewind, Julius. "ἀγγελία, κτλ." *TDNT* 1:56–73.
Schrage, Wolfgang. "συναγωγή, κτλ." *TDNT* 7:798–852.
Schweizer, Eduard. "πνεῦμα, κτλ." *TDNT* 6:332–455.
Seidl, T. "שְׁלָמִים, šᵉlāmîm." *TDOT* 15:105–16.
Seitz, Christopher R. *Word Without End: The Old Testament as Abiding Theological Witness*. Grand Rapids: Eerdmans, 1998.
Selman, Martin J. *1 Chronicles: An Introduction and Commentary*. TOTC. Leicester: IVP, 1994.
Shedd, Russell R. "Worship in the New Testament Church." In *The Church in the Bible and the World*, edited by D. A. Carson, 120–53. Grand Rapids: Baker, 1987.
Simkins, Ronald A. *Creator and Creation: Nature in the Worldview of Ancient Israel*. Peabody, MA: Hendrickson, 1994.
Skoglund, John E. *A Manual of Worship*. Valley Forge, PA: Judson, 1968.
Sly, Randy and Wayne Boosahda. "The Convergence Movement." In *Twenty Centuries of Christian Worship*, edited by Robert Webber, 134–41. Nashville: Abbott Martyn, 1994.
Smith, Gary V. "Prophet; Prophecy." *ISBE* 3:986–1004.
Smith, George. *Chaldean Account of Genesis*. New York: Scribner, Armstrong, 1876; Reprinted Whitefish, MT: Kessinger, 2003.
Smith, Mark S. *The Early History of God: Yahweh and the Other Deities in Ancient Israel*. 2nd ed. Grand Rapids: Eerdmans, 2002.
Sternhold, Thomas, John Hopkins et al. *The Whole Booke of Psalmes Collected into Englishe Metre*. London: John Daye, 1584.
Stevens, R. Paul and Michael Green. *Living the Story: Biblical Spirituality for Everyday Christians*. Grand Rapids: Eerdmans, 2003.
Stott, John R. W. *Between Two Worlds: The Art of Preaching in the Twentieth Century*. Grand Rapids: Eerdmans, 1982. = *I Believe in Preaching*. London: Hodder & Stoughton, 1982.
———. *The Message of Ephesians*. BST. Leicester: IVP, 1984.
———. *The Message of Romans*. BST. Leicester: IVP, 1994.
———. "2 Timothy." In *The Message of Timothy and Titus*. BST. Leicester: IVP, 1997.
———. *The Spirit, the Church and the World: The Message of Acts*. Downers Grove: IVP, 1990.
Stott, Wilfred. "Sabbath, Lord's Day." *NIDNTT* 3:405–15.
Strathmann, H. "λατρεύω, κτλ." *TDNT* 4:58–65.
Talley, Thomas J. *The Origins of the Liturgical Year*. Collegeville, MN: Liturgical, 1991.
The Protestant Episcopal Church. *The Book of Common Prayer*. New York: The Church Pension Fund, 1945.
Thompson, J. Arthur. "Covenant (OT)." *ISBE* 1:790–3.
Thompson, R. J. "Sacrifice and Offering: I. In the Old Testament." *IBD* 3:1358–66.
Towner, Philip H. *The Letters to Timothy and Titus*. NIGTC. Grand Rapids: Eerdmans, 2006.
Turner, Max. "Spiritual Gifts." *NDBT* 789–96.

Verhey, Allen. *Reading the Bible in the Strange World of Medicine*. Grand Rapids: Eerdmans, 2003.
Wainwright, Geoffrey. "Ecumenical Convergences." In *The Oxford History of Christian Worship*, edited by Geoffrey Wainwright and Karen B. Westerfield Tucker, 721–54. Oxford: Oxford University Press, 2006.
Waltke, Bruce K. "Cain and His Offering." *WTJ* 48 (1986) 363–72.
———. *Genesis*. Grand Rapids: Zondervan, 2001.
Waltke, Bruce K. and James M. Houston. *The Psalms as Christian Worship: A Historical Commentary*. Grand Rapids: Eerdmans, 2010.
Walton, John H. *Old Testament Theology for Christians: From Ancient Context to Enduring Belief*. Downers Grove: IVP Academic, 2017.
Warfield, B. B. *Counterfeit Miracles*. New York: Charles Scribners, 1918.
Webber, Robert E. *Signs of Wonder: The Phenomenon of Convergence in Modern Liturgical and Charismatic Churches*. Nashville: Abbot Martyn, 1992.
———. *Worship Old and New*. Revised. Grand Rapids: Zondervan, 1994.
Weiser, Artur. *Psalms*. OTL. London: SCM, 1962.
Wenham, Gordon J. *The Book of Leviticus*. NICOT. Grand Rapids: Eerdmans, 1979.
———. *Genesis 1–15*. WBC. Waco, TX: Word, 1987.
———. "Sanctuary Symbolism in the Garden of Eden Story." In *Proceedings of the Ninth World Congress of Jewish Studies, Division A: The Period of the Bible*, 19–25. Jerusalem: World Union of Jewish Studies, 1986.
———. "The Theology of Old Testament Sacrifice." In *Sacrifice in the Bible*, edited by Roger T. Beckwith and Martin J. Selman, 75–87. Carlisle: Paternoster, 1995.
Westermann, Claus. *Creation*. London: SPCK, 1974.
———. *Genesis 1–11: A Commentary*. London: SPCK, 1984.
———. *Isaiah 40–66*. OTL. Philadelphia: Westminster, 1969.
———. *Praise and Lament in the Psalms*. Atlanta: John Knox, 1981.
———. "הלל *hll* pi. to praise." *TLOT* 1:371–6.
———. "עָבַד *'ebed* servant." *TLOT* 2:819–32.
Westminster Confession of Faith. Glasgow: Free Presbyterian, 1985.
White, James F. "The Spatial Setting." In *The Oxford History of Christian Worship*, edited by Geoffrey Wainwright and Karen B. Westerfield Tucker, 793–816. Oxford: Oxford University Press, 2006.
White, R. E. O. *Biblical Doctrine of Initiation*. London: Hodder & Stoughton, 1960.
White, Susan J. *Christian Worship and Technological Change*. Nashville: Abingdon, 1994.
Wilkinson, Bruce. *The Prayer of Jabez: Breaking Through to a Blesssed Life*. Sisters, OR: Multnomah, 2000.
Williamson, Paul R. "Covenant." *DOTP* 139–55.
Wilson, Marvin R. *Our Father Abraham: Jewish Roots of the Christian Faith*. Grand Rapids: Eerdmans, 1989.
Witvliet, John D. *The Biblical Psalms in Christian Worship: A Brief Introduction and Guide to Resources*. Grand Rapids: Eerdmans, 2007.
———. *Worship Seeking Understanding: Windows into Christian Practice*. Grand Rapids: Baker Academic, 2003.
Wright, N. T. "Worship and the Spirit in the New Testament." In *The Spirit in Worship—Worship in the Spirit*, edited by Teresa Berger and Bryan D. Spinks, 3–24. Collegeville, MN: Liturgical, 2009.

Zevit, Ziony. "The Earthen Altar Laws of Exodus 20:24–26 and Related Sacrificial Restrictions in their Cultural Context." In *Text, Temples, and Traditions: A Tribute to Menahem Haran*, edited by Michael V. Fox, Victor Avigdor Hurowitz, Avi M. Hurvitz, Michael L. Klein, Baruch J. Schwartz, and Nili Shupak, 53–62. Winona Lake, IN: Eisenbrauns, 1996.

Subject Index

Absolution, 69, 161, 218, 243–44
Advent, ix, 163–64, 269, 271, 278
adventus, 271
aineō, 135
ainos, 135
agapē, 208–9, 216, 276
Alexandria, 275, 277
Alms-giving, 235
Altar(s), 60–61, 73–78, 80–81, 87–89, 101, 125, 167–70, 175–80, 182–83
Amalekites, 75
Anabaptist(s), 113, 194, 219, 281
Analepsis, 278
Ancient Near East, 8, 16–17, 20–23, 79, 106, 171, 195
Angel(s), 5, 8, 26, 32, 34, 37, 40–42, 48–50, 66–67, 88–89, 103, 116, 133, 145, 148, 192, 214, 259, 261
angelos, 66
Anglican, 241, 274, 280
Antioch, 70, 112, 261, 267
Apostles' Creed, 45
Aramaic, 4, 97, 215, 235, 277
Ark of the Covenant, 79, 81, 124
Armed Forces Day, 282
Ascension, 36, 40, 51, 90, 111, 146, 226, 269, 278–79, 281
Ash Wednesday, 274–75
Asia Minor, 266, 277
Assemblies of God, 194
Atonement, 80, 82, 107, 123–27, 130, 167–68, 173, 178, 180–81

Azazel, 125
'*āšam*, 174–75, 179
'*ābad*, 6–8
'*ăbôdâ*, 8

Baal, 11, 27, 130
Babylon, 74, 97, 128
Baptism, xi, 35, 51, 57, 102, 112, 122, 191–207, 220, 223, 257, 265, 267, 273, 275, 277–79
Baptists, 70, 113, 195, 202
Bay Psalm Book, 152
bārûk Yhwh, 143, 145
Benediction, 88, 97, 246–47, 266
Benedictus, 145
Bethel, 75
Bethesda, 111
Bethlehem, 38, 272
Book of Common Prayer, 214, 241, 243–44
Bow down, 3–6, 9–10, 12, 26, 32, 38, 144, 262
Brethren, 70, 203, 266
Buddhism, 15
Burnt offering, 60, 64, 73–74, 76–77, 84, 121, 123, 128, 166–67, 169–70, 174, 176, 181–85

Cana, 33
Canaan, 28, 62, 64, 73, 75, 81, 112, 117, 137, 167, 170–71, 182, 225
Canaanite(s), 5, 11, 16, 27, 39, 68, 75, 138, 173
charismata, 250

charismati, 250
Charismatic, x, 2, 249, 282
Cherubim, 20, 79
Christian year. *See* Church year.
Christmas, 130, 163–64, 271–74, 281
Church, ix–x, xiii, 1–3, 7, 10–15, 27–28, 36, 42–43, 45, 48–49, 51–52, 54–57, 64–66, 68–70, 74, 77–78, 83, 86, 90, 92–95, 98–103, 107, 112–13, 116, 118, 120, 122, 130–31, 145, 147, 149–53, 156–57, 161–66, 186, 188, 191–93, 195, 199–211, 215–21, 224–30, 232, 235–36, 238–39, 241, 243, 245–46, 249–58, 261–62, 267–83
Church year, 119, 131, 163, 193, 241, 265–83
Circumcision, 6, 53–54, 62, 68, 87, 89, 109–10, 112, 114, 145, 192, 195, 203
Clean, 9, 24–25, 38–39, 42, 48, 57, 59, 61, 63, 69, 74–75, 81, 86, 89, 91–92, 118, 124–25, 129, 168, 170–73, 175, 178–79, 181, 187, 190, 195–96, 200–201, 205, 240
Clergy Appreciation Day, 282
Collect, 241–42
Colossae, 99, 116
Communion. *See* Lord's Supper.
Confession (prayer), 69, 153, 158, 161–62, 197, 217, 243–44
Confirmation, 193, 278
Corinth, 28, 70, 99–100, 118, 120, 208, 211, 216, 218, 252
Council of Carthage, 225
Council of Constantinople, 45, 58
Council of Florence, 193
Council of Hippo, 225
Council of Jerusalem, 65, 111, 267
Council of Laodicea, 152
Council of Nicea, 45, 269, 277
Council of Ravenna, 202
Council of Trent, 193, 219–20
Covenant, 3, 5–6, 16–17, 21–24, 27, 29–30, 37, 53, 61–62, 65–66, 78–81, 87, 92, 107, 109, 112, 114, 116, 118, 121–22, 124–27, 130–31, 144, 169–71, 174, 177–78, 182–84, 188–90, 192, 203, 210–13, 218, 224, 265
Creation, 5, 16–22, 29–30, 33, 37, 43, 45–46, 49, 51, 54, 60, 62, 66–68, 84, 98, 108, 112–14, 122–23, 131, 134, 137, 139–43, 149, 153, 184, 189, 200–201, 212, 215, 222, 227, 233, 258, 260, 262–63
Creator, 1, 5, 10, 12, 13, 16–19, 21, 27, 29, 67, 103, 107–8, 113–14, 116, 121, 140–41, 149, 153, 163, 190, 212, 243, 256, 262
Cross, 34–35, 51, 77–78, 103, 114, 118, 126–27, 130, 146, 156, 165, 189–90, 192–93, 200, 208, 210, 212–13, 218, 227, 243, 260, 276
Crucifixion, 34–36, 40, 117–18, 120, 164, 187–88, 200, 207, 212, 224, 226, 270, 275–77

Damascus, 76, 136, 204
Dancing, 47, 73, 87, 106, 132, 136, 144
Day of Atonement, 107, 123–27, 130, 167, 173, 178, 181
Dead Sea Scrolls, 195
Decalogue. *See* Ten Commandments.
Deist, 18, 29
Demon, 31, 35–36, 39, 98, 146–47, 222
Devil, 32, 51, 232, 237
diakoneō, 32
diakonia, 226
didache, 232
Didache, 112, 202, 209, 214, 217–18, 270
dies natalis, 280
douleuō, 8
doxa, 135
doxazō, 135

Easter, 103, 119, 126, 163–64, 273–79, 281
Eastern Orthodox, 67, 192, 203, 207, 238, 272–73
Eastertide, 278
Ecumenical, 45, 70, 216, 282
Eden, 20, 29, 59, 73, 260

SUBJECT INDEX   297

Egypt, 4, 8, 16, 32, 62, 73, 78–80, 84, 107–8, 112, 116–18, 120–21, 130, 182, 192
Egyptian, 27, 78, 85, 116, 137
Eighteen Benedictions, 97, 266
ekklēsia, 95, 98, 239
El Elyon, 63
Elohim, 16–17, 21, 66, 79
energēma, 250
epaineō, 135
epainos, 135
Ephesus, 54, 99–100, 147, 198
epiphaneia, 273
Epiphany, 241, 271–75
Eschatology, 65, 100, 112, 118, 122, 139, 163, 201, 212, 214, 235
eskēnōsen, 38
Essenes, 195–96
Eucharist. *See* Lord's Supper.
eucharisteō, 208
eucharistia, 209
eulogētos, 145
Evangelical, 70, 282
ex opere operato, 193, 201
Exodus (event), 16, 62, 112, 119, 130, 210
exomologeō, 147
‘*ebed*, 7, 9
‘*edah*, 95

Fasting, 3, 9, 32, 35–36, 89, 112, 124–25, 129, 163–64, 184, 223, 235, 261, 271, 274–75, 278
Fat, 166–67, 175–80, 275
Father's Day, 282
Fear, 3, 5–7, 10, 12–14, 18, 26, 32, 36, 39–40, 47, 64, 66, 94, 98, 106, 136, 140, 155, 159–162, 199, 258, 261–62, 281
Feast of Tabernacles, 107, 123, 127–28, 183
Feast of Trumpets, 107, 123
Feast of Unleavened Bread, 107, 116, 119–21, 130, 184
Feast of Weeks, 107, 120–21, 279
Firstfruits, 107, 121–23, 166
Forgiveness, 58, 69, 77, 125–27, 161, 164, 166, 168–70, 195, 205, 212–13, 215, 224, 234, 236–37, 241, 243–44, 247, 257, 275–76
Fourth Lateran Council, 219
Freewill offering, 121, 175, 177–78
Funeral(s), 51, 105, 161, 223

Galilee, 40, 51, 128, 146, 261
Gethsemane, 33, 156, 276
Gibeon, 73, 81, 183
Gilgal, 81, 182
Gloria, 278
Good Friday, 126, 164, 274, 276, 278, 281
Gospel, 9, 13, 28, 52–53, 55–58, 64–66, 69, 85, 90, 98–99, 101, 103, 112, 122, 146–48, 161, 187, 199, 206, 212, 214–15, 217–18, 224, 226–27, 230, 232, 236, 244, 260, 262, 274, 279
Grain offering, 123, 166–67, 169, 174, 176–77, 179, 181
Grandparents' Day, 282
Great Commission, 198, 204, 261
Guilt offering, 166–67, 175, 179–81, 183

Haftarah, 97
Haggadah, 117–19
hagioi, 65
hālal, 133, 135
halĕlû-yāh, 133, 143
Hanukkah, 87, 107, 129–30
Harvest Festival, 130, 282
Healing, 31, 35, 39, 63, 90, 98, 106, 110–11, 146, 156, 162, 193, 228, 245–46, 249–51, 257, 260
Heaven, 3, 16–18, 26, 33, 40–43, 45, 64, 66–67, 80, 86, 92, 101, 106, 112, 138, 140–42, 147–50, 163, 187, 197–98, 212, 214, 219–20, 242–43, 259–60, 278, 280–81
Hellenistic, 37, 226
heortas, 95
High priest, 25, 80, 82, 124–28, 173, 220
Holiness, 7, 12, 23–27, 59, 61, 65, 69, 85–87, 94, 102, 125, 171–73, 182, 188, 190, 236–37, 259

Holy of Holies, 76, 79–82, 124–26, 173, 187
Holy place, 58–59, 79–82, 95, 102, 110, 126, 179
Holy Spirit, ix, xi, 3, 25–26, 28–30, 43–58, 60, 65, 68, 88, 91, 93, 122, 128–29, 147–48, 188–91, 194, 197–99, 202, 204–6, 212, 223, 226–28, 231, 233–35, 240, 243–47, 249–50, 252, 254, 256–58, 260–262, 273, 279–80
Holy Thursday. *See* Maundy Thursday.
Hope, 3, 47–48, 103, 112, 128, 139, 148, 160, 162–65, 200, 263
Hosanna, 146, 214, 276
hoti, 147
Hymn, 50, 53, 100, 118, 136, 141, 158, 161, 164, 192, 232, 278
hymneō, 136
hymnos, 136
ḥag hammaṣṣôṭ, 119
ḥag haqqāṣîr, 121
ḥag hassukkôt, 127
ḥag hā' āsîp, 127
ḥag šābu' ôṭ, 120
ḥaṭṭā't, 174–75, 178
ḥāwâ, 3–6
ḥesed, 23
ḥillēl, 171
ḥōdeš, 114

Idol(s), 4, 8, 11, 18, 24, 27–28, 32, 59, 66, 84–85, 111, 182–83, 199–200, 252
Image of God, 21, 260
Immanence, 18–19, 79, 212
Immanuel, 37, 46, 85, 213
Immorality, 57, 94, 111, 267
Incense, 75–77, 80, 88, 124–25, 174–76, 179, 189, 248, 269
Intercession, 36, 85, 238
Invocation, 60, 68, 158, 233, 240–42
Israel, 2–9, 14, 16–20, 22–23, 25, 27–28, 30–32, 37, 39–40, 42, 46–49, 51, 60–65, 68, 73–87, 89–90, 96, 102, 105–17, 120–21, 123–30, 135, 137–42, 144–45, 147, 153, 157, 162, 164, 166–74, 180, 182–83, 185, 192, 195–96, 203, 213, 227, 232, 234, 256, 265, 269–70, 279, 283
' îš hārûaḥ, 47

Jericho, 62
Jerusalem, 20, 30–31, 34, 40, 50, 52, 64–65, 72–74, 81, 86–94, 96, 103, 111, 115, 117, 128–29, 145–46, 183–84, 186–87, 196, 199, 209–10, 226, 261, 266–67, 275–76, 279
Jidu Jiao, 15
Jordan River, 63, 75, 81, 182, 196, 198, 266
Joy, 3, 40, 57, 90, 115, 118, 121, 128, 136, 140, 143–50, 155–57, 160–61, 163, 205, 241, 244, 255, 257–58, 261, 263, 271, 273, 276, 278–79
Judaism, 28, 37, 41, 93, 109, 112, 195, 266–67, 270
Judea, 24, 64, 128, 131, 196, 198, 266

kafara, 167
kālîl, 176
kappōret, 124, 168
Kebar River, 74
keneset, 95
Kingdom of God, 31, 67, 118, 146, 196, 214, 255
Kingdomtide, 280
koinōnia, 208, 210, 216
kōper, 168
kurios, 38
kerygma, 232

Labor Day, 282
Lament, xi, 26, 35, 48, 60, 87, 134, 139, 142, 152, 155–65
Laodicea, 54, 99, 152
Last Supper, 117, 119, 191, 207, 209, 212–14, 276
latreia, 252
latreuō, 8, 54
Law, ix–x, 3, 7, 14, 25, 27–28, 32, 39, 48, 50, 52–53, 60–62, 73, 75,

78, 87, 89–90, 93, 106, 109–11, 113, 116, 121–22, 126, 128, 130, 136, 152, 169–70, 172, 179, 181, 184–85, 188, 192–93, 201, 213, 225, 244, 270, 281
Lectionary, 164, 274
leitourgeō, 8
Lent, 163–64, 274–78
Levite(s), 8–9, 13, 25, 64, 73, 80, 85, 121, 144, 172, 182–83, 253
Litany, 241–43
Liturgical year. *See* Church year
Liturgy, 2, 8, 11, 28, 51, 60, 96, 118, 145, 149–50, 197, 205, 207, 214, 216, 232, 258–59, 268, 270, 278, 283
Lord's Prayer, 25, 36, 235–39
Lord's Supper, xi, 11, 13, 68, 77, 100, 102, 112, 118–19, 189, 191–95, 204, 207–21, 223, 228, 232, 257, 265, 267, 276, 278, 281

Magi, 38, 40, 273–74
mandatum novum, 276
maranatha, 214–15
Mass. *See* Lord's Supper.
Matrimony, 193
Maundy Thursday, 274, 276
Memorial Day, 282
Mennonite, 70
Methodist, 70
methorion, 67
minḥâ, 174, 176
miqdāš, 79, 82
Mishnah, 111
miškān, 78–79
missa, 209
Mission, 35, 52, 56, 58, 66, 255, 260–62
Missionary, 15, 55–56, 64, 98, 120, 188–89, 246, 261–62
mizbēaḥ, 75
mizmôr, 135
môʿēd, 79, 95
Monotheism, 36–37, 199
Morality, 7, 10, 12, 18, 24, 27, 57, 113, 118, 185, 201, 262
Mothering Sunday, 282
Mother's Day, 282

Mt. Gerizim, 91, 103
Mt. Moriah, 75
Mt. Sinai. *See* Sinai.
Music, 9, 13, 47, 53, 68, 73, 135–36, 138, 140, 144, 151–53, 235, 255
mysterium, 191–92

Natalis Solis Invicti, 272
Nazareth, 31, 51, 97
Nazirite, 61, 88, 172–73, 179, 181, 186
nĕšāmâ, 46
New creation, 122, 200–201, 260, 262
New heaven and new earth, 3, 66, 92, 259
New moon, 106–7, 110–11, 114–16, 120–21, 123, 181, 183
New year, 105, 123, 127, 282
Nicene Creed, 45, 58
Nob, 81
Nunc Dimittis, 51, 145

Offering(s), 20, 31, 34, 43, 56–57, 60–62, 64–65, 72–77, 80, 84, 112, 121–25, 127–28, 134, 145, 166–71, 174–90, 207, 210, 213, 220, 232, 246, 252, 257
Ordinance(s), 117, 191, 195, 204, 207, 219, 221
Ordinary Time, 274, 279–80
Ordination, 178, 181, 193
ʾ*ōlâ*, 174, 176

Palestine, 78, 97, 119, 141, 267
Palm Sunday, 274–76
paraklētos, 52
Pascha. *See* Easter.
Passover, 9, 30–31, 62, 90, 107, 116–21, 130, 178, 182, 184, 186–87, 192, 210, 214, 267, 277, 279
Passover lamb, 30, 116–18, 186, 267
Pastor(s), x, xiii, 1, 188, 204, 220, 228, 231–32, 245, 251, 253, 255
Patriarchs, 76, 95, 272
Peace offering, 31, 43, 77, 121, 167, 169–70, 175, 177–78, 181–85, 189
Penance, 193–94
Penitence, 161, 164

SUBJECT INDEX

Pentateuch, 84, 97, 106
Pentecost, 26, 28, 46, 48, 52, 56, 64, 93, 120–22, 130, 198–99, 226, 266, 278–81
Pentecostal(s), 70, 249, 282
pentēkostē, 120
pesaḥ, 116, 277
phanerōsis, 250
Pharisee(s), 89, 96, 110–11, 196, 204, 238
Philippi, 70, 99, 120
Philistine(s), 136, 181
phobeō, 5
pneuma, 44
pneumatika, 250
ponēros, 237
Praise, ix, xi, 3–4, 8, 19, 23, 25, 41, 43, 47–48, 50, 53–54, 60, 63–64, 67–69, 74, 78, 89, 99, 101, 132–56, 158–65, 185, 187–90, 215, 220, 228, 234, 259, 262–63, 270
Prayer(s), ix–xi, 1, 3–4, 9, 11, 13, 25–26, 28, 34–36, 38–39, 41–43, 47–48, 50–51, 53–54, 60, 65, 68–69, 74, 76–78, 86, 88–91, 96–100, 102, 110, 112, 114, 129, 134, 138–39, 143–44, 146–53, 156–62, 164, 181, 184–86, 189–90, 193, 209–10, 212, 214–18, 223, 226, 228, 231–48, 255, 257, 259, 261, 263, 265–66, 268–71, 274, 276, 278, 280
Preaching, 1, 9, 13, 35–36, 51–52, 57, 65, 69, 90, 93, 102, 122, 128, 146, 153, 194, 196–97, 215, 218, 223–33, 240, 252–53, 260, 266–67, 279
Presbyterian, 70, 152
Priest(s), 4, 8–9, 22–23, 25–26, 33, 36, 39, 42, 46, 50, 56, 60–61, 63–65, 67, 73–74, 76–77, 79–82, 84, 87–89, 92, 96–97, 109–10, 117, 120–21, 123–28, 149, 166, 168–70, 172–85, 187–90, 193, 196, 220, 248, 253
Prophecy, 13–14, 47–50, 63, 65, 88, 92, 97, 118, 122, 128–29, 136, 144–45, 196–97, 200, 214, 250–53, 258, 266
Prophet(s), 5, 24, 34, 36, 42, 46–49, 54, 58, 62, 64, 74, 87–92, 96–97, 110, 115, 144, 146, 156, 182–83, 185–86, 196–97, 210, 213, 224, 228, 232, 251, 253, 259
Proselyte(s), 63, 65, 98, 195–96
proskuneō, 4–5, 38
Protestantism, 15, 69, 113, 192–94, 203, 216, 220, 223, 274, 278, 281–82
psallō, 135–36
Psalm(s), x, 3, 5–6, 12, 14, 48, 53, 60, 63–64, 97, 100, 102, 132–36, 138–44, 147, 150–53, 156–65, 182, 184, 223, 230, 234–35
psalmos, 136
pûr, 129
Purim, 107, 129
Purity, 24, 27, 118–20, 130, 195, 273
Puritan(s), 102, 113, 223, 259

qādēš, 27
qādôš, 23, 171
qahal, 95
qĕdēšâ, 27
qōdeš, 79, 82
qorbān, 167
Quinquagesima, 274–75
Qumran, 195

Redemption, 30, 43, 57, 108, 116, 118–19, 123, 130–31, 142, 145–47, 192, 205, 222, 281
Reformation Day, 282
Reformers, 76, 113, 193–94, 219–20, 228, 281
Remembrance Day, 282
Rest, 20, 61, 105, 108–15, 125, 162, 182
Resurrection, 32, 37, 40, 42–43, 58, 65, 88, 90, 111–13, 119, 148, 163–64, 186, 201, 205, 223, 225–26, 260, 273–74, 277–78
Righteousness, 24–25, 43–44, 52, 55, 58, 62, 65, 69, 77, 102, 135, 140, 148, 186, 197, 201, 222, 224, 235

SUBJECT INDEX

Roman Catholic(ism), 15, 192–94, 216, 220, 241, 273, 275, 282
Rome, 28, 99–100, 126, 147, 235, 275, 277
rûaḥ, 44–47

Sabbath, 20, 31, 40, 87, 96, 102, 106–16, 120–21, 125, 130, 181, 223, 265, 269
Sacrament(s), 69, 102, 191–95, 204–5, 207, 209, 211, 213, 216, 219–21, 223, 237
sacramentum, 191–92, 194–95
Sacrifice, xi, 3, 5, 7–9, 11, 20, 23–25, 30–31, 34, 42–43, 50–51, 56, 60–64, 68, 70, 72–78, 82, 84–86, 89, 92, 96, 108–10, 114–21, 123–29, 134, 146, 148, 166–90, 207–10, 212–13, 215, 218, 220, 227, 238, 252, 257, 268–70
Sadducees, 96, 196
sāgad, 4
Saints' days, 280–82
Salvation, 29, 38, 45, 49–50, 55–56, 66, 70, 89–91, 99, 130, 134, 136–37, 143, 145–47, 149–50, 163–64, 189, 193–94, 196, 200, 218, 224, 226–28, 254, 260, 268–69, 271
Samaria, 64, 74
Samaritan(s), 64, 72, 91, 93, 199
Sanctuary, 60–62, 78–79, 81–82, 87, 91, 94, 124–26
Scapegoat, 124–25
Second Vatican Council, 193, 275
sĕgid, 4
Septuagesima, 273–75
Septuagint, 4, 8, 32, 66, 95, 98, 120, 133, 135–36, 145, 147, 252
Sermon on the Mount, 38, 235
Serpent, 21, 259
Serve, ix, 3, 6–10, 12–14, 22–23, 25, 27, 30–35, 43–44, 46–47, 49–51, 53–58, 60–61, 64, 66–68, 70, 82, 86, 88, 99–100, 102, 108–9, 118, 124, 149, 155, 170, 183, 186, 188–90, 193, 199, 204–5, 209, 220, 247–48, 250–55, 257–60, 262
Seventh Day Adventists, 113
Seventh Day Baptists, 113
Sexagesima, 274–75
Shechem, 75
Shema, 27–28, 96–97
Sheol, 139, 143, 185
Shiloh, 81, 87
Showbread, 110, 177
Shrove Tuesday, 274–75
Sin, 12, 21, 23–24, 30, 34, 37, 43–44, 47–48, 50–52, 55, 57–59, 61–62, 64–65, 67–69, 78, 87, 114, 118, 120, 124–27, 130, 139, 142, 152, 155–58, 161–70, 172–76, 178–81, 183–85, 187, 190, 193–97, 199–201, 205, 212–13, 215, 217–18, 222, 224, 227, 232, 234, 237, 243–44, 247, 257, 260, 275
Sin offering, 31, 121, 123–25, 128, 166–67, 175, 178–79, 181, 187, 211–13, 237–38
Sinai, 16, 22, 78, 80, 82, 107, 109, 118, 121, 130, 138, 171, 227, 233
skēnoō, 85
Slavery, 8, 13, 57, 65, 70, 107–9, 114, 120–21, 130, 179, 182, 187, 200–201
Song, x, 1, 8, 12–14, 23, 26, 47, 53, 58, 60, 67, 69, 132, 134–38, 140, 142, 144–45, 149, 151–53, 158, 257–58
Songs of Ascents, 60
Sorrow, 3, 154, 156, 160, 164, 180, 193, 234, 271
Spiritual gifts, xi, 13, 44, 49, 57–58, 101, 189, 245, 249–55, 267
sukkôt, 127
Sunday, ix, 112–13, 119, 210–11, 228, 241, 271–72, 274–82
synagōgē, 95
Synagogue, 6, 26, 31, 39, 51, 74, 87, 90, 93–99, 110, 137, 146, 152–53, 184, 245, 265–67
šāḥah, 3
šākan, 79

šārat, 8
šĕlāmîm, 174–75, 177

Tabernacle, 7–9, 20, 24–25, 38, 47, 72–86, 92, 94, 101–2, 110, 124–25, 127, 168, 170, 172–73, 175–76, 178, 181–83, 190
Targumim, 97
tĕhillâ, 133, 136
tĕhillîm, 133
Temple(s), 4, 9, 20, 30–32, 37, 48, 50, 57, 60, 72–74, 76–77, 79, 81, 85–96, 98, 101–3, 110, 115, 117, 119, 121, 128–31, 139, 145–46, 152–53, 181, 183–84, 186–90, 265–67, 269
Ten Commandments, 6, 12, 22, 77, 107, 130, 171, 236
Tent of meeting, 9, 79–81, 95, 125
tersanctus, 149
Thank offering, 134, 184
Thanksgiving, 4, 53, 77, 134, 139, 147, 152–53, 161, 175, 177–78, 184, 189–90, 209–10, 215, 220, 242, 271, 282
Theophany. *See* Epiphany.
thusiastērion, 75
Tian Zhu Jiao, 15
tôdâ, 134, 184
Tongues, 101, 249–52, 279
Torah, 96–97, 122, 162, 185, 279
Transcendence, 17–19, 21, 24, 27, 29, 212
Trinitas, 45
Trinity, 28, 37, 44–45, 49, 57–58, 203, 243, 280
Trinity Season, 280
Trinity Sunday, 279–80

Trisagion, 149
Troas, 120, 210
Tyre, 39, 136
ṭāhôr, 171
ṭāmē', 171

Unclean, 24, 26, 39, 61, 65, 81, 94, 115, 124, 168, 170–74, 178, 190
Unleavened bread, 107, 116–21, 130, 184

Veterans Day, 282
Vows, 5, 86, 184–85, 223, 278

Westminster Confession of Faith, 101, 113, 223
Westminster Shorter Catechism, 194
Whit Sunday, 279
Wine, 33, 88, 115, 118, 127, 166, 176, 189, 207–12, 214–20, 266
Wisdom, 6–7, 44, 46, 48, 52, 55, 70, 187, 226, 251
Wisdom literature, 6–7, 106, 182, 185

Yamin, 141
yādâ, 134–35, 147
yārē', 5
yôm habbikkûrîm, 121
yôm hakkippurîm, 123
Yom Kippur, 123

zāmar, 135
zāmîr, 135
zamrû Yhwh, 143
Zaphon, 141
zimrâ, 135
zebaḥ, 167, 177, 184
Zeus, 87, 129

Name Index

Aaron, 61, 76, 84
Abel, 60, 73, 166
Abraham, ix, 4, 13, 16, 22–23, 30, 60–65, 73, 75, 77, 107, 128, 155, 170–71, 200, 233–34
Adam, ix, 20–21, 29, 31, 59, 73, 155, 233
Agrippa, 98
Ahaz, 76
Aland, Kurt, 203
Allen, Leslie C., 143
Allen, Ronald B., 150
Amos, 186
Anderson, Bernhard W., 16, 152–53, 157
Anna, 89–90, 146
Antiochus IV Epiphanes, 87, 129
Aquila, 99–100
Araunah the Jebusite, 63
Armerding, Carl A., 114
Asa, 76
Asaph, 73, 144
Augustine of Hippo, 192, 194, 215, 237, 249
Aune, David E., 55
Aurelian, 272
Averbeck, Richard E., 79–80, 168, 177

Balchin, J. A., 245
Baldovin, John F., 112, 268, 272–73
Ball, Edward, 75
Barak, 137–38
Barnabas, 74, 261
Barrett, C. K., 252, 268

Barth, C., 135
Barth, Karl, 203, 236, 239
Bathsheba, 48, 156
Beale, Gregory K., 123
Beasley-Murray, George R., 203
Becket, Thomas à, 280
Beckwith, Roger T., 96, 98
Begbie, Jeremy, 33
Behm, Johannes, 209, 214
Beyer, Hermann W., 32
Blocher, Henri, 18–19
Bloesch, Donald G., 54, 217, 234, 238–39
Blomberg, Craig L., 31, 197
Blue, B. B., 208
Boaz, 62
Boling, Andrew, 6
Boosahda, Wayne, 282
Bradshaw, Paul F., 96, 267–68, 270, 275, 277, 283
Braun, Joachim, 144
Bromiley, Geoffrey W., 203
Broyles, Craig C., 158, 161
Bruce, F. F., 65, 187, 199, 209, 237, 266
Brueggemann, Walter, 109, 156–57, 159
Buchanan, C. O., 194

Cabié, Robert, 204
Cain, 60, 73, 155, 166
Calvin, John, 151, 194, 203, 219
Carson, D. A., 196
Chapell, Bryan, 246
Childs, Brevard S., 23, 80
Christ. *See* Jesus Christ.

NAME INDEX

Clarkson, David, 259
Clifford, Richard J., 17, 185
Cornelius, 41, 269
Courtman, Nigel B., 184
Craigie, Peter C., 5
Cranfield, C. E. B., 190, 252
Crawford, A. G., 202
Cyprian, 200
Cyrus, 87, 183

Daniel, 60, 74
Dau, W. H. T., 202
David, ix, 22, 37, 39, 47–48, 73–74, 76, 81, 86, 88, 92, 138, 142, 144, 146, 149, 156, 183, 214
Davids, Peter, 98, 122, 245
Deborah, 137–38
Delling, Gerhard, 136
Dillard, Raymond B., 76, 171
Doeg the Edomite, 63
Dombek, David A., 229
Dumbrell, William J., 22, 24
Durham, John I., 22, 75, 79

Eichrodt, Walter, 22
Elijah, 8, 35, 50, 76, 88, 115, 196
Elisha, 8, 63, 196
Elizabeth, 50
Esther, 129
Eusebius, 270
Eve, ix, 20–21, 31, 59, 73
Evely, Louis, 237
Ezekiel, 48, 74, 115, 186, 200
Ezra, 116, 128, 183–84, 225

Fee, Gordon D., 208, 218, 250–51, 253, 268
France, R. T., 36–37, 93, 199
Fretheim, Terence E., 16, 19
Fokkelman, J. P., 151

Gaius, 99
Garrett, Duane A., 123
Geldenhuys, J. N., 237
Gideon, 60, 76, 238–39
Green, Michael, 99, 205
Greeven, Heinrich, 38
Grenz, Stanley J., 35, 238

Grudem, Wayne, 200
Gunkel, Herman, 17
Gunton, Colin, 19

Haggai, 183, 186
Hannah, 127, 156
Harakas, Stanley S., 67
Harrell, Daniel, 83
Harrison, R. K., 171
Hartley, John E., 24, 115
Hasel, Gerhard, 17
Heidel, Alexander, 17
Heman, 144
Herod the Great, 38, 77, 87–88, 120
Hess, Richard S., 17
Hezekiah, 76
Hiley, David, 151
Hippolytus, 112, 270
Hobbs, T. R., 76, 115
Hopkins, John, 152
Houston, James M., 48
Hurowitz, Victor A., 76
Hurtado, Larry W., 36, 215

Ignatius of Antioch, 112
Irenaeus, 45
Isaac, 4, 16, 60, 73, 75, 77
Isaiah, 24, 26, 34, 62, 64–65, 91–92, 97, 180, 197
Ittai the Gittite, 63

Jabez, 238
Jacob, 16, 32, 37, 75, 156
Jairus, 39
Jeduthun, 144
Jenson, Philip P., 124
Jeremiah, 91, 186
Jeremias, Joachim, 129, 203, 235, 237
Jesus Christ, x, 3, 7, 12–15, 25–46, 49–58, 63–68, 70–72, 74, 77–78, 85, 88–93, 97–100, 102–3, 107, 110–12, 114, 116–20, 122, 126–30, 135, 137, 145–49, 156, 161–62, 164, 166, 180, 186–93, 195–202, 204–5, 207–16, 218–20, 224–27, 230–39, 241–47, 250, 252–53, 258, 260–63, 265–67, 269, 271–82

Jinkins, Michael, 157
Job, 6, 46, 63–64, 74, 185
John Chrysostom, 112, 267
John the Apostle, 33–34, 37, 39–42 54,
    71, 85, 111, 117–18, 136, 187,
    192, 198, 230, 263, 269
John the Baptist, 31, 35, 50–52, 88, 93,
    118, 122, 145, 187, 196–98, 273
Johnson, Maxwell E., 196, 270, 272
Johnston, Philip S., 156
Joseph, 8, 30–31, 37, 50, 89–90, 145,
    156, 186
Joshua, 9, 46, 76, 81, 182, 196
Jounel, Pierre, 204
Judas Maccabeus, 87
Justin Martyr, 112, 200, 210, 217, 228

Kelly, J. N. D., 200
Kendall, R. T., 228
Kittel, Gerhard, 235
Kiuchi, N., 168
Knierim, Rolf, 16
Kraus, Hans-Joachim, 79, 110, 117,
    138–39, 171, 184
Kugel, James L., 151
Kuhn, K. G., 215
Kunzler, Michael, 280

Ladd, George Eldon, 197, 224
Laymon, Charles M., 235
Leah, 62
Lewis, C. S., 133, 136, 150–51
Lincoln, Andrew T., 53, 147–48
Lind, Millard C., 182
Lindsay, T. M., 202
Lohmeyer, Ernst, 235, 237
Lohse, Eduard, 107
Lombard, Peter, 192–93
Longman, Tremper, III, 151–52, 171,
    182
Longenecker, Richard N., 122, 209, 269
Lot, 234
Lucas, Ernest C., 185
Luke, 31, 35–36, 39–40, 49, 56, 64, 88,
    90, 121–22, 135–36, 145–46,
    210, 235, 269
Luther, Martin, 151, 194, 219
Lydia, 99, 203

Mack, Edward, 129
Mark, 39, 92
Marshall, I. Howard, 31, 50, 55–56,
    117, 146–47, 187, 226
Martimort, A. G., 204
Martin, Ralph P., 117
Mary, 25–26, 30–31, 37–38, 50–51,
    89–90, 145, 186, 238, 281
Mary Magdalene, 40, 260
Matthew, 31–32, 38–40, 45, 198, 235,
    237, 261, 271
Mays, James L., 141
McComiskey, Thomas Edward, 47
McConnell, Walter Leslie, III, 16, 19,
    63, 102, 223, 261
McGrath, Alister, 45
McKelvey, R. J., 95
Melchizedek, 63
Metzger, Bruce M., 36, 208
Meye, R. P., 225
Micah, 47, 182, 185
Michaelis, Wilhelm, 85
Milgrom, Jacob, 169, 177–78
Miller, Patrick D., 108, 134, 143, 182
Miriam, 137
Moberly, R. W. L., 157
Morris, Leon, 33, 55, 57
Moses, 4, 16, 31, 42, 46, 73, 75, 78–82,
    84–86, 92, 95–96, 112, 116–17,
    121, 137, 169, 213, 225, 233–34
Motyer, J. Alec, 54, 64, 180
Murphy, Roland, 157

Naaman, 63, 74, 77, 196
Naomi, 62
Nehemiah, 87, 128, 225
Noah, 22, 60, 62, 74, 155, 166, 169–70,
    200
Nocent, Adrien, 204
Nolland, John, 38
North, R., 24
Nympha, 99

Obed-Edom, 73
O'Brien, Peter T., 53–54
Oden, Thomas C., 203
Okholm, Dennis L., 234
Origen, 204

NAME INDEX

Ornan the Jebusite, 183
Osborne, Kenan B., 193
Otto, Rudolf, 209

Packer, J. I., 225
Paul, 7, 9, 28, 41, 46, 53, 55–57, 65,
    70, 74, 90, 92, 94, 98–101,
    111, 116, 118, 120, 122, 125,
    147–48, 186–90, 198, 200–201,
    204–5, 207–8, 210–17, 224–25,
    227, 230, 234–35, 250–54,
    267–68, 271, 273
Peter, 25–26, 35, 39, 41, 48, 65, 118,
    120, 148, 187–88, 200, 269, 279
Peterson, David, 31
Pharaoh, 108, 137
Philemon, 99
Philip, 199, 204
Piper, John, 260
Polycarp of Smyrna, 280
Pope John XXII, 280
Preisker, Herbert, 136
Preuss, Horst Dietrich, 3
Priscilla, 99–100
Procksch, Otto, 24, 26
Prokurat, Michael, 67
Provan, Ian W., 63

Qohelet, 7, 105–6, 185

Rachel, 62
Rad, Gerhard von, 20, 60, 81, 141, 182
Rahab, 62
Reid, Daniel G., 182
Ringgren, H., 136
Robertson, A. T., 202
Ross, Allen P., 144
Rowley, H. H., 96, 127, 167
Ruth, 62

Samson, 47, 136
Sanders, J. Oswald, 52
Satan, 32, 101, 110, 130, 197
Saul, 47, 204, 261
Schaff, Philip, 58
Schmemann, Alexander, 265
Schniewind, Julius, 218
Schrage, Wolfgang, 95–96, 98

Schweizer, Eduard, 44, 56
Seidl, T., 177
Seitz, Christopher R., 29
Selman, Martin J., 144
Shedd, Russell R., 66
Sicard, Damien, 204
Simeon, 50–51, 89–90, 145–46
Simkins, Ronald A., 17
Skoglund, John E., 241
Sly, Randy, 282
Smith, Gary V., 47
Smith, George, 17
Smith, Mark S., 27
Solomon, ix, 4, 20, 24, 64, 74, 76, 81,
    86, 89, 94, 181, 183
Stephanus, 203
Stephen, 92–93, 97, 280
Sternhold, Thomas, 152
Stevens, R. Paul, 205
Stott, John R. W., 55–56, 122, 147, 190,
    231
Stott, Wilfred, 107
Strathmann, H., 54
Studd, C. T., 189

Talley, Thomas J., 277
Tertullian, 45, 58, 200, 204
Thomas, 40, 42
Thompson, J. Arthur, 22
Thompson, R. J., 177
Timothy, 227
Titius Justus, 99
Titus, 88
Towner, Philip H., 100
Tsumura, David Toshio, 17
Turner, Max, 250

Uriah the Hittite, 63
Uzzah, 73

Verhey, Allen, 161

Wainwright, Geoffrey, 282
Waltke, Bruce K., 48, 63, 167
Walton, John H., 17
Warfield, B. B., 249
Webber, Robert E., 267, 282
Weiser, Artur, 66

Welch, Thomas B., 207
Wenham, Gordon J., 17–18, 20, 125, 168, 171–72, 180
Westermann, Claus, 9, 18, 20, 60, 64, 133–34, 142–43, 147, 151, 159
White, James F., 77
White, R. E. O., 203
White, Susan J., 207
Wilkinson, Bruce, 238
Williamson, Paul R., 22

Wilson, Marvin R., 266
Witvliet, John D., 132, 150–51, 160
Wright, N. T., 49

Zadok, 73
Zechariah, 48, 50, 77, 88–90, 129, 145, 183, 186
Zerubbabel, 87, 115, 183
Zevit, Ziony, 75, 77
Zwingli, Ulrich, 194–95, 219

Scripture Index

Genesis

1	17
1–2	19
1:1	16
1:2	45
1:14–15	19
1:22	18
1:28	18
2	19
2:2–3	108
2:5	8
2:7	46
2:15	8
3	21
3:1	21
3:8	20
4:3–4	60
4:4	176
4:26	60, 233
6:5	169
6:18	22, 170
8:20–21	75
8:20	60, 170
8:21	169
9:9–17	22, 170
12	107
12:1–3	61, 170
12:2–3	62
12:7–8	60, 75
12:15	136
13:4	60
13:18	60, 75
14	63
15:1–20	171
15:1	13
15:8–18	22
15:17	171
17:1–14	22
17:9–14	62
18:20–33	234
21:33	60
22:9	60, 75
23:7	4
23:12	4
24:12	23
24:26–27	4, 23
24:26	60
26:25	60, 75
29:15	8
31:54	181
33:20	75
35:1–3	75
35:7	75
39:4	8
42:6	4
43:26	4
43:28	4

Exodus

3:12	8, 80
4:23	8
4:31	4
5:1–9	108
5:2	85
7:16	8
7:26	8

10:10	109	25:40	82
10:26	8	26:30	82
12	116	27:1–2	75
12:14	117	27:8	82
12:19	62	27:21	79
12:21	116	29	181
12:25–26	9	29:18	169
12:26–27	117	29:19–21	61
12:38	62	29:33	168
12:43–49	62	29:36–37	168
12:46	118	29:38–41	176, 181
12:49	62	29:42	81
13:8	117	30:1–10	76
15:1–18	137	30:7–8	88
15:1–3	137	31:2–11	47
15:13–16	6	31:12–17	109
15:13	23	31:13	25
15:20	144	31:14–15	109
16:23–30	107	32	82
17:15	75	32:2–4	84
19:5–6	22, 61	32:4–5	84
19:6	23	32:6	84, 177
19:8	107	32:25	84
20	77, 107	33:7	79
20:1–17	22	33:11	81
20:3–5	27	34:21	109
20:3	21	34:26	79
20:4–5	18	35–40	78, 84
20:4–6	5, 9	35:2	109
20:8–11	20, 108	35:3	109
20:8	107	38:24	79
20:10	62	39:32	79
20:24–26	77		
20:24	75	**Leviticus**	
20:25–26	75	1:1–17	176
21	77	1:2	176
21:1—23:33	22	1:4	167, 176
23:12	62	2:1–16	176
23:14–17	117	2:2	169, 184
23:16	121	2:3	176
23:19	79	3:1–17	177
24:4	54	3:5	169
24:5	177	4:1—5:13	178
24:6–8	61	4:2	178
24:8	213	4:20	167–68
25–31	78, 84	4:26	167
25:8	79	5	179
25:9	82		

Leviticus (continued)

5:14—6:7	179
5:15	179
6:1–5	179
6:7	167
6:8–13	176
6:14–23	176
6:19–23	176
6:24–30	178
7	181
7:1–7	179
7:11–34	177
7:11–21	177
7:19–21	173
8–9	181
9:4	176
10:17	168
12–15	178
12:1–8	181
12:3	30, 110, 186
12:7–8	168
12:8	30, 186
13:6	172
13:13	172
13:17	172
14:1–32	181
14:1–20	61
14:12–28	179
14:19–20	167
14:20	168
16:16	125
16:18–20	125
16:29	124
17:4	79
17:11	168
18:20–30	173
19:2	23, 25, 61
19:19–22	179
20:2–5	173
20:3	23
20:8	25, 172
20:26	23
21:8	25, 172
21:15	172
21:23	172
22:2	23
22:3	173
22:9	172–73
22:16	172
22:32	23, 172
23:2	107
23:16	120
23:22	121
23:27–32	124
23:29	124
23:42–43	127
24:7	184
24:8	110
24:22	62
26	22
26:12	20
26:31	169
26:32–33	169

Numbers

2–3	80
2:2	80
3:7–8	9
3:12–16	121
4:4	9
4:23–24	9
4:30–33	9
6:9–21	181
6:9–12	179
6:13–20	186
6:17	176
6:24–26	97, 246
7:89	79
9:12	118
10:10	114
10:21	82
11:2	234
11:16–17	46
11:24–27	47
11:25	46–47
11:29	47
15:7	169
15:14–16	62
15:29	62
15:32–36	109
17:13	79
18:29	82
21:7	234
24:2	47

27:18–23	46
28:1–8	176, 181
28:9–10	109–10
28:11–15	115
28:18	120
28:25	120
28:26	121
29:1	123
29:2–5	123
29:7	124
31:47	79
35:16–21	173
35:31	173

Deuteronomy

4:10	7
4:15–19	18
5:12–15	20
5:14	62, 109
5:15	108
6	31
6:4	28, 96
6:13	12, 32
6:16	32
7:6	61
7:9	23
8	31
8:2	32
8:3	32
9:20	234
9:26–29	234
10:12	12
10:20	12
14:2	61
14:23	7
16:2	117
16:3	120
16:5–7	117
16:10–11	62
16:10	121
16:12	121
16:16	117
16:17	116
17:9	7
18:15	48
18:18–19	48
23:15	20

23:17	27
27:5–6	75
27:9—28:28	22
29	22
31:14	81
34:9	46

Joshua

2:11	62
4:15–19	81
5:10–12	182
6:3–4	110
6:25	62
7:7–9	159
8:30–35	73, 182
8:30–31	75–76
8:30	73
9:6	22
9:11	22
9:15	22
18:1	73, 81
22:10–11	75
22:19	81
22:21–29	182
22:27–28	75
22:27	81, 177
22:29	81
24	22
24:14–24	8
24:15	9

Judges

2	22
3:9–10	46
5:1–5	137–38
5:2–31	137
5:3	135
6:18–21	176
6:24–26	77
6:25–29	73
6:25–26	182
6:34	46
6:36–40	238
7:15	60
11:29	46
11:30–40	182

Judges (continued)

13:19	75
13:25	46
14:6	46
14:19	46
15:14	46
16:20	47
16:24	136
17:1–13	182
20:26–27	81
21:3	159

Ruth

1:16	62
4:11	63

1 Samuel

1:1–5	181
4:4	79
7:17	73, 182
10:1–13	47
10:6–8	47
10:6	46
10:10	46
10:27	176
11:1	8
11:14–15	178, 181
11:15	177
15:13–22	170
16:13	46
16:14	47
19:18–24	47
19:23	47
20:5–26	115
21	81
21:7	63
24:9	4
25:32	147

2 Samuel

5:1–3	22
6	73
6:1–19	181
6:2	79
6:12–14	144
6:17–18	177
7:6–7	20
7:12–17	22
11:3–24	63
14:25	136
15:19–21	63
22:4	10
22:50	135
24:16–24	63
24:18–25	77, 181

1 Kings

1:9	181
1:25	181
1:48	145, 147
4:21	176
6–7	76
8:1–11	86
8:4	81
8:15	147
8:27–30	86
8:38	96
8:44	96
8:48	96
8:62–64	181
18:29	181
18:30–32	77
19:21	8
22:24	47

2 Kings

1:8	196
2:9	47
3:20	181
4:23	110, 115
5:2–3	63
5:15	63
7–23	183
11	22
16:10–15	76
16:13	177
16:15	76, 181
17	5, 22
19:15	79, 86
19:22	23
22:11–20	183
23:3	22

1 Chronicles

4:10	238
6:32	8
9:32	110
13	73
15–16	73
15:16–24	144
16	81
16:4	8
16:9	135
16:25	10
16:37	8, 73
16:39–42	73
16:39	81
17:1–14	183
18:2	8
18:6	8
18:13	8
21:24–29	183
24:1–19	88
25:1	144
28:2	79
28:18	76
29:10–13	142

2 Chronicles

1:3	73, 81
1:3–6	81
3–4	76
4:1	76
6:34	96
6:38	96
7:3	4
7:1–7	183
8:12–13	117
8:13	128
15:1	47
15:8	76
20:14–17	144
29:10	22
29:17	76

Ezra

1:1–2	87
3:1–6	115
3:2–5	183
3:4	128
3:10–11	183
5:1–2	183
6:14	183
8:15–36	184

Nehemiah

8–10	225
8:2	116
8:14–18	128
9:6	5
10:31	110
11:1	86
11:18	86
13:15–22	110
13:19–21	110

Esther

3:7	129
9:24	129
9:26	129

Job

1:1	6, 64
1:3	64
1:5	64, 185
1:6	66
1:8	64
1:21–22	64
2:1	66
2:3	64
5:1	66
6:10	23
15:15	66
27:3–4	46
28:28	6
29–31	157
33:4	46
38:7	66
42:8–9	185
42:7–9	64

Psalms

1:1–2	152
2:11	12

Psalms (continued)

Reference	Page
3	139
5:7	12
6	161
6:3	158
6:5	143, 185
7	135
7:2	139
7:6–9	139
7:15	139
7:17	135
8:3	141
8:5	141
8:6–8	141
9:1	132, 134
9:4	134
9:7	141
9:11	86
9:15	139
10:1	159
10:16	141
11:4	141
12:11	135
13:1–2	158, 160
13:1	159
13:2	159
13:5–6	160
15	59
18:3	10
18:4–5	139
19:1–6	67
19:1	141
19:3	141
20	162
22:1	35, 156
22:3	23
22:6–8	159
22:12–13	159
22:16–18	159
22:20–21	159
22:23	6
22:24	134
22:25	184
22:27	5, 64
22:28	141
22:29	5
24	141
24:1–2	141
24:1	18
24:3–4	86
24:3	59
24:4	59
24:7–10	141
29:1–2	5, 67
29:1	66
29:3–9	141
29:10	141
30:3	139
30:4	23, 134
30:5	135
31:4	139
31:5	156
32	161
33	140–41
33:1–9	140
33:1	132, 144
33:2	135
33:6	45, 141
34:20	118
35:17	158
38	159, 162, 184
40:6–8	184
40:14	147
41	159, 162
41:7	144
41:13	145
42:8	86
42:9	159
43:2	159
44:9	159
44:10–16	159
44:23	159
44:24	159
45:6	141
46:4	86
46:5	20
47:2	141
47:6	135
47:7	141
47:8	141
48:1	10
50	184
50:5	184
50: 8–14	184
50:8	184

50:16	184	86	241
50:23	184	86:9	5
51	48, 161	86:12	132
51:11	44, 48	86:13	139
54:6	184	87:3	86
55:17	270	88	159
55:20–21	139	89:5	143
56:1	139	89:9	141
56:10–13	139	89:11	141
56:12	184	89:12	141
58:1–2	159	89:22–23	138
59:1–4	139	89:46	158
59:6	139	90:13	158
59:14	139	91	139
60:10–11	138	94:3	158
63:4	144	95:5	141
65:1	184	95:6–7	144
66:2	135	96:4	10
66:4	64	96:5	141
66:13–15	184	96:9	5
68:5	135	96:10–13	139
68:33	135	96:11–13	67
69:30–31	134	96:11–12	143
69:34	143	96:13	143
69:35–36	143	97:7	66
70	184	97:9	5
71:18	147	97:12	134
71:22	23	98:2	50
72:11	64, 141	98:4–9	67
72:18	145	98:5–6	144
74:1	159	98:5	135
74:8	95	98:7–8	143
74:10	158	98:9	143
74:13–17	140	99:1–2	86
74:16	141	99:1	79
74:17	141	100	184
78:60	81	102	161
79:5	158	103:1	23
79:6	138	103:19	141
80	164	103:20–21	67, 143
80:1	79	103:21	8
80:4	158	104:35	133
80:7	164	105:2	135
80:17	164	105:3	24
80:19	164	105:48	147
81:2–3	144	106:48	145
81:3	114	108:3	134
83:6–11	138	108:4	134

Psalms (continued)

110:1	138
110:4	63
110:5	138
111:1	132
111:10	6
113–18	118
113:1	133
115–18	118
115:11	6
115:17	143, 185
116:17	184
116:18	184
117:1	133
118:21	134
118:25	146
118:27	184
119:62	270
119:164	270
119:175	143
120–34	60
130	161
132:7	79
134:2	144
135:1	133
135:3	135
135:20	6
136	242
136:1–3	134
137	138
141:2	189, 248
143	161
145:3	10
145:13	141
146:6	141
147:1	132
147:7	135
148	67
148:1–12	143
148:1	133
148:2–4	134
148:2	67
148:7	133
148:14	143
149:3	87, 144
150:1–5	134
150:3–5	144
150:4	87, 144
150:6	143

Proverbs

1:7	6
1:8	7
1:11–12	7
1:13–14	7
1:16–18	7
1:19	7
2:1	7
2:5	6
2:16–19	7
3:1	7
3:7	6
4:1–4	7
5:1	7
5:3–23	7
6:17	7
6:24–35	7
7	185
7:5–27	7
7:6–23	185
8:13	6
9:10	6
12:8	136
15:8	185
20:30	7
21:27	185
27:2	136
28:4	136
28:9	185
31:28	136
31:30	136
31:31	136

Ecclesiastes

1:9	105
3:1–8	106
3:14	106
5:1	185
5:13–14	106
6:1–2	106
7:14	106
8:14	106
9:10	185

9:11–12	106	64:1–9	164
12:13	7	66:1–2	92
		66:19	64
Isaiah		66:20	64–65
		66:21	64
1:4	23	66:23	64, 115
1:10–17	185		
1:13–14	115	**Jeremiah**	
2:2–3	64		
4:3	62	2:21	164
5:1–7	164	7:2	87
6:3	23–24, 149	7:3–8	87
6:5	24	7:11	91
6:7	24	7:12–15	87
11:1–5	48	7:21–28	170
11:10	64	7:21–23	185
12:5	135	7:30–31	185
25:6–9	214	11:18—12:6	157
30:8	54	15:10–21	157
32:15	48	16:7	209
37:16	86	17:12–18	157
38:18	143	17:22	109
40:3–5	197	17:26	186
42:1	48	18:18–23	157
42:6	51	19:14	87
44:15	4	20:7–18	157
44:17	4	20:13	133
44:19	4	22:8–9	5
45:14	5	26:2–13	87
45:18–23	27	26:2	87
45:22–23	64	26:6	87
46:6	4	31:31–37	22
48:2	86	31:31–34	118, 213
48:16	47	31:32	22
49:6	51	31:33	213
49:7	5	49:25	136
52:1	86		
52:10	50	**Lamentations**	
53:3	156		
53:4–12	180	2:7	159
53:10	180	4:4	209
55:12	67		
56:3–8	64	**Ezekiel**	
56:7	91		
60:3–6	64	3:15–23	74
61:1–2	97	10:18–19	87
61:1	51	11:5	47
63:10–11	44	11:19–20	48
		15:1–8	164

Ezekiel (continued)

18:31	48
20:12–20	109
26:1	115
26:17	136
29:17	115
31:1	115
32:1	115
36:25–27	201
36:26–27	48
43:13–17	76
43:18–27	186
45:17	115
46:1–9	110
46:1–7	115
46:1–24	186
46:13–14	181
47	20

Daniel

3:5–7	4
3:10–12	4
3:14–18	4
3:28	4
6:10	60, 74, 96, 270
7:13–14	49

Hosea

2:11	115
8:11–13	185
9:7	47
11	22

Joel

2:28–29	47–48
2:32	48

Amos

5:21–25	185
5:24	186
8:5	115

Jonah

1:5–16	5

Micah

3:5–8	47
3:11–12	87
4:1–3	64
4:5	88
6:6–8	186

Habakkuk

1:2–4	157

Zephaniah

2:11	5, 64
3:9	60

Haggai

1:1	115

Zechariah

2:11	64
4:1–6	48
7:12	47
14:9	27
14:16–19	128

Malachi

3:1	196
4:5–6	196

Matthew

1:18	50
1:20–21	50
1:21	37
1:23	37, 85
2:2	38
2:8	38
2:11	38
3:1–3	197
3:4	196
3:5	196
3:7	196
3:11	51, 197
3:14–15	197
3:16–17	197, 273
4:1	51

4:2	35	19:4	224
4:4	32	19:13–15	35
4:7	32	19:29	40
4:10	32	20:20	40
4:11	32	20:26	34
4:17	197	20:28	34
4:23	31	21:9	146
5:16	135	21:12–13	89
5:23–24	89, 186	21:13	91
5:39	237	21:14	90
5:44	36	21:16	135, 224
5:45	237	21:23	90
6:5–8	235	21:42	224
6:5–6	35	22:31	224
6:9–13	36, 235	22:44–45	63
6:9	25	23:11	34
6:13	237	23:18–20	77
7:7–11	234	23:21	89
8:2	38	24:1–2	92
9:8	135, 146	25:14–30	254
9:18–26	39	26:17	120
10:17	97	26:26–27	35
11:14	196	26:27	209
11:25–27	146	26:28	213
11:28–30	111	26:29–44	234
11:28	162	26:29	214
12:1–8	111	26:30	118, 136
12:3	224	26:36–44	35
12:5	109, 224	26:39	34
12:6	91	26:42	34
12:7	111	26:53	34
12:8	111	26:55	90
12:9	31	27:46	35, 156, 276
13:19	237	27:51	126
13:54	31	28:8	261
14:19	35	28:9	40
14:23	35	28:16–20	40
14:27	39	28:17	261
14:30–31	39	28:18–20	198
14:30	234	28:19–20	32
14:33	39	28:19	28, 45, 192
15:6	226	28:20	226
15:22	39		
15:25	39	**Mark**	
15:31	135, 146	1:2–4	197
15:36	35	1:4	196
17:12–13	196	1:6	196
18:26	38		

Mark (continued)

1:7	197
1:8	51
1:10–11	197
1:12	51
1:21	110
1:24	26
1:35	35
2:12	146
2:23–28	111
2:27	111
3:1–5	110
3:4	111
3:13–19	35
3:14–15	35
5:22	39
6:41	209
6:46–48	35
7:13	226
8:6	209
9:28–29	36
10:45	34
11:15–17	89
11:27—13:2	92
11:27–33	93
11:27–32	196
12:1–12	93
12:13–34	93
12:28–29	28
12:35–44	93
12:35	90
13:1–2	92
13:1	92
14:1	120
14:12	117, 120
14:23	209
14:25	214
14:26	136
14:34	156
14:36	235
15:34	35, 156, 276
15:38	126

Luke

1:8–10	50
1:10	269
1:11	77
1:15–17	50
1:15	51, 88
1:17	196
1:32–33	37
1:35	26, 50, 85
1:46–55	50, 145
1:49	25
1:64	147
1:67–79	50
1:68–79	145
1:68	145
2:13	135
2:14	145, 278
2:18	145
2:20	135, 145
2:21–38	90
2:21–24	30, 87, 186
2:25–27	50
2:25–26	89
2:29–33	146
2:29–32	145
2:30	89
2:36–38	146
2:37	9–10, 89
2:41–42	30, 89
2:46	90
3:2–6	197
3:2	226
3:3	196
3:6	50
3:7–14	196
3:16	51, 122, 197
3:21	35
3:22	51, 197
4:1	51
4:8	32, 51
4:14–15	51
4:15	146
4:16–21	97, 110
4:16	31, 110
4:18–19	51
4:34	26
5:16	35
5:25–26	146
6:1–5	111
6:6–10	110
6:12–16	35
6:12–13	35

6:12	35	23:34	35–36, 276
7:16	146	23:40	7
7:26–27	88	23:43	276
8:41	39	23:45	126
9:18–22	35	23:46	35, 156, 276
9:20	35	23:47	146
9:23	190	24:30	209
9:28–29	35	24:35	209
10	146	24:44	136
10:2	36	24:45	224
10:17	146	24:49	52
10:19–20	147	24:52–53	90
11:1–2	35	24:52	40
11:2–11	235	24:53	146
11:2–4	235		
11:13	51, 55	**John**	
12:11	97		
13:10–13	110	1:1–14	37
13:13	146	1:1	33
13:14–16	110	1:6–9	51
14:1–4	110	1:14	33, 38, 85
17:8	32	1:18	33
17:15	146	1:19–34	51
17:18	146	1:21	196
18:1–8	36	1:23	197
18:2–8	234	1:25	196
18:2	7	1:27	197
18:4	7	1:29	118, 187
18:9–14	89	1:32–33	197
18:43	135, 146	1:35–37	198
19:9	99	1:36	118, 187
19:37	135, 146	2:11	33
19:45–46	89	2:13	89, 118
19:47	90	2:14–22	91
20:1–7	196	2:14–17	89
20:1	90	2:19–20	88
20:42	136	3:16	260
21:5–6	92	3:22–23	198
21:12	266	3:30	198
21:37–38	90	4:1–2	198
22:1	120	4:20–24	91
22:7	120	4:21	72
22:16	118, 214	4:53	99
22:17	209	5:1–9	110
22:19	118, 192, 209–10	5:1	89, 118
22:20	210	5:17	111
22:32	35	5:18	128
22:40–46	35	5:24	226

John (continued)

5:41	135
5:44	135
6:4	118
6:33	237
6:35	42, 237
6:63	46
6:69	26, 85
7	128
7:10–14	89
7:16–17	33
7:22	110
7:28–29	33
7:37–38	128
8:12	42
8:16	33
8:18	33
8:28	33
8:29	33
8:50	135
8:54	135
9:1–38	39
9:1–14	110
10:7	42
10:9	42
10:11	42
10:14–18	33
10:14	42
10:22–39	130
10:22–23	89
10:22	107
10:25	33
10:35	226
10:37	33
11:25	42
11:41–42	35
12:1	118
12:2	32
12:43	137
12:44	33
12:45	33
12:49	33
13:20	33
13:34	276
14	52
14:6	42
14:7	42
14:9	42
14:15–26	43
14:15–18	52
14:16	52, 55
14:23	33
14:26	43, 52
14:31	33
15:1–7	164
15:16	238
15:18–21	266
15:26–27	52
15:26	43, 52
16:7–15	52
16:7–11	52
16:7	52
16:8	43–44, 52
17:11–17	36
17:11	25
17:15	237
17:20–23	36
19:26–27	276
19:28	276
19:30	35, 276
19:36	118
20:19–20	40
20:28	41

Acts

1:3	278
1:4–5	52
1:4	55
1:8	52, 64
1:11	279
1:13–14	99
1:13	74
1:14	269
1:20	136
2	121–22
2:1	120
2:12–13	266
2:14–41	52
2:15	270
2:22–42	28
2:27	26, 85
2:29–30	47
2:33	55
2:34–35	63

2:38	199	11:24	52
2:41	199	12:1–3	280
2:42	65, 209–10, 226	12:3	120
2:44–45	210	12:12	74
2:46–47	99	13:1	70
2:46	90, 209	13:2	261
2:47	135	13:3	261
3:1	90, 266, 269–70	13:14–48	110
3:8–9	135	13:14–44	266
3:12–26	90	13:16	6
3:14	26	13:26	6
4:1–22	266	13:33	136
4:1–2	90	13:35	26
4:18	93	14:14–15	41
4:24–30	242	15	65, 267
4:27	26	15:1–29	187
4:30	26	15:21	110–11
4:31	52	16:12–34	70
5:13	93	16:13	74, 110
5:40	93	16:14–15	99
5:42	90, 99–100, 266	16:15	99, 203
6:1	226	16:24–25	74
6:2	226	16:25	136
6:4	226	16:30–33	99
6:9	98	16:31	203
7:42	8	16:40	99
7:49–50	92	17:2–3	110
7:57—8:2	280	17:5	99
7:59–60	41	17:6	66
8:12	199	17:11	226
8:13–24	199	18:4	110
8:13	199	18:7–8	99
8:16	199	18:7	99
8:25	226	18:8	99
8:36	199	18:26	99
8:38	199, 204	19:1–5	198
9:17–22	52	19:5	199
9:18	199, 204	20:7	111–12, 210, 277
10	65	20:11	209
10:2	6	20:16	89, 120
10:3	269	20:20	99–100
10:9	269–70	20:29–32	227
10:22	6, 74	21:23–26	90, 186
10:25–26	41	24:17	187
10:30	269	24:17–18	90
10:35	6	26:11	98
10:48	199	27:9	126
11:14	99		

Acts (continued)

27:35	209
28:17–31	99

Romans

1:5	250
1:7	65, 250
1:9	9
1:11	250
1:18–25	28
1:25	8
2:5	100
2:29	135–36
3:9–18	7
3:25	187
5:2	250
5:11	147
6:3–4	201, 277
6:3	199
6:4	201
6:5	201
6:11	201
8	123
8:3	187
8:15–16	53
8:15	235
8:19	100
8:23	122
8:26	234
8:34	33, 36, 234
9:2	156
9:5	41
10:17	224, 227
12	251
12:1—15:13	252
12:1–2	65
12:1	9, 188, 190, 252
12:6–8	250–51
12:6	250
14:5–6	112
15:11	135
15:15–16	56
15:16	65, 188
15:25–31	65
15:27	9
16:3–5	99
16:3	100
16:20	250
16:25	101

1 Corinthians

1:2	42, 65
1:7	100, 250
1:11–13	70
1:13–17	267
1:16	99, 203
1:18	227
3:3–17	94
3:3–9	70
3:16–17	92, 95
4–5	52
4:5	136
5:6–9	120
5:7–8	267
5:7	116, 118, 187
5:8	118
6:9–11	57
6:18	57
6:19–20	57, 94
6:19	92
8:4–6	28
9:19–23	187
10	208
10:16–17	216
10:16	208
10:21	207
11:2–16	267
11:17–34	267
11:20–34	211
11:20–22	208
11:20	207, 211
11:23–26	210
11:23–27	212
11:24–25	192
11:26	214, 218
11:27	211
11:28–30	217
11:33–34	208
12–14	250–51
12	252
12:1–31	267
12:1	250
12:2	252
12:3	252

12:4–6	250, 252
12:4	250
12:5	250
12:6	250
12:7	57, 250
12:8–10	251
12:11	57, 254
12:28–31	252
12:31	250, 253
14	101, 252
14:1–25	267
14:1	250, 252
14:3	253
14:12	57
14:26–40	267
14:26	100, 136, 253
14:29	253
14:36	226
14:40	220, 253
15:20	122
15:23	122
16:1–4	65
16:2	111–12
16:8	120
16:19	99–100
16:22	214
16:51	99

2 Corinthians

1:3	147
1:8	156
3:6	46
3:14–16	224
5:21	187, 213
6:16	92, 94
6:17–18	94
7:1	7, 94
8–9	65
11:31	147
12:1	101
12:7–9	234
12:8–9	41
13:14	28, 45, 246

Galatians

2:2	101
2:10	65
2:11–14	65
3:27	199
3:28–29	65, 200
4:6–7	53
4:6	235
5:16–17	57
5:22–23	57
6:6	226

Ephesians

1:3–14	147
1:3–10	147
1:3	147–48
1:9–10	191
1:12–14	148
2:10	189
2:14	70, 95
2:19–22	92
3:3	191
3:4	192
3:9	192
4:4–6	28
4:5	205
4:11–16	253
4:11–13	250
4:11	57, 250–51
4:12	57
5:2	187
5:14	53
5:18–20	53, 100
5:19	136
5:21	13
5:31–32	191
6:19	192

Philippians

1:9–11	148
2:5–6	41
2:6–11	53
2:16	227
2:17	188
2:25	9
3:2	53
3:3	9, 53–54
4:18	189

Colossians

1:15–20	53
1:15–17	41
1:19–20	41
2:9	41
2:11–12	203
2:12	201
2:16–17	111
2:16	116
3:16	100, 136
4:15	99
4:16	100, 225

1 Thessalonians

1:8	226
3:11–12	41
5:17	271
5:27	225

2 Thessalonians

1:7	100
3:5	41
3:16	41
3:18	41

1 Timothy

1:17	28
2:5–6	28
2:5	28, 126
3:4–5	100
3:9	192
3:12	100
3:16	53, 192

2 Timothy

1:3	9–10
1:10	273
3:14–17	55
3:15	224
3:16–17	55, 224
4:2	227
4:6	188

Titus

1:11	100
3:7	201

Philemon

2	99

Hebrews

1:1–12	41
1:1	54
1:6	67
1:14	66
2:11	25
2:12	136, 146
3–4	112
3:3	10
4:1–11	112
4:12	229
5:6–10	63
6:20	63
7:1–17	63
7:25	36, 234
7:26–28	126
8:1–13	42
8:2	33
9:4	9–10, 77
9:6–14	126
9:6–10	126
9:7	126
9:11–12	126
9:12	126
9:14	9–10, 51
9:24–26	126
9:24	126
9:26	126
10:1–18	127
10:1–10	42, 187
10:10	25
10:14	25
10:19–22	126
10:22	200
10:25	104
12:22–29	92
13:10–12	77–78
13:10	75
13:11–13	126

13:15–16	148, 189–90
13:15	78

James

1:18	122
2:2	98
2:21	77
3:9–10	148
5:13–15	245
5:14	245
5:15	245
5:16	69

1 Peter

1:3	147
1:7	136, 148
1:14–16	65
1:15–19	119
1:15–16	25
1:15	85
1:16	25, 61
1:19	187
2:4–5	188
2:5	92, 189
2:9	65
3:15	41
3:20–21	200
3:21	200
4:16	148

2 Peter

2:13	208
3:15–16	225

1 John

1:1–2	227
1:7	187
1:9	69, 243
2:1	36, 52
2:2	187
2:16	31

Jude

12	208

Revelation

1:4–6	28
1:10–11	54
1:10	277
1:20	192
2:13	280
4	259
4:6–11	67
4:8	23, 26, 149
4:10	71
4:11	10, 41, 149, 259
5	259
5:5	149
5:6–14	41, 67, 187
5:6–13	119
5:8	189, 248
5:9–10	149
5:9	10, 41, 259
5:11–14	41
5:12	10, 259
5:13	28, 41, 149
6:10	26
6:16	41
7	259
7:10–12	28
7:10	41
7:11–12	67
7:15	10
7:17	41
8:3–4	189, 248
10:7	192
11:8	6
11:15–18	67
14:1–4	122
14:1	41
14:4	41
14:7	12
15:4	12, 26
17:5	192
17:6	280
17:7	192
17:14	41
19:5	6, 135
19:7–9	119
19:9	214
21:1–2	92
21:22–23	28, 41

Revelation (continued)

21:22	20, 92
22:1–2	20
22:1	41
22:3	41
22:4	92
22:7	262
22:8–9	41
22:12–13	262
22:20	215, 263
20:21	263

www.ingramcontent.com/pod-product-compliance
Lightning Source LLC
Chambersburg PA
CBHW061845300426
44115CB00013B/2518